BURGUNDY
AND THE RHÔNE VALLEY

Signpost
Guides

Titles in this series include:

- Andalucía and the Costa del Sol
- Australia
- Bavaria and the Austrian Tyrol
- Brittany and Normandy
- Burgundy and the Rhône Valley
- California
- Catalonia and the Spanish Pyrenees
- Dordogne and Western France
- England and Wales
- Florida
- Ireland
- Languedoc and South-west France
- New England
- New Zealand
- Portugal
- Provence and the Côte d'Azur
- Scotland
- Tuscany and Umbria
- Vancouver and British Columbia
- Washington DC and Virginia, Maryland and Delaware

and

- Selected Hotels and Inns in North America
- Bed and Breakfast in France 2001

For further information about these and other Thomas Cook publications, write to Thomas Cook Publishing, PO Box 227, Thorpe Wood, Peterborough PE3 6PU, United Kingdom

Signpost
Guides

BURGUNDY
AND THE RHÔNE VALLEY

The best of Burgundy and the Rhône
Valley, from the Romanesque churches
of Vézelay and Auxerre to the
vineyards of Beaune, and from the
big-city attractions of Lyon to the
charming backwaters of the Brionnais,
with suggested driving tours

Andrew Sanger

The
Globe
Pequot
Press

Thomas
Cook
Publishing

Published by Thomas Cook Publishing
A division of Thomas Cook Holdings Ltd
PO Box 227
Thorpe Wood
Peterborough PE3 6PU
United Kingdom

Telephone: +44 (0)1733 503571
Fax: +44 (0)1733 503596
E-mail: books@thomascook.com

For further information about
Thomas Cook Publishing, visit our website:
www.thomascook.com

ISBN 1 841570 31 1

Published in the USA by
The Globe Pequot Press
PO Box 480
Guilford, Connecticut USA
06437

ISBN 0 7627 0691 0

Text: © 2000 Thomas Cook Publishing
Maps and diagrams:
Road maps supplied by Lovell Johns Ltd, OX8 8LH
Road maps generated from Bartholomew digital database © Bartholomew Ltd, 2000
City maps prepared by Polly Senior Cartography, © Thomas Cook Ltd

Publisher: Donald Greig
Commissioning Editor: Deborah Parker
Map Editor: Bernard Horton
Series Editor: Christopher Catling
Copy Editor: Lucy Thomson
Proof-reader: Jan Wiltshire
Written and researched by: Andrew Sanger

Managing Director: Kevin Fitzgerald

About the author

Andrew Sanger is a well-established travel writer who has contributed many hundreds of articles to British national newspapers and magazines. He has also written over 20 guidebooks, most about regions of France. From 1991 to 1999 Andrew was editor of French Railways' travel magazine *Rail Europe*, and he has twice been a winner at the prestigious Travelex Travel Writers' Awards in London (1994 and 1996).

Andrew's most recent books include *Thomas Cook Signpost Guide Provence & the Côte d'Azur* (2000), *AA Explorer Israel* (2000), *Brussels and Bruges* (1999), *South-west France* (1998) and *Languedoc & Roussillon* (1997), as well as pocket guides to *Tenerife* (2000), *Lanzarote & Fuerteventura* (1999) and *Channel Hopping* (1999), and a children's guidebook to Paris.

France is Andrew's special subject and special love. His lifelong involvement with the country started with his primary education at the Lycée Français in London. He began to visit France on his own from the age of 14, when he travelled by train to the Massif Central. The next trip was to Six-Fours-la-Plage, on the Mediterranean coast, which he chose 'purely because of the name'. Since then he reckons to have walked, cycled, driven and travelled by train over almost the whole of France, with accommodation ranging from mobile homes to five-star hotels, from sleeping rough to luxury villas – as well as acquiring a home in a medieval village near Montpellier.

'Living in the south of France, I worked as vineyard labourer, truck driver and anything else that came to hand. For a while I scraped a living as a private English tutor. One of my students was an airline instructor, who preferred to take his lessons over a coffee in the local bar, or strolling in the village. His English was terrible, and he made little progress – I'm not much of a teacher – and we usually ended up chatting in French, about life, France and everything.

'I became good friends with Guy, and his wife Annie, and when he moved to a job in Burgundy, my wife and I often visited them and their children at their new home in the Charolais area. On countless outings, by car, on foot and even by plane, we explored this glorious region together, summer and winter, learning about its wine, food and countryside, its rural customs and its high culture. Certainly my French improved, even if his English didn't!'

Acknowledgements

Andrew Sanger would like to thank Guy and Annie Gatty 'for introducing me to Burgundy'; Eurotunnel, for its fast Channel crossings; and tour operator Inntravel, of York, for its help and knowledge of rural France.

Contents

About Signpost Guides   8
Burgundy and the Rhône Valley at a glance   10
Introduction   12
Travel facts   14
Driver's guide   24
Getting to Burgundy and the Rhône Valley   30
Setting the scene   32
Highlights   40

The Sénonais and Gâtinais   42
The rolling green northern edge of Burgundy

Puisaye   50
A place of wildlife, beloved of the writer Colette

Chablis   58
Highly prized wines and old stone and timber buildings

Auxois and the Seine Valley   68
Gallo-Roman sites and museums

The Cure and Cousin valleys   76
Monumental architecture and unspoiled wilderness

The Morvan   86
The high granite massif at the heart of Burgundy

Dijon   98
Burgundy's lively capital, jam-packed with art

The Côte d'Or   110
Source of Burgundy's world-famous wines

Beaune   122
Narrow cobbled streets and Flemish-Burgundian architecture

The Chalonnais   132
Prestige wines and hard-working villages

The Mâconnais   140
Southern warmth and first-rate white wines

● **Beaujolais** 150
A tangle of narrow lanes, wooded hills and wine hamlets

● **The Loire in Burgundy** 162
Bridges and riverside towns along Burgundy's western edge

● **The Charollais and Brionnais** 170
Charolais cattle and monastic grandeur

● **West of Lyon** 178
Popular centre for gastronomic restaurants

● **Bresse** 186
Village markets full of old-world charm and character

● **La Dombes** 194
Lakes, meadows and wildfowl reserves

● **Lyon** 202
France's second city and a World Heritage Site

● **Vienne** 214
Former capital of Roman Gaul

● **The Haut-Vivarais** 222
Volcanic region of profound rusticity

● **The southern Ardèche** 230
The jewel of the Rhône Valley for its dramatic scenery

● **Côtes du Rhône: Vienne to Valence** 242
Vineyards and immense views to the Alps

● **Bas-Dauphiné** 254
Fresh air and pre-Alpine slopes

● **Diois** 262
The flavour of Provence combined with ski resorts

● **The border of Provence** 270
Café tables on tree-shaded squares, with high peaks behind and
the former Roman towns of Orange and Vaison to the south

Language 282
Index 283
Feedback form 287

About Signpost Guides

Thomas Cook's Signpost Guides are designed to provide you with a comprehensive but flexible reference source to guide you as you tour a country or region by car. This guide divides Burgundy and the Rhône Valley into touring areas – one per chapter. Major cultural centres or cities form chapters in their own right. Each chapter contains enough attractions to provide at least a day's worth of activities – often more.

Star ratings

To make it easier for you to plan your time and decide what to see, every sight and attraction is given a star rating. A three-star rating indicates a major attraction, worth at least half a day of your time. A two-star attraction is worth an hour or so of your time, and a one-star attraction indicates a site that is worth visiting, but often of specialist interest. To help you further, individual attractions within towns or theme parks are also graded, so that travellers with limited time can quickly find the most rewarding sights.

Chapter contents

Every chapter has an introduction summing up the main attractions of the area or town, and a ratings box, which will highlight its appeal – some places may be more attractive to families travelling with children, others to wine-lovers visiting vineyards, and others to people interested in finding castles, churches, nature reserves, or good beaches.

Each chapter is then divided into an alphabetical gazetteer, and a suggested tour or walk. You can select whether you just want to visit a particular sight or attraction, choosing from those described in the gazetteer, or whether you want to tour the area comprehensively. If the latter, you can construct your own itinerary, or follow the author's suggested tour, which comes at the end of every area chapter.

The gazetteer

The gazetteer section describes all the major attractions in the area – the villages, towns, historic sites, nature reserves, parks or museums that you are most likely to want to see. Maps of the area highlight all the places mentioned in the text. Using this comprehensive overview of the area, you may choose just to visit one or two sights.

One way to use the guide is to find individual sights that interest you, using the index, overview map or star ratings, and read what the author has to say about them. This will help you decide whether to visit the sight. If you do, you will find plenty of practical information, such as the telephone number for enquiries and opening times.

Symbol key

🛈 Tourist Information Centre

Ⓦ Website

🚆 Advice on arriving or departing

🅿 Parking locations

🚘 Advice on getting around

➲ Directions

🎫 Sights and attractions

🍴 Eating

🅒 Accommodation

🛍 Shopping

🅟 Sport

🅐 Entertainment

Practical information

The practical information in the page margins, or sidebar, will help you locate the services you need as an independent traveller – including the tourist information centre, car parks and public transport facilities. You will also find the opening times of sights, museums, churches and other attractions, as well as useful tips on shopping, market days, cultural events, entertainment, festivals and sports facilities.

Alternatively, you can choose a hotel, with the help of the accommodation recommendations contained in this guide. You can then turn to the overall map on pages 10–11 to help you work out which chapters in the book describe the cities and regions closest to your touring base.

Driving tours

The suggested tour is just that – a suggestion, with plenty of optional detours and one or two ideas for making your own discoveries, under the heading 'Also worth exploring'. The routes are designed to link the attractions described in the gazetteer section, and to cover outstandingly scenic coastal, mountain and rural landscapes. The total distance is given for each tour, and the time it will take you to drive the complete route, but bear in mind that this indication is just for driving time: you will need to add on extra time for visiting attractions along the way.

Many of the routes are circular, so that you can join them at any point. Where the nature of the terrain dictates that the route has to be linear, the route can either be followed out and back, or you can use it as a link route, to get from one area in the book to another.

As you follow the route descriptions, you will find names picked out in bold capital letters – this means that the place is described fully in the gazetteer. Other names picked out in bold indicate additional villages or attractions worth a brief stop along the route.

Accommodation and food

In every chapter you will find lodging and eating recommendations for individual towns, or for the area as a whole. These are designed to cover a range of price brackets and concentrate on more characterful small or individualistic hotels and restaurants. In addition, you will find information in the 'Travel facts' chapter on chain hotels, with an address to which you can write for a guide, map or directory.

The price indications used in the guide have the following meanings:

€   budget level
€€   typical/average prices
€€€ de luxe

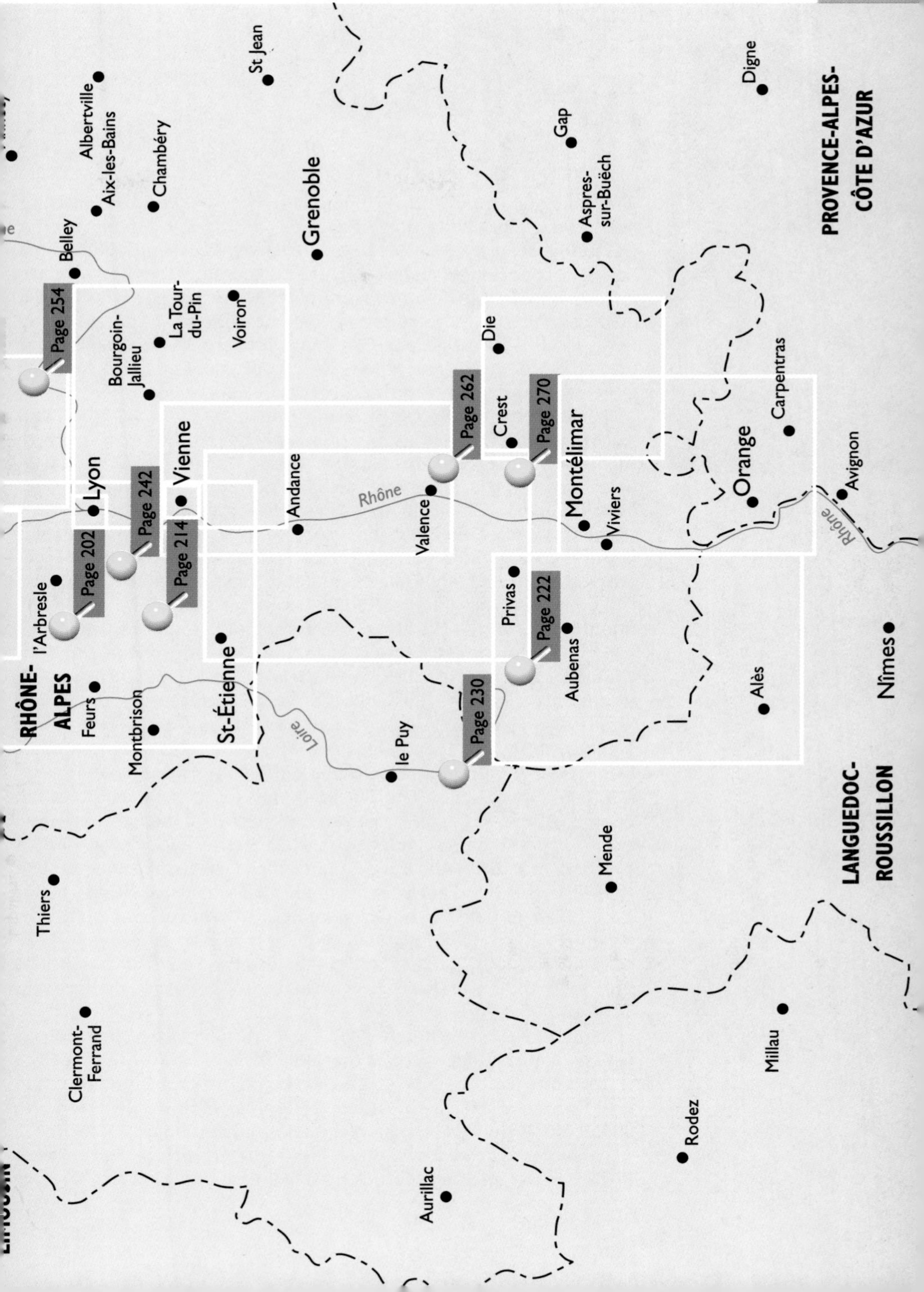

St Jean

Digne

Albertville

Gap

Aix-les-Bains

Chambéry

Aspres-
sur-Buëch

Grenoble

PROVENCE-ALPES-
CÔTE D'AZUR

Belley

La Tour-
du-Pin

Page 254

Voiron

Die

Carpentras

Bourgoin-
Jallieu

Page 262

Page 270

Crest

Vienne

Montélimar

Orange

Lyon

Page 242

Andance

Avignon

Rhône

Page 202

Page 214

Valence

Viviers

Rhône

l'Arbresle

Privas

Page 222

RHÔNE-
ALPES

Aubenas

Alès

Feurs

St-Étienne

Nîmes

Montbrison

Loire

Page 230

le Puy

Thiers

Mende

LANGUEDOC-
ROUSSILLON

Clermont-
Ferrand

Millau

Rodez

Aurillac

Introduction

The name of Burgundy brings to mind ancient, vaulted wine cellars, or dusty, venerable old bottles of precious vintages, treasured until a great moment of celebration arrives. The cork is carefully pulled, the rich dark wine poured and sipped and tasted and the gods invoked to bring long life, fortune and happiness. Many people, who have a prestigious bottle they are saving, or wish they had, know nothing more about Burgundy than this – that for centuries the region has produced the greatest of wines. Perhaps there is no need to know more, for that one fact reveals a great deal.

Green, prosperous Burgundy is one of the most thoroughly civilised places on earth. Not just France, but the whole world owes a debt to this well-watered land. In many ways, the Duchy extending almost from Paris to Lyon represents the height of human accomplishment. From farming to fine art, Burgundy established a norm of excellence.

The Gauls made their last stand here, to try to preserve their ancient culture against the might of Rome. The Roman towns flourished. Burgundy's poignant Romanesque abbeys and churches – Cluny, Cîteaux, Vézelay, Paray-le-Monial and the country churches of the Brionnais – achieved the highest expression of the medieval era. Some survive almost intact; others are majestic, awe-inspiring ruins. In Gothic architecture, too, the region excelled. And the influence of the Renaissance – that great explosion of art and creativity, learning and ideas – is still clear in Burgundy's towns and cities and châteaux.

For centuries, the dynasty of Dukes who ruled here stood quite apart from the French monarchy. By the end of the Hundred Years War (1337–1453), during which Burgundy joined with England against France, the Dukes had an empire of their own, which extended throughout Franche-Comté, Alsace, Lorraine, Picardy and all of Flanders into Holland. Burgundian patronage helped to establish Flemish artists and craftsmen as the leaders of their day, and it was from Flanders that the tradition came of decorated roof tiles, now regarded as typically Burgundian (and rarely seen in Flanders). In 1477 the marriage of the Duke's daughter divided the Burgundy possessions into two, and the French crown finally took control of the great Duchy.

Impressive abbeys, churches and castles rising up from the medieval streets of tiny villages recall the past. In many ways, the Duchy's sturdy self-reliant character, its richness and love of the finer things in life, remain unchanged. In the little country towns there is an abundance of good *pâtisseries*, *charcuteries* and restaurants.

To Burgundy, add the Rhône Valley – the great river highway that flows south from Lyon towards the Mediterranean. Together, the two make a single grand region renowned for food, wine, art, refinement, culture and good living.

Where does Burgundy end and the Rhône Valley begin? The city of Lyon links the two. From the high Alps, the Rhône runs cool and lively into Lake Geneva, and pours out the other side to descend into the heart of Lyon. There it meets and absorbs the darker waters of the Saône coming from Burgundy. Despite notorious industrial suburbs, Lyon remains a fascinating town of character, with an extensive riverside Renaissance quarter. Above all, it is the great gastronomic capital of France. The old streets and lanes are packed with discreet restaurants. Here the cooking has no Provençal bravura about it and is not based on oil, garlic and herbs. It's too close to Burgundy for that. Rather, the Lyonnais make good use of the highest-quality traditional farm produce from the attractive surrounding country districts – butter and cream, Charolais beef, fish and fowl from La Dombes, Bresse pork and capons.

The contented diners of Lyon have long looked upon a modest Beaujolais as their local *vin de table*. The wine comes from pretty, vine-covered hills just northwest of town, a delightful area, rural yet prosperous. One of the leading chefs in France, Paul Bocuse, has his restaurant at Collonges, where the hills touch the city limits. Here, customers might turn instead to the local Côte du Rhône and Côte d'Or wines.

Follow the Beaujolais hills west and descend through the pastures of Charollais into workaday Roanne. On a busy ring road, in front of the railway station, stands another of Europe's most celebrated restaurants, where the brothers Troisgros offer dinner and decor that are both resolutely modern. The Loire runs right through the town. Indeed, it's something of a surprise to discover how close France's two greatest rivers are to each other, particularly from here up to the source of the Loire, in the Ardèche. Confusingly, though, the Loire *département* is actually in the Rhône-Alpes region!

For millions of people each summer, the Rhône Valley is a mere corridor to the south. Its *routes nationales*, *autoroutes* and TGV railway lines, flanking the fast-flowing river, are filled with travellers hurtling to the beaches. Don't be rushed. The Rhône is a region, not just a route. The river itself brims with history. Its first Greek and Roman settlers planted grapevines and gardens alongside it, and the cultivation has continued ever since. Today this valley is one of France's richest provinces, a region of industry, productive orchards, horticulture and great vineyards, famous restaurants and classical ruins. To either side of the Rhône rise little-visited uplands and rustic backwaters, and villages that look down on visitors as if from another age.

Travel facts

Accommodation

Accommodation in Burgundy and the Rhône Valley ranges from some of the world's most sumptuous and palatial five-star hotels to simple country campsites. In between, there are hundreds of small, moderately priced, independent family-run hotels. Every little town, and many a tiny village, has at least one clean, adequately comfortable, unpretentious hotel (or sometimes, a *restaurant avec chambres*, 'restaurant with rooms'). Standards range from the extremely basic to the height of luxury. Pricing is normally for the room, not per person. A star system is in force, but some traditional hotels in both town and country fall far short of even a single star, while others far exceed the requirements for the maximum grade 'four-star luxe'. Most are two to three stars. There are many self-catering *gîtes* – usually country cottages – which often represent a bargain, though facilities can be basic.

Outside high season (July to August), booking hotels and other accommodation far ahead is rarely essential; throughout the region – except during local festivals or special events or on national holidays – it is usually sufficient to phone a few days before to reserve a room.

The major international hotel chains are represented in Burgundy and all down the Rhône Valley. The big French chains, all with several hotels in the region, include:

• **Campanile** – popular national chain of motels with restaurant: reliable, all identical, mid-price.

• **Balladins, Bonsaï, Etap Hôtel, Formule 1, Liberté, Première Classe** – all economy motels: modern but minimalist.

• **Ibis** – modern, functional, town hotels: mid- to low-budget.

• **Meridien** – smart, modern, high-quality chain.

• **Sofitel** – luxurious, modern hotels.

Useful accommodation and restaurant federations include:
• **Relais & Châteaux** – independently owned; top of the market, old-fashioned luxury, with excellent food (especially those designated as *Relais Gourmand*). Free handbook available from French tourist offices abroad.

• **Relais Routiers** – truck-drivers' stops; inexpensive roadside restaurants, generally with a few basic rooms. Recognisable by a blue-and-red circular sign outside.

• **Relais du Silence** – top-quality hotels in especially quiet locations. Bookable in France; *tel: 01 44 49 90 00*.

• **Logis et Auberges de France** – a great resource; almost 5 000 small,

Websites

France (*for Burgundy and the Rhône Valley websites, see page 20*): *www.francetourism.com/* (French Tourist Office site in the US with useful accommodation and trip-planning pages); *www.fr-holidaystore.co.uk/tourops/* (UK tour operators specialising in France); *www.gites-de-france. fr/csomang/general* (Gîtes de France site); *www.logis-de-france. fr/us/index* (English-language pages of Logis et Auberges de France site).

Camping

France has over 11,000 approved campsites. They are graded with stars: anything above two stars will have hot showers and good facilities. **Camping à la Ferme**, campsites on farms, tend to be more basic. Four-star and the even better four-star *Grand Comfort* sites have excellent amenities. **Castels et Camping** (*www.les-castels.com*) is a federation of top-quality camps, mainly in superb locations.

Thomas Cook Exchange Bureaux

Thomas Cook Travellers Cheques free you from the hazards of carrying large amounts of cash. Thomas Cook Foreign exchange bureaux are listed below. They all provide full foreign exchange facilities and will change currency and travellers' cheques (free of commission in the case of Thomas Cook Travellers Cheques).

Thomas Cook Bankers
*Gare De Lyon Perrache
10 Cours de Verdun
Hallde Gare No1
Lyon 69002
Tel: 04 78 38 38 84*

Thomas Cook Bankers
*Gare de Lyon Part Dieu
Boulevard Vivier Merle
Lyon 69003
Tel: 04 72 33 48 55*

unpretentious, family-run independent hotels, nearly all with a good inexpensive restaurant (half of them specialise in regional dishes). Rooms are adequate and reasonably priced. Free handbook available from French tourist offices abroad.

• **Gîtes** are simple cottages, rented as inexpensive, self-catering, vacation accommodation. They are bookable in the UK; *tel: 0990 360360, e-mail: info@gites-de-france.fr*
• **Villages des Vacances** ('holiday villages'), either for all the family or for children only, are popular with the French. Details from national and regional tourist offices.
• **Chambres d'Hôtes** ('guest rooms'), often announced by a simple hand-made sign on a front gate, are homely bed-and-breakfast stopovers (often with evening meal too), usually in ordinary family homes in rural areas.
• **Café-Couette** ('coffee and quilt') is a scheme to pre-book bed and breakfast at ordinary homes and *chambres d'hôtes*. Bookable in France; *tel: 01 42 94 92 00, fax: 01 42 94 93 12.*

Airports

Lyon-Saint Exupéry is the principal airport of Burgundy and the Rhône Valley region, handling scheduled international and internal flights (*see page 30, Getting to Burgundy and the Rhône Valley*). **Geneva**, in Switzerland, is another international airport on the border of the region and with excellent rail and road connections. **Dijon-Bourgogne Airport** handles flights from London and French provincial cities.

Children

French children may strike their British, American and Australasian counterparts (and their parents) as very well behaved and fairly strictly disciplined. Children are expected to sit quietly at table and eat grown-up food. On the other hand, there are plenty of facilities and entertainment for kids and – as long as they know how to behave – they are welcomed everywhere.

Climate

The region enjoys a long, warm, sometimes rather humid summer from around May to September, with daytime temperatures often reaching above 20°C. Autumn is bright, mild and comfortably warm. Temperatures are lower at higher altitudes. Occasional heavy downpours are a feature of the later summer and autumn. Spring is mild and pleasant. In winter it can be damp and sometimes very cool, January and February being the coldest and wettest months. In the large river valleys, winter is generally milder.

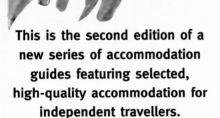

Currency

French money is the French franc (FF), divided into 100 centimes. There are coins of ½, 1, 2, 5, 10 and 20 francs, and notes of 20, 50, 100, 200 and 500 francs.

The franc is a denomination of the Euro, although there is no cash form of the Euro before 2002. The franc will be completely replaced by the Euro at the end of 2002.

French money is readily available from ATMs (cash dispensers) accepting all credit cards and bank cards displaying the appropriate international symbols.

There's no limit on the amount of money that can be taken into or out of France.

Customs regulations

Non-EU citizens aged over 15 and spending less than 6 months in France may be able to reclaim **VAT** (*TVA* in French) on any items costing over 2 000F purchased for export. At the time of the purchase, present your passport and ask for a *bordereau* form. On leaving France, have the *bordereau* validated by French Customs.

• For travellers returning to the **UK and other EU countries** there are no restrictions, except that all goods brought back must be for personal consumption. In the UK, HM Customs & Excise still maintain limits on the amount of alcoholic drinks and tobacco that will be considered reasonable 'for personal use'. These propose up to 90 litres of wine, 10 litres of spirits and 800 cigarettes. More information on: *www.hmce.gov.uk*.

• Travellers returning to the **USA** have an allowance of up to $400 for goods for personal use, but most plants or foods are prohibited. For US Treasury customs information consult *www.customs.ustreas.gov/ travel/travel*.

• In general, goods for personal use or gifts up to $300 may be brought back to **Canada**. Call 1-800-461-9999 for more information.

• **Australian** Customs allow up to $400-worth of goods, including 250 cigarettes and 1 bottle of alcoholic drink. Foods and anything containing wood or plant material may be prohibited.

• In **New Zealand** you are allowed $700-worth of goods, including 200 cigarettes and 6 bottles of alcoholic drink. Prohibited items include foods and anything containing wood or plant material.

• **South Africans** can bring back up to 1 250 rand-worth of goods tax-free, including 1 litre of spirits, 2 litres of wine and 400 cigarettes. Above that limit, an additional 10,000 rand-worth of goods is allowed but is taxed at 20 per cent for all goods.

For visitors entering France there are no limits on legal articles for ordinary personal use.

Electricity

The power supply in France is 220 volts. Circular two-pin plugs are used.

Entry formalities

Travellers from the UK, USA, NZ and Canada do not need a visa for visits of less than 90 days. Australians and South Africans must apply for a visa from a French embassy.

Festivals

Major and minor festivals take place throughout Burgundy and the Rhône Valley all year long. In the wine villages in autumn, look out especially for *paulées* – festivals to celebrate the end of the grape harvest.

End of Jan:
• *Fête de St-Vincent* in many Burgundy wine villages;
• *St-Vincent Tournante* festival at a different village each year, Côte d'Or;
• *Fête des Conscrits* (Army Conscripts' Festival) with *La Vague race*, Villefranche-sur-Saône.

Begin Feb: *St-Vincent Tournante* among the Chablis villages.

Mar: *Florissimo* – a huge flower event that takes place every three years, Dijon (see page 106).
16–24 Mar: Carnival, Chalon-sur-Saône.

Whitsun: International Boules Tournament, Lyon.

Information is provided on *www.info-france-usa.org/america/embassy/customs/cover.*

Drinking

Burgundy and the Rhône Valley are famous for fine wine, but everyday drinking in Burgundy is similar to elsewhere in France. The French do not usually drink with the intention of getting drunk at all, but to enhance appetite, conversation and companionship. In any bar or *brasserie*, not only alcoholic and soft drinks are served but also coffee (including decaffeinated), hot chocolate, tea and herbal tea.

Drinks

de l'eau minérale – mineral water
eau gazeuese or *eau plate* – sparkling or still water
une bière – any name-brand German or Belgian beer
un demi or *une bière à la pression* – a glass of draught lager-style beer
un café – espresso (the French keep going with frequent shots all day)
un café-crème (usually *un grand crème*) – coffee with milk (the French usually drink this only for breakfast)
un déca – decaffeinated coffee
un thé (*nature*, *citron* or *au lait*) – tea (black, with lemon, or with milk)
une tisane – herbal tea
un chocolat chaud – hot chocolate
un Miky – cold chocolate drink
un kir – a Burgundy speciality, correctly made with local Aligoté wine and crème de cassis (blackcurrant liqueur)
Suze, Noilly Prat, Dubonnet and *Martini* – popular brand-name aperitifs
un panaché – shandy (mixed beer and lemonade)
un coca/un coca light – Coca Cola/Diet Coke
un diabolo menthe (green) or *diabolo grenadine* (red) – lemonade mixed with brightly coloured syrup
un jus d'ananas, jus de poire – pineapple juice or pear juice are both popular
un jus d'orange – bottled orange juice
une orange pressée – freshly squeezed orange juice
une Orangina – fizzy orange drink
sirop – fruit-flavoured sweet drink served in either still or fizzy water
du vin (rouge/blanc/rosé/doux/mousseux) – wine (red/white/rosé/sweet/sparkling). No need to ask for dry – it's all dry unless you specify sweet
un pichet/demi-pichet (d'eau/de vin blanc/de vin rouge/de vin rosé) – 1-litre carafe/half-litre carafe (of water/white wine/red wine/rosé wine)
See also pages 34–6 for regional wines.

Third Sun after Whitsun: Sacré-Coeur Pilgrimage to Paray-le-Monial.

May: *Montgolfiades* – annual hot air balloon show, Chalon-sur-Saône.
31 May: *Fête de la Bague* – traditional horse race, Semur-en-Auxois.

Fri nearest 24 June: Midsummer Night Fair, Villefranche-sur-Saône.
July: Baroque music festival, Beaune.

1–15 July: jazz festival, Vienne.
14 July: jousting on the River Yonne, Clamecy, and on the Rhône, Condrieu and Tournon.
15–31 July: Morvan Music Festival, Autun.
22 July: Ste-Madeleine Pilgrimage, Vézelay.

15 Aug: jousting on the Yonne, Coulonges-sur-Yonne.
Weekend after 15 Aug: flower festival, St-Honoré-les-Bains; horse show, Cluny.

Early Sept: vineyard festival and popular music festival, Dijon. Ste-Reine Pilgrimage, Alise-Ste-Reine.
8 Sept: Beaujolais Vinegrowers' Pilgrimage to Mont Brouilly Chapel.
Sept: vineyard festival, Beaune.

Nov: *Les Trois Glorieuses* – wine trade and growers' celebrations, Beaune, Vougeot and Meursault. Chablis Wine Festival, Chablis.

8 Dec: Festival of Light, at Lyon.

Eating out

Most French eating places offer a choice of about three *menus*, that is, three *prix fixe* (fixed price) set meals, as well as the à la carte menu, a list of individually priced dishes. The price difference reflects not differences in quality but in the number of courses and difficulty of preparation. In general, to get the best out of a French restaurant, order one of the *menus*. Prices will usually be higher if you pick and choose from the *carte*. The day's menus are always displayed outside the restaurant.

Prices must include service and all taxes. It's not necessary to give any extra tip, though a few centimes or 1F is often left for the waiter on a café table. *Vin compris* means wine included (usually about a quarter or third of a litre of house wine per person).

Away from resorts and big cities, it can be difficult to find something to eat outside normal mealtimes. The lunch break lasts from 1200 to about 1400. Sunday lunch, often taken *en famille* at a local restaurant, lasts until 1500. A little more flexibility comes into dinner hours, from 1900 to 2200, though 2000 is still the usual time to start dinner. *Brasseries* are bars that generally serve food at any time. A *salon de thé* serves pastries and other light snacks with tea or coffee.

Health

It's usually possible to see a general practitioner without an appointment, or to phone to request a visit. For doctors, medicines and hospital treatment, payment must be made on the spot. Keep receipts – you will need them when claiming reimbursement, whether through Form E111 (available to UK citizens – instructions on the form and accompanying leaflet) or from your travel insurance.

Burgundy and the Rhône Valley on the Web

www.burgundy.net/indexa Burgundy business, culture, news and tourism. *www.burgundy-today.com/* Online food and wine magazine about Burgundy. *www.burgundy-tourism.com/* The regional tourist office site. *www.cr-bourgogne.fr/* Burgundy regional council site with latest news and information about the region. *www.europe-france.com/France/22* About the Rhône-Alpes. *www.fgtousa.org/regional/bur* The Burgundy page of the French Tourist Office in the USA. *www.maregion.com/* Eclectic French site about Burgundy, mainly for locals. *www.rhone-en-decouverte.com* Rhône département site. *www.tourisme-rhone-alpes.com* Rhône-Alpes Tourist Office.

Information

- **UK** Maison de France (French Government Tourist Office), *178 Piccadilly, London W1V 0AL. Tel: 0891 244123, fax: 020 7493 6594.*
- **Ireland** Maison de France (French Government Tourist Office), *38 Lower Abbey Street, Dublin 1. Tel: 01 703 4046, fax: 01 874 7324.*
- **USA** Maison de France (French Government Tourist Offices), *444 Madison Avenue, 16th Floor (between 49 and 50th Street), New York, NY 10022-6903. Fax: 212 838-7855.*
- **Australia** Maison de France (French Government Tourist Office), *BNP Building, 12 Castlereagh St, Sydney, NSW 2000. Tel: 61 2 231 5244, fax: 61 2 221 8682.*
- **Comités Régionaux du Tourisme (Regional Tourism Committees) in Burgundy and the Rhône Valley** CRT Bourgogne, *12 blvd de Brosses, Dijon. Tel: 03 80 50 90 00, fax: 03 80 30 59 45. CRT Rhône-Alpes, 104 route de Paris, Charbonnières-les-Bains. Tel: 04 78 42 50 04, fax: 04 72 38 42 18.*

Maps

Tourist offices have free city and country maps printed in French and sometimes in English. City brochures usually have a map of the city printed inside. Michelin regional maps 243 (Bourgogne-Franche Comté) and 244 (Rhône-Alpes) cover most of Burgundy and the Rhône Valley in detail. The annual Michelin motoring atlas is useful for touring in Burgundy, the Rhône-Alpes and further afield. The Michelin *Atlas Autoroutier* (Motorway Atlas) is a handbook detailing facilities, junctions, etc, on the *autoroutes*. IGN regional maps are an alternative to Michelin, and IGN local large-scale maps are ideal for walking.

Insurance

UK citizens should travel with Form E111, entitling reimbursement of part of any medical expenses incurred, as well as travel insurance covering medical emergencies. Other visitors are advised to have full medical cover as part of their travel insurance policy. For motorists, third-party insurance is compulsory (see page 27).

National parks

www.parcs-naturels-regionaux.tm.fr website of the Fédération des Parcs Naturels Régionaux de France (French Regional Nature Parks).

The offices of the region's parks are:
Parc Naturel Régional du Morvan Maison du Parc, 58230 St-Brisson; tel: 03 86 78 79 00, fax: 03 86 78 74 22, e-mail: contact-@parcdumorvan.org, website: www.parcdumorvan.org

Parc Naturel Régional du Pilat Maison du Parc, Moulin de Virieu, BP 57, 42410 Pelussin; tel: 04 74 87 52 01, fax: 04 74 87 52 02. Tourist information: 04 74 87 52 00.

Museums

Basic opening times for most museums in the region are 0900–1200, 1400–1800, closed Monday or Tuesday and some national holidays, with many variations (sometimes with different opening times on different days and different months). Hours are often extended in July and August.

Opening times

Shops: typically Tue–Sat 0900–1200 or 1230, 1500–1900. Food shops may open earlier in the morning, but later in the afternoon, and some (especially *pâtisseries*) open on Sunday morning. In cities and resorts, shops may keep longer hours.
Department stores: Mon–Sat 0900–1830 (often with one or more late evenings per week).
Hypermarkets: Mon–Sat 0900–2200.
Banks: either Mon–Fri or Tue–Sat 0900–1200, 1400–1700, with local variations.
Petrol stations: usually daily around 0700–2200.
Post offices: Mon–Fri 0800–1900, Sat 0800–1200. Stamps and envelopes can usually be bought from newsagents.
Tourist offices: usually Mon–Sat 0900–1200, 1400–1800. Longer hours, and no midday closing, in season.
Businesses: Mon–Fri 0900–1200, 1400–1800.
Bars: 0700 or 0800 to 2300 or 2400. Some stay open later, especially in resorts.
Restaurants: 1200–1400, 1900–2200. Most restaurants have at least one day off per week.
Churches: usually daily 0900–1700.

Packing

Bring a hat, sunglasses, light clothes and cool footwear, plus a warmer jacket or raincoat just in case. If you're planning to visit up-market nightspots, casinos or classical concerts, a smart dress, jacket or smart casual wear could be appropriate. A light sweater is invaluable as it can be cool even on summer evenings. In winter, take a thick sweater and coat.

Postal services

Postcards and letters are charged at the same rate for all EU destinations, with delivery within a few days. Stamps are available in newsagents and tobacconists. Airmail rates for letters to other destinations are much higher and items have to be weighed at a post office (indicated by a PTT sign).

Sport

Canals and rivers – canal and river cruising is a major holiday activity in Burgundy. With three large rivers, the Saône, Loire and Rhône, and a network of 17th-century canals running alongside and between them, there are over 1200km of navigable rivers and canals open to pleasure craft. The Burgundy Comité Régional du Tourisme (CRT) produces a brochure dedicated to canal and river boating.

Cycling – locals like it and so do visitors, and many areas are ideal either for touring or more strenuous mountain biking. Especially popular in the Morvan.

Golf – there are around 20 excellent golf courses in Burgundy and the Rhône Valley.

Rock climbing and potholing – in the river gorges and hill areas, especially west of the Rhône.

Walking – the region is criss-crossed with over 5000km of marked footpaths.

Watersports – the region's major sporting activity with sailing on lakes and canoeing on the rivers. All waterside resorts have facilities for equipment hire and tuition. Especially popular in the Ardèche Valley.

Public holidays

I Jan: New Year's Day
Mar/Apr: Easter Monday
I May: Labour Day
8 May: VE Day
May: Ascension
May/June: Pentecost (Whit Monday)
14 July: National Day
15 Aug: Assumption
I Nov: All Saints' Day
11 Nov: Armistice Day
25 Dec: Christmas
Where national holidays fall on a Sunday, the next day is taken as a holiday instead.

Telephones

Public transport

Town buses – called *bus* – are available in all cities from about 0700–2100.

Trains are useful for excursions, with stations in almost all towns. Scenic rail services run in the Ardèche and Haut-Vivarais areas.

Generally, public phones in France require a pre-paid phonecard (*une télécarte*), available from newsagents, *tabacs* and other shops.

Directory enquiries: 12.
Operator: 13.
Police: 17.

To call the UK from France, the international dialling code is 00 44. The code for Australia is 00 61, USA and Canada 00 1 and New Zealand 00 64. Calling from the UK or any other country, the code for France is 00 33.

Safety and security

Apart from certain districts in Lyon away from the city centre, all the other towns and rural areas included here are generally very safe. However, it is wise to take certain precautions: do not wear ostentatious jewellery, openly handle large sums of cash, or leave anything of value on view in cars. To call the Police, dial 17.

Tipping

Restaurants – included, not necessary.
Bars – included, but you could leave some small change.
Taxis – about 10 per cent.
Room service – included, not necessary.
Tour guides – tip at your discretion.
Toilet attendants – small change.

Toilets

Usually called WC (pronounced 'Vay-Say') or *toilettes*. Free or small charge in bars. Small charge for attended public toilets, no charge if not attended. Many are automatic self-cleaning, charging 1F (not really safe for children).

Time

France observes Central European Standard Time and Central European Daylight Saving Time. These are one hour ahead of Greenwich Mean Time (GMT) throughout the year. French Daylight Saving Time (Summer Time) starts at 0200 on the last Sunday in March and ends at 0300 on the last Sunday in October.

Travellers with disabilities

For parking, the orange card scheme applies in France. Vehicles modified for a disabled driver and showing 'disabled' on the registration document are entitled to lower *autoroute* tolls.

Accessibility information for tourists is available from:
Association des Paralysés de France, *17 blvd Auguste Blanqui, 75013 Paris. Tel: 01 40 78 69 00.*
CNFLRH, *236bis r. de Tolbiac, 75013 Paris. Tel: 01 53 80 66 66, fax: 01 53 80 66 67, website: www.whanditel.jouve.fr.*
RADAR, *12 City Forum, 250 City Rd, London EC1V 8AF. Tel: 020 7250 3222.*

Driver's guide

Accidents

Breakdowns

Hazard warning lights or a warning triangle are compulsory (motoring organisations recommend you have both). On *autoroutes* (motorways), use the red emergency phones provided every 2km. Approved recovery vehicles will be sent and a fixed fee charged (around 400F; more at night, at weekends and during holidays). On other roads, members of motoring organisations with European cover should contact their emergency phone number. Those without European cover should simply make contact with a local garage.

If you are involved in a road accident you must stop your vehicle immediately, with minimum obstruction to traffic. If anyone has been injured, or either party is under the influence of alcohol, the police must be called. French motorists will probably complete a *constat* (an insurance form verifying the facts) and all parties must sign to show that it is an accurate account. Non-French motorists should simply exchange details with the other parties.

It's worth knowing that, if a motor accident involves a pedestrian under 16 or over 70, or a severely disabled person, they cannot be held responsible for the accident.

If the accident is due to a bad road surface or faulty traffic light, a claim may be made against the Ponts et Chaussées (bridges and roads) authority.

A hitch-hiker may claim against his driver even though the driver was not responsible for the accident.

Autoroutes in Burgundy and the Rhône Valley

In Burgundy and the Rhône Valley the main road artery is the *Autoroute du Soleil* (the 'Sunshine Motorway') – the A6 from Paris to Lyon, continuing beyond Lyon as the A7. It is the principal highway linking Provence and the Riviera with northern France, and suffers heavy congestion on holiday weekends throughout the year and at the start and end of the main summer holiday period (mid-July and end of August). In northern Burgundy the A19 and A5 give access to the Autoroute du Soleil from the A26, the *Autoroute des Anglais* – so-called because it runs directly out of the ferry terminal at Calais.

An alternative little-used north–south *autoroute* is the A31/A39/A40/A42, running along the eastern edge of Burgundy all the way to Lyon. Other *autoroutes* in Burgundy are the A31 from Beaune and Dijon into northeastern France, the A36 heading east from Beaune, and Dijon's A38 and A39 spurs connecting the city to other *autoroutes*. The A40 runs from Mâcon to Bourg-en-Bresse.

South of Lyon, the A7 continues down the Rhône into Provence. The A43, A48 and A49 turn east from the A7 to the Alps, while the A47/A72 heads west via St-Étienne into the Auvergne.

Driving conditions

Motorways (A roads), called *autoroutes* in French, are of high standard, with frequent service stations where food and sometimes accommodation is available. Main roads (N or RN) are called *routes nationales*. Secondary roads (D) are called *routes départementales*. The extensive network of clearly marked, straight, well-maintained D roads in France makes it easy to avoid busy main highways.

Main highways are generally well maintained and of high standard and are kept clear in snowy weather. Roads in town may be of poor standard, and are often cobbled. While locals may drive normally over cobbles, it would be wiser to protect your car's suspension by driving gently on these streets. Some country lanes may be poor. On peak summer days, the A6 and A7 (passing through Burgundy and the Rhône Valley) are notorious for dense traffic and hold-ups. Roadside panels warn of dates to avoid, when exceptionally heavy traffic is expected.

The website at *www.autoroutes.fr* gives full information (in French) on *autoroutes*, including tolls.

Caravans and camper vans

On hills, watch out for signs applying a lower speed limit for caravans. Before setting out, check that brake and other cables to the caravan are firmly in place and correctly adjusted, and that caravan tyres are of the same size and type and in sound condition. The make and serial number of a caravan must be clearly displayed. When making stops, remember that stopping overnight in a caravan or camper van is only permitted on campsites or other authorised locations.

Car hire

Car hire is widely available all over France from both major international and local firms. Prices are generally higher than in other countries.

Driving rules

The *Priorité à Droite* (give way to the right) rule is the main cause of accidents involving foreign drivers in France. The rule is this: drive on the right and always give way to anything approaching from the right, except where signs indicate to the contrary. There is one other exception: vehicles emerging from private property don't have priority over traffic on the public highway.

Be especially careful in the following situations:
• where two major highways merge – watch out for priority signs;
• in towns, where traffic coming from side roads on your right may drive out as if on a 'green light' even if you are on the main road;
• at roundabouts. Most roundabouts now give priority to vehicles already on the roundabout (as in the UK). If you see signs reading *Vous n'avez pas la priorité* and/or *Cédez le passage* ('You don't have priority' or 'Give way'), this is the case. If there are no such signs, the usual priority rule applies, and traffic already in the roundabout has to give way to traffic entering it. Remember to go round in an anticlockwise direction!

Generally, take extra care when overtaking – driving on the right in a right-hand drive car makes it difficult to see oncoming traffic.

Documents

Insurance and car registration papers and a driving licence must always be carried when driving. A full UK or other west European or US driving licence is accepted. The minimum driving age for a car or motorcycle is 18.

Drink-driving laws

In France the maximum legal level of alcohol in the blood is 0.05 per cent. Depending on the amount of excess, penalties range from on-the-spot fines, impounding of the vehicle, confiscation of driving licence, and so on, up to prison sentences of varying severity.

Fuel

Regular unleaded (*essence sans plomb*), high-octane unleaded (*super sans plomb*) and diesel (*gasoil* or *diesel*) are all widely available. Leaded petrol is hard to find. Petrol prices are a little higher than in the UK except for diesel, which is much cheaper. Credit cards are widely accepted at petrol stations, but not universally; customers are sometimes required to 'verify' the card by tapping in their PIN on a keypad. Travellers' cheques cannot usually be used to pay for petrol.

Seat belts

Seat belts must be worn at all times in both the front and back of the car, except in older vehicles which do not have seat belts fitted. Children under 10 are not allowed to travel in the front seats (except for babies up to 9 months weighing under 9kg and seated in a rear-facing baby seat). Even in rear seats, all children must use seat belts. Although children over a certain age may travel in the front of a car, remember that airbags can kill a child or small adult.

Information

The *Bison Futé* organisation provides traffic information and alternative routes (*Routes Bis*) to avoid congestion. It publishes an annual map, available free from tourist offices and some gas stations. Call 08 36 68 20 00 (2,23F per minute) for up-to-the-minute information.
• RAC Roadworks in Europe: 0891 500 241 (premium rate)
• RAC European Touring Information: 0891 500 243 (premium rate)

Insurance

Third-party insurance is compulsory. Comprehensive insurance issued by UK insurers is valid in the EU (a Green Card is no longer required, although a few insurers still wish to be informed that you are going abroad).

Lights

Dipped lights and main beam must be adjusted using headlight deflectors, to avoid dazzling oncoming drivers when driving on the right. Dipped lights must also be used in rain and poor visibility as well as after dark. Motorcycles over 125cc must use a dipped headlight at all times.

Parking

The Burgundy and Rhône Valley regions are predominantly rural, with few busy urban areas. Parking is not usually a problem outside large towns. However, in town centres, especially Lyon, cars left in no-parking zones are generally quickly towed away without warning – often within ten minutes of parking. Kerbside signs always make it clear what the parking regulations are in each street.

Police

Law enforcement in France is perfunctory and severe. French police (*gendarmes*) have generally not been to charm school and have considerable powers. Many offences, including speeding, not stopping at a Stop sign, overtaking where forbidden, driving with worn tyres, not wearing a seat belt, or a helmet (for motorcyclists) are punishable by an immediate on-the-spot fine that may be as much as 1 000F, payable in cash. Issuing a receipt is part of the on-the-spot procedure – always be sure to get one, and keep it carefully. Serious motoring offences such as drink-driving are liable to lead to confiscation of the car, heavy fines, or imprisonment. Drink-driving enforcement has recently been tightened up.

Tolls

Tolls are levied on most *autoroutes*, except where bypassing large cities. Foreign currency is generally accepted. Credit cards can be used to pay motorway tolls; signatures are not normally required. Travellers' cheques cannot usually be used for tolls.

Security

Crime is not known to be a big problem in Burgundy or the Rhône Valley, except in some districts of Lyon, but it's a wise precaution everywhere to put all valuables out of sight when leaving your car parked.

Speed limits

Speed limits reflect road conditions, and variable limits are used on some busy roads, so watch signs. In normal circumstances, limits are generally 50kph (31mph) in town, 90kph (55mph) out of town. The limit is generally 110kph (68mph) on dual carriageways, and 130kph (80mph) on motorways (sometimes lower on toll-free motorways). Motorways often also have a minimum fast-lane speed limit of 80kph (49mph). Signs sometimes indicate lower speed limits for wet weather or fog, and new drivers (in their first two years) must also keep to limits about 10kph lower than indicated.

What to take

You must have a red warning triangle or hazard warning lights in case of accident. Your car's headlights must be adjusted to avoid dazzle when driving on the right; you can buy stick-on headlight deflectors. You'll also need a GB sticker, a first-aid kit, a torch, a petrol container and spare headlight bulbs. Spectacle wearers are advised to carry a spare pair.

Getting to Burgundy and the Rhône Valley

From the UK

Option one: just get in your car and go

Dozens of operators cross the Channel each day and a network of roads runs direct from the ferry terminals. The fast route is the A26 (*Autoroute des Anglais*) direct from Calais to Troyes in Champagne, on the border of northern Burgundy (3–4 hours). It's a further 2-hour drive to Dijon and the Côte d'Or. This option is by no means the cheapest.

Option two: book a self-drive package holiday

Widely available, and good value for money, all packages include Channel crossings and accommodation (whether hotel, self-catering, or camping in pre-erected tents) in Burgundy and the Rhône Valley. Some include hotel stops en route. The cheapest packages may use poor-quality campsites in unattractive areas, while the most expensive put you up in luxurious châteaux-hotels with famous restaurants. This option is generally the most economical.

Option three: fly and drive

There are frequent charter and scheduled flights to Lyon-Saint Exupéry from London and British regional airports. Lyon is about 2 hours' flying time from London. Car hire from major international and local companies is available at the airport.

Roissy-Charles de Gaulle and Orly airports in Paris, Saint Exupéry Airport at Lyon, Geneva and Bâle-Mulhouse airports are all linked to Burgundy by motorway or TGV.

Dijon-Bourgogne Airport, 6km southeast of Dijon, is served by internal flights to Clermond-Ferrand, and from there to Angoulême, Bordeaux, Lille, Limoges, Madrid, Marseilles, Nantes, Pau, Rennes and Toulouse. For flight information and reservations at Dijon Airport, tel: 03 80 67 67 67, fax: 03 80 63 02 99.

Option four: rail and drive

It's easy to reach Burgundy and the Rhône Valley by rail (Eurostar to Lille, TGV direct from Lille to Dijon, Lyon, or Valence) and hire a car on arrival. Even on ordinary express trains, most of Burgundy is under 2 hours by train from Paris.

By high-speed train
- London to Paris takes 3 hours, to Lille 2 hours
- Lille to Lyon takes 3 hours, Paris to Lyon 2 hours
- Lille to Dijon takes 2 hours 40 minutes, Paris to Dijon 1 hour 40 minutes
- Paris–Dijon–Beaune–Chalon-sur-Saône takes 2 hours 10 minutes altogether
- Paris to Mâcon-Loché TGV station takes 1 hour 40 minutes
- Paris to Le Creusot-Montceau-Montchanin TGV station takes 1 hour 25 minutes.

AutoTrain to Lyon

There is no Motorail (cars and passengers on the same train) into Burgundy, but you can still travel by train and have your own car on arrival. Overnight AutoTrain allows your car to travel from Paris to Lyon overnight while you travel during the day by TGV. The rail journey is much less stressful than the long drive, so this option is especially useful for those with children. For information, tel: Rail Europe *08705 848 848*.

From outside Europe

There are frequent direct scheduled flights to Paris (and Geneva in Switzerland) from over 30 North American cities, and from Australia and New Zealand. On arrival, there are fast and simple TGV rail connections from Paris and Geneva airports to Dijon and Lyon.

From other regions of France

Autoroutes and *routes nationales* provide easy access from all other regions.
From the north, west and east
- A26 and A5 from Calais
- A6 or A5 from Paris
- A31 from Luxembourg, Metz and Nancy
- A36 and A39 from Mulhouse and Besançon
- A40 from the Alps and Geneva
From the south
- A7 from Provence and the southeast
- A9 from Languedoc and the southwest

Car hire

Car hire is relatively expensive in France. It is widely available in all big towns, at Lyon-Saint Exupéry Airport and at many railway stations, from the major international companies. Do-it-yourself car hire is much more expensive than taking it as part of a package.

Setting the scene

Burgundy and the good life

The culture of Burgundy and the Rhône Valley results from over two millennia of civilisation in a generous and productive land. Not for nothing has 'Burgundy' become the name of a rich, dignified colour: a deep red, close to purple, suggestive of pomp, power and prosperity. Of course, it is supposed to represent the colour of Burgundy's famous dark red wines. The white wines would have to be represented by an equally noble colour – gold, perhaps. But these colours are also themes of Burgundy's heritage, easily picked out in its religious paintings, medieval tapestries, ecclesiastical robes and decorated roof tiles.

Even modern Burgundy evokes intoxicating images of opulence, luscious pasture with heavy cattle, rich fabrics, civilised towns, refined and generous cuisine, cream sauces and fine wines. Certainly all that is there, and is part of what the French call *l'art de vivre*, the art of living. However, there are other elements to the art of living, and in these, too, Burgundy excels: architecture, the love of nature and the open air, physical energy, sport and activity.

Then of course, there is art itself. Flanders, while a possession of the Dukes of Burgundy, was the home of the greatest artists and craftsmen of the Middle Ages. Much of their work made its way into Burgundy's castles and churches, where it can still be seen. Music, painting, drama and literature continue to be highly prized here, celebrated in festivals, in theatres, galleries and museums. And although 'Rhône' is not yet the name of a colour – perhaps it should be – along the Rhône Valley, too, art and the art of living have been cultivated for centuries, together with a dynamic commerce and industry.

Hills, valleys and plains

Burgundy and the Rhône Valley form a broad band through France from north to south, stretching from Paris to Provence. Its approximate borders are the River Loire on the west, and the uplands of eastern France (Jura and Alps) on the east. This wide swathe of countryside divides roughly into two parallel strips.

Its western half is mostly hilly and varied, and cut through by many rivers. There are several plateaux (for example, Morvan, Auxerrois, the Arrière Côte) and hill ranges (Monts du Lyonnais, Monts du Beaujolais, the Vivarais upland), where the landscape can be wild and open, populated with rustic communities or small industrial centres.

The eastern half is the broad river plain of the Rhône and its major Burgundian tributary, the Saône. The terrain is mainly flat or gently undulating, and divided into regions of primarily historical significance (Bresse, Dombes, Bas-Dauphiné) that stretch as far as the foothills of the Alps. Although the flatter eastern terrain is also predominantly rural, along the Rhône and Saône valleys most of the industrial and urban development has taken place over more than 20 centuries. The principal transport corridor between northern and southern France has run alongside the two rivers throughout all that time.

Who goes?

Burgundy and the Rhône Valley is green, provincial France. It offers an eclectic portfolio of attractions for the francophile, gourmet and nature-lover, among others, and exerts a strong appeal for a generally more discerning type of visitor. Many come again and again for short breaks of a few days or week.

Only the southern Ardèche features in the brochures of major European tour operators as a full-length family holiday destination – and even then as a rural, connoisseur's choice. Those who love wild hill country, who enjoy a cool river swim, canal and river cruising or long walks may head for its open spaces. Others visit its Roman remains, Romanesque architecture, picturesque villages and ancient cities. Those who enjoy the good life of Burgundy and the Rhône Valley come to enjoy winetasting, château-hotels and the world's greatest gastronomic restaurants.

When to come

Generally warm, mild and humid, with prevailing westerly breezes and moderate rainfall year-round, Burgundy's climate is comfortable throughout spring, autumn and most of summer too. Only in July and August do temperatures sometimes hit uncomfortably hot and muggy highs. In contrast, January days can be bitingly cold, especially in the Morvan and other uplands.

At Lyon, the Rhône Valley begins, and at Valence the weather becomes more distinctly Mediterranean, sunnier and drier, with each step south. The valley's most striking characteristic is the bone-dry Mistral wind. In winter it can lash down the Rhône Valley (most of the trees are leaning southward), but in the summer months this wind shows its kinder face, as smooth and tender as silk, keeping the air balmy and skies clean and blue.

In spring, both northern Burgundy and the Rhône Valley are pretty with fruit trees heavy with blossom. Best months throughout the region are May, June and September. Autumn is a joyous time in the wine areas, from Chablis to the Côte d'Or, to Beaujolais to the Côtes du Rhône, a season of harvesting and feasting, when the leaves turn to dazzling gold and purple.

The main wine regions of Burgundy and the Rhône Valley

Auxerrois

South of Auxerre along the River Yonne. Modest rosés and reds, and fizzy Crémant de Bourgogne (see page 84).

Chablis

Northern Burgundy, near Champagne. Dry and elegant whites. The same region produces modest red and rosé wines, but these are not 'Chablis' (see page 60).

Côte d'Or

The long, east-facing slope extending 60km south from Dijon to Santenay; divided into Côte de Nuits, for highest grade reds, and Côte de Beaune, for highly prestigious reds and whites (see page 118).

Côte Chalonnaise

Lying west of Chalon-sur-Saône, the last southern slope of the same escarpment as the Côte d'Or. A few superb whites and reds (see page 132).

Memories of Rome

Two thousand years ago, the Rhône Valley provided the avenue for the armies of Rome to stride north from Provence. In their wake came the Empire's civil engineers, architects, administrators, temple-builders, circuses and wine-makers. The Roman invasion started in 59 BC. In 58 BC Caesar set out to conquer the whole of Gaul. In 52–51 BC the 'Gaulish War' represented the largest concerted effort by the disparate Gallic tribes, under Vercingetorix, to throw off Roman rule. Their defeat at *Alisia* marked the start of a rapid Roman colonisation of Burgundy. In the 1st century AD, most Gallic settlements were converted into Roman towns. Grapes and orchards were planted and cities laid out. Much survives from that era, both on the ground and in museums. A few Roman structures remain standing to this day, in Vaison and Orange. In some towns, like Vienne, Lyon and Autun, the ruins are extensive and impressive. At excavated *Alisia* (now Alise), the memory lingers of the last stand of Gaul against Rome.

Romanesque Burgundy – cathedrals, abbeys and monasteries

A great part of Burgundy's inheritance comes from the religious zeal of the Middle Ages. Up to the 9th century, many abbeys and churches were built, and rebuilt in the more imposing Burgundian Romanesque style. The vast church of the Benedictine abbey at Vézelay, founded in 864, was rebuilt in 1100 and still stands.

Under the Dukes, Burgundy led the way in the growth of monasticism in western Christendom. The greatest of the monasteries was established at Cluny in 910. Its building style was distinctive for plain and simple elegance, and the church itself was the largest in Europe. Cluny also adhered to the Benedictine Rule, but modified to demand more prayer, less abstinence. Owing allegiance only to the Pope, and sufficiently far away from him to be virtually self-governing, yet endowed with his authority, Cluny attracted numerous substantial donations. Within two centuries it had set up over 1000 daughter communities. Scores of churches were built in the same style (Brionnais is noted for them).

In 1112, a group of austere monks rebelled against Cluny's luxury-loving abbots, and set up their own community at Cîteaux. Following a life of harsh self-denial, they established the Cistercian Order. Within 30 years, 350 abbeys adhered to their Order, and constructed among the finest monastic buildings in Burgundy, several with later additions spanning the transition from Romanesque to Gothic, such as Fontenay and Pontigny.

Mâconnais

On the east bank of the Saône, north and east of Mâcon. Outstanding whites, everyday reds (see page 145).

Beaujolais

From the hills south of the Mâconnais, east of the Saône. Ninety-nine per cent is highly drinkable, uncomplicated red, with some standing out from the rest (see page 153).

Val de Loire

Separate from the rest of the province's vineyards, these are right-bank Loire Valley wines that are technically in Burgundy. Mostly crisp, fruity whites of quality (see page 162).

Ardèche

In southern Ardèche. Light, ordinary reds, the region's cheapest wines, good value (see page 230).

Côtes du Rhône

Divided into Côtes du Rhône Septentrionales, north of Valence, and Côtes du Rhône Méridionales, south of Valence. With many different *appellations*, both north and south produce a variety of reds, rosés and whites ranging from the highest quality to large quantities of *vin ordinaire* for everyday drinking (see pages 245, 246 and 247).

Many of Burgundy's monasteries and abbey churches were badly damaged in the 16th- and 17th-century Religious Wars, with even more damage done during the Revolution, yet to this day – whether intact or in ruins – they are awesome in size, dignity and beauty.

On the water

A key to Burgundy's early prosperity was its waterways. The Rhône, Saône and Loire and numerous navigable smaller rivers were the highways of former ages. They were joined by a network of canals in the 17th to 18th centuries, creating in total some 1200km of navigable waterways. Today the network has little commercial significance, but is an invaluable resource for leisurely touring in unique style. The canals have the elegance of their times – fine stone embankments, poplar-lined waterways, cast iron metalwork, park-like towpaths – and, together with the rivers, give traffic-free access to town centres and major sights. As well as the Rivers Yonne and Saône, highlights of Burgundy's seven canals are the Bourgogne (from Yonne to Saône – 189 locks, fine sightseeing, and many changes of scene), the Nivernais (Yonne to Loire – reserved for pleasure cruising) and the Centre (Chalonnais and Charollais – still busy with commercial craft). You are free to moor anywhere on the waterways. Many companies both on the spot and around the world organise boating in Burgundy. An easier option, also available on the Rhône, is cruise-style *Péniche-Hôtels* (hotel barges).

Grand tour

The suggested tours of Burgundy's regions can be linked to make a single grand tour of the heart of Burgundy, as follows: Sénonais and Gâtinais, Cure and Cousin, Morvan, Mâconnais, Beaujolais, Brionnais and Charollais, West of Lyon, Lyon, Dombes, Beaujolais, Bresse, Côte d'Or, Dijon, Auxois and the Seine Valley, Chablis.

In the Rhône Valley, a circular trip to the south and back can be made by linking Lyon, Vienne, Côtes du Rhône, Diois, The Borders of Provence, Southern Ardèche, Haut-Vivarais, West of Lyon, Lyon, Dombes, Beaujolais, Bresse, Côte d'Or, Dijon, Auxois and the Seine Valley, Chablis.

Burgundy in a glass

Quite apart from enjoying world-famous local wines with lunch or dinner, a great treat in Burgundy and the Côtes du Rhône wine country is to visit cellars or vineyards to sample their produce. In towns, there are premises where visitors can taste and buy regional wines. Touring in wine country, you'll see signs at vineyard gates, or at the end of their access roads, offering *Dégustation* (tasting). Take

A drink before and a drink after

For an aperitif, try a kir, properly made with the blackcurrant liqueur Cassis de Dijon in a glass of sharp white Bourgogne Aligoté wine. As a *digestif* (drink after dinner), Burgundy's *marc* (brandy made by distilling the residue of grape pressing) is reckoned the best and smoothest in France.

them up on it. It's usually free of charge, and is an opportunity to taste several varieties. You don't need to be a wine expert, and there's no obligation to buy – though it may be polite to buy at least one bottle after a tasting session.

Burgundy on a plate

Few regions are so much associated with rich, refined cooking as Burgundy. A great abundance of high-quality animal and vegetable produce has encouraged the development of a generous and sophisticated cuisine. Meat cooked in a cream and wine sauce is the local tradition, giving rise to such well-known regional specialities as *coq au vin* (chicken cooked with onions and mushrooms in wine), *boeuf bourgignon* or *à la bourguignonne* (beef – usually Charolais – cooked with onions and mushrooms in wine) and *saupiquet* (ham in cream and wine sauce). Crayfish are also very popular in wine and cream sauce. Sauces are often laced with mustard.

A great speciality of the region is the famously tender chicken from Bresse, just northeast of Lyon. Bresse hens and capons are given every indulgence in life – reared on the best maize and wheat – and even in death are washed in milk before being cooked in cream.

In the same area is Dombes, a lakeland teeming with fresh fish and wildfowl, which often end up on a plate. River fish are plentiful, and they too are cooked with wine, for example as fish-and-wine stew (*pauchouse* or *pôchouse*). Game is common: *lapin* (rabbit) is served either *rôti* (baked with mustard) or *à la moutarde* (in a creamy mustard sauce). *Escargots* (snails) cooked in various ways – usually with garlic and parsley butter – are tremendously popular as a starter: they are

usually served either six or twelve at a time and may be listed on the menu simply as a number, or for example, *les six de Bourgogne*.

Gougère (rich pastry mixed with cheese) may be served in large or small portions as an *amuse-gueule*, starter or side dish. Puff pastry features strongly in the regional cuisine, used for encasing snails, mushrooms or cheese, or for dessert served with *fromage blanc* or seasonal fruits.

Other classic Burgundy dishes include *potée* (a thick stew of beef, bacon and vegetables), *jambon persillé* (pressed ham and parsley in white wine jelly), *oeufs en meurette* (eggs poached with onions in red wine and served in the liquid – fish can be cooked *en meurette*, too), terrines and pâtés, rustic, home-cured hams and *andouillette* sausages and other charcuterie.

Some dishes and ingredients belong particularly to certain areas. For example, in Chablis and the northern cheese-making districts, cheese flan is served. In Beaujolais and La Dombes, local hams, frogs' legs (with parsley butter) and duck are especially seen. Lyon is especially fond of charcuterie. In Bas-Dauphiné expect to see *gratin dauphinois* (slices of potato baked in milk). Ardèche has its potato pancakes and makes good use of the abundant local fruits and delicious wild mushrooms and wild chestnuts, while the Diois and the borders of Provence feature the truffles of Tricastin and the olives of Nyons.

Burgundy and the Rhône Valley on the cheeseboard

Just a few cheeses are made, notably the strong *Epoisses*, which is washed with *marc*, *Pierre-Qui-Vire* from northern Burgundy and Chaource from the Burgundy–Champagne border. From the same area come *Soumaintrain* and *St-Florentin*. From south of Dijon come *Cîteaux* and the impossibly acrid *Bouton-de-Coulotte* (literally 'trouser buttons' – with unsavoury connotations).

Watch out for *Fromage Fort*, a powerful concoction of strong cheese mixed with all sorts of herbs, spices, pungent oils and *eau-de-vie*, sealed up and allowed to ferment. Just when any normal person would expect to throw it away as totally inedible, it is deemed perfect by Burgundians as a snack on toast. At the other end of the region, the Ardèche and Provençal borders of the Rhône Valley are noted for different versions of the piquant goats' cheese, *Picodon*.

Snacks, treats, self-catering – and where to buy a picnic

An *alimentation* is a general grocery, for food, wine and all other drinks (there are almost no off-licences/liquor stores). They are often arranged as a 'mini-supermarket' with *Libre-Service* (self-service).

Supermarché usually means nothing more than a big *alimentation*, but the huge out-of-town *hypermarchés* are open long hours, sell just about everything, at good prices, and often have a cheap and popular self-service cafeteria as well.

Except in emergencies, buy bread only at a *boulangerie*, where it is freshly baked on the premises twice a day. There will be a selection of white breads and rolls, *pain complet* (wholemeal) and *pain de siègle* (rye). Most have morning *croissants* and *pains au chocolat*. Note that a *dépôt de pain* sells bread but does not bake it; theirs is usually factory-made. A *pâtisserie*, literally a 'pastry-cook's', has better *croissants*, a selection of delicious little pastries and ice cream, everything being made on the premises by a qualified *pâtissier*. Instead of making British or American-style cakes and cream-filled pastries, they make light pastries with delicious fillings or toppings, and rarely use fresh cream.

In all cities, most towns and even villages, skilled speciality confectioners called *chocolatiers* or *confiseurs* make high-quality

Contact your local Thomas Cook shop to arrange your

CONTINENTAL MOTORING ASSISTANCE

- Assistance due to breakdown / accident

- Hire car

- Legal protection

- Comprehensive Personal Travel Insurance

- And much more . . . . .

Full details available at Thomas Cook Shops in the UK.

Only for sale to UK Residents

chocolates on the premises. They also make other sweets, often including some local speciality. Ice-cream shops, called *glaciers*, sell delicious freshly made ice cream. These shops are everywhere, and the ice cream is superb ... but they often only have three flavours (vanilla, chocolate or strawberry).

Boucherie means 'butcher's', or *boucherie chevaline* if it sells horse meat. A boon for picnics, a *charcuterie* (a pork butcher's) sells a wide variety of cooked meats and other prepared foods, including salads. A *traiteur* is like a delicatessen, again with plenty of prepared meats.

The ordinary town or village *marché* (market) consists mainly of stalls selling fresh fruit and vegetables; traders' vans with dozens of cheeses, big rounds of butter, cold meats and *charcuterie*; other stalls with goats' cheese, cakes, honey, perhaps chickens alive or dead. Larger markets have traders selling workclothes, fabrics, household goods, excellent kitchenware, freshly gathered herbs, dried fruit and nuts, and much more. You'll rarely see a fishmonger, *poissonier*, except in markets. Common in rural areas is the travelling general stores van, which turns up at the village once or twice a week.

Bringing it all back home – where and what to buy

- In Burgundy: *moutarde de Dijon* (or *de Beaune*), *pain épice* (spiced honey bread), liqueurs and fine wines.
- In Lyon and the northern Rhône Valley: silk, puppets, fine wines.
- In the southern Rhône Valley: Nyons olives, lavender and lavender products, herbs, truffles and fine wines.

Wine bargains

Remember that if any of the famous-name wines are being sold at knockdown prices, they're probably too old, too young or from a poor year.

Tourist offices

Local tourist offices have various names:
- *Office de* (or *du*) *Tourisme*;
- *Bureau de* (or *du*) *Tourisme*;
- *Syndicat d'Initiative*;
- *OTSI* (stands for *Office du Tourisme/Syndicat d'Initiative*).

In this book, for clarity, we call them all 'Tourist Office'. Opening hours are generally Mon–Sat 0900–1200, 1400–1800, with longer hours in July and August.

Highlights: the best routes for...

Winetasting
1 Chablis – *see page 58*
2 Cure and Cousin – *see page 76*
3 Côte d'Or – *see page 110*
4 Beaune – *see page 122*
5 Chalonnais – *see page 132*
6 Mâconnais – *see page 140*
7 Beaujolais – *see page 150*
8 Côtes du Rhône – *see page 242*
9 Diois – *see page 262*
10 The border of Provence – *see page 270*

Fine dining
1 Dijon –*see page 98*
2 Côte d'Or – *see page 110*
3 Beaune – *see page 122*
4 Chalonnais – *see page 132*
5 Mâconnais – *see page 140*
6 Beaujolais – *see page 150*
7 West of Lyon – *see page 178*
8 Bresse – *see page 186*
9 Lyon – *see page 202*
10 Côtes du Rhône – *see page 242*

Wilderness, solitude and wildlife
1 Sénonais and Gâtinais – *see page 42*
2 Morvan – *see page 86*
3 La Dombes – *see page 194*
4 Haut-Vivarais – *see page 222*
5 Diois – *see page 262*

Gallo-Roman sites and museums
1 Alise-Ste-Reine and Châtillon-sur-Seine – *see pages 68* and *70*
2 Autun, St-Père and *Bibracte* – *see pages 86, 91* and *94*
3 Lyon – *see page 202*
4 Vienne – *see page 214*
5 Vaison-la-Romaine and Orange – *see pages 277–9*

Scenery
1 Cure and Cousin – *see page 76*
2 Morvan – *see page 86*
3 Beaujolais – *see page 150*
4 Loire – *see page 162*
5 West of Lyon – *see page 178*
6 Haut-Vivarais – *see page 222*
7 Southern Ardèche – *see page 230*
8 Côtes du Rhône – *see page 242*
9 Diois – *see page 262*
10 The border of Provence – *see page 270*

Children
1 Dijon – *see page 98*
2 Beaune – *see page 122*
3 Lyon – *see page 202*
4 Haut-Vivarais – *see page 222*
5 Southern Ardèche – *see page 230*

The very best ...
The unmissables of Burgundy and the Rhône Valley:
1 Sit down to a bottle of the best local wine you can afford and a classic local dish
2 Visit a vineyard or a wine village and try a *dégustation* (tasting)
3 Explore the Palais des Ducs, Dijon
4 Stand in the courtyard of the Hôtel Dieu, Beaune
5 In Lyon, walk through a *traboule*, see Guignol and go to a *bouchon*
6 Take in a Romanesque masterpiece – eg, Vézelay, Fontenay, Paray-le-Monial
7 Rediscover the Romans – eg, at Autun, Alise, Orange or Vaison
8 See the Pont d'Arc, a natural stone archway spanning the River Ardèche
9 Take a river boat ride (eg, at Valence or Lyon)
10 Go into a *grotte* or *aven* (eg, Aven d'Orgnac)

Architectural heritage
1 Cathedral, Sens – earliest of the great French Gothic cathedrals – *see page 46*
2 Château d'Ancy-le-Franc and Château de Tanlay – Renaissance palaces – *see pages 58 and 64*
3 Fontenay – Cistercian monastery – *see page 72*
4 Basilica of Ste-Madeleine, Vézelay – Romanesque world heritage site – *see page 80*
5 Place de la Libération district, Dijon – Renaissance mansions – *see page 98*
6 Hôtel Dieu, Beaune – medieval charity hospital – *see page 124*
7 Paray-le-Monial and Brionnais villages – Romanesque churches – *see pages 170–5*
8 Brou church, Bourg-en-Bresse – flamboyant Gothic and Renaissance extravaganza – *see page 186*
9 Pérouges – fortified medieval village – *see page 197*
10 Vieux Lyon – Renaissance quarter of Lyon, a World Heritage Site – *see page 208*

The Sénonais and Gâtinais

Ratings

Activities	●●●●
Châteaux	●●●●
Medieval architecture	●●●●
Restaurants	●●●●
Wildlife	●●●●
Scenery	●●●
Villages	●●●
Children	●●

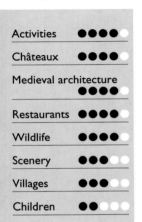

Sénonais takes its name from the historic town of Sens, while Gâtinais is the neighbouring watery, half-wild plateau that once belonged to the counts of Sens. This low, rolling, green northern edge of Burgundy, with its countless streams, woods, fields and rough pastures, merges into the Île de France and rubs shoulders both with the Loire Valley and Champagne. Sometimes parts of the Gâtinais and Sénonais rural plateau have fallen within Burgundy's borders and occasionally outside them. For those arriving from Paris, it's a first sight of the duchy – but is far from typical. In places profoundly rustic, with a multitude of varied and productive little farms, in other areas it becomes quite austere and desolate. These domains, especially in the Gâtinais, are rich in game, and their unspoilt forests and lakes are much appreciated by hunters and anglers.

CHÂTEAURENARD*

ⓘ Châteaurenard Tourist Office 22 pl. de la République; tel: 02 38 95 39 53, fax: 02 38 95 39 53, www.coeur-de-france.com/chateaurenard.

🏛 Musée Vivant de l'Apiculture Gâtinaise €€ Tel: 02 38 95 35 56, fax: 02 38 95 20 45; open May–Aug, daily 1000–1800, 1 Sept–15 Nov Wed, Sat and Sun only, rest of the year by appointment.

This little Gâtinais country town, bordering the Puisaye region to its south, has several fine old houses and a ruined 10th-century hilltop castle, built by the Count of Sens who was known as Renard. On the riverside stands the (privately owned) 17th-century Château de la Motte. Partly brick and partly stone, and with eight massive round towers, it was built for the second wife of William of Orange. Also in the town is the **Musée Vivant de l'Apiculture Gâtinaise* (Museum of Gâtinais Bee-keeping)**, where you can watch bees going about their business, learn about bee-keeping and buy some of their honey.

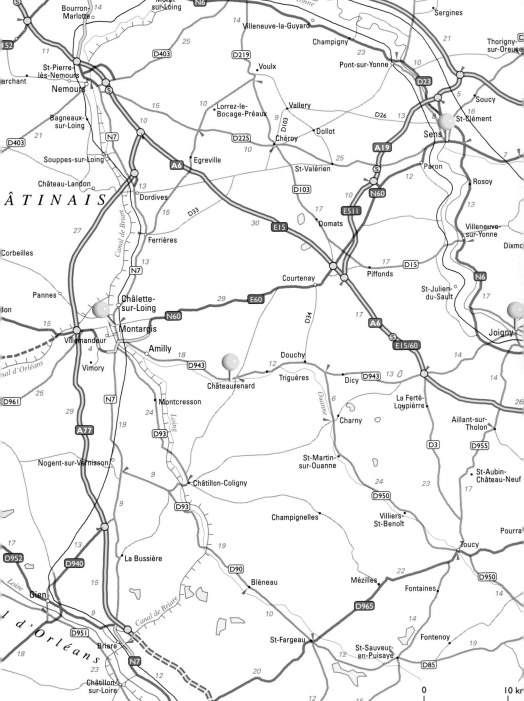

JOIGNY✦✦

ⓘ Joigny Tourist Office *4 quai Ragobert; tel: 03 86 62 11 05, fax: 03 86 91 76 38, www.ville-joigny.fr/; open Mon–Sat 1400–1700, July–Aug, open daily.*

🚗 *The town lies off the N6. Approaching on the D943, cross the Yonne and turn either left or right to park.*

Ⓟ *There is riverside parking close to the centre, especially off Quai du Dragons, a few metres upriver from the Yonne Bridge.*

⬛ *There is a **market** on Wed and Sat am.*

⬥ *Festivals: Les Nuits Maillotines shows in July and Aug (information from tourist office); Local fête in June and Fête des Vendanges (wine harvest festival) in Oct.*

Stand on the 18th-century bridge spanning the Yonne for the best view of Joigny. The little town rises in terraces from the river, with narrow lanes weaving up and down the slopes between the old houses. From the bridge, walk up to the historic centre, passing several superb old timbered houses. The most striking, called the *Arbre de Jessé* ('Tree of Jesse'), stands on a corner on the left beside r. Gabriel Cortel: turn left here for Église St-Thibault, a Gothic and Renaissance church with an attractive 17th-century campanile. The interior looks strangely skewed, with asymmetrical vaulting and a choir that turned slightly to the left. Continue up to the Porte du Bois, the 12th-century gateway that was once part of Joigny's castle. The people of Joigny are correctly called by the appealing name of *Joviniens*, but in the 15th century they weren't so jovial and acquired a new name. Oppressed by the local lord, Guy de la Tremoille, the *Joviniens* invaded his castle and beat him to death with vineyard tools known as *mailles*. Ever since, *Joviniens* have preferred the name *maillotins*; a *maille* – it's a sort of mallet – even features in the town's crest. The town took a battering itself soon after in the 15th and 16th centuries, first during the Hundred Years War (1337–1453), when it was attacked by the English, and then in the Wars of Religion (1562–98), when it was set ablaze. In this century too it has been hammered by wartime bombing, though the town centre was impeccably reconstructed afterwards. In 1981 a major gas explosion ripped through the heart of the old quarter and again the houses were reconstructed.

Accommodation and food in Joigny

À la Côte St-Jacques €€€ *14 faubourg de Paris; tel: 03 86 62 09 70, fax: 03 86 91 49 70.* One of the great names of Burgundy (and France), passed from father to son almost without change, this classic, beautifully decorated, gastronome's paradise chooses the best of ingredients to make dishes of flair and skill. It's also a luxurious hotel, made from several handsome old riverside houses with balconies and gardens beside the Yonne.

Hôtel Modern and Restaurant Godard €€ *17 av. Robert Petit; tel: 03 86 62 16 28, fax: 03 86 62 44 33.* Traditional, comfortable and well-run provincial hotel with its own excellent relaxed good-quality restaurant.

MONTARGIS❖❖

❶ Montargis Tourist Office *Pl. du 18 juin (next to the bus station, off blvd Paul Baudin); tel: 02 38 98 00 87, fax: 02 38 98 82 01; open 0830–1230, 1400–1800 (July, Aug and Sept 0900–1230, 1400–1900).*

❷ Montargis is a large town. The N7 runs into town on the east side of the River Loing and the canal, the D94 on the west side.

❸ A convenient place to park, near the tourist office and the main sites but outside the central one-way system, is in pl. du 18-juin-1940, a large square off r. du Port, between the Canal de Briare and the river.

An industrial town, yet with an attractive centre and a pleasant atmosphere, Montargis straddles the River Loing and has long been considered the 'capital' of the Gâtinais. It is especially known for its confectioners, and for the *pralines*, sugared burnt almonds, devised here in the 17th century by the Duke of Plessis-Praslin's cook. The town's ancient château, once a royal castle, now a school, is still the principal landmark. Handsome bridges are everywhere, as the river, small canals and the larger Canal de Briare, busy with pleasure craft, enclose and thread through the central quarter. Next to the château lies the old tannery district and one of the former tanners' houses has been made into the **Musée des Tanneurs❖ (Tanning Museum)**. Cross the road to find, in a former tanning factory, the **Musée du Gâtinais❖ (Gâtinais Museum)**, concentrating not so much on the landscape and culture of the region but on archaeological finds made here. Walk the short distance to the other side of the town centre to a pleasant public park called Jardin Durzy, where there's a 13th-century Templar archway. Also in the park, the **Musée Girodet❖** is a worthwhile art museum with French and Italian paintings from the 15th to 18th centuries, notably the neo-classical 18th-century painter Anne-Louis Girodet.

Accommodation and food in Montargis

Hôtel-Restaurant de la Gloire €€ *74 av. du Gén. de Gaulle; tel: 02 38 85 04 69, fax: 02 38 98 52 32.* The small family-run hotel is convenient and comfortable, if a little close to the busy road and the station, but its restaurant is highly rated for outstanding, accomplished cooking of dishes such as lobster, fish ravioli, *pigeonneau* and sweetbreads of calf.

Musée des Tanneurs € *Tel: 02 38 98 00 87; open Sat (and first Sun of each month) only, 1430–1730, or by appointment.*

Musée du Gâtinais €€ *Tel: 02 38 98 07 81; open Wed, Sat and Sun 0900–1200, 1330–1730 (Fri 1700), closed hols and 26 July.*

Musée Girodet €€ *Hôtel Durzy; tel: 02 38 98 07 81; open Wed–Sun 0900–1200, 1330–1730 (Fri 1700), closed hols and 26 July.*

The dog of Montargis

As well as its confectionery, Montargis has entered the French consciousness for another reason – the legendary dog of Montargis. In the story, a man was murdered at Montargis. Later, as the army marched through town, the murdered man's dog identified the killer among the ranks. He attacked the soldier, who confessed to his crime and was subsequently executed. Unfortunately, nobody knows whether the story is true or false, when it happened, or who either of the two men were. Undeterred, local confectioners celebrate the tale with another creation – little chocolates called *crottes du chien* (dog shit).

SENS✦✦

Sens Tourist Office *Pl. Jean Jaurès; tel: 03 86 65 19 49, fax: 03 86 64 24 18; www.mairie-sens.fr/*

Turn off the N6 on to the N360 to reach the town centre.

Where the N360 reaches pl. Jean Jaurès, there is parking to the right.

The **market** takes place on Mon, Fri and Sat.

Tree-lined boulevards in this tranquil, contented country town run on the ruins of the daunting ramparts that stood here for 2000 years and the town itself was a majestic ecclesiastical centre famed throughout Christendom. The once-grand old town of Sens (pronounced 'Sanss') was the chief settlement of the *Sénones*, a ferocious Gallic tribe who – in 390 BC – earned the distinction of having marched on Rome, attacked it and taken the city. How Europe would have been different if the Gauls had destroyed Rome then and there! It was the geese, not the guards, who awoke as the *Sénones* moved into the city and began to sack it under cover of darkness. The Romans, unable to beat off the invaders, tried buying them off instead. Enriched with a tribute of gold, the *Sénones* happily returned to Sens. Later, when Rome conquered Gaul, there was a grudging regard for the people of Sens and the Romans made the town into a wealthy provincial capital within massive ramparts. The town's importance was assured for centuries to come.

With the coming of Christianity, it became a powerful archbishopric, with authority over Paris. In 1130 the construction of the first Gothic cathedral in France was begun here, and the architect, William of Sens, used it as a model for his work at Canterbury Cathedral. In 1234 it served as the setting for the marriage of Louis IX of France (St-Louis) to Margaret of Provence. Sens rose to the height of its prominence in the 13th and 14th centuries, began its decline during the Wars of Religion (1562–98), and was already eclipsed by Paris in the 1600s. During the French Revolution, much of its grandeur was erased. In the 19th century the ancient ramparts were demolished to make way for boulevards, and a statue of Brennus, the Gaul who led the attack on Rome, was erected on the town hall.

Cathédrale St-Étienne € *Pl. de la République; tel: 03 86 65 19 49; open daily.*

Musée de Sens, including Treasury €€ *Pl. de la Cathédrale; tel: 03 86 64 46 22; open June–Sept, daily, except Tue, 1000–1200, 1400–1800 (July and Aug 1000–1800), rest of the year Wed, Sat and Sun 1000–1200, 1400–1800, Mon, Thur and Fri 1400–1800 only.*

Festivals: *Foire* at the end Apr/beginning May; *Les Synodales* (dance festival) every summer; *Fête de la St-Fiacre* in Sept.

On the menu

The abundance of game and fish, together with a traditional countryside of small farms, makes for some good eating in the Sénonais and Gâtinais. Menus are often dependent on *la saison et la chasse* (the hunting and the time of year). Autumn – start of the hunting season – is the high point of the year for freshly killed meat. High-quality fruit and vegetables, rustic farm-made produce and salted meats, too, are characteristic of the region. The area looks to the upper Loire, just as much as to Chablis, for its source of local wine, but more typical of the region is its rustic farm-pressed cider.

Right
Covered market, Sens

Cathédrale St-Étienne◆◆◆ stands at the very heart of the oval-shaped old centre. Despite evident damage, it is a magnificent sight. The building, and most of the extensive sculpture, dates from the 12th to 15th centuries, showing the evolution of the Gothic style from its earliest phase. That said, the distinctive tall south tower with its campanile was built later; the two bells inside it weigh 14 and 16 tons. In the high, light interior, there's beautiful stained glass. The oldest glass, of the 12th century, includes several images of Thomas à Becket with Henry II of England, the king who, perhaps unwittingly, ordered his assassination. Becket's vestments can be seen in the **Cathedral Treasury**◆◆, among a sumptuous collection of medieval tapestries, liturgical items, silks and ivories. Access to the treasury is via the **Musée de Sens**◆, housed in the former Archbishop's Palace, devoted to the full range of the town's history and prehistory.

Facing the cathedral across place de la République, there's a fine wood-and-iron 19th-century covered market. Among several historic houses in the town, notice especially the astonishing carved timberwork of the 16th-century Maison d'Abraham and Maison du Pilier on the corner of r. de la République and r. Jean Cousin. Many half-timbered houses stand along Grande Rue, which continues to the River Yonne.

Accommodation and food in Sens

Hôtel l'Esplanade € *2 blvd du Mail; tel: 03 86 83 14 70, fax: 03 86 83 14 71.* A low-budget favourite with simple little rooms in an old town-centre building, decently renovated and with a bar downstairs.

Hôtel de Paris et de la Poste €€ *97 r. de la République; tel: 03 86 65 17 43, fax: 03 86 64 48 45.* This solid, traditional, well-kept hotel, with a reliable and reasonably priced classic restaurant, is ideally placed in the town centre.

Restaurant Le Soleil Levant € *51 r. Émile Zola; tel: 03 86 65 71 82.* Try the excellent seafood and fish dishes at this inexpensive, traditional provincial restaurant near the station.

Suggested tour

Auberge de la Clé des Champs €€
Route de Joigny, les Quatres Croix; tel: 02 38 97 42 68, fax: 02 38 97 38 10.
Buried in greenery and tranquillity on the edge of the Gâtinais village of **Courtenay**, this appealing auberge is somehow both rustic and elegant. Its classic, high-quality restaurant is devoted to the best of regional ingredients and specialities.

Total distance: 132km, or 150km if you take the detour.

Time: The driving will take only a couple of hours, but this makes a full day if you take in all the sights.

Links: From Châteaurenard to Dicy on the D943. This route follows the same road as the Puisaye route (*see page 56*).

Route: From **SENS ❶**, leave town on the D58 on the left bank of the Yonne and turn left on to the D26 to head west through the countryside to **Vallery**. Pause here to see the 16th-century château, then make a straight route across the Gâtinais countryside on minor roads (D103, D33) through **Chéroy**, with its medieval barns, to **Ferrières**. Close to the River Loing, this is a historic town with several handsome old buildings, washhouses and remnants of its ancient monastery. The busy N7 heads south from here beside the River Loing – or, for a more leisurely ride, cross to the more peaceful left-bank lanes – to **MONTARGIS ❷**. Leave the Loing, taking the main road, D943, along the River Ouanne to **CHÂTEAURENARD ❸**. Stay on the D943 to the crazy La Fabuloserie at **Dicy** (*see page 53*).

Below
Cathédrale St-Étienne, Sens

From Dicy, either take the detour or turn back (4km) to the junction with the D34 and turn right to **Courtenay**, where an 18th-century mansion stands on the site of the fortress of the local feudal lords. Bear right to join the N60, the main road that cuts across the middle of the Gâtinais, and goes back into Sens.

Detour: This longer return journey leaves the heart of the Gâtinais and takes a route along its edge, via the Yonne Valley. From Dicy, stay on the D943 all the way into **JOIGNY ❹**. From here follow the River Yonne downstream to the agreeable riverside town of **Villeneuve-sur-Yonne**, where sections of the old ramparts survive, Gothic gateways stand at each end of the main street and an old bridge crosses the Yonne. Continue back into Sens.

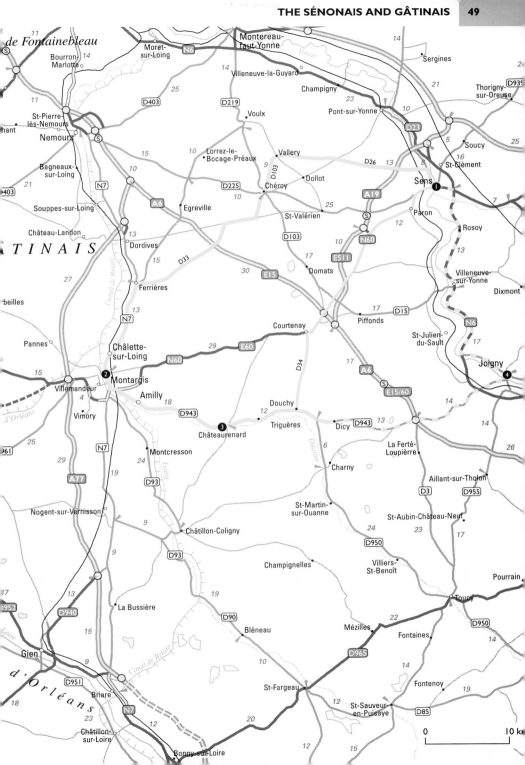

de Fontainebleau

Moret-sur-Loing
Montereau-faut-Yonne
Sergines
Bourron-Marlotte
Villeneuve-la-Guyard
Thorigny-sur-Oreuse
Champigny
St-Pierre-lès-Nemours
Voulx
Pont-sur-Yonne
Nemours
Soucy
Bagneaux-sur-Loing
Lorrez-le-Bocage-Préaux
Vallery
St-Clément
Dollot
Sens
Souppes-sur-Loing
Chéroy
Paron
Egreville
St-Valérien
Rosoy
GÂTINAIS
Château-Landon
Domats
Villeneuve-sur-Yonne
Dordives
Dixmont
Ferrières
Piffonds
Courtenay
St-Julien-du-Sault
Pannes
Joigny
Châlette-sur-Loing
Montargis
Villemandeur
Amilly
Douchy
Vimory
Châteaurenard
Triguères
Dicy
La Ferté-Loupière
Montcresson
Charny
Aillant-sur-Tholon
Nogent-sur-Vernisson
St-Martin-sur-Ouanne
St-Aubin-Château-Neuf
Champignelles
Villiers-St-Benoît
Pourrain
La Bussière
Toucy
Bléneau
Mézilles
Fontaines
Gien
Fontenoy
Briare
St-Fargeau
St-Sauveur-en-Puisaye
Châtillon-sur-Loire
d'Orléans
Bonny-sur-Loire

0   10 k

Puisaye

Ratings

Activities	●●●●
Medieval architecture	●●●●
Wildlife	●●●●
Châteaux	●●●
Children	●●●
Museums	●●●
Scenery	●●●
Villages	●●●

Puisaye, beloved of the writer Colette (*see page 54*), is a sparsely inhabited, little-known landscape in the northeast of the duchy, which in places seems as much water as earth. Here are fresh, clean lakes, ponds, rivers, streams and marshy heaths. There are, too, great expanses of forest and rough pasture. The River Loing, close to its source, runs through the heart of the region that lies between the Yonne and the Loire. Lonely farms are hidden from view by mature hedges. It's a place of wildlife, of the simple life, of escape from modern life. Yet this is a 'civilised wilderness', where small forestry industries are thriving, where the great white wines of the Loire and of Chablis are both local, where the moist woodlands have footpaths and bridleways and where the farmers are contented stockbreeders, raising Burgundy's top-quality Charolais beef cattle.

 For information about Puisaye try: *Maison de la Puisaye, 3 pl. de la République, St-Fargeau;* tel: 86 74 15 72, fax: 86 74 15 82. Typical tourist office opening times throughout the region are: *Mon–Fri 1000–1200, 1400–1700 (or 1800), Sat 1000–1200 (or 1230).*

Right
Canal de Briare

10 km

N60   E60   29

N6

E15/60

A6   17   S

18

Châteaurenard

D37   D93

osson

18   12   Douchy   D943   13

Triguères   Dicy

Piffonds   17   D15

St-Julien-   du-Sault   17

Bussy-en-Othe

Brienon-sur-
Armançon

Yonne   9   18

Joigny   Migennes   Armançon

11   4   Cheny

14   Charmoy   D91

14   Seignelay

26   10

Monéteau

La Ferté-
Loupierre

6   Charny

D3   D955

Aillant-sur-Tholon

8

St-Martin-
sur-Ouanne

St-Aubin-Château-Neuf   Auxerre

24   23   17

St-Denis-
sur-Ouanne   D950

Champignelles   Villiers-
St-Benoît   Dracy

Châtillon-Coligny

St-Georges-sur-Baulche

23

Pourrain   Champs-sur-Yor

Toucy

Rogny-les-
Sept-Écluses   19

D90

Bléneau

Ouanne   D950   17

22   Coulanges-
la-Vineuse

Mézilles

Fontaines   14   6

D965   D955   Ouanne

14   6

10

St-Fargeau   Fontenoy   19   10

12   St-Sauveur-   D85
D85   en-Puisaye   Courson-les-
Carrières

le-Cl

20   D185

PARC NATUREL
DE BOUTISSANT

onny-sur-Loire   12   Château de   15
Guedelon   Druyes-les-   11
D955   Château de   Belles-Fontaines
Ratilly   Treigny-   N151
D957   21   Perreuse
St-Amand-   Étais-   Coulanges-
en-Puisaye   la-Sauvin   sur-Yonne

16   D955   P   U   I   S   A   Y   E   Clamecy   7

Léré   17   D9

18   17   N151

Entrains-
sur-Nohain   24

D957   Canal du Nivernal

D13   4   Cosne-Cours-   D19
sur-Loire   D5   19

12   La Chapelle-
St-André   17   Tannay

Bannay   14   N7   Pougny   20   D33   Menou   7   Varzy
Donzy

CHÂTILLON-COLIGNY❖

Main tourist office
2 pl. Coligny; tel: 02 38 96 02 33, fax: 02 38 96 09 44; open Mon–Fri 1000–1200, 1400–1700, Sat 1000–1230. **Guided tours** of the town are available from the tourist office.

Point i (annexe) *La Halte Fluviale, r. de la Lancière; open 15 May–15 Oct, Mon–Fri 0930–1130, 1715–1930, Sat 0930–1130, 1600–1930, Sun 1600–1930.*

**Musée € ** *In the old hospital; tel: 02 38 92 64 06; open Apr–Oct, Tue–Fri 1400–1730, Sat–Sun (and hols) 1000–1200, 1400–1730, rest of the year Sat–Sun (and hols) only 1400–1730.*

There is a **market** on Fri am.

Festival: Cattle Fair on 1st Sun in July at Ste-Geneviève-des-Bois.

An unusual, rather grand little canalside town, Châtillon-Coligny has a five-sided old quarter contained within a moat of water drawn from the nearby River Loing. Within this ensemble, a web of narrow streets radiates from a central square. At the water's edge stand several old *lavoirs* or washhouses. There are ruins, too, of a Renaissance château with a much older Romanesque keep and underground passageways. A 15th-century hospital has become the town's **Musée (Museum)**❖, which tells the town's story with good collections of local archaeology, historical documents and fine old furniture and porcelain. Colette (*see page 54*) lived for a while in the town with her brother, until her first marriage in 1893.

DICY❖❖

On the D943 between Montargis and Joigny.

La Fabuloserie €€ On D943; tel: 03 86 63 64 21; open Easter to All Saints (except July–Aug): Sat, Sun and hols, 1400–1800, July–Aug: daily 1400–1800. Guided tours available.

To discover how one man's crazy hobby can end up putting his home town on the map, call at **La Fabuloserie❖❖❖** in the village of Dicy. This makes – quite literally – a fantastic visit for children and grown-ups alike. Here, local architect Alain Bourbonnais has transformed his private collection of artwork into a museum, both inside and outside the house, which he subtitles the Musée de l'Art Hors-les-Norms (Museum of Abnormal Art). It's as bizarre an art gallery as most people will ever see, with everything in it – strange forms, amazing figures, ensembles and dreamlike imaginings – created by uneducated people entirely without any knowledge of the norms of art. It's what Bourbonnais calls 'Raw Art'. Arranged inside and outside his museum, it is a disturbing, captivating, amusing world that you must leave before it starts to look normal!

ST-FARGEAU❖❖

St-Fargeau Tourist Office 3 pl. de la République; tel: 03 86 74 15 72, fax: 03 86 74 15 82; open in summer Mon–Sat 1000–1200, 1400–1800, Sun 1000–1200, 1500–1900, rest of the year Mon–Sat 1000–1200, 1330–1730.

Château €€€ Tel: 03 86 74 05 67, fax: 03 86 74 18 63; open for guided tours 1 Apr–11 Nov 1000–1200, 1400–1800.

Ferme du Château €€ Tel: 03 86 74 03 76; open Apr–Sept only, daily 1000–1900.

Church Free access when open; open daily.

Musée du Reproduction du Son €€ In the old town hall; tel: 03 86 74 13 06; open Apr–Sept, daily 1000–1200, 1400–1800, rest of the year by appointment.

The main town of the Puisaye is dominated by a sombre, unusual moated **château❖** in red brick and white stone, with five sturdy towers. Within the daunting exterior is a large, elegant courtyard. The first castle on the site was built over one thousand years ago. The present château was originally 15th century, but was completely redesigned and refurbished in the 17th century by La Grande Mademoiselle – the soubriquet of Anne-Marie Louise d'Orléans, the imperious and

impulsive cousin of King Louis XIV. The château had its own farm, the **Ferme du Château❖**, now restored as an enjoyable low-key family entertainment with farm animals, trailer rides and a museum of rural life. The town's **church❖** has fine 16th-century stained glass and contains several high-quality 14th- to 16th-century paintings and woodcarvings. The fascinating **Musée du Reproduction du Son (Museum of Sound Reproduction)❖❖**, in a former 17th-century convent, has a wonderful (formerly private) collection of hundreds of sound-reproducing machines, from music boxes and barrel-organs to ingenious prototype record players.

St-Sauveur-en-Puisaye❖❖

🛈 **Communauté de Communes de St-Sauveur** *Tel: 03 86 45 57 93, fax: 03 86 45 63 13; open 1000–1200, 1400–1800, except Tue.*

🏛 **Musée Colette** €€ *Le Château; tel: 03 86 45 61 95, fax: 03 86 45 55 84; open Apr–Oct 1000–1800 (closed Tue), rest of the year weekends 1000–1800 and during school holidays 1400–1800, except Tue.*

In the heart of the Puisaye region, in a typical untamed landscape of heath, woodland and small lakes, St-Sauveur was the birthplace and the home of Colette (*see below*). Although the tempestuous writer is more often associated with Paris, she retained an enduring love for her native home town, described in detail in *La Maison de Claudine*, though she would not recognise the place today. The Renaissance château is still here, with its oval 12th-century Tour Sarrazine (Saracen Tower) and its fine gardens, but today it houses the intriguing aesthetic **Musée Colette**❖❖, an attractively laid out collection of photos, manuscripts and memorabilia donated by the family of her second husband, and a reproduction of her Paris apartment. The nearby street where she was born has been named r. de Colette, and the house bears a simple plaque *Ici Colette est née* ('Colette was born here').

Colette

Always known only as Colette, the country girl whose name was Sidonie Gabrielle Colette was born in St-Sauveur-en-Puisaye on 28 January 1873, and spent her whole childhood in the village where she received only an ordinary elementary school education. At the age of 19 she left to share a home with her brother in a nearby village but within a year met and married Henry Gauthier-Villars, thereafter known by Colette's nickname for him, Willy. Her first four novels were written under his name, and he took full credit for them and kept the money they earned. For this, Colette divorced him. She then became a risqué music-hall entertainer, moving on to become a serious actress, and remarried to Henri de Jouvenel. Although they had a daughter, Colette divorced again and set up home with fellow author Maurice Goudeket, marrying him in 1935. In 1936 she was elected to the Académie Goncourt. By now a successful, controversial author and dramatist, Colette moved between the Riviera and Paris, spending her old age in her luxurious Paris apartment until her death in 1954 at the age of 80. Her best known work is probably *Gigi* (1944). She was a productive author, specialising in short, intense, passionate, sensual pieces concerned with the emotional life of women. Many of her works evoke poignantly the love of nature and the countryside of her youth: 'J'appartiens à un pays que j'ai quitté ... dont mon âme a soif', 'I belong to a land I have left ... for which my soul thirsts'. Ask at Puisaye tourist offices for the 'Colette pas à pas' (Colette step by step) guide to discover Puisaye sites that were important in Colette's life.

Toucy❖

🛈 **Toucy Tourist Office** *20 pl. des Frères-Genêt; tel: 03 86 44 15 66; www.urich. edu/~jpaulsen/toucy; open June–mid-Oct 0930–1230, 1430–1800.*

This quiet little country town, resting on a wooded hillside, with its medieval lanes and old houses, stands at the eastern edge of Puisaye. The most striking feature is the two towers of a castle of the Bishops of Auxerre, one massive and powerful, the other narrower and more elegant, which now form part of the 15th-century parish church. Linguists and francophiles should pause here to pay homage to a local lad, Pierre Larousse (1817–75), creator of the definitive French

Train touristique €
Av. de la Gare; tel: 03 86 44 05 58.

There is a traditional weekly market on Sat am, and a bigger monthly market on the first Sat of the month.

dictionary. A jolly little **train touristique**✦ runs on summer weekends from here to Villiers-St-Benoît, 9km away (*see page 56*).

Accommodation and food in Toucy

Hôtel-Restaurant Le Lion d'Or € *37 r. Lucille-Cormier; tel: 03 86 44 00 76.* In a once-grand old mansion, this simple but well-kept *restaurant avec chambres* is a find. Modest rooms, good cooking of local dishes, and all at moderate prices.

TREIGNY-PERREUSE✦✦

www.perso.wanadoo.fr/ treigny_si/.

Château de Ratilly
€ 2km from village on the D185; tel: 03 86 74 79 54; open 19 June–12 Sept 1000–1800.

Parc Naturel de Boutissant €€ *On the D185, 7km from Treigny, 9km from St-Fargeau; tel: 03 86 74 07 08, fax: 03 86 74 17 19; www.boutissant.com/.*

Château de Guedelon €€€ *On the D955; information and reservations at Château de St-Fargeau: tel: 03 86 74 19 45, fax: 03 86 74 19 46; www.guedelon.org; open Apr–June, Mon–Fri 1000–1800, Sat, Sun and hols 1000–1900 (closed Wed), July and Aug, daily 1000–1900, 1 Sept–15 Nov 1000–1730 (closed Wed). A two-hour guided tour of the site is also available (very expensive).*

Château de Ratilly✦✦✦ is hidden in a lovely, quiet, rustic setting just outside the village of Treigny, deep in the Puisaye. This is not only a fascinating and imposing 13th-century fortress, complete with high walls and massive conical towers, all of rosy stone, and enclosed by a dry moat, it's also a centre of culture, education and entertainment. Inside, there are modern art exhibitions, concerts and shows, and, in one wing, a stonecarving *atelier* producing Puisaye crockery where you can watch the work and buy pieces if you wish.

Within the *commune* of Treigny, lying just 7km from the village, the **Parc Naturel de Boutissant**✦✦ is a 400-hectare animal park which has only native species, notably deer. It is in no sense a place of protection for the animals though, as one of the attractions on offer is a day's hunting. Also well away from the village, but within its *commune*, **Château de Guedelon**✦✦✦ is the scene of an extraordinary enterprise: the reconstruction of the 13th-century fortified farm which used to belong to the Château de St-Fargeau, using only the original medieval materials and techniques. As if that were not enough, the workers are also all dressed in the costume of the time. Stand and watch the strange and wonderful lifting gear, the intricate and time-consuming craftsmanship, the beasts of burden and the painfully slow progress … the work is scheduled to continue for at least another 25 years.

Pottery in the Puisaye

The area south of St-Sauveur-en-Puisaye is the traditional Puisaye pottery district. Since the Middle Ages potters have made good use of the heavy Puisaye earth, which consists of clay and crushed flint. Today pottery is still a thriving local trade. Many Puisaye towns and villages have pottery sellers, though the best place to see and buy high-quality local crockery is St-Amand-en-Puisaye, where there are several potters' workshops. On the edge of St-Sauveur-en-Puisaye, the village of Mouitiers-en-Puisaye is known for fine chinaware and that of La Batisse for stoneware.

Accommodation and food in Puisaye

Contact tourist offices at Auxerre or St-Fargeau for *chambres d'hôte* accommodation at farms and villages along the route.

Suggested tour

Auberge du Point du Jour €€ *Pl. de la Mairie; tel: 03 86 74 94 38, fax: 03 86 74 85 92.* At **Bléneau**, a village in the heart of Puisaye countryside, this smart restaurant is the place to discover the region's traditional local cuisine.

Hostellerie Blanche de Castile €€ *17 r. d'Orléans; tel: 03 86 74 92 63, fax: 03 86 74 94 43.* This is a comfortable, modern, family-run small hotel, with its own restaurant, that offers excellent value for money.

Son-et-lumière shows at the château in St-Fargeau: *2200 every Fri and Sat from 16 July–28 Aug.* Dramatic costume re-enactments of key moments in French history, with a cast of 600. *Tel: 03 86 74 05 67.*

Total distance: 96km, or 123km if you take the detour.

Time: One day. The starting point, the village of Toucy, is 23km from Auxerre (*see page 77*). As there is little accommodation on the route, it may be convenient to make this tour from Auxerre.

Links: From Dicy to Châteaurenard the route follows the same road as the Sénonais and Gâtinais route (*see page 48*). The two routes could easily be combined into one longer tour.

Route: From **TOUCY** ❶, take the D950 beside the River Ouanne, following it downstream through a succession of waterside villages – Dracy, **Villiers-St-Benoît** (where there is a **Museum of Puisaye** and a useful tourist office), St-Denis and St-Martin-sur-Ouanne to slightly larger Charny. Just north, accessible by several different small roads, it's fun to visit **DICY** ❷. Turn left on to main road D943, staying with the Ouanne as it heads into **Châteaurenard**.

Turn south here on to the D37, which goes straight to **CHÂTILLON-COLIGNY** ❸, where our route rejoins the River Loing. Follow the river upstream, on either side of the valley, to **Rogny-les-Sept-Écluses**. The name means 'Rogny of the Seven Locks', and you'll see why at the attractive confluence of the Canal de Briare and the River Loing, although today six locks have replaced the original seven. The town puts on a huge firework display at the end of July. The D90 continues via **Bléneau** through a watery landscape, again following the course of the Loing, to **ST-FARGEAU** ❹. It's just 11km on the main road to **ST-SAUVEUR-EN-PUISAYE** ❺, or you may prefer the longer, interesting detour through the district of Treigny.

Detour: Leave St-Fargeau on the D85 and turn right straight away on to the D185, skirting the Bourdon reservoir, to the **Parc Naturel de Boutissant** (*see Treigny, page 55*). Continue on D185, crossing the D955, to reach **TREIGNY-PERREUSE** ❻. Turn off just before the village to visit the **Château de Ratilly** (*see Treigny, page 55*). Return as far as the D955, where you turn right, soon arriving at the **Château de Guedelon** (*see Treigny, page 55*). Carry on from here into St-Sauveur-en-Puisaye.

Again, water dominates the scene on the drive from St-Sauveur back into Toucy.

10 km

Piffonds
17 D15
N6
Courtenay
St-Julien-
du-Sault
Bussy-en-Othe
Brienon-sur-
Armançon
N60 *29* E60
17 A6
17
18
Douchy
Joigny
9
Migennes
12
Cheny
2 D943
13
E15/60
S
Charmoy
11
4
châteaurenard
Triguères
Dicy
14
14
D91
D37
La Ferté-
Loupière
26
10
Seignelay
6
Charny
D3
D955
Aillant-sur-Tholon
Monéteau
St-Martin-
sur-Ouanne
St-Aubin-Château-Neuf
8
Châtillon-Coligny
24
23
17
St-Georges-sur-Baulche
Auxerre
St-Denis-
sur-Ouanne
D950
8
Champignelles
Villiers-
St-Benoît
Pourrain
23
Dracy
Champs-sur-Yonne
Rogny-les-
Sept-Écluses
Toucy
1
19
D90
Ouanne
D950
17
Coulanges-
la-Vineuse
Bléneau
Mézilles
22
14
Fontaines
6
St-Fargeau
4
D965
D955
Ouanne
10
14
6
Fontenoy
19
Courson-les-
Carrières
12
St-Sauveur-
en-Puisaye
5
D85
10
D85
PARC NATUREL
DE BOUTISSANT
11
N151
Château de
Guedelon
Château de
Ratilly
D955
6 Treigny-
Perreuse
Druyes-les-
Belles-Fontaines
Coulanges-
sur-Yonne
D957 *21*
15
20
St-Amand-
en-Puisaye
Étais-
la-Sauvin
7
Clamecy
D955
P U I S A Y E
17
18
17
Entrains-
sur-Nohain
D957
24
D19
N151
D951
Cosne-Cours-
sur-Loire
D5
19
4
P
12
La Chapelle-
St-André
17
annay
N7
Pougny
14
Donzy
20
D33
Menou
7
Varzy
Tannay

Chablis

Ratings

Architecture	●●●●●
Winetasting	●●●●●
Châteaux	●●●●
Country towns	●●●●
History	●●●●
Restaurants	●●●●
Scenery	●●●
Children	●●

The mild and rural Chablis country lies along and between the Serein and Armançon rivers, flowing calmly through this little land close to the border of Champagne. At its fringes, it rises to spacious, but soft countryside. In some areas, wide cornfields open out, though generally the region is rustic and old-fashioned, with many old stone, timber or brick farm buildings with stables and orchards, and cows standing in small fields of rough pasture. Occasionally the skyline is broken by little copses or patches of mature deciduous woodland. Then there are the vineyards, confined only to sun-catching valley slopes. True Chablis wines come only from the tranquil, appropriately named River Serein (serene), which flows through the town of Chablis itself. Highly prized, immaculately tended, arranged in neat rows, the precious vines seem to have an almost self-conscious air in such a pastoral setting.

ANCY-LE-FRANC❖❖

ⓘ Ancy Tourist Office *La Faïencerie; tel: 03 86 75 03 15; open daily Easter–All Saints (1 Nov), 1030–1230, 1430–1900.*

One of the finest of Burgundy's **châteaux**❖❖❖ stands here alongside this small town beside the River Armançon and the Burgundy Canal. It's a neat square, and technically it marks the first signs of a distinct French Renaissance style, although to the ordinary observer Ancy is thoroughly ornate and Italian. Built in 1554, Ancy copies the style of an Italian palazzo and even had an Italian architect, but was designed in response to a growing French taste for Renaissance design. The interior décor is glorious, and is mainly the work of Primaticcio, who also decorated the palace of Fontainebleau. The workmanship of ceilings and wall panels is exquisite, sometimes overwhelmingly richly decorated, and there are remarkable frescos. On the ground floor, highlights are the vaulted Salle de Diane and the château kitchens, while upstairs are elaborate bedrooms and lounges. Particular highlights are the Salon Bleu et Or (The Blue and Gold Room); the Galerie de Pharsale, with a large original 16th-century fresco; the

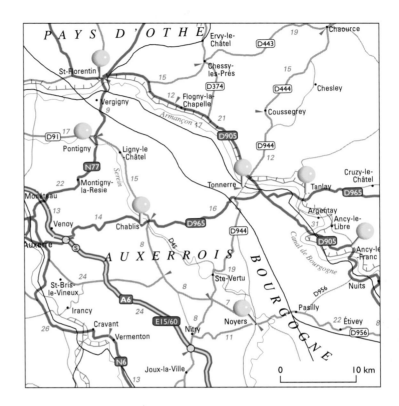

Château €€€ *Tel: 03 86 75 14 63; open une–20 Sept 1000–1200, 1400–1800, 25 Mar–31 May and 21 Sept–11 Nov closes at 1700, closed rest of the year.* Guided tours several times daily lasting 45 mins.

Musée de l'Automobile et de l'Attelage €€ *Tel: 03 86 75 14 63; open May–Sept only, 1000–1200, 1400–1800.*

Chambre des Fleurs, so-called for its decorative panels; and the Chambre des Arts, with a series of acclaimed oval medallions and coffered ceiling. Outside, the gardens were laid out by Le Nôtre (who also created Versailles). A small **Musée de l'Automobile et de l'Attelage (Museum of Vintage Vehicles)***, including a collection of antique bicycles and 60 carriages, as well as 100-year-old motor cars, has been created in some château outbuildings.

The town itself is a thriving and congenial little market centre and river port with some attractive old stone houses. It's a popular stopover for people boating on the waterways. One of its attractions is the restored 18th-century **Faïencerie** (earthenware factory), now housing the tourist office.

Accommodation and food in Ancy

Hôstellerie du Centre €€ *34 Grande Rue; tel: 03 86 75 15 11, fax: 03 86 75 14 13.* A good little town-centre family-run hotel, well equipped and welcoming, with an enjoyable traditional restaurant serving classic French cooking.

CHABLIS✦

ⓘ **Chablis Tourist Office** / Quai Biez; tel: 03 86 42 80 80, fax: 03 86 42 41 79, e-mail: otchablis@chablis.net, www.chablis.net/; open 1000–1230, 1330–1800 (closed Mon Oct–Mar).

☾ **Hôtel de l'Etoile** € 4 r. des Moulins, Chablis; tel: 03 86 42 10 50, fax: 03 86 42 81 21.

Though in some ways an unremarkable small agricultural town, quiet and sleepy, with remnants of fortifications, some historic buildings on a broad main street and a medieval core of narrow backstreets, Chablis possesses the aura of fame. Many of its doorways have a sign, *Viticulteur* (winemaker), where one of the great white Burgundy wines can be tasted and bought direct from growers. The village, the wine, and its Église St-Martin, all date from about the 12th century. Notice the church doorway with its horseshoes left by pilgrims and passers-by. Why horseshoes? Because in the Middle Ages, it was St Martin, not St Christopher, who was thought to protect travellers. Though interesting for a stroll, if you'd like to try a typical local meal with a decent bottle of Chablis, you might be better off at a quieter, neighbouring village, where prices are more reasonable.

Chablis wine

The name Chablis has been abused and misused around the world, in some countries meaning any crisp, dry, aromatic white wine of character. In France, the name is protected by the *appellation* rules and cannot be used to describe wines from other regions. Among the most prestigious and best-known of white Burgundies, Chablis *appellation* wine is made from just one grape variety – Chardonnay – and all of it comes from the vineyards of just 19 *communes* around the small town of Chablis. If you're looking to buy a good bottle, remember that in the hierarchy of Chablis *appellations*, confusingly, Premier Cru takes second place to Grand Cru. Both of these may be aged several years. Premier Cru, less rich and savoury than the Grand Cru, is considered to represent the best, most typical flavour of Chablis. Next down the scale comes the standard Chablis *appellation*: a pale gold with just a hint of green in the colour, it should be drunk cool, usually under three years old. Next step down is Petit Chablis, a crisp, fresh, less expensive wine to be drunk very young and chilled.

NOYERS***

Noyers Tourist Office *Point d'Acceuil at the Mairie; tel: 03 86 82 83 72, fax: 03 86 82 63 41; open June–Sept only, Tue–Fri 1400–1900, Sat and Sun 1000–1200, 1400–1900.*

Museum € *R. de l'Église; tel: 03 86 82 89 09; open June–Sept, daily 1100–1830, Oct–May, Sat and Sun only, same hours.*

Festival: Annual summer festival of 30 choral music concerts.

Pronounced 'Noyaire', this splendid example of a medieval fortified village, protected by a river and ramparts, has staunchly resisted modernisation. The pretty Serein curves around the little town, while the walls are reinforced by 16 round towers. Within the fortifications, Noyers is a cluster of half-timbered houses, gables and arcades, several houses adorned with statuary or carvings, dating mostly from the 14th to 17th centuries. Walk along main street, r. de la Petite-Étape-aux-Vins, admire the postcard-perfect place de l'Hôtel de Ville, with its arcaded Renaissance timbered houses. Wander from there, to place du Marché-au-Blé, to r. du Poids-du-Roy and, opening off it, tiny place de la Petite-Etape-aux-Vins. The town's **museum***** in r. de l'Église contains a surprising collection of modern naïve painting, including over 100 important works donated by art historian Jacques Yankel.

Accommodation and food in Noyers

Hôtel de la Vieille Tour € *Pl. du Grenier-à-Sel; tel: 03 86 82 87 69.* Comfortable and pleasing rooms at this unpretentious hotel by the river, and good set meals in the restaurant, all at low prices.

PONTIGNY❖❖

ⓘ **Pontigny Tourist Office** (also serving Ligny-le-Châtel and the surrounding area) *Opposite the abbey at 22 r. Paul Desjardins; tel: 03 86 47 47 03, fax: 03 86 47 58 38; open Easter–15 Oct 1030–1230, 1500–1900, rest of the year Mon–Fri 0900–1300.*

ⓘ **Abbaye de Pontigny** € *Beside main street; tel: 03 86 47 54 99, fax: 03 86 47 84 66; open daily 0900–1900.*

❍ **Festivals:** 15 Aug – *Journée d'Artisanat d'Art et Gastronomique* (Day of Art and Gastronomy); summer concerts in Pontigny Abbey.

It used to be said that on the old bridge that crosses the River Serein on the edge of this village, three bishops, three counts and an abbot could sit down to dine and all be on their own territory. Here was a meeting of ecclesiastical and political domains that today have faded from memory, as one crosses the bridge unaware of any borders (there is, though, a perfect spot at the bridge where the party could dine!). Close to the bridge, an avenue of trees leads past surviving monastic buildings to the huge church of the old Cistercian **Abbaye de Pontigny**❖❖, founded in 1114. The lower part of the pale, heavy structure is Romanesque and austere, the upper part early Gothic, with a single low and uneven octagonal tower on one corner. The abbey provided refuge to Thomas à Becket, Archbishop of Canterbury, during his exile in 1164 (two years later, back in Canterbury, Becket was murdered).

Accommodation and food in Pontigny

Moulin de Pontigny € *Tel: 03 86 47 44 98.* Beside the Serein Bridge, this beautifully situated bar and restaurant has a lovely waterside terrace, and some inexpensive *menus*.

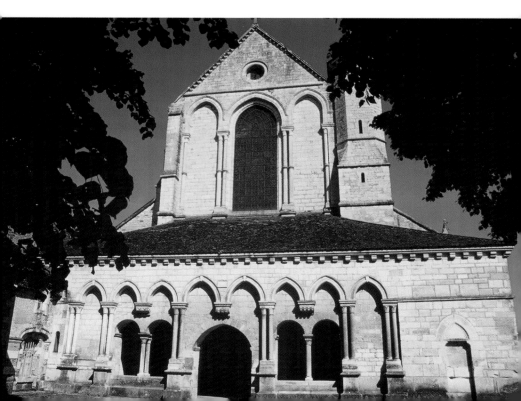

ST-FLORENTIN✥

ℹ️ **St-Florentin Tourist Office** 8 r. de la Terrasse; tel/fax: 03 86 35 11 86; open all year.

On the cheeseboard

The dairy pastures of northern Burgundy produce some of France's greatest connoisseur cheeses. The style here is soft, rich, cow's milk cheese made in rounds, wrapped in paper, and sold in wooden boxes. The cheese rinds are washed and edible. *Chaource*, from just across the Champagne border, is a succulent, tasty, creamy cheese of fine texture with a slightly pink-tinted crust. The little town of St-Florentin lies at the centre of the area producing its own tangy, brine-washed *St-Florentin* cheese. In the same area, the cheese called *Soumaintrain* is the traditional farm-made version, sold wrapped in vine leaves.

The busy and appealing town – where *Soumaintrain* and *St-Florentin* cheeses are made – rises from a pretty canal and the delightful River Armançon close to the confluence with the Armance. Head up the hill to the old part of St-Florentin, with remains of its old fortifications. Here are busy little shops, bars and a useful tourist office. The back lanes make a picturesque jumble, a mix of stone, wattle-and-daub and timber houses. Step into the church to see some excellent Renaissance stained glass.

Accommodation and food in St-Florentin

Hôtel-Restaurant de l'Est €–€€ *Route de Troyes; tel: 03 86 35 10 35, fax: 03 86 43 45 77.* A simple two-star close to the town centre, with a slightly shabby air; most rooms are very inexpensive. The *patron* is an accomplished chef and his restaurant reaches a far higher standard than the hotel.

La Grand Chaumière €€€ *3 r. des Capucins; tel: 03 86 35 15 12, fax: 03 86 35 33 14.* A much grander hotel than others in town, this comfortable place has a lovely garden with trees and an excellent restaurant.

Hôtel-Restaurant des Tilleuls €€ *3 r. Decourtive; tel: 03 86 35 09 09, fax: 03 86 35 36 90.* A two-star *logis* up a little side turn off the Troyes road, this endearing hotel has an adorable little flowery garden and terraces and an elegant, ambitious restaurant.

Left
Abbaye de Pontigny

Above
Timber house, St-Florentin

TANLAY❖❖

Château de Tanlay
€€€ *Tel: 03 86 75 70 61; open for one-hour guided tours Apr–mid-Nov six to seven times daily 0930–1715 (1745 in July and Aug), closed Tue.*

Standing incongruously beside a simple canalside village, **Château de Tanlay**❖❖❖ is a large, stately Renaissance palace of sumptuous classical elegance. Approached by a long avenue of trees through a park, it's surrounded by broad moats of running water and adorned with a wealth of decoration. You first arrive at the Petit Château, in fact a glorified gatehouse, and then cross the lily-covered water on a stone bridge to the Cour d'Honneur of the main château, with its arcades and domed towers. The combining of the original medieval fortifications with an opulent 16th-century mansion – for the château stands on the site of Tanlay's earlier feudal fortress – creates an extraordinary and pleasing building. The interior Renaissance decoration and carvings include extravagant frescos, particularly in the Tour de la Ligue, where there is a bizarre and fascinating allegorical mural about the conflict between Protestants and Catholics. The figures are real people: Catherine de Medici appears naked as Juno, and Diane de Poitiers as Venus. The château, property of the Protestant organiser Gaspard de Coligny, played a key role in those wars, as the meeting place of leading Protestant nobility. De Coligny was murdered in the St Bartholomew's Eve massacre of 1572, the night when thousands of French Protestants were slaughtered.

Above
Château de Tanlay

TONNERRE✣

Tonnerre Tourist Office 12 r. François Mitterrand; tel: 03 86 55 14 48, fax: 03 86 54 41 82, www.tonnerre89.com/; open 0930–1230, 1430–1830, closed Sun out of season. **Guided tours** are organised by the tourist office.

Ancien Hôpital €€ Tel: 03 86 54 33 00; open June–Sept 1000–1200, 1300–1830 (closed Tue), Apr, May, Oct Sat, Sun and hols only, 1330–1830, rest of the year closed.

Hôtel de Uzès R. des Fontanilles. Access to exterior only.

Fosse Dionne R. de la Fosse-Dionne.

Main town of the Chablis region, Tonnerre is the cheerful, busy centre of a wine-growing area producing red, white and rosé wines that are not 'Chablis' at all but come under the Tonnerre and Epineuil *appellations*. In the lofty old quarter with its 11th-century Église St-Pierre, some other medieval buildings have survived, notably the 13th-century **Ancien Hôpital (Former Hospital)**✣✣✣, a vast and gloomy building. Inside, it has a high and beautifully timbered barrel-vaulted roof with oak framework rising over the stone walls and floor of the main hospital ward. It looks a grim place in which to lie sick. Patients were arranged so that they could see the altar at one end, with its notable carving of the Entombment. Just round the corner from the Ancien Hôpital, a savings bank now occupies the aristocratic Renaissance **Hôtel de Uzès**✣, birthplace of the enigmatic Chevalier d'Eon (*see below*). A great oddity on the edge of town is the **Fosse Dionne**✣✣, a large circular *lavoir* around a clear, wide, unfathomable pool fed by a deep underground stream.

Right
Chablis wine fair

The Chevalier d'Eon

Tonnerre's oddest native was the young, and strangely christened, Charles Geneviève Louise Auguste Andrée Timothée Eon de Beaumont. Bearing the title Chevalier d'Eon (1728–1810), Charles Geneviève grew up to become a French spy living in Russia as Mademoiselle Lia de Beaumont; he became the closest and most intimate lady friend of the Tsarina. Later living in England as a man, he returned to France to live as a woman. His (or her) sex was a hot topic among high society in both England and France; at one point a panel of Ladies of Quality, after intimate examination, declared that he was a she. On his death (in London) in 1810, the post-mortem – subject of fierce betting at the time – revealed that the Chevalier d'Eon had been a man all along

Above
Château de Tanlay

Suggested tour

Total distance: 142km, or 178km if you take the detour.

Time: 1 day.

Links: At Auxerre this route meets the Cure and Cousin route (*see page 84*).

Route: Leave Auxerre (*see page 77*) by crossing the Yonne, following signs for the N6 (direction Avallon) and the D956 (direction Chaumont). Turn away from the N6 to follow the Chaumont and Chablis signs, at last passing under *autoroute* A6 and continuing into **CHABLIS ❶**. Follow the little D45, the winding Chablis wine road, through the Serein villages, to **NOYERS ❷**. Leaving the village, rejoin the D956, turning left and staying on this road for just 10km to the D12 (just after Pasilly), where you turn left to **ANCY-LE-FRANC** ❸, beside the Armançon. A country lane runs straight to Ancy-le-Libre; there rejoin the river and canal and go via Argentay to **TANLAY** ❹. Alternatively, reach Tanlay by taking the main D905 (direction Tonnerre) and turning right after 8km on to D118, signposted Tanlay. From Tanlay, the D956 takes you to **TONNERRE** ❺.

The D905 follows the Armançon and the canal from Tonnerre to **ST-FLORENTIN** ❻.

Detour: From Tonnerre, take the D944 in the Troyes direction. It's just 9km to the border of Champagne, and another 18km, much of the way through forest, to **Chaource**, close to the source of the River Armançon. The countryside round about, called the Chaourçois, broadly continues the Chablis region, lying in the well-watered gap between the Othe and Châtillonais uplands. Take the D443, returning to the main route at St-Florentin.

From St-Florentin, the N77 quickly reaches **PONTIGNY** ❼ and continues back into Auxerre.

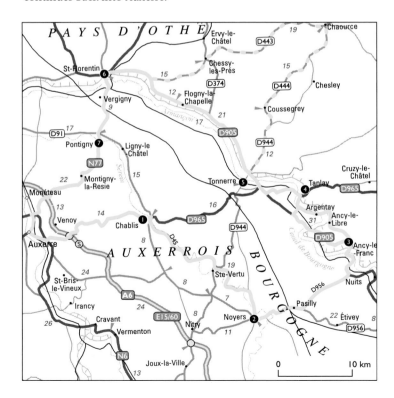

Auxois and the Seine Valley

Ratings

Archaeology	●●●●●
Châteaux	●●●●●
History	●●●●●
Medieval architecture	●●●●●
Activities	●●●○○
Folklore	●●●○○
Scenery	●●●○○
Children	●●○○○

The fertile Auxois region, centred on Mont Auxois, lies between the higher uplands of Morvan, Othe and Châtillonais. On its eastern edge the Seine gathers pace as it flows to the northern rim of Burgundy. The road on this route is interspersed with bright, open hills, broad landscapes of pasture and enticing deciduous forests stretching away to either side. Gallo-Roman sites and museums abound, some of them archaeological excavations such as Alésia, others intriguing relics such as the Vix treasure at Châtillon-sur-Seine. There is much later history too: medieval and Renaissance, secular and religious. Heading south, the countryside is laced with springs and streams and dashing little rivers – some of which flow straight into the River Seine, others preferring the Armançon, which reaches the Seine later via the River Yonne.

ALISE-STE-REINE✠✠

 www.alesia.asso.fr/.

Fouilles d'Alésia €€ Tel/fax: 03 80 96 10 95; open July and Aug, daily 0900–1900, Sept, Oct, Easter–June 1000–1800, rest of the year closed. Joint ticket with Musée Alésia available.

Musée Alésia € R. de l'Hôpital; tel/fax: 03 80 96 10 95. Same opening times as archaeological site.

The **Fouilles d'Alésia (Alésia archaeological site)**✠✠ on Mont Auxois is where the great Gaulish leader Vercingetorix made his last stand against the Roman conquest. A huge, impressive statue of the warrior chief stands on top of the hill. It was erected in 1861, at which time Napoleon III ordered that excavations begin here; they have been continuing ever since. In the village of Alise-Ste-Reine at the foot of the hill, the **Musée Alésia**✠ displays numerous objects found on the site.

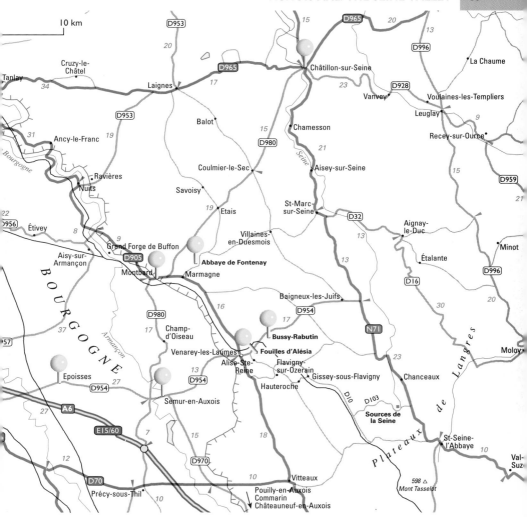

10 km

D953

D965   15   D965   20   13

20   D996

Cruzy-le-
Châtel   D965   Châtillon-sur-Seine   La Chaume

Tanlay   Laignes   17   23   D928

34   Vanvey   Voulaines-les-Templiers

D953   Balot   Leuglay   9

31   Ancy-le-Franc   19   15   Chamesson   Recey-sur-Ource

Bourgogne   D980   21   15

Coulmier-le-Sec   Aisey-sur-Seine   D959

Ravières   Savoisy   21

Nuits

22   19   Etais   St-Marc-
sur-Seine   D32   Aignay-
le-Duc

956   Étivey   8   9   Villaines-
en-Duesmois   13   Étalante   Minot

Aisy-sur-   Grand Forge de Buffon   D905   Abbaye de Fontenay   13   D996

Armançon   Montbard   Marmagne   D16

B O U R G O G N E   Baigneux-les-Juifs   30   20

D980   16   D954

37   17   Champ-
d'Oiseau   17   Bussy-Rabutin   N71   Moloy

57   Venarey-les-Laumes   Fouilles d'Alésia   23

Epoisses   13   Alise-Ste-
Reine   Flavigny-
sur-Ozerain   Gissey-sous-Flavigny   Chanceaux

27   D954   D954   Hauteroche   D10   D103

A6   Semur-en-Auxois   Sources de
la Seine   St-Seine-
l'Abbaye   10

27   E15/60   7   15   18   P l a t e a u x   Val-
Suz

12   D970

D70   10   Vitteaux   598 △
Mont Tasselot

Précy-sous-Thil   10   Pouilly-en-Auxois
Commarin
Châteauneuf-en-Auxois

The death of Vercingetorix

Early in 52 BC, the army of Caesar, beaten by Gauls at Gergovie, took refuge at Sens and joined forces with the troops of Labienus. Marching south together, the Roman soldiers were ambushed at Alésia by Vercingetorix and his men. Despite Vercingetorix's previous victories, this time the Gauls were beaten off. Caesar insisted on getting revenge. He ordered that Alésia be beseiged and conquered. The *oppidum* was enclosed by rings of Roman troops protected by fortified earthworks. Reinforcements arrived to see off a rescue attempt by other Gaulish armies. After six weeks, Vercingetorix realised that he had no hope of victory, and personally surrendered to Caesar. He was taken in triumph to Rome to be publicly paraded in chains, tortured and humiliated, imprisoned for six years and finally strangled to death.

Bussy-Rabutin✦✦

Take the D954 from Venarey-les-Laumes for 6km. Pass through the village of Grésigny-Ste-Reine and turn right after 2km for the château.

Château de Bussy-Rabutin €€ Tel: 03 80 96 00 03; open Apr–Sept 0930–1130, 1400–1700 (1800 in July and Aug and no midday closing at weekends in those months), Oct–Mar 1000–1100, 1400–1500 (closed Tue and Wed). 45-min guided tours.

A 15th-century feudal fortress transformed into a 17th-century Renaissance **château**✦✦ protected by towers and moats and surrounding woodland, this palatial country residence was the luxurious 'prison' of exiled Count Roger de Bussy-Rabutin. Famed as a libertine, poet and satirist of the Grand Siècle, he was banished here, first for being involved in an orgy at which he improvised songs poking fun at Louis XIV and his mistress, and then – after a year in the Bastille – confined here again for composing his *Histoires Amoureuses des Gaules* (1665), a series of bawdy satirical writings about Royal Court life. The lavish interior, gilded and polished, is studded with allegorical paintings, portraits and sharp-tongued *devises* (captions, couplets and caustic epigrams) – all done by Bussy-Rabutin himself during his bitter years of exile.

Châtillon-sur-Seine✦✦

Châtillon Tourist Office Pl. Marmont; tel: 03 80 91 13 19, fax: 03 80 91 21 46, www.parisgifts.com/chatillon; open daily 0900–1200, 1400–1800 (closed Sun and hols out of season).

Église St-Vorles € Off r. du Recept; tel: 03 80 91 24 67; open mid-June–Sept, daily 1030–1200, 1430–1730, Apr–mid June Wed, Sat and Sun only, Sept–Nov Sat and Sun only, otherwise closed.

Source de la Douix (Douix Spring) € R. de la Douix.

Musée du Châtillonais €€ R. du Bourg; tel: 03 80 91 24 67; open mid-June–Sept, daily 0900–1200, 1330–1800, Apr–mid-June and Sept–Nov 0900–1200, 1400–1800, closed Tue, rest of the year 1000–1200, 1400–1700, closed Tue.

At Châtillon the Seine splits into two and the façades and spires of the medieval heart of the town rise attractively from both arms of the river. The historic Bourg quarter lies around **Église St-Vorles**✦, which dates from the 10th century, though most of the building was built two or three hundred years after that, while the cumbersome belfry was added in the 17th century. Close by is the delightful promenade beside the **Source de la Douix (Douix Spring)**✦, where water gushes from the foot of a rocky cliff. Walk parallel to the Seine to reach the 17th- to 18th-century Renaissance quarter around Église St-Nicolas. Just here is the **Musée du Châtillonais**✦✦ in a Renaissance mansion. Dominating the museum is the astonishing Trésor de Vix (Treasure of Vix) collection. Close to the town are extensive woods, especially the Forêt de Châtillon, with paths and trails to explore and the beautiful buildings and gardens of the 12th-century former Cistercian abbey **Val des Choues**✦✦.

Accommodation and food in Châtillon

Val des Choues Abbey € *21290 Essarois; tel: 03 80 81 01 09; open 1 Mar–12 Nov 1000–1800 (closed Tue except in July and Aug).*

Ask at the tourist office for *chambres d'hôtes* and *gîtes* in the area. There are campsites close to the town centre.

Hôtel du Jura €–€€ *19–21 r. Dr Robert; tel: 03 80 91 26 96, fax: 03 80 91 10 52.* Decent, simple, family-run hotel (no restaurant) on the main through-road in the town centre, close to the St-Nicolas quarter.

Val des Choues Abbey €€ *Tel: 03 80 81 01 09.* Deep in the Châtillon forest, this historic abbey has some delightful, simple, elegant accommodation in the former abbey buildings.

Restaurant le Bourg-à-Mont € *27 r. du Bourg-à-Mont; tel: 03 80 91 04 33, fax: 03 80 93 12 02; closed Sun pm and Mon except in summer.* Classic regional dishes such as snails, terrines and *oeufs en meurette* (eggs poached in wine and rich stock) are nicely prepared at this homely, inexpensive restaurant.

EPOISSES✤

Château €€ *Tel: 03 80 96 40 56; exterior open daily 0900–1900, interior July and Aug only, 1000–1200, 1500–1800 (closed Tue).*

Impressive double fortifications and a double moat protect the ancient fortress on the edge of this farming village on the Auxois plateau. The structures within the **château✤** walls almost have the air of a hamlet in their own right, with a 13th-century church and a large 16th-century dovecote with 3 000 nesting holes.

Accommodation and food in Epoisses

Hôtel-Restaurant La Pomme d'Or €€ *In village; tel: 03 80 96 43 01.* A former coaching inn, this *brasserie* and hotel has a 17th-century interior and features *Epoisses* cheese dishes on the menu.

Epoisses cheese

The village of Epoisses gives its name to one of the great cheeses of France, created by 15th-century monks and described by the diplomat and gastronome Brillat-Savarin as the King of Cheeses. Matured in caves, then washed in *marc* (the spirit made from grape pressings), it's strong enough to make your eyes water, yet rich, runny and creamy.

ABBAYE DE FONTENAY❖❖❖

ⓘ Abbaye de Fontenay €€ *The abbey is 5km from Montbard, and 3km from the village of Marmagne on D32; tel: 03 80 92 15 00, fax: 03 80 92 16 88, www.abbayedefontenay. com/; open daily for 45-min guided visits every hour (except 1300) from 0900–1700.*

The approach to this famous Cistercian abbey, along a lane through the village of Marmagne and alongside the quiet green and wooded valley of a little stream, is itself a joy. Eventually a small bridge crosses the stream and leads to the abbey, elegant and pale, and arranged around neat gardens and fountains. The abbey was founded in 1118 by the Bishop of Norwich, who came here as abbot. Much damaged during the French Revolution and then turned into a paper factory, the building was purchased in 1906 by a family member of the paper mill owners. He stopped production and extensively restored the abbey, all trace of the factory being carefully removed.

Accommodation and food near the Abbaye de Fontenay

Château de Malaisy €€ *At Fain-les-Montbard; tel: 03 80 89 46 54, fax: 03 80 92 30 16.* This grand and peaceful 17th-century country house (and modern annexe) 5km from Montbard, set back from the D905 close to the Fontenay turning, has spacious accommodation, a good restaurant and an 'animal park' with sheep, goats and geese.

MONTBARD❖❖

ⓘ Montbard Tourist Office *R. Carnot; tel: 03 80 92 03 75, fax: 03 80 92 03 75; open Mon–Sat 0900–1200, 1400–1800.*

ⓘ Parc Buffon € *Tel: 03 80 92 50 42; open 1015–1600 in winter, 1015–1700 in summer (1800 in July and Aug), closed Tue in winter.*

Musée Buffon € *R. du Parc Buffon; tel: 03 80 92 50 42; open daily except Tue, 1000–1200, 1400–1800 (1700 Nov–Mar).*

Grande Forge de Buffon €€ *7km from Montbard on the D905; tel: 03 80 92 10 35; open Apr–Sept 1000–1200, 1400–1800 (closed Tue).*

The pride and joy of this hardworking, industrial little town is Georges-Louis Leclerc, the Count of Buffon (1707–88), distinguished scientist and naturalist of his day. At the age of 28, he bought the local 10th- to 13th-century château, a former residence of the Dukes of Burgundy, and proceeded to knock most of it down. In its place he put a handsome park and botanical gardens, now called the **Parc Buffon**❖❖, and turned the two remaining château towers into a library, laboratory and museums. Buffon's life's work was to write a complete history of nature, the 36-volume *Histoire Naturelle* which took him 50 years to complete. His stables are now the **Musée Buffon**❖, which deals with the man himself rather than his scientific work. In old age, Buffon created the out-of-town **Grande Forge de Buffon**❖❖, a small riverside ironworks designed both for scientific research into the ores and for their commercial exploitation.

Accommodation and food in Montbard

Le Cyclamen €–€€ *6 av. Maréchal Foch; tel: 03 80 92 06 46; closed Sun pm and Mon.* In an attractive house and garden, this good-quality restaurant ably prepares the local regional dishes.

Semur-en-Auxois**

ⓘ Semur Tourist Office *Beside the fortified gateway at 2 pl. Gaveau; tel: 03 80 97 05 96, fax: 03 80 97 08 85, e-mail: tourisme.pays. auxois@wanadoo.fr, www. parisgifts.com/semur; open Mon–Sat 0830–1200, 1400–1830, Sun and fêtes 1000–1200, 1500–1800 (June–Sept 0900–1900). During the summer months, a little 'tourist train' makes a tour of the town at 1700 and 2200, starting from the tourist office.*

ⓘ Église Nôtre-Dame *€ Rue Nôtre-Dame; open daily: guided tours in summer.*

Cobbled lanes, four mighty towers, a massive stone gateway into the fortified old quarter: many remnants of the Middle Ages survive at this appealing little country town. Walk through the 15th-century barbican in r. Buffon and beneath the double gateway of Guillier (13th century) and Sauvigny (15th century). To either side, old houses of stone and timber line the way. **Église Nôtre-Dame***, though much damaged, is a good example of the Burgundian architecture of the 13th and 14th centuries. Continue past the massive Tour de l'Orle d'Or, split from top to bottom, via r. des Remparts and past the little hospital, to the small park on top of the 15th-century **ramparts***. From here the extraordinary position of the town can be fully appreciated: perched on a high spur, it rises from a bizarre loop in the River Armançon. It looks especially picturesque from the bottom of the hill: pause on the **Pont Joly*** that crosses the river on the D954 on the north side of town, to get the full effect of the towers and houses clustered on the pink granite.

Accommodation and food in Semur

Ask the tourist office for details of several *gîtes* and *chambres d'hôtes* in the area.

La Côte d'Or €–€€ *3 pl. Gaveau; tel: 03 80 97 03 13, fax: 03 80 97 29 83; closed Jan and Wed (except in summer).* This is a simple, old-fashioned, family-run hotel with rooms that are a little shabby but with a rather good traditional restaurant.

Hostellerie d'Aussois €€ *Route de Saulieu; tel: 03 80 97 28 28, fax: 03 80 97 34 56; closed Sun pm in winter.* Good family-run, out-of-town, country hotel, with a restaurant (Le Mermoz) that's popular with locals.

Hôtel Les Cymaises €€ *7 r. Renaudot; tel: 03 80 97 21 44, fax: 03 80 97 18 23.* Down a backstreet in the old quarter, this modernised 18th-century mansion within a courtyard makes an appealing hotel (no restaurant). It's comfortable, quiet, furnished with style and makes a good base.

Suggested tour

Why 'les Juifs'?

There is no trace now in Baigneux-les-Juifs of the large Jewish community that once lived here and at some other villages in this corner of Burgundy. From the 5th century, Jews – previously mainly living in Provence – moved into Burgundy, settled at Dijon, and in the 8th century began to create large communities in southern Champagne around Troyes, as well as in Alsace. By the 11th century, the Jewish community living within a radius of a few kilometres of Troyes, including Chablis and Baigneux, was among the largest and most densely populated in the world (the great 11th-century Talmudic authority Rashi was a *viticulteur* living at Troyes). Every north Burgundy town with a r. des Juifs was probably part of this population. All the communities were broken up and decimated with the start of the Crusades, but some, such as Baigneux, survived until Jews were expelled from Burgundy in 1394.

Total distance: 157km, and a 23km detour.

Time: 1 day. For those *en route* to Dijon, the route makes an interesting one-way journey from Châtillon-sur-Seine to St-Seine l'Abbaye (27km from Dijon).

Links: This links with Dijon (*see page 98*).

Route: Leave **CHÂTILLON-SUR-SEINE** ❶ on the D980, towards Montbard. At the village of Etais, it is possible to turn off left for a cross-country route to **ABBAYE DE FONTENAY** ❷, but it is badly signposted, and a simpler approach is via **MONTBARD** ❸. Take in a trip to La Grande Forge de Buffon, 7km west of town, before heading south on the D980 again to **SEMUR-EN-AUXOIS** ❹.

Detour: There's a pleasant drive west from town on the D954 through dairy country to **EPOISSES** ❺, crossing half-a-dozen streams which all flow into the Armançon.

From Semur, cross Pont-Joly and follow the road round on to the D954 to **Venarey-les-Laumes**. Continue on the same road to visit **BUSSY-RABUTIN** ❻, then double back to the D103 for the **Fouilles d'Alésia** and the adjacent village **ALISE-STE-REINE** ❼. The tiny D103 threads along beside the Ozérain River, turn right for the 2km climb up to **Flavigny-sur-Ozerain**, then return to the D103. Turn off left for a precipitous ascent into **Hauteroche**, then a sharp descent and another climb – passing the remains of a Gallo-Roman villa – to the village of **Gissey-sous-Flavigny**, on the D10 beside the River Oze, where you turn right. Stay on this road as far as D103, where you turn left for the twisting 9km drive to the **Sources de la Seine (source of the Seine)**.

The road that passes the source continues as far as the N71 main road. Turn left here, skirting old **Baigneux-les-Juifs**, with its *lavoirs*, and continue back to Châtillon-sur-Seine.

Also worth exploring: There is much to see in the southern Auxois, especially around **Pouilly-en-Auxois**, 34km south from Semur-en-Auxois on the D970 near the interchange of the A6 autoroute and the A38 Dijon spur. A high, rolling landscape of green valleys, wide open fields, reservoirs and small copses, southern Auxois has many medieval châteaux and manor houses. One of the most striking is the dreamlike **Commarin**, an opulent little palace rising straight from the water of its wide mirror-like moat, while the old village of **Châteauneuf-en-Auxois** is dominated by its large 12th-century fortress.

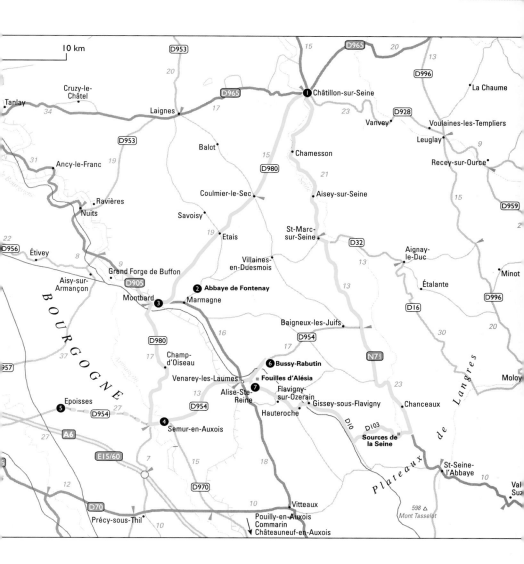

10 km

D953

D965 15

D965 20

13

D996

Cruzy-le-Châtel

La Chaume

Tanlay

34

Laignes

17

D965

❶ Châtillon-sur-Seine

23

D928

Vanvey

Voulaines-les-Templiers

Leuglay

9

D953

Balot

15

Chamesson

Recey-sur-Ource

Ancy-le-Franc

19

31

D980

21

15

D959

Ravières

Coulmier-le-Sec

Aisey-sur-Seine

2

Nuits

Savoisy

St-Marc-sur-Seine

22

19

Etais

D32

Aignay-le-Duc

D956

Étivey

8

Villaines-en-Duesmois

13

Minot

9

Grand Forge de Buffon

13

Étalante

Aisy-sur-Armançon

D905

Montbard ❸

❷ Abbaye de Fontenay

Marmagne

D16

D996

B O U R G O G N E

Baigneux-les-Juifs

D980

16

D954

957

37

17

Champ-d'Oiseau

17

D954

N71

30

20

P l a t e a u   d e   L a n g r e s

❻ Bussy-Rabutin

Moloy

Venarey-les-Laumes

❼ Fouilles d'Alésia

13

Alise-Ste-Reine

Flavigny-sur-Ozerain

23

Epoisses

D954

Gissey-sous-Flavigny

Chanceaux

❺

27

Hauteroche

❹ Semur-en-Auxois

D10

D103

A6

27

Sources de la Seine

E15/60

7

St-Seine-l'Abbaye

10

12

15

18

Val-Suz

D970

D70

10

Vitteaux

598 △
Mont Tasselot

Précy-sous-Thil

10

Pouilly-en-Auxois
Commarin
Châteauneuf-en-Auxois

The Cure and Cousin valleys

Ratings

Medieval architecture	●●●●●
Roman remains	●●●●●
Scenery	●●●●●
Activities	●●●●○
History	●●●●○
Restaurants	●●●●○
Winetasting	●●●○○
Children	●●○○○

All the richness of Burgundy old and new can be found on this route: busy, enticing towns, monumental medieval Christian architecture, unspoiled wilderness and sumptuously fertile farm country. This is *Bourgogne profonde*, 'deep rural Burgundy', where two pretty, rustic little valleys cut through northern and central Burgundy. The Cure and Cousin rivers, like the Yonne into which their waters flow, spring up in the Morvan uplands. The Cure runs briskly past the landmark abbey church at Vézelay and down to meet the fields, vineyards and orchards of the Yonne Valley below Auxerre. The Cousin, skirting the eastern Morvan, is an even prettier gem. Its deep valley skirts the town walls of Avallon. From there it carves a route through the limestone terrain to join the Cure just south of Vézelay.

ARCY-SUR-CURE✦

Ⓗ Manoir de Chastenay €€ *Val Ste-Marie; open for guided tour Mon–Sat in morning and afternoon, closed in winter.*

Grottes d'Arcy (Arcy Caves) €€ *Off the N6, south of Arcy; tel: 03 86 81 90 63 in season, 03 86 40 92 24 out of season, fax: 03 86 81 91 07; guided tours Mar–Nov only, 0930–1200, 1400–1800.*

A hump-backed bridge straddles the River Cure as it pours through this village with a 14th-century château. Just outside the village, at Val Ste-Marie, stands a one-time château of the Knights Templar, now called **Manoir de Chastenay**✦. Beyond Val Ste-Marie the **Grottes d'Arcy (Arcy Caves)**✦✦ dig deep into the River Cure's limestone escarpment. Inside them, visitors follow a 900m-path to see two underground lakes and ten caverns, including an area with traces of the people who sheltered here at the beginning of the Stone Age.

Accommodation and food in Arcy

Hôtel-Restaurant Les Grottes € *On the N6; tel: 03 86 81 91 47, fax: 03 86 81 96 22.* Simple, adequate one-star *logis* and a decent restaurant serving a hearty low-priced menu.

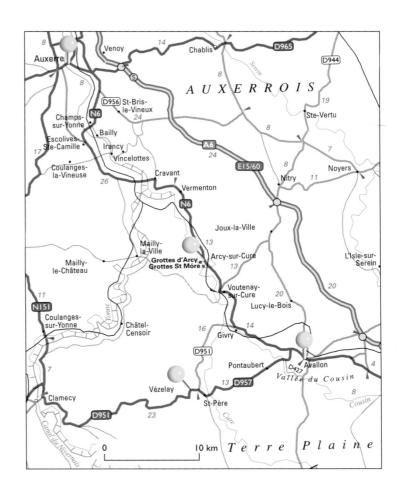

AUXERRE***

Auxerre Tourist Office 1–2 quai de la République; tel: 03 86 52 06 19, fax: 03 86 51 23 27, www.webhdo.com/bourgogne /89/auxerre/tourisme, and www.auxerre.com/; open Mon–Sat 0900–1230, 1400–1830, Sun 1000–1300, in summer Mon–Sat 0900–1300, 1400–1900, Sun and hols 0930–1300, 1500–1830.

Though halfway between Paris and Dijon, Auxerre (pronounced 'Ossaire') turns its face resolutely towards the Burgundian capital. This is a thoroughly Burgundian town, beside a thoroughly Burgundian river that vanishes into the Seine as soon as it leaves the duchy. The footbridge over the Yonne gives a lovely view of the town and the river.

The old quarter, defended by high terrace walls, is wonderfully picturesque, with narrow, winding, cobbled lanes climbing between uneven, tall, timbered houses with steep tiled roofs. At the foot of the hill are the *quais* beside the Yonne. This part of the old quarter, especially attractive along its steep lanes centred on r. Cochois, is

Two exits leave the A6 *autoroute* for Auxerre. The N6 bypasses the town. There are extensive commercial suburbs. A busy ring road within the town encircles the central districts. Much of the town lies on the right bank of the Yonne, but for the old centre you must cross to the left bank.

It's difficult to park in Auxerre, especially in the old quarter, where there are pay-and-display charges and time limits. Place St-Étienne and place des Cordeliers, by the cathedral, have parking places. There are long narrow car parks beside the main roads that run round the perimeter of the quarter, with over 2000 free parking places. Quai de la Marine has over 300 places.

Ancien Abbaye St-Germain €€ *Tel: 03 86 51 09 74; open daily, except Tue, June–Sept 1000–1200, 1400–1800, Oct–May 1000–1830.*

Cathédrale St-Étienne € *Tel: 03 86 52 23 29; open June–Sept 0900–1800, Oct–May 0900–1200, 1400–1800.*

Festivals: *Fête de la St-Vincent* – Jan; *Spring Fair* – May; *Jazz Festival* – June; *Piano Festival* – Sept; *Foire de la St-Martin* – Nov; *Auxerrois Wine Festival* – Nov.

Above
Stained-glass window, Cathédrale, Auxerre

called 'Quartier de la Marine'. Beside the river here, the 49m-high 12th-century belfry of the **Ancien Abbaye St-Germain**✦✦, almost destroyed during the Religious Wars but now housing a museum of archaeology, is a beautiful landmark. Beneath the abbey-church, historic tombs lie in an atmospheric crypt, with Carolingian frescos that are nearly 1200 years old – the oldest in France.

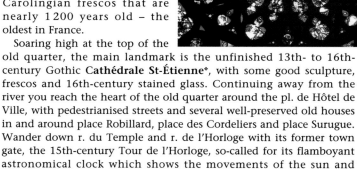

Soaring high at the top of the old quarter, the main landmark is the unfinished 13th- to 16th-century Gothic **Cathédrale St-Étienne**✦, with some good sculpture, frescos and 16th-century stained glass. Continuing away from the river you reach the heart of the old quarter around the pl. de Hôtel de Ville, with pedestrianised streets and several well-preserved old houses in and around place Robillard, place des Cordeliers and place Surugue. Wander down r. du Temple and r. de l'Horloge with its former town gate, the 15th-century Tour de l'Horloge, so-called for its flamboyant astronomical clock which shows the movements of the sun and moon, as well as the time of day.

Accommodation and food in Auxerre

There are many chain hotels (€–€€€) along the N6 and the ring road. In the town centre, Quai de la Marine, the riverside main road below the old quarter, has several restaurants and hotels with river views.

Parc des Maréchaux €€ *6 av. Foch; tel: 03 86 51 43 77, fax: 03 86 51 31 72.* Stylish accommodation in a grand Second-Empire mansion, at amazingly reasonable prices. Piano concerts in the grounds are a bonus.

Brasserie Le Quai €–€€ *Pl. St-Nicolas.* This large well-placed *brasserie* beside the river in the Quartier de la Marine is a cheerful and inexpensive place for a drink or a meal.

Restaurant Jean-Luc Barnabet €€€ *Quai de la République; tel: 03 86 51 68 88, fax: 03 86 52 96 85.* Decorated in clear, calm style, this great Auxerre restaurant beside the river is acclaimed for a light, fresh approach to Burgundy's rich and meaty classic gastronomy, often combining things in startling ways.

Restaurant Le Maxime €€ *3–5 Quai de la Marine; tel: 03 86 52 04 41.* An accomplished, satisfying local favourite offering well-prepared classic dishes.

AVALLON✤✤✤

ℹ️ **Avallon Tourist Office** *4–6 r. Bocquillot; tel: 03 86 34 14 19, fax: 03 86 34 28 29, e-mail: pays-avallonnais@ respublica.fr/, www.collines.ifrance and www.ville-avallon.fr/.*

🅿️ *Park opposite Église St-Lazare.*

⛪ **Église St-Lazare** € *Corner of r. St-Lazare and r. Bocquillot.*

Musée de l'Avallonnais (Avallon Regional Museum) €€ *R. du Collègiale; tel: 03 86 34 03 19; open May–Oct 1000–1200, 1400–1800 (closed Tue). Rest of the year by appointment.*

Musée de Costume €€ *R. Belgrand; tel: 03 86 34 19 95; one-hour guided tours Easter–Oct daily 1030–1230, 1330–1730.*

A small and ancient town, Avallon is superbly situated high in beautiful country. Avallon's 'new town', with several wide roads, tree-lined squares and 17th- to 18th-century buildings, is bustling, while the atmosphere of the older part of town, within the ramparts, is calm and peaceful. There are many unfaced stone houses and narrow cobbled streets – hardly anything dates from later than the 1700s.

Grande Rue A. Brind is the main street through the old town, though it has practically no traffic. It passes beneath a handsome 15th-century bell tower and continues to the fascinating 12th-century **Église St-Lazare**✤✤, which stands, most unusually, slightly below street level and has to be entered by going down steps. The exterior is in terrible condition, with mouldy columns and a badly damaged tympanum, but the portals are fine none the less, with much detailed carving. Looking into the gloom, the interior is hard to appreciate at first, but notice the interesting frescos and domes.

The **Musée de l'Avallonnais (Avallon Regional Museum)**✤ has varied collections evoking the art, culture and history of the area, including a lovely 2nd-century AD Roman mosaic. The **Musée de Costume**✤ uses its extensive collection of period clothing to hold interesting exhibitions focusing on the dress of a particular era.

Pass through the ramparts between Tour Gaujard and the Bastion de la Petite Porte to a delightful esplanade of lime trees. From this high, fresh vantage point there are precipitous views across the plunging wooded valley of the Cousin. From here a walk round the outside of the ramparts begins, going from one fortified tower to another.

Accommodation and food in Avallon

Avallon and its neighbourhood are well served with good places to stay and eat, though bargain prices are few within the town walls or along the Cousin Valley. On the busy N6 either side of town, low-budget chain hotels offer plenty of basic, cheaper accommodation.

Les Capucins €€ *6 av. P. Doumer, in town; tel: 03 86 34 06 52, fax: 03 8634 58 47.* A more modest place, though solidly reliable and satisfying, is this small two-star *logis* with a good restaurant.

Hostellerie de la Poste €€ *13 pl. Vauban, in town; tel: 03 86 34 36 99, fax: 03 86 31 66 31.* This early 18th-century coaching inn in the main square is rather grand, with carefully tended gardens and much character. It has been attractively restored and upgraded, and is remarkably good value. The restaurant specialises in rich, substantial classic cooking.

Moulin des Ruats €€ *Cousin Valley, near town; tel: 03 86 34 97 00, fax: 03 86 31 65 47.* One of the most enticing of the peaceful, charming old small hotels along the River Cousin, indeed verging on the idyllic, with its restaurant and riverside gardens.

Moulin des Templiers €€ *Cousin Valley, near Pontaubert; tel: 03 86 34 10 80.* A delightful little watermill beside the Cousin, now a blissfully romantic and homely place to stay.

VÉZELAY✦✦✦

ℹ Vézelay Tourist Office *R. St-Pierre; tel: 03 86 33 23 69, fax: 03 86 33 34 00, www.collines.ifrance.com, www.multimania.com/ vezelay/, www.morvan.com/ vezelay/vezelay and www.cef.fr/sens-auxerre/vezelay/; open daily 1000–1300, 1400–1800 (closed Thur out of season).*

Picturesque, ancient, its steep lanes of stone cottages perfectly restored, with lovely ramparts and medieval gates, it's hard to believe that this north Morvan hilltop village overlooking the River Cure was completely abandoned and crumbling just 100 years ago. Since then it has been transformed into a chic, up-market little haven of tourism, boasting top-quality restaurants, expensive hotels, art galleries and the usual craft shops. But the reason for it all, the awesome **Basilique Ste-Madeleine (Basilica of Mary Magdalene)**✦✦✦, has remained unscathed by the commercialism.

Considered one of the greatest masterpieces of Romanesque architecture, the basilica has been listed by Unesco as a World Heritage Site. From outside, the basilica – originally the abbey-church of the Vézelay abbey founded here in the 9th century – appears deceptively plain. However, the interior is stunning: immense, light, overwhelming. From a vast vestibule, huge double doors lead into the nave, the scale and proportions of which make the people inside look tiny. Apart from the stonework itself there is almost no decoration, no distraction. Around the choir, dim traces of old frescos on some

Right
Interior of Basilique
Ste-Madeleine

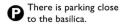

P There is parking close to the basilica.

Basilique Ste-Madeleine (Basilica of Mary Magdalene) €
For information: Fraternité Monastique de Jérusalem, Service des Visites, Vézelay; tel: 03 86 33 26 73, fax: 03 86 33 36 93. If you can, try to visit Vézelay sometime outside the crowded months of July and August and, if possible, come soon after breakfast to be here before the streams of tour buses start to arrive.

columns and parts of the ceiling show that it was not always so bare. Simple wooden crosses fixed to the walls were put there after the Second World War in 1946. A side chapel, slightly less plain, is used for ordinary services.

In the dark crypt a little shrine contains relics once thought to be the bones of Mary Magdalene, brought here from St-Maximin in Provence. After centuries of inspiring vast pilgrimages and intense devotion, it was realised that these are not the Magdalene's bones at all – whose they are has never been established, yet, oddly, they are still the object of reverence. After the pilgrimage era, Vézelay went into a rapid decline, and subsequently was badly damaged by Protestants and then by French Revolutionaries. By the time Viollet-le-Duc came here and decided to have it restored, the abbey itself had completely disappeared and its church was almost in ruins. Using old texts and plans, Viollet-le-Duc rebuilt the church between 1840 and 1861. Whether it did originally look like this is hotly debated; what is undeniable is that the abbey-church today is an exceptionally beautiful building.

Accommodation and food in Vézelay

Le Compostelle €€ *Pl. du Champ-de-Foire; tel: 03 86 33 34 34.* Welcoming and comfortable village hotel with modern, well-equipped rooms. It's at the foot of Vézelay, with rooms with views over either the garden or the countryside. No restaurant.

Hôtel-Restaurant l'Espérance €€€ See St-Père (*see page 94*).

Hôtel-Restaurant de la Poste et du Lion d'Or €€ *Pl. du Champ-de-Foire; tel: 03 86 33 21 23, fax: 03 86 32 30 92; restaurant closed Tue and Thur midday, and Mon.* This attractive and comfortable former coaching inn has views of the basilica on one side. Its excellent restaurant offers regional specialities such as snails, roast pigeon or *oeufs en meurette*, and the cheapest menu is a bargain.

Right
River Cousin, Avallon

Whose bones?

Medieval Christianity depended on the worship of cult objects, vital to encourage the pilgrimages that built up patronage, prestige and prosperity for religious centres. The Second and Third Crusades effectively started from Vézelay (in 1146 and 1190) because of the abbey's collection of human bones, which it claimed were those of Mary Magdalene, supposedly brought here in the 9th century, for safekeeping, from St-Maximin-la-Sainte-Baume in Provence. Because of the great pilgrimages to see and worship the Vézelay bones, the tyrannical and extortionate abbots, much hated by the local people who periodically rose up against them, became enormously rich. It all came to an abrupt end in 1280 when it was discovered that the 'real' relics of Mary Magdalene were still in the church at St-Maximin (although even those have no historical basis).

Suggested tour

Total distance: About 70km, plus a 10km detour.

Time: Allow 1 day for the drive and the short walk at the Grottes d'Arcy.

Links: At Auxerre, this route connects with the Chablis route (*see page 66*). At Avallon and Vézelay, it connects with Morvan (*see page 94*).

Route: Leave **AUXERRE** ❶ on the N6, turning off left on to country road D956, to climb through an open landscape of vine-covered hills, dotted with pretty orchards. Soon you come to the pleasing 11th-century fortified village of **St-Bris-le-Vineux**, an aptly named and extraordinarily handsome flower-decked winegrowers' community. Almost all the houses are of white stone, while a few older cottages are half-timbered. Inside the 13th-century Gothic church there's a striking 500-year-old fresco. Try the wines of St-Bris at the *cave co-opérative*. Continue to **Irancy**, similar but smaller, and arguably prettier, nestling sweetly among its vine slopes, producing the best red wines in this white wine region. Several houses have *Viticulteur* signs, where it's possible to taste and buy from the grower. Follow the road round and descend to **Vincelottes**, another lovely wine village, with a perfect spot to pull over beside the river.

Detour: Double back along the Yonne's right bank for about 3km to the **Caves de Bailly** (wine cellars of Bailly, *tel: 03 86 53 77 77*), a fascinating arrangement of underground caverns that were once important limestone quarries, mined by hand for over 800 years. The 4-hectare site was then taken over by St-Bris winemakers as a cellar, and now the tunnels are lined with some 5 million bottles of Crémant de Bourgogne wine. Continue beside the Yonne to the N6, where you turn left to cross the river and enter the village of **Escolives-Ste-Camille**. Here is a remarkable archaeological and historical site (*tel: 03 86 53 34 79; open Apr–Oct*) covering the Gallo-Roman and Merovingian periods, with baths, a 2nd-century AD mural and everyday items such as a pair of Roman shoes.

Carry on to little **Cravant** on the N6. Once fortified and standing at the confluence of the Rivers Yonne and Cure, it's another pretty village with a fine abbey-church. The N6 hugs the boisterous River Cure, through more vineyards and orchards, to **Vermenton**. Notice the fine 12th-century tower on the village church here. Stay with the Cure river to enter **ARCY-SUR-CURE** ❷. Carry on via Val-Ste-Marie, rejoining the N6 close to the Grottes d'Arcy.

Getting out of the car: On reaching the Grottes d'Arcy, pause to visit these limestone caverns. Leaving the Great Cave after the visit, there's an enjoyable and impressive riverside walk at the foot of the weather-carved cliffs, passing several other caves and caverns.

Follow the Cure on the N6. Soon after Voutenay-sur-Cure, there's a fine view of distant Vézelay on its hill. Stay on the N6 to **Givry**, at the confluence of the Cure and Cousin rivers. Turn south here along the D951 to follow the valley of the River Cure to **VÉZELAY** ❸. Now take the D957 towards Avallon, but only as far as **Pontaubert**. At Pontaubert, turn on to the little D427 to follow the **Vallée du Cousin**.

The Cousin is exquisite, twisting and changing, sometimes rushing, sometimes calm, always shaded by mossy trees. A narrow winding road (D427) with hardly any traffic runs between a wooded rocky escarpment on one side and the river on the other. Along the way are several old watermills, a few now turned into enviable private homes. The road skirts Avallon, whose ramparts rise above. At last, as the river turns away from the town, take a left on Route de Lormes through the new town into the centre of **AVALLON** ❹.

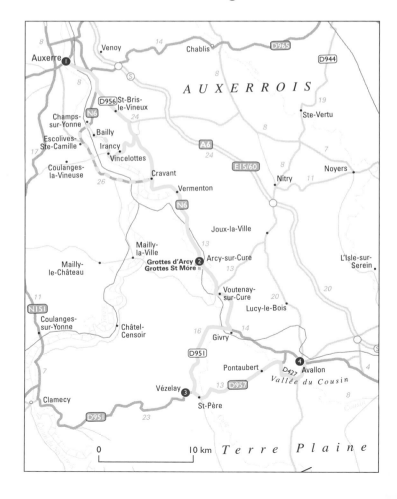

The Morvan

Ratings

Medieval architecture	●●●●●
Roman remains	●●●●●
Scenery	●●●●●
Activities	●●●●○
Folklore	●●●●○
History	●●●●○
Restaurants	●●●●○
Children	●●○○○

In France, any large area of open countryside that has never been much use for farming tends now to acquire a 'leisure' aspect. Certainly this is true of Le Morvan, the high granite massif, which lies at the heart of Burgundy. Much of the area, 1730sq km, was made a regional nature park in 1970 – one way in which the government has tried, by attracting tourism, to breathe life into the economy of such an unspoiled, sparsely populated rural region. Here are clear, clean rivers and tranquil lakes, small empty villages, rolling tracts of oak, beech and pine woods, heathland and high pasture with broad airy views. Though steep in places, in general the hills are not too severe (never above 1000m), and lovers of walking, riding, canoeing, or just gentle touring, are being encouraged to come and enjoy the wild landscape and fresh air.

Autun✦✦✦

ⓘ Autun Tourist Office *Main office: 2 av. Charles de Gaulle; tel: 03 85 86 80 38, fax: 03 85 86 80 49, e-mail: office.du. tourisme.autun@wanadoo.fr, www.autun.com/; open weekends in May, June–Sept daily 0900–1900, Oct– Apr Mon–Sat 0900–1200, 1400–1800.*

A thriving little country town with a pleasant atmosphere, and a focal point for visitors to the Morvan, Autun centres on its huge main square, the Champs de Mars. The town hall contains the important **Library of Ancient Manuscripts✦**. Highlight of the town is its superb Romanesque **Cathédrale St-Lazare✦✦✦**, topped with a wonderful Gothic stone spire. The cathedral, constructed to welcome the thousands of credulous pilgrims who flocked here to see the supposed tomb of Mary Magdalene's brother Lazarus, was consecrated by Pope Innocent II in 1132.

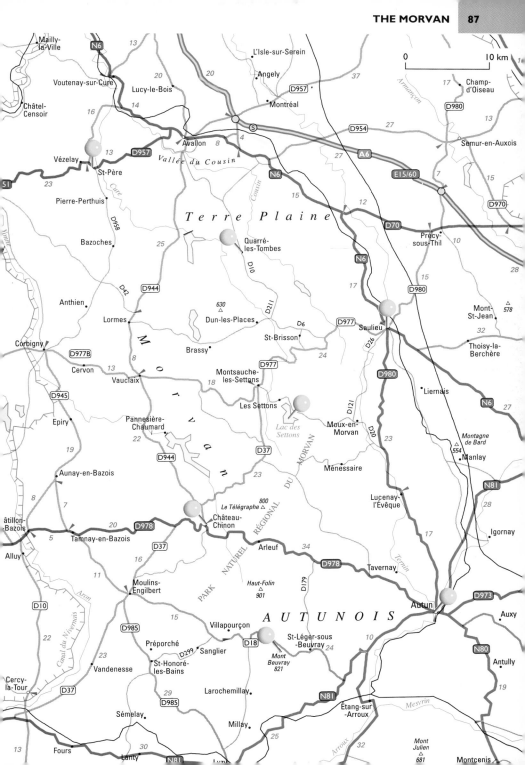

0   10 km

Mailly-la-Ville
N6
L'Isle-sur-Serein
Angely
13
Champ-d'Oiseau
17
Voutenay-sur-Cure
20
20
D957
Montréal
D980
Lucy-le-Bois
D954
27
13
14
Châtel-Censoir
16
S
27
Semur-en-Auxois
Avallon
8
4
A6
Vézelay
13
D957
Vallée du Cousin
E15/60
7
St-Père
N6
15
51
23
Cure
15
Pierre-Perthuis
Cousin
12
D70
10
D970
Bazoches
D958
Terre Plaine
N6
Précy-sous-Thil
Corbigny
D944
25
Quarré-les-Tombes
17
15
28
Anthien
D42
D10
D980
Mont-St-Jean
578
Lormes
630
Dun-les-Places
D211
D6
D977
Saulieu
32
D977B
M
Brassy
St-Brisson
D26
Thoisy-la-Berchère
Cervon
13
8
o
D977
24
Vauclaix
18
Montsauche-les-Settons
D980
Liernais
N6
27
D945
r
Les Settons
D121
Moux-en-Morvan
Epiry
Pannesière-Chaumard
22
v
Lac des Settons
23
Montagne de Bard
19
a
D37
Ménessaire
554
Manlay
Aunay-en-Bazois
n
23
DU
Lucenay-l'Évêque
N81
8
7
MORVAN
28
âtillon-Bazois
20
D978
Le Télégraphe
800
Château-Chinon
17
Igornay
Alluy
5
Tamnay-en-Bazois
D37
16
Arleuf
34
D978
Tavernay
Termin
11
RÉGIONAL
D73
Moulins-Engilbert
Haut-Folin
901
D179
Autun
Auxy
D10
Aron
PARK
AUTUNOIS
15
Villapourçon
N80
22
NATUREL
D985
Préporché
D18
St-Léger-sous-Beuvray
10
Antully
23
Sanglier
24
Canal du Nivernais
Vandenesse
D299
St-Honoré-les-Bains
Mont Beuvray
821
19
Cercy-la-Tour
29
Larochemillay
D37
D985
Sémelay
Millay
Mesvrin
Mont Julien
681
25
13
Fours
Lanty
N81
30
32
Montcenis
Étang-sur-Arroux
N81
Arroux

P In Champs de Mars and off blvd Latouche just east of it.

Library of Ancient Manuscripts €–€€
Town Hall; tel: 03 85 86 80 35; usually open weekday afternoons in summer or by appointment.

Cathédrale St-Lazare €
5 pl. du Terreau; open daily.

Musée Rolin €€ 3 r. des Bancs; tel: 03 85 52 09 76, fax: 03 85 52 47 41; open Apr–Sept daily 0930–1200, 1330–1800 (closed Tue), Oct–Mar Wed–Sat 1000–1200, 1400–1600 (Oct 1700), Sun 1420–1700 (closed Mon, Tue and hols).

Musée Lapidaire (Archaeological Museum) € R. Ile St-Nicolas; tel: 03 85 52 09 76; open at irregular hours or by appointment.

Ramparts walk € Runs between blvd des Résistants-Fusillées on the west side and Tour des Ursulines on the south side.

Théâtre Romaine (Roman theatre) € Av. du 2ème Dragon.

Events and festivals: Musique en Morvan oratorio festival – July; Il Était Une Fois Augustodunum: spectacular costume entertainment in the Roman theatre as locals re-enact ancient times – July/Aug. Tel: 03 85 86 80 38 for both events.

Above
Tympanum of the Cathédrale St-Lazare

Right
The roofs of Autun

Outside the cathedral, on the other side of an amazingly elaborate 16th-century Renaissance fountain, **Musée Rolin**✤✤ occupies a fine mansion. Named after Nicolas Rolin, the 15th-century local lawyer who became Chancellor to the Dukes of Burgundy (and had the spire put on the cathedral), this is the most important of Autun's museums. It has rich collections of Gallo-Roman art and artefacts, with fascinating everyday objects, as well as exceptional medieval and 15th-century sculpture and religious art.

Autun has a long and illustrious history. Before Roman colonisation in 15 BC it was the principal settlement of the powerful *Aedui* tribe of Gauls, who under Vercingetorix had defeated the Romans in battle at nearby *Bibracte* (see page 91). After their eventual defeat, the town was built partly to subdue and partly to honour them and bring them into Roman life. As *Augustodunum* – 'Rome's sister', Caesar called it – the Gallo-Roman town became a great centre of education, art, entertainment and commerce.

Just north of the main square there's a small, old medieval district, Quartier Marchaux, enclosed by 15th-century fortifications; it's centred around the Romanesque Chapelle St-Nicolas, now a **Musée Lapidaire (Archaeological Museum)**✤. The original medieval town walls follow the line of the Roman fortifications. There's a **ramparts walk**✤✤ for part of the way round. Beside the ramparts on the east side lie the scant remains of what was once Gaul's largest **Roman theatre**✤ – with seating for over 12,000 spectators, and thousands more standing!

Two of the four Roman city gates survive. Porte St-André is large, designed for a considerable passage of people, with two big arches for traffic and two smaller arches for pedestrians. Porte d'Arroux is smaller and more graceful, though not as well preserved. In Roman times, the main road ran through this gate to the *Via Agrippa*, the great north–south highway of eastern Gaul.

Accommodation and food in Autun

Hôtel des Ursulines and **Restaurant Le Capitole €€** 14 r. Rivault; tel: 03 85 86 58 58, fax: 03 85 86 23 07. In the tranquil and impressive surroundings of a former Ursuline convent, this is a delightful hotel and good restaurant.

Le Chalet Bleu €€ 3 r. Jeannin; tel: 03 85 86 27 30, fax: 03 85 52 74 56. This excellent town-centre restaurant has reasonable prices and imaginative cuisine.

CHÂTEAU-CHINON❖

ℹ Château-Chinon Tourist Office *Porte Nôtre-Dame; tel/fax: 03 86 85 06 58; open irregular hours, but open all year.*

🏛 Musée du Septennat €€ *6 r. du Château; tel: 03 86 85 19 23; open July–Aug daily 1000–1300, 1400–1900, May, June and Sept daily 1000–1300, 1400–1800, other months (except Jan and Feb) Sat, Sun, national hols and school hols 1000–1200, 1400–1800, closed Jan and Feb.*

Musée du Costume €€ *Hôtel du Buteau-Ravisy, 4 r. du Château; tel: 03 86 85 18 55; open same times as Musée du Septennat.*

For several years Château-Chinon made much of the fact that President Mitterrand (1916–96) came from here, had been the town's mayor and used to return for his annual vacation. **Musée du Septennat**❖❖ (*septennat* refers to the seven-year presidential term of office) pays homage to Mitterand, but surprisingly ends up not just being about him as it contains numerous gifts that he received from other heads of state, making an eclectic, priceless collection of artistic and ethnographic treasures from around the world. The **Musée du Costume**❖ focuses on French interiors, fashions and popular clothing of the 18th and 19th centuries.

Accommodation and food in Château-Chinon

Hôtel-Restaurant Le Vieux Morvan €€ *8 pl. Gudin; tel: 03 86 85 05 01, fax: 03 86 85 02 78.* A decent two-star *logis*, the restaurant has good cooking and a low-priced set menu.

Right
Lac des Settons

LAC DES SETTONS❖

ℹ Les Settons Tourist Office *Pl. de l'Ancienne Gare, Montsauche-les-Settons; tel/fax: 03 86 84 55 90.*

⇄ *The lake is reached on the D193 south of Montsauche-les-Settons.*

The result of damming the River Cure more than a century ago, the beautiful Lac des Settons with its wooded islands has become an established home to waterbirds and attracts watersports enthusiasts. The prettily placed waterside resort village of Les Settons, close to the dam, makes a good base for enjoying the area.

MONT BEUVRAY❖❖

❖ *www.perso.*
wanadoo.fr/bibracte/.

❖ Access is via a one-
way road, the D274,
which encircles the base of
the mountain.

❖ **Bibracte €€** Tel:
museum (see below);
1-hour guided tours (in
French) available only if the
weather is suitable, no tours
in winter, June–Sept daily at
1400, 1500, 1600, rest of
the year and weekends and
hols at 1500 or by
appointment.

Bibracte Museum €€ St-
Léger-sous-Beuvray; tel: 03
85 86 52 35, fax: 03 85 82
58 00, e-mail: bibracte
@wanadoo.fr; open daily
1000–1800, closed Tue
from mid-Sept to mid-June.

Mont Beuvray was the site of **Bibracte**❖❖, the most important *oppidum*
(walled settlement) of the *Aedui* tribe of Gauls. Under their fearsome
chief, Vercingetorix, it was a centre of the Gauls' resistance against
Roman occupation. The *Aedui* actually succeeded in defeating the
Romans in battle. Eventually beaten, Vercingetorix was taken to Rome
to be publicly tortured and eventually executed (*see page 69*). The
Romans then pacified the *Aedui* by creating the new city of
Augustodunum (now Autun) close to *Bibracte*. Little survives of the pre-
Roman period, but Beuvray is none the less a striking spot. The
summit, 821m high, allows a tremendous sight of the wild woodlands
and peaks of the southern Morvan. At the foot of the hill there is a
museum❖ devoted to the site.

Right
Festival dancing in the Morvan

QUARRÉ-LES-TOMBES✣

ⓘ **Quarré Tourist Office** *Mairie; tel: 03 86 32 23 38, fax: 03 86 32 23 43, www.morvan.com/villages/quarré; open July–Aug daily 1000–1200, 1500–1800, other months Sat only 1400–1700.*

The strange name of this quiet Le Morvan village above and between the Cure and Cousin valleys comes from the startlingly large number of curious sarcophagi found here near the church. All dating from the 7th to the 10th centuries, many were removed, and now 112 *éléments* (either the tops or the bottoms of the sarcophagi) are arranged around the exterior of the village church. The most likely explanation, researchers theorise, was simply that this happened to be the place where such tombstones were made for sale to other communities.

That doesn't ring true to some people, who point out that the stone for the sarcophagi comes from 20 to 40km away. Many believe that there may well have been some sort of necropolis here. The only objection to that, say the academics, is that all the sarcophagi were empty. Perhaps they were looted, comes the answer.

Accommodation and food in Quarré

Auberge de l'Atre €€ *Les Lavault; tel: 03 86 32 20 79, fax: 03 86 32 28 25.* About 5km from the village on the D10, this highly rated *restaurant avec chambres* is a quiet and peaceful top-of-the-range *logis*, with attractive gardens.

Hôtel-Restaurant Le Morvan € *6 r. des Ecoles; tel: 03 86 32 29 29, fax: 03 86 32 29 28.* A good, family-run country hotel and restaurant with modest prices.

Above
Sarcophagi in Quarré-les-Tombes

Right
Morvan landscape

SAULIEU✣

ⓘ **Saulieu Tourist Office** *24 r. d'Argentine; tel: 03 80 64 00 21, fax: 03 80 64 21 96, www.bienpublic.com/cociel/saulieu.*

ⓘ **St-Andoche Basilica €** *Centre of town; open daily.*

A popular, pleasing little market town, Saulieu has a long history as a halt for travellers, and in that tradition it still has a number of good restaurants and hotels. Worth a look is the **St-Andoche Basilica✣**, where pilgrims have stopped on their journeys since the 12th century. Next door, the **Musée Pompon✣** tries to capture the soul of Saulieu with two distinct themes – stonecarving (sculpture, sarcophagi and milestones) and gastronomy (*haute cuisine* and local specialities). The museum is named after local sculptor François Pompon, whose work *Le Taureau* stands in pl. Charles de Gaulle.

Accommodation and food in Saulieu

Musée Pompon €€
Beside the basilica; tel: 03 80 64 19 51; open Apr–Sept daily (except Tue) 1000–1230, 1400–1800 (Sun and hols 1700), Oct–Dec daily (except Tue) 1000–1230, 1400–1730 (Sun, hols and all Jan and Feb, closes at 1700).

La Poste €€ *1 r. Grillot; tel: 03 80 64 05 67, fax: 03 80 64 10 82.* In a handsome 17th-century building, this former coaching inn has become a classic provincial hotel: substantial, reliable, with good food, attractive, comfortable rooms and a pleasant atmosphere.

La Côte d'Or €€€ *2 r. d'Argentine; tel: 03 80 64 07 66, fax: 03 80 64 08 92, www.integra.fr/relaischateau/loiseau.* Most notable of the many Saulieu eating places is this chi-chi, ultra-pricey, highly rated 17th-century hotel and restaurant. The owner-chef, Bernard Loiseau, now reckoned one of the best in France, offers imaginative unconventional cooking according to a philosophy of utter simplicity.

St-Père❖❖

www.morvan.com/villages/st-pere.

Église Nôtre-Dame
In village; tel: 03 80 64 66 07; open daily 1000–1830.

Musée Archéologique Régional (Regional Archaeological Museum) €€ *Presbytery in village; tel: 03 86 33 37 31; open Apr–Oct 0930–1230, 1330–1830, rest of the year closed. Ticket also covers Fontaines Salées.*

Fontaines Salées €€ *2km from village; tel: museum (above); open same times as museum.*

For such a tiny place, St-Père, just outside Vézelay, boasts a surprising number of attractions, with picturesque old houses and one of the most lauded restaurants in France, L'Esperance. The extraordinary village church **Église Nôtre-Dame❖**, which took almost 300 years to build, is a mass of Gothic ornament, with a superb belfry considered a masterpiece of medieval stonecarving. In the presbytery, the **Musée Archéologique Régional❖** contains interesting items discovered in the Morvan area. Just outside the village, the **Fontaines Salées❖** are above a saltwater spring, worshipped by Gauls and Romans. The fountains were in continuous daily use from the Iron Age to the end of the Middle Ages until, in an example of bureaucratic madness, they were destroyed and filled in by order of the 17th-century Salt Tax Office for not paying any tax. They are now the focal point of an archaeological site, while water from the spring is once again in use.

Accommodation and food in St-Père

L'Esperance €€€ *In village; tel: 03 86 33 39 10, fax: 03 86 33 26 15.* For many years praise, stars and accolades have been heaped on this restaurant and its famous owner-chef Marc Meneau. The cooking is classic, correct, in grand style. There are rooms as well, but note that meals and the impeccable, tranquil accommodation are both very expensive.

Above
Roche Perchée at
Pierre-Perthuis

Suggested tour

Total distance: About 250km, plus a 55km detour.

Time: Allow 2 days for the driving. Sightseeing, walking, and other activities will be extra.

Links: At Avallon and Vézelay, this route connects with Cure and Cousin (*see page 84*).

Route: Leave Avallon (*see page 79*) on the D957, a high, hilly road with expansive views across the farmland and woods of the northern Morvan. The Basilique Ste-Madeleine, the great abbey-church standing high above the rest of **Vézelay** (*see page 80*), is clearly visible from several kilometres away. From Vézelay return 2km down the hill to

ST-PÈRE ❶. Turn right (D958) just before the bridge over the River Cure, into the old village. The road leaves St-Père and shortly passes tiny **Pierre-Perthuis**, beautifully situated on the rushing Cure. Turn off the road for a moment, or walk down, to see the old bridges and the river in its narrow gorge; on the opposite bank you'll see the 'pierced rock' which gives the village its name. Between high fields of pasture continue on the D958 through **Bazoches**. After 8km turn left (D42) to hillside **Lormes**. Take the D944 south towards CHÂTEAU-CHINON ❷, perhaps pausing on the way at the dam and lake of **Pannesière-Chaumard**, one of the Morvan's largest.

Detour: There's an attractive road (D37–D977) directly from here to Saulieu through the heart of the park, allowing an easy detour to beautiful **LAC DES SETTONS** ❸ and the hill-village **Montsauche-les-Settons**, the highest village in the Morvan.

Take the D978 west out of Château-Chinon, turning left (D37) to **Moulins-Engilbert** with its old houses and market. Two kilometres after the village take the D985 on the left to **St-Honoré-les-Bains**. A narrow, winding and picturesque route runs over and around the hills from this spa town to Mont Beuvray: first, from St-Honoré take the D299; at Sanglier turn left on to the D227, then turn right at the junction with the D18. The steep D3 then struggles to the 821m-summit of **MONT BEUVRAY** ❹, which allows a tremendous sight of the wild woodlands and peaks of the southern Morvan. In the nearby village of St-Léger-sous-Beuvray take the left turn (D179), another narrow, hilly and unfrequented road, which leads eventually through the twisting gorges of the little River Canche and on to the busier D978, where you turn right towards AUTUN ❺.

Leave Autun by passing through the Porte d'Arroux on the D980 and continue towards Saulieu. For a more scenic route part of the way, after 24km turn left on to the D149, following this country lane (which becomes the D20, D121 and D26) all the way into **SAULIEU** ❻.

Return towards Avallon not on the N6 but on the attractive smaller road, which starts out from Saulieu as the D977. After 10km take the D6 (right), which soon reaches **St-Brisson**, the Morvan Regional Park's main information and exhibition centre.

Getting out of the car: the Maison du Parc at St-Brisson used to be a walled Morvan farm. In a delightful, airy, unspoiled setting, it has herb gardens, a play area, an observation post beside a shallow lake and marked footpaths. Also in the grounds, there is a Musée de la Résistance – the Resistance was very important in the Morvan – housed in a small cottage in the grounds.

At a junction 10km further, take the D211, which becomes the D10, into **QUARRÉ-LES-TOMBES**. The D10 continues from here back into Avallon.

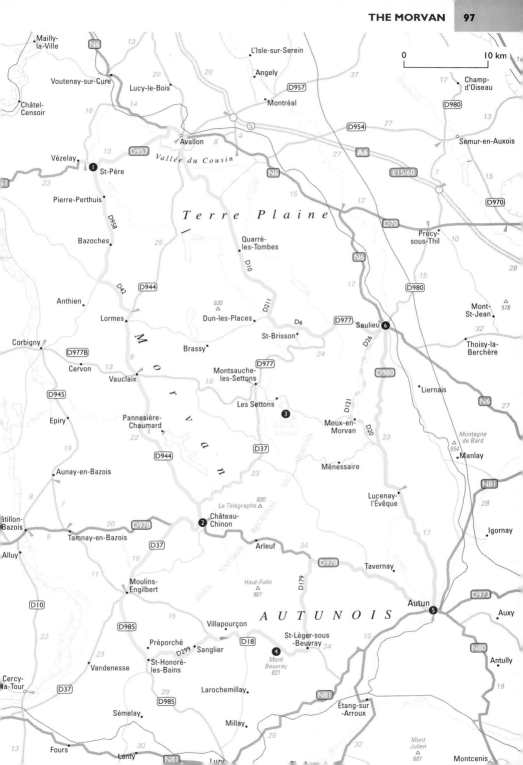

0   10 km

Mailly-la-Ville

N6

Voutenay-sur-Cure

Lucy-le-Bois

Châtel-Censoir

L'Isle-sur-Serein

Angely

Montréal

D957

Champ-d'Oiseau

D980

Semur-en-Auxois

D954

Avallon

Vézelay

St-Père

D957

Vallée du Cousin

N6

A6

E15/60

Pierre-Perthuis

D958

Terre Plaine

D70

Précy-sous-Thil

D970

Bazoches

Quarré-les-Tombes

D10

N6

D980

Anthien

D42

D944

Lormes

630

Dun-les-Places

D211

D6

St-Brisson

D977

Saulieu 6

Mont-St-Jean 578

Corbigny

D977B

Cervon

Vauclaix

Brassy

Montsauche-les-Settons

D977

D26

Thoisy-la-Berchère

D945

Epiry

Pannesière-Chaumard

Les Settons

3

D37

Moux-en-Morvan

D121

D980

Liernais

N6

Montagne de Bard 554

Manlay

Aunay-en-Bazois

Ménessaire

D20

Lucenay-l'Évêque

N81

Châtillon-Bazois

Tamnay-en-Bazois

D978

Le Télégraphe 800

D37

Château-Chinon 2

D37

Arleuf

D978

Tavernay

Igornay

Alluy

Moulins-Engilbert

Haut-Folin 901

D179

Autun 5

D973

Auxy

D10

AUTUNOIS

Villapourçon

St-Léger-sous-Beuvray

N80

Antully

D985

Préporché

D299

Sanglier

D18

Mont Beuvray 821 4

Cercy-la-Tour

Vandenesse

St-Honoré-les-Bains

D37

D985

Sémelay

Larochemillay

Étang-sur-Arroux

N81

Fours

Lanty

Millay

Mont Julien 681

Montcenis

Dijon

Ratings

Architecture	●●●●●
History	●●●●●
Restaurants	●●●●●
Museums	●●●●○
Shopping	●●●●○
Street life	●●●●○
Children	●●●○○
Entertainment	●●●○○

It's a pleasure to explore this dignified, civilised city, the ancient seat of the Dukes of Burgundy. Today – despite a rather sedate first impression – it's Burgundy's lively modern capital, a centre of *haute cuisine*, the only major city between Paris and Lyon and prefecture of Côte d'Or *département*. Head into the central old quarter to the Palais des Ducs, the imposing palace that the powerful Dukes of Burgundy called home. Sumptuously furnished in 17th-century style, it's a museum jam-packed with art treasures. The entrance faces place de la Libération, a magnificent semicircle of grand old honey-tinted stone houses and handsome Renaissance backstreets with museums, galleries and boutiques. Although a large, populous and industrial town, Dijon's central quarter has a welcoming and walkable feel, with great atmosphere and scores of fine old buildings, the focal point being place François Rude.

Getting there and getting around

ⓘ Dijon Tourist Office *Head office: Hôtel Chambellan, 34 r. des Forges; tel: 03 80 44 11 44, fax: 03 80 30 90 02, e-mail: infotourisme@ot-dijon.fr; open May–15 Oct, Mon–Sat 0930–1300, 1400–1800,16 Oct–Apr, Mon–Fri 1000–1300, 1400–1800, closed national hols. With information and hotel booking for Dijon and the whole of Burgundy.*

By rail
Dijon is especially accessible by train, with TGVs direct to Paris and Lyon and to Lille.

By road
Autoroutes approach Dijon from every direction. A series of boulevards make up a ring road around the city centre. The Palais des Ducs (Ducal Palace) is regarded as the city's central point. In the heart of the city, driving is difficult, with narrow streets, a complicated one-way system and a pedestrian zone.

There is plenty of car parking in the city centre, including at pl. de la Libération, off r. Condorcet, at pl. Grangier and adjacent to pl. Darcy.

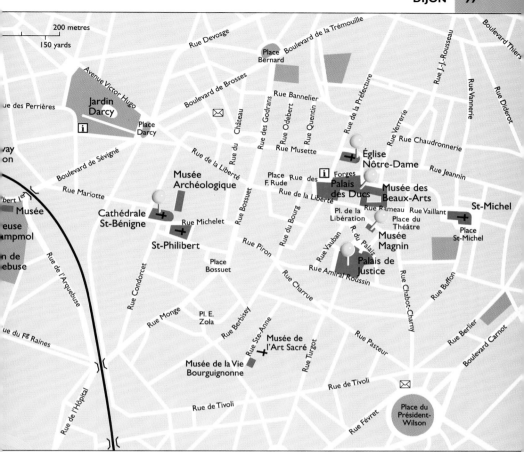

200 metres

150 yards

Rue Devosge

Avenue Victor Hugo

ue des Perrières

Jardin Darcy

Place Darcy

Boulevard de Brosses

Boulevard de la Trémouille

Place Bernard

Rue Bannelier

Rue des Godrans

Rue Odebert

Rue Quentin

Rue du Château

Rue Musette

Rue de la Préfecture

Boulevard Thiers

Rue J.-J.-Rousseau

Rue Vannerie

Rue Diderot

Rue Verrerie

Rue Chaudronnerie

Église Nôtre-Dame

Rue Jeannin

vay on

Boulevard de Sévigné

Rue Mariotte

Rue de la Liberté

Musée Archéologique

Place F. Rude

Rue des Forges

Palais des Ducs

Musée des Beaux-Arts

St-Michel

bert Ier

Musée

euse mpmol

n de ebuse

Rue de l'Arquebuse

Cathédrale St-Bénigne

St-Philibert

Rue Michelet

Rue Bossuet

Rue de la Liberté

Rue du Bourg

Pl. de la Libération

Rue Rameau

Rue Vaillant

Place du Théâtre

St-Michel

Place St-Michel

Musée Magnin

Place Bossuet

Rue Piron

Rue Vauban

R. du Palais

Palais de Justice

Rue Condorcet

Pl. E. Zola

Rue Monge

Rue Berbisey

Rue Charrue

Rue Amiral Roussin

Rue Chabot-Charny

Rue Buffon

Rue Berlier

Musée de l'Art Sacré

Rue Ste-Anne

Rue Turgot

Rue Pasteur

Boulevard Carnot

Musée de la Vie Bourguignonne

Rue de Tivoli

Rue de l'Hôpital

Rue de Tivoli

Rue Févret

Place du Président-Wilson

ue du Fg Raines

 Main office (for personal callers only) *Pavillon du Tourisme, pl. Darcy; open all year round, May–15 Oct, daily 0900–2000, 16 Oct–Apr, daily 0900–1300, 1400–1900. With information, currency exchange, tickets for shows and hotel booking for Dijon, Burgundy and the whole of France.*

Right
Église Nôtre-Dame

Sights

🛈 **Cathédrale St-Bénigne** € *Pl. St-Bénigne; tel: tourist office on 03 80 44 11 44; open daily (crypt is open Easter–Oct only, 0900–1900). There is a pilgrimage to the cathedral every 20 Nov.*

Musée Archéologique (Archaeological Museum) € *5 r. du Docteur Maret; tel: 03 80 30 88 54, fax: 03 80 30 71 57; open daily (except Tue) June–Sept 1000–2000, Oct–May 0900–1200, 1400–1800.*

Chartreuse de Champmol € *1 blvd Chanoine Kir; tel: 03 80 42 48 48; open daily 0800–2000. Follow signs to Puits de Moïse.*

Église Nôtre-Dame € *R. de la Chouette; open daily.*

🅦 *www.ot-dijon.fr/ (useful main tourist office site); www.ville-dijon.fr/ (the city in detail); www.dijon-by-night.com (mix of items including names and addresses of a few late-night bars and discos).*

Cathédrale St-Bénigne and Musée Archéologique**

A former abbey-church of the 11th, 13th and 14th centuries, the **Cathedral of St-Bénigne**** is an excellent example of the Burgundian Gothic style, though with survivals of its Romanesque predecessor. The third great church to stand on this site, it was much damaged during the French Revolution. Its external buttresses, towers and coloured tiles are in contrast to the plain, austere interior. St-Bénigne, said to have converted Burgundy to Christianity, is buried in the crypt.

Part of the former church cloisters and the abbey's vaulted dormitory have become the city's **Archaeological Museum***, displaying a mix of medieval and Gallo-Roman religious and ancient artworks.

Chartreuse de Champmol*

Today it's Dijon's psychiatric hospital, but once it was a grand monastery, fit for a king to pray in or be buried in. Little more than a fine 15th-century doorway survives. A little away from the centre of things, it's where the Dukes of Burgundy lie buried (though the tombs have been moved to the Palais des Ducs/Musée des Beaux-Arts). In the courtyard at the back stands the Puits de Moïse (Well of Moses), so-called for the striking sculptures of Biblical characters, including Moses, around this elaborate hexagonal stonework. Despite the name, it's not a well – it was the base of a large 14th-century calvary, now vanished.

Église Nôtre-Dame**

The most famous family in Dijon resides in one of the two belltowers of this distinctive 13th-century Dijon church. The father is called Jacquemart: he is the mechanical man who sounds the hours by striking a bell with his hammer, and has been doing so (in various incarnations) since the year 1382. In fact, Jacquemart is from Courtrai, in Flanders, and was kidnapped by Philip the Bold, Duke of Burgundy, after he had put down a revolt by his Flemish subjects. A century later Jacquemart found a female partner to live with him and strike bells together. After another 100 years had passed, by some mechanical means the two produced their son Jacquelinet, who strikes the half-hours. But it took almost 170 years more to have their second child, Jacquelinette, the daughter who strikes the quarter-hours and first appeared in 1881.

The façade of the church has exquisite arcaded galleries, each with a row of very odd gargoyles perched along the edge. The interior contains much fine stonework and craftsmanship, and in here resides another important Dijon figure – Nôtre-Dame de Bon Espoir (Our Lady of Good Hope). It's claimed she often saved the town from

Right
Cathédrale St-Bénigne

Musée Magnin € *4 r. des Bons-Enfants; tel: 03 80 67 11 10; open daily (except Sat) 1000–1200, 1400–1800.*

Palais de Justice € *R. du Palais; no tel; open 0900–1200, 1400–1700.*

Palais des Ducs, Les États de Bourgogne et Musée des Beaux-Arts €€ *Pl. de la Ste-Chapelle; tel: 03 80 74 53 59; open daily (except Tue) 1000–1800, certain sections, including the kitchens, close 1145–1345.*

invaders, besiegers and occupiers, starting with the Swiss on 11 Sept 1513 and continuing until the liberation of Dijon from Nazi occupation on 11 Sept 1944.

Musée Magnin*

Step through the door of this grand 17th-century mansion into another age, another lifestyle. Former home of magistrate Maurice Magnin and his art-loving wife, it still contains their extensive private collection (over 1500 items) of distinguished middle-rank painters, including many 16th-century Flemish and 19th-century French works. The house also contains much fine original 18th- and 19th-century furniture.

Palais de Justice (Law Courts)*

The Palais de Justice was the central point of the Romans' fortified colony *Divio*, the original Dijon. There are several impressive 16th- and 17th-century mansions in the streets around the Palais de Justice, once an aristocratic district. The Law Courts themselves were once Burgundy's parliament building and have kept a Renaissance façade. Inside, the lobby, called the Salle de Pas-Perdus – once a grand meeting place for wealthy people – has an exquisite vaulted panelled ceiling.

Palais des Ducs, Les États de Bourgogne et Musée des Beaux-Arts (Palace of the Dukes, The Estates of Burgundy and Fine Arts Museum)***

If memories of the Dukes of Burgundy are still alive in Dijon, then their ghosts are actually walking the corridors and courtyards of this vast edifice in pale stone. Technically, the Palais des Ducs is now Dijon's town hall. This most notable of all Dijon's grand historic buildings is where the modern administration is still located, together with the city's outstanding Fine Arts Museum.

The front of the building is set back around a majestic Cour d'Honneur. Inner courtyards lie within the blocks to both sides – west is the Cour de Flore, east the Cour de Bar. Rising from the palace alongside the Cour de Bar, the sturdy square Tour de Bar is emblematic of the city and the duchy. The name recalls the most famous prisoner confined here by Duke Philippe le Bon – 'Good King René' of Sicily, Anjou, Provence, Bar and Lorraine.

The palace fell into disrepair after the death of Charles the Bold in 1477, when the French took over Burgundy. Two hundred years later, it was restored and enlarged by the Estates of Burgundy from 1682 onwards, a time when French control over the duchy was being consolidated. Much has been added since then: the Palais des Beaux-Arts, on the east side, is only 150 years old.

Most of the palace is occupied by the extensive Musée des Beaux-Arts (Museum of Fine Art), one of the leading provincial collections.

Right
Roofs of Dijon

Burgundy vs France

Burgundy's relationship with the kingdom of France was stormy right up to the outbreak of the French Revolution in 1789. Large and prosperous, the territory always felt itself to be free and independent. The duchy – evolving out of the land first occupied by the *Burgundii* tribe – began to take shape in the 9th century. In 1384, through marriage, inheritance and alliances, Philippe the Bold took control of the whole of Burgundy and turned the duchy into a separate kingdom within France, which (although it was loyal to France) the kings of France were unable to command. In 1477, on the death of Duke Charles the Bold, the French invaded and conquered Burgundy. However, when Philippe II of France died, his daughter Isabelle inherited Burgundy. She married the Archduke of Austria, which once more took the duchy out of French control. In 1678, the French again had to invade and conquer Burgundy. One century later, the French Revolution at last turned France into a single nation.

Here are numerous religious pictures and sculptures, paintings representing most major European schools (including Impressionist, Post-Impressionist and Modern art), ceramics, glasswork and numerous other works. In addition to its art collection, the place is fascinating for its glimpses into the workings of the palace, with the relics of the dukes and their life. It deserves a visit just to see the magnificent rooms and lavish décor.

On the west side of the palace, the superb Escalier Gabriel (Gabriel Staircase) ascends from the Cour de Flore to the Salle des États, grandiose meeting hall of the Estates of Burgundy, the name given to the Burgundian parliament, loyal to the French Crown.

Right
Place F. Rude

Dinner in Dijon

Dijon is the gastronomic capital of a gastronomic region and created many of the best-known traditional French dishes. The city's name is synonymous with the best of French mustard – *moutarde de dijon* – as well as the best *crème de cassis* (blackcurrant liqueur). Other local products of Dijon and its area include *pains d'épices* (gingery spice breads), *jambon persillé* and *escargots*. French food guides heap their awards on the town's restaurants, where the great Burgundian classics – such as *coq au vin* (chicken, onions, mushrooms, wine), *boeuf bourguignon* (Charolais beef in onions, mushrooms and wine) and *pauchouse* (fish and wine stew) – are properly made and correctly served. In addition to the wines of nearby Chablis and the Côte d'Or, the classic French aperitif, *kir*, comes from here.

Shopping

The main shopping streets are r. de la Liberté and its turnings, r. Bossuet, down to place Bossuet, all especially good for high-quality food and drinks as well as fashions and accessories. La Boutique Maille (*tel: 03 80 30 41 02*), at 32 r. de la Liberté, has been a specialist mustard shop since 1777 and is the place to choose a jar – the jars themselves can be works of art – from the immense range of Dijon mustards. In place Bossuet is the *pain d'épices* specialist Mulot et Petitjean, founded in 1796. Vedrenne, in r. Bossuet, specialises in liqueurs.

Accommodation and food in Dijon

La Cloche €€–€€€ *14 pl. Darcy; tel: 03 80 30 12 32, fax: 03 80 30 04 15*. This renowned, traditional hotel-restaurant overlooking the gardens of place Darcy has been referred to as a 'national monument'. Lately it's been criticised for making the menus too 'touristic', but it's still a good place to enjoy a classic meal, well prepared and at a moderate price, in the centre of the city.

Hôtel du Nord €€ *Pl. Darcy; tel: 03 80 30 58 58, fax: 03 80 30 61 26*. Charming, simple old hotel in the city centre, welcoming and inexpensive. Wine bar in the vaulted basement.

Hôtel Wilson €€ *Pl. Wilson, tel: 03 80 66 82 50, fax: 03 80 36 41 54*. Among the best, most comfortable and reasonably priced places in town to stay and to eat, a modernised establishment in a former 17th-century coaching inn.

Bistrot des Halles € *10 r. Bannelier; tel: 03 80 49 94 15, fax: 03 80 38 16 16*. For a good meal at a modest price, head for this excellent wine bar and restaurant.

Pré aux Clercs €€ *13 pl. de la Libération; tel: 03 80 38 05 05, fax: 03 80 38 16 16; closed Mon, and Sun pm*. In handsome historic premises in the elegant place opposite the Palais des Ducs, this is where acclaimed chef Jean-Pierre Billoux creates his imaginative dishes based on classic local specialities.

Restaurant Thibert €€€ *Pl. Wilson; tel: 03 80 36 41 54*. The top-flight Thibert goes in for the most rarefied and elegant of gastronomic dining.

Simpatico € *30 r. Berbisey; tel: 03 80 30 53 33; closed Mon*. Among the eateries of this popular area, this convivial Italian is one of the very best, with authentic dishes at modest prices.

Suggested walk

Total distance: About 2km, or 3km including the detour.

Time: The main walk will take all day, allowing time to visit museums, admire façades, and step down side turns. Allow at least an extra hour to include the detour to the botanic gardens.

Route: Start from **Jardin Darcy**, the town-centre gardens. At the entrance stands the unmissable polar bear statue by animal sculptor François Pompon (1855–1933). Pass through 18th-century archway **Porte Guillaume** to take pedestrianised shopping street **r. de la Liberté**. Reaching the junction with r. Bossuet, you come upon the busy little focal point known as the Coin du Miroir (Mirror Corner). Look out for the 15th-century houses **Maison aux Trois Visages** (the Three-Sided House) and, opposite, **Hôtel Millière**, an old shop with its decorated roof and Renaissance turret.

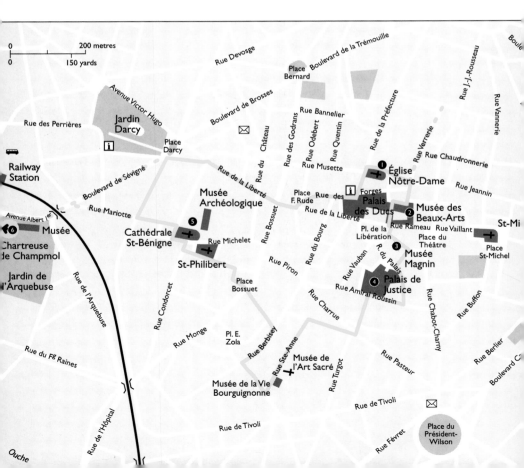

Now walk into **place F. Rude**, the lively and agreeable centre point of the pedestrianised zone. In the middle of the square is the naked *Bareuzai* (winemaker) trampling grapes. All around are picturesque half-timbered houses and café tables where visitors and locals gather. Turn up **r. des Forges**, where there are several exceptional medieval and Renaissance houses. Most striking of all, **Hôtel Chambellan** has a remarkable inner courtyard open to the public, with galleries and an open spiral staircase in Flamboyant Gothic style. On the left rises **ÉGLISE NÔTRE-DAME ❶**. Pass to the north side of the church to find **r. de la Chouette**, named (it means 'Owl Street') after a little owl set into a niche in a wall, which passers-by stroke for good luck.

The road leads into place des Ducs. But first take a step back to see r. Verrerie and r. Chaudronnerie – this area is known for its many antique shops. The remarkable early 17th-century **Maison des Cariatides**, at 28 r. Chaudronnerie, has a dozen caryatids in front. Return to place des Ducs for the **PALAIS DES DUCS, LES ETATS DE BOURGOGNE AND MUSÉE DES BEAUX-ARTS ❷**.

On the south side of the Palais des Ducs, the elegant 17th-century **place de la Libération** – once place Royale – makes an attractive semi-circle of pale Renaissance mansions. Step a few paces up r. des Bons-Enfants to visit **MUSÉE MAGNIN ❸**. Walk south on r. du Palais to the **PALAIS DE JUSTICE ❹**.

Continue south via r. Hernoux, place des Cordeliers and r. Dumay to reach r. Ste-Anne. In this street you find **Ste-Anne Chapel**, housing the **Musée d'Art Sacré (Museum of Sacred Art)**. Here too is the **Musée de la Vie Bourguignonne (Museum of Burgundian Life)**. Turn right into r. du Chaignot, right again into r. Berbisey and left into r. Brulard, to pass **Église St-Jean**, then **Église St-Philibert**, to reach **CATHÉDRALE ST-BÉNIGNE AND MUSÉE ARCHÉOLOGIQUE ❺**. Walk up r. Maret to return to place Darcy or take the detour.

Detour: Take r. Mariotte, pass beneath the railway bridge and cross r. de l'Arquebuse to reach the **Jardin de l'Arquebuse**. If you have the energy – though this trip might be better by car or bus (no 12, direction Fontaine d'Ouche, bus stop Hôpital des Chartreux) – continue east beyond the gardens to see the **CHARTREUSE DE CHAMPMOL ❻**. Return along avenue Albert 1er and boulevard de Sévigné to place Darcy.

Right
Palais des Ducs

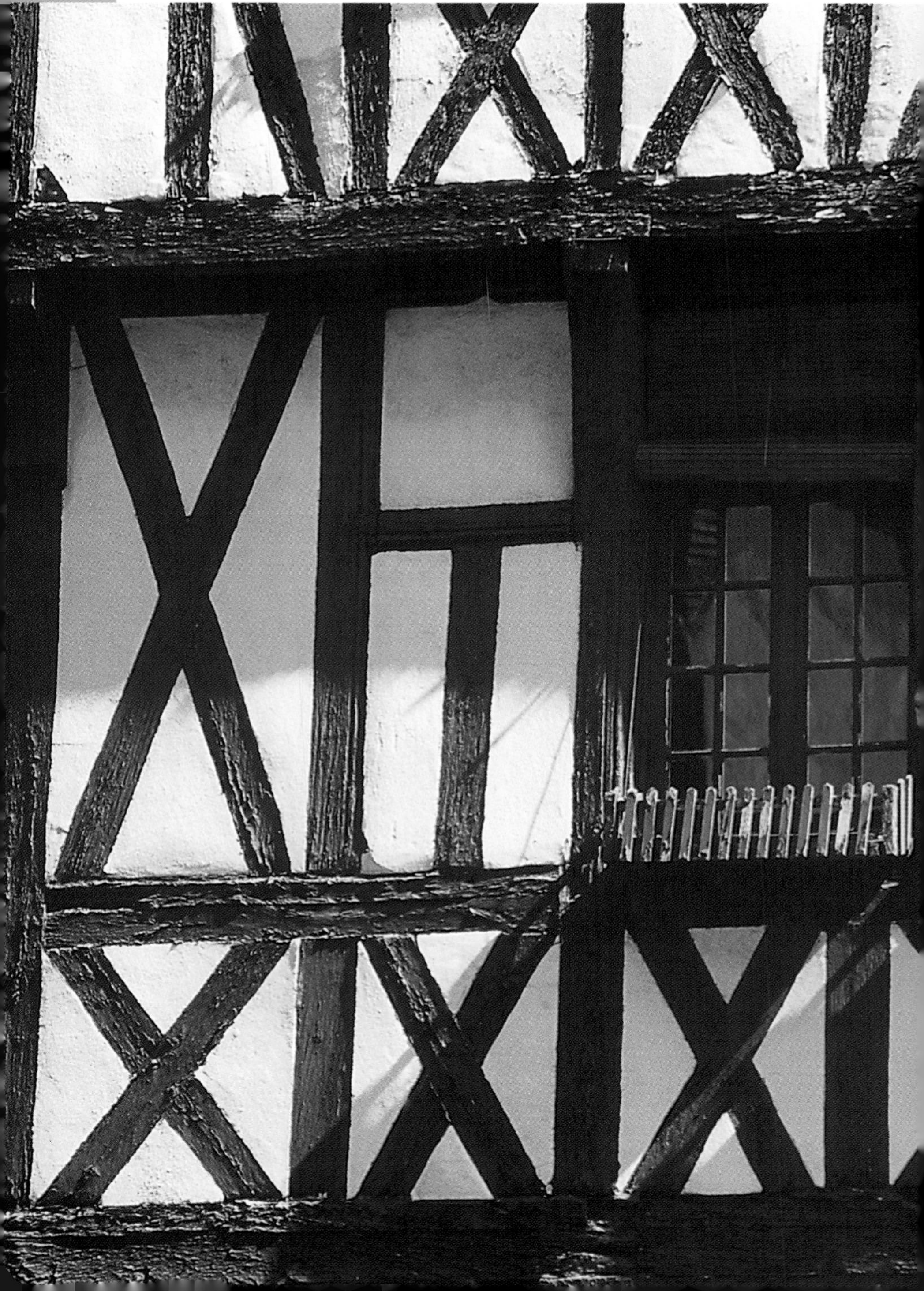

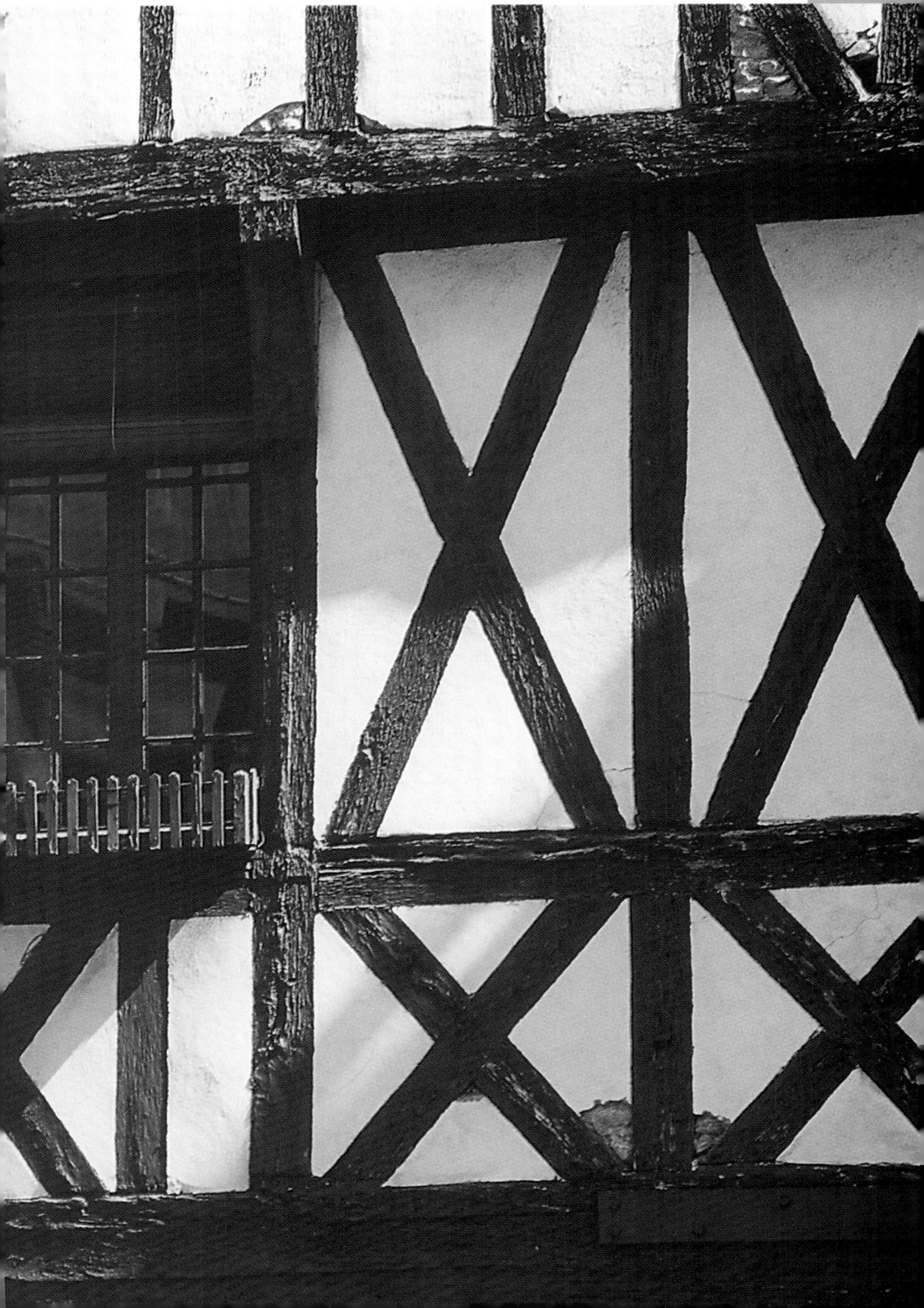

The Côte d'Or

Ratings

Restaurants	●●●●●
Villages	●●●●●
Winetasting	●●●●●
History	●●●●
Scenery	●●●●
Folklore	●●●
Shopping	●●
Children	●

It's not called the Côte d'Or for nothing. The name means 'Golden Slope', and this gorgeous 60-km hillside is brilliantly luminous, gold-tinted in morning sunlight. This is the most famous part of Burgundy. From its steep slope come the celebrated wines that have made the name of Burgundy famous throughout the world. The hillside runs from Dijon into the countryside beyond the fortified market town of Beaune. Along its length, villages are strung like gems along a country road. Each one is simple, charming, blessed with some modest sight or attraction, and surrounded by immaculate fields of vines. Every village, or even individual vineyards, will claim – with justification – to produce quite distinct wines with a character all their own. Many a label bears the name of a particular *clos*, sometimes known locally as a *climat*, being a tiny area of grapevines, often a walled field.

ⓘ Côte d'Or Tourist Office *Hôtel du Département, Dijon; tel: 03 80 63 66 00, fax: 03 80 49 90 97, e-mail: cdt21@wanadoo.fr.*

Ⓦ *www.burgcellar.com/ bvillage* (wine website about Côte d'Or local *appellations* and vineyards); *www.avco.org/index_uk* (site of Côte d'Or winegrowers' association, AVCO).

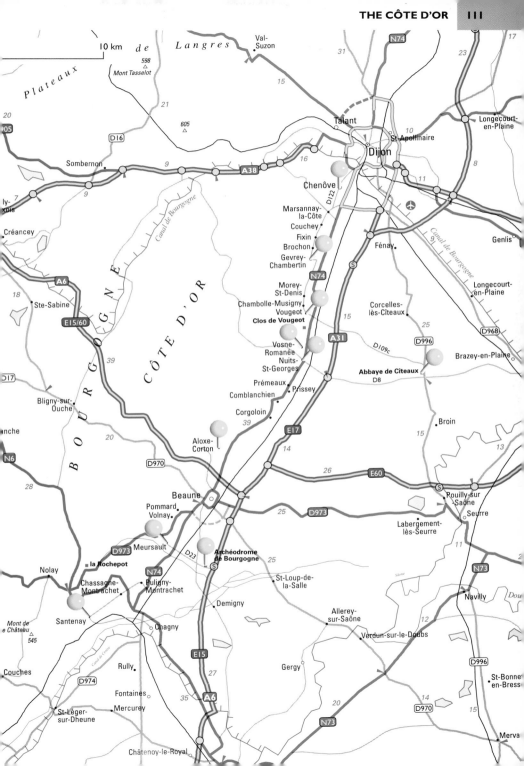

ALOXE-CORTON**

At pretty Aloxe-Corton (pronounced 'Alosse'), one of the world's oldest and greatest wine names, Charlemagne had a vineyard; today – in a village noted for red wine – it still produces an acclaimed white wine, with the *appellation* Corton-Charlemagne. This village marks the start of the Côte de Beaune, the Côte d'Or's southern area where white wines excel (though reds are still world class!).

Accommodation and food in Aloxe-Corton

Villa Louise €€€ *In village; tel: 03 80 26 46 70, fax: 03 80 26 47 16*. A charming, comfortable, stylish and welcoming 17th-century house among the prestigious Corton vineyards. No restaurant.

L'Ermitage Corton €€€ *Route de Digne, Chorey; tel: 03 80 22 05 28, fax: 03 80 24 64 51*. Between Aloxe-Corton and Beaune, this grand, old, sumptuously decorated restaurant serves rich, classic cuisine expertly prepared. It's a small, lavishly luxurious hotel, too.

ARCHÉODROME DE BOURGOGNE**

Archéodrome de Bourgogne €€ *Aire de Beaune-Tailly, 6km from Beaune on autoroute A6; tel: 03 80 26 87 00, fax: 03 80 21 40 95, e-mail: info@archeodrome-bourgogne.com, www.archeodrome-bourgogne.com; open Mar 1000–1700 (1800 on Sat and Sun), Apr–Oct (except July and Aug) Mon–Fri 0930–1800, Sat and Sun 0930–1900, July and Aug daily 0930–1900, with guided visits every afternoon, currently closes Nov–Feb, with plans to open occasionally – phone first.*

The Archéodrome Restaurant €€ serves 'Roman-style meals'.

Set right beside the *autoroute*, this museum park offers 'edutainment' with reconstructions of Gaulish dwellings, life-size models, mock archaeological digs, and audio-visual shows explaining what has been discovered from several nearby archaeological sites. It's intended to give an overview of life at this spot from Stone Age times right up to the year AD 1000.

Right
Aloxe-Corton

CHENÔVE❖

ⓘ **Cuverie des Ducs de Bourgogne** € 8 r.
Roger Salengro; tel: 03 80 52 82 83; open June–Sept daily 1400–1900 for free 45-min tour in French, rest of the year visit by appointment only.

Now a populous suburb of Dijon, Chenôve has ancient vineyards and its impressive Clos du Roy winecellar, the **Cuverie des Ducs de Bourgogne**❖, was once the cellar of the Dukes of Burgundy. It has two giant-sized 13th-century wine presses, in use until 1927, which are worked by an ingenious counterbalancing system and capable of pressing 30 tonnes of grapes between them.

Right
Vineyards

The Vinegrowers' Festival

The Festival of St-Vincent Tournante, the biggest village festival in Burgundy, takes place in the Côte d'Or's villages on the first Saturday after 22 January, traditionally the vinegrowers' least busy month. The festival is based in a different village each year (*tournante* means 'rotating'). For a week, the vinegrowers feast, have fun and honour their patron saint. *For information, tel: 03 80 61 07 12.*

Food in Chenôve

Le Clos du Roy €€ *35 av. du 14 juillet; tel: 03 80 51 33 66, fax: 03 80 51 36 66, closed Sun pm and Mon.* A good, rather lavish meal is attractively served at a modest price, at this unlikely looking Dijon suburban location.

ABBAYE DE CÎTEAUX✤✤

Abbaye de Cîteaux
€ *3km from Cîteaux village; tel: 03 80 62 15 00; open daily 0900–1200, 1400–1645 for 45-min guided tour in French.*

Cistercians

Cistercians believed that a simple life was most appropriate for those serving God, and in the centuries after their abbey had been established it became more and more austere. The order attracted many adherents: within a century there were over 1 000 Cistercian monasteries, which eventually grew to number 3 600. Four popes came from the abbey at Cîteaux, and one of its abbots was the ecclesiastical head of the brutal Albigensian Crusade, which savaged the Languedoc region in the 12th century.

Cîteaux (the name comes from *cistels*, 'reeds') is where the Cistercian Order was founded in 1098 by three monks dissatisfied with the comfortable existence offered at Cluny (*see page 142*). The new order they created elevated unostentatious simplicity to an art form. Yet, despite the spartan regime of the monks, they developed the cultivation of the grapevine on the Côte d'Or, and built the Château du Clos de Vougeot (*see page 118*), which was in effect their farmhouse. Most of the wine produced was consumed by the monks themselves, though any which was surplus to their appetites was given away to influential and useful friends.

The abbey was closed down in the 18th century by French Revolutionaries and subsequently almost entirely destroyed. At this time the Cistercians underwent changes and a new strict, contemplative order was started – the Trappists. Since the late 19th century, a reunified Cistercian Order has returned to Cîteaux, where, in what's left of the abbey and in new buildings, together with a considerable area of land, they again live a simple monastic life, undertake charitable work and concentrate now on producing a cheese to go with the wine!

Right
Countryside around the Abbaye de Cîteaux

GEVREY-CHAMBERTIN❖❖

ℹ️ **Gevrey-Chambertin Tourist Office** *Pl. de la Maire; tel: 03 80 34 38 40, fax: 03 80 34 15 49; open Mon–Sat 0930–1230, Sun 0930–1230.*

🏰 **Fortress** *€€ Beside village; tel: 03 80 34 36 13; open Mon–Sat 1000–1200, 1400–1800 (Oct–Mar 1700), Sun and hols 1100–1200, 1430–1730 (Oct–Mar 1700), closed some national hols.*

Combes

The famous Côte is just a hillside, no more or less. Narrow wooded valleys with little streams run down from the top of the hill, cutting the 'golden' slope with little valleys called *combes*; these make superb walks and drives off the main route. At the top, you reach the rustic Haute Côte plateau.

Well-travelled wine

On 22 July 1999 French astronauts Claude André-Deshay and Jean-Pierre Haigneré were launched into space. They took with them a bottle of Chambertin 1989.

Gevrey-Chambertin, 12km south of Dijon, is one of the really great names of the Côte, some say the best of them all. Prize-winning vineyards encircle the village, which in turn clusters round its 13th-century church and 10th-century **fortress**❖, which once belonged to the monks of the abbey at Cluny. There are several distinct *appellations* within this one village: Chambertin and Clos de Bèze are the pick of the crop, but some others are good too and represent better value. A nicely aged bottle of a good vintage Chambertin was, it is claimed, Napoleon's favourite tipple. The village is a good starting point for walks or drives. Beside the village a *combe* sweeps down the slope through the vines, and a steep attractive road, the D31, follows it up the hillside.

Accommodation and food in Gevrey-Chambertin

Les Arts et Terroirs *€€ 28 route de Dijon; tel: 03 80 34 34 76, fax: 03 80 34 11 79.* A good little hotel with attractive rooms, bearable prices and a flourishing garden where breakfast is served.

Les Grands Crus *€€ Route des Grands Crus; tel: 03 80 34 34 15, fax: 03 80 51 89 07.* A pretty hotel in a peaceful setting overlooking the vines, with breakfast in the garden.

Les Millésimes *€€€ 25 r. de l'Église; tel: 03 80 51 84 24, fax: 03 80 34 12 73.* Vaulted, atmospheric restaurant with first-class regional cooking, top-notch wines and lovely location, but special-occasion prices.

Rôtisserie du Chambertin *€€ R. du Chambertin; tel: 03 80 34 33 20, fax: 03 80 34 12 30.* In an evocative, historic setting of tapestries and old timber, this is the place to enjoy classic Burgundian dishes, superbly prepared.

MEURSAULT✣

ℹ **Meursault Tourist Office** *Pl. de l'Hôtel de Ville; tel: 03 80 21 25 90, fax: 03 80 21 26 00; open May–Nov only, 1030–1300, 1400–1830.*

Slightly off the beaten track between the D973 and N74, the famed village of Meursault with its beautiful Gothic church spire is where the *Trois Glorieuses* celebrations (*see page 126*) come to an end. Some of the very best white wines come from here – it's considered the 'capital' of white Burgundy – and several wine producers and sellers may give tours of their magnificent old premises.

Accommodation and food in Meursault

Hôtel des Charmes €€€ *Pl. Murger; tel: 03 80 21 63 53, fax: 03 80 21 62 89.* An attractive 18th-century house in the village centre, with a lovely breakfast terrace.

NUITS-ST-GEORGES✣

ℹ **Nuits Tourist Office** *R. Sanoys; tel: 03 80 61 22 47, fax: 03 80 61 30 98.*

Nuits, as it is usually called, is the small commercial hub of the Côte de Nuits, a lively and bustling, though not an especially lovely town, straddling the busy *route nationale*. The wines of Nuits became fashionable among Europe's aristocracy after 1680 when they were prescribed for Louis XIV by his physician 'to restore his strength'. He was advised to drink several glasses of both Nuits and Romanée wines every evening with dinner. The town's own vineyards are 1000 years old.

Accommodation and food in Nuits

Hôtel-Restaurant la Gentilhommière €€ *13 vallée de la Serré; tel: 03 80 61 12 06, fax: 03 80 61 30 33.* Just out of town in a deliciously quiet setting with its own river and gardens, and a notable restaurant.

Right
Grape picking

SANTENAY✣

ℹ **Santenay Tourist Office** *R. des Sources; tel: 03 80 20 63 15, fax: 03 80 20 65 98.*

🎰 **Casino des Sources** *R. des Sources; open daily 1000–0300. Free entry.*

The village spreads along the River Dheure, at the southern tip of the Côte d'Or, in three separate districts – Santenay le Bas, Santenay le Haut and Santenay St-Jean. Santenay is better known for health-giving waters (from Le Bas) than for its modest wines (from Le Haut). The salty waters are used to treat rheumatism. Visit the 15th-century castle keep with its glazed rooftiles and the beautiful little medieval church of St-Jean-de-Narosse, enclosed by cliffs and with good views.

VOSNE-ROMANÉE✧

Between the Château du Clos de Vougeot and Nuits-St-Georges, just off the road at Vosne-Romanée, is what probably qualifies as the most distinguished vineyard estate in the whole of Burgundy, Domaine de la Romanée-Conti, with lands covering seven of the top *appellations*. The most sought after of its prestigious labels, called simply 'Romanée-Conti', comes from under two hectares. No wonder the price is high – though much of the appeal is the scarcity.

VOUGEOT✧✧✧

Château du Clos de Vougeot €€ *Outside village; tel: 03 80 62 86 09, www.closdevougeot.com; open Apr–Sept daily, 0900–1830 (Sat 1700); Oct–Mar 0900–1130, 1400–1730 (Sat 1700), closed 1 Jan, 24, 25 and 31 Dec. 35-min guided tours, in English if required.*

Just outside the village, the **Château du Clos de Vougeot**✧✧✧ stands splendidly amidst its vineyards. The château was constructed in the 12th century, then largely rebuilt in the 16th, by the Cistercians at Cîteaux, who developed vine-growing and winemaking into a fine art. No longer the home of monks, since 1944 the château has been the base of the international wine 'brotherhood', the Confrérie des Chevaliers du Tastevin. This awesomely named 'Brotherhood of the Knights of Winetasting' is a Burgundian growers', winemakers' and merchants' association dedicated to the art of banqueting. The Confrérie gathers here at various times throughout the year for its

ritualised *chapitres* – sumptuous and jolly banquets, notably during the first night of the *Trois Glorieuses*, the 'three glorious' days at the end of the annual harvest in November, when there are usually about 600 people at a sitting.

The Côte's principal wine districts

The Côte d'Or is divided broadly into two large regions: the Côte de Nuits, from near Dijon down to Corgoloin, and then, by a slight change in conditions, it becomes the Côte de Beaune. With some exceptions, the red wines from the Côte de Nuits tend to be considerably better: richer, longer lasting and more sought after than those of the Côte de Beaune; while the Côte de Beaune excels for whites. On both Côtes, the best wine comes from the oldest vines and from those nearest the top of the hill – but not *on* the top, of course, since steepness is all-important here.

Suggested tour

An excellent restaurant in Marsannay-la-Côte is Les Gourmets (8 r. du Puits de Tet; tel: 03 80 51 91 31, www.Les-Gourmets.fr).

Total distance: About 60km, plus a 30km detour.

Time: At least 1 full day will be needed to do justice to this drive, including the detour to Cîteaux. This is one to savour, with visits to the sights on the way, a leisurely lunch among the vines, and perhaps a winetasting.

Links: At Chagny, this route connects with the Chalonnais (*see page 132*) and Beaune (*see page 122*).

Route: From Dijon (*see page 98*), leave town on the N74, but soon turn right for **CHENÔVE** ❶, a wine village which has become a populous Dijon suburb. From here follow the D122, the small country road which threads through the wine villages. **Marsannay-la-Côte**, the next village, has several modest hotels and restaurants; it produces an excellent rosé wine (a rarity in Burgundy) by rapid fermentation. The

Above
Montrachet

road passes through Couchey, with its decorated church roof, to **Fixin** (pronounce the 'x' as 'ss'), a pretty little place. **Brochon** is the first village reached that is properly entitled to use the Côte de Nuits *appellation*, signifying the northern half of the Côte d'Or, where red wines tend to be richer and more long-lasting than further south.

Brochon's neighbour **GEVREY-CHAMBERTIN** ➋ is one of the really great names. Continuing on the D122, village signposts read like a collection of distinguished wine labels. Pass through **Morey-St-Denis** and **Chambolle-Musigny**, with centuries-old lime trees and a church with an interesting tower, to reach **VOUGEOT** ➌.

Detour: From Vougeot, take the D109c to **CÎTEAUX** ➍. Either return on the same road, or – better, unless you are keen to see the Romanée vineyards – return to the route on the D8 to **NUITS-ST-GEORGES** ➎.

The D122 turns on to the N74, passing **VOSNE-ROMANÉE** ➏, which has Burgundy's most prestigious vineyards, the Romanée-Conti. Just beyond is the small, busy town of Nuits-St-Georges. Stay on the N74. The last villages of the Côte de Nuits are **Prémeaux**, **Prissey**, **Comblanchien** and **Corgoloin**. At **ALOXE-CORTON** ➐ you enter the Côte de Beaune, and almost at once, the road comes to **Beaune** (*see page 122*).

Pass through the town centre or take the ring road, and leave Beaune on the N74. Take the D973 on the right. Some of the world's greatest white wine names are here, just south of the town. The D973 passes through **Pommard**, built around an unusual square bell tower. At **Volnay**, its neighbour, Our Lady of the Vines, looks down on to the fields from the hillside church. Turn off the D973 to **MEURSAULT** ➑. Take the D23 from here – straight across the N74 – to visit the **ARCHÉODROME DE BOURGOGNE** ➒.

Returning from the Archéodrome, turn left on to the N74 and left after 5km to reach the grandest white wine names of all, **Puligny-Montrachet** and **Chassagne-Montrachet**. Immediately below them, in an imposing rocky setting, which marks the end of the Côte d'Or, and spread beside the River Dheure, is **SANTENAY** ➓. It's 5km on a tiny road into Chagny (*see page 134*), end point of the Côte d'Or.

Dégustation

Fancy a taste? As you follow the route, signs beckon you to try *dégustation*, a tasting. Tourist offices in Dijon, Beaune and the villages offer a list of over 200 vineyards that currently welcome visitors. You'll be plied with examples of some excellent vintages. There may be a charge of about 35F (though your first one or two tastes may be free) until the pressure to buy a few bottles becomes irresistible!

Puligny-Montrachet

One of the best white wines of the Côte comes from Puligny-Montrachet, south of Beaune. Alexander Dumas, author of *The Three Musketeers*, said the wine of Puligny-Montrachet should be drunk 'while kneeling with the head uncovered'.

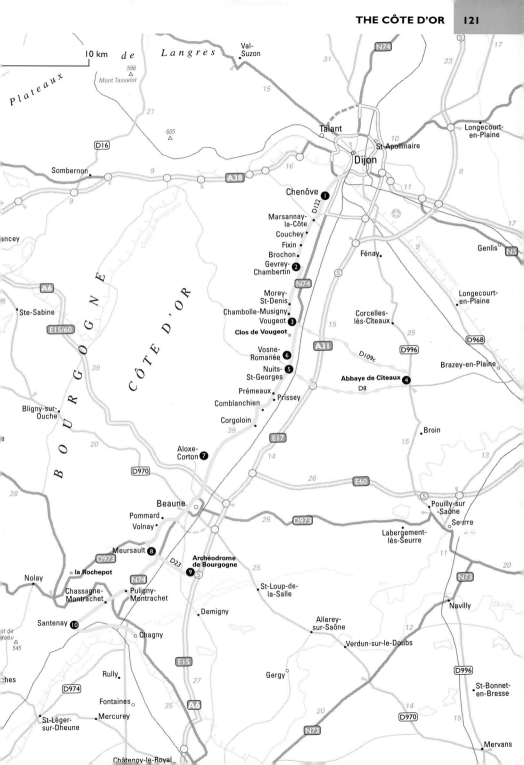

10 km

Plateaux   *de*   *Langres*

Val-Suzon

598 △ Mont Tasselot

605 △

D16

Sombernon

A38

Talant

Dijon

St-Apollinaire

Longecourt-en-Plaine

Chenôve ❶

D122

Marsannay-la-Côte

Couchey

Fixin

Brochon

Gevrey-Chambertin ❷

Fénay

Genlis

N5

Morey-St-Denis

N74

Chambolle-Musigny

Vougeot ❸

Clos de Vougeot

Corcelles-lès-Cîteaux

Longecourt-en-Plaine

D968

Ste-Sabine

A6

E15/60

B O U R G O G N E

C Ô T E   D ' O R

Vosne-Romanée ❻

A31

D109c

D996

Brazey-en-Plaine

Nuits-St-Georges ❺

Abbaye de Cîteaux ❹

D8

Prémeaux

Comblanchien

Prissey

Bligny-sur-Ouche

Corgoloin

Broin

Aloxe-Corton ❼

D970

E17

E60

Beaune

Pouilly-sur-Saône

Pommard

Seurre

Volnay

D973

Labergement-lès-Seurre

Meursault ❽

D23

N73

D973

Archéodrome de Bourgogne

la Rochepot

N74 ❾

Nolay

Chassagne-Montrachet

Puligny-Montrachet

St-Loup-de-la-Salle

Navilly

Demigny

Santenay ❿

545 △

Chagny

Allerey-sur-Saône

Verdun-sur-le-Doubs

Doubs

E15

D974

Rully

Gergy

D996

St-Bonnet-en-Bresse

Fontaines

A6

St-Léger-sur-Dheune

Mercurey

N73

D970

Mervans

Châtenoy-le-Royal

Beaune

Ratings

Architecture	●●●●●
History	●●●●●
Restaurants	●●●●●
Winetasting	●●●●●
Museums	●●●●○
Street life	●●●●○
Children	●●●○○
Entertainment	●●●○○

Despite tourist crowds and terrible traffic problems, Beaune is a glorious little town, set amid rich vineyards enclosed by ancient ramparts and ornamented with fine medieval buildings – the best of them under the duchy's distinctive Flemish-Burgundian patterned tile roofs. Much of the town centre is pedestrianised, the right size for strolling, is packed with bars and restaurants and has a manageable handful of don't-miss sights, so seeing everything is easy, enjoyable and rewarding. The central area is a maze of narrow cobbled streets and attractive busy squares. Until the 14th century, Beaune was the home of the Dukes of Burgundy, and even after they officially moved to Dijon, it continued to serve as their capital of wine. It remains the centre of the Burgundy wine trade. Set into the walls of the tree-covered ramparts around the town centre are the *caves* of wine growers.

Getting there and getting around

ℹ **Beaune Tourist Office** *1 r. de l'Hôtel Dieu; tel: 03 80 26 21 30, fax: 03 80 26 21 39, e-mail: ot.beaune@wanadoo.fr; open Jan–Mar, mid-Nov–Dec, daily 0930–1800, Apr–mid-June, Mon–Thur 0900–1900, Fri–Sat 0900–2000, Sun 0900–1800, mid-June–mid-Sept, Mon–Sat 0900–2000, Sun 0900–1900, mid-Sept–mid-Nov 0900–1800 (Fri and Sat till 1900). With information and hotel booking for Beaune and the whole of Burgundy.*

By road
Beaune is close to the meeting point of three busy *autoroutes*: the A6 (Paris–Lyon), the A31 (to Dijon) and the A36 (for Alsace, Switzerland and Germany). It's also on the *route nationale* from Dijon, the N74, and is not far from the N6, the old Paris–Lyon main road, still much used.

On arrival at Beaune, all traffic is fed on to the ring road of boulevards that runs around the town ramparts and gives entry to the central area through openings in the town walls.

Within the walls, many roads are narrow, one-way and congested, so it's best to avoid driving within the town itself.

By rail
Beaune is a frequent stop for TGVs and classic trains on the Paris–Lyon line.

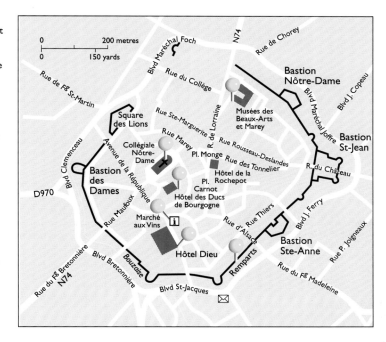

www.perso.club-internet.fr/funjam/ ('not in any way the official site of Beaune' says the intro, but 'one man's view' of the town – interesting and useful); *www.perso.club-internet.fr/crums/AVB/index* 'site of the Friends of Old Beaune association); *www.beaune.cci.fr/* (Beaune Chamber of Commerce site, in French, for the business community).

Collégiale Nôtre-Dame € *Pl. Leclerc; open daily.*

Hôtel des Ducs de Bourgogne (or **Musée du Vin)** €€ *R. d'Enfer; tel: 03 80 24 56 92; open daily 0930–1800 (Dec–Mar, closed Tue).* Ticket gives entry to Musées des Beaux-Arts et Marey.

Parking
Parking is difficult within the ramparts, but there is plenty of parking space off the boulevards around the perimeter.

Collégiale Nôtre-Dame (Nôtre-Dame Collegiate Church)*
In the oldest part of the town, Église Nôtre-Dame dates from 1120. It has a striking triple doorway in the Cluniac style (*see page 142*) and a later Gothic spire rising above. Inside, there's a lovely apse with three radiating Romanesque chapels, and on the south side a Renaissance chapel. There's plenty of fine stonecarving and artwork, including 15th-century frescos. Most of all, the church is noted for the five large 15th-century Flemish wool and silk tapestries, in the choir by the altar. Depicting the Life of the Virgin, they were donated by Nicolas Rolin.

Hôtel des Ducs de Bourgogne (or Musée du Vin)**
The grand 14th- to 16th-century former residence of the Dukes of Burgundy is now given over entirely to Beaune's prestigious wine museum. It has comprehensive displays on the whole story of winemaking in Burgundy, including such treasures as medieval tapestries, statuary and gold plate. In the cellars, huge wine presses and a curious collection of implements used in the trade look as though everything was made for the use of giants.

Hôtel Dieu €€ *R. de l'Hôtel Dieu; tel: 03 80 24 45 00, fax: 03 80 24 45 99, www.hospices-de-beaune.tm.fr/htgb/home; open end Nov–end Mar, daily 0900–1130, 1400–1730, rest of the year daily 0900–1830. The last visitors may remain inside for one hour after 'closing' time. Guided visits on request (€€€).*

Son et Lumière €€ *Le Rêve de Nicolas Rolin (Nicolas Rolin's Dream) is the nightly sound-and-light show in the Cour d'Honneur of the Hôtel Dieu. Shows Apr–Nov in different languages at different times each evening. Times of English shows vary from 2215 to 2345 according to the day and month.*

Festivals include: *Fête de la Vigne, Folklore Parade – 2nd Sat in Sept; auction of new wines at the Hospices de Beaune as part of the Trois Glorieuses – 3rd Sun in Nov; International Festival of Baroque Music – July, in the Hôtel Dieu and Église Nôtre-Dame; film festivals – Aug and Oct; Anim'Été – annual programme of summer outdoor entertainments and street events.*

Hôtel Dieu (of the Hospices de Beaune)✦✦✦

After all the build-up, the first reaction on reaching the Hôtel Dieu could almost be surprised disappointment. From outside, the façade of the old building, topped by a Gothic spire, conveys nothing of its charm. But step into the courtyard, the Cour d'Honneur, and there you discover – all around the lovely cobbled square with its ornate well – one of the duchy's best examples of the traditional Flemish-Burgundian coloured roof tiles. The glazed and patterned roof, with gilded weather vanes, descends steeply over dormer windows and over a timbered first-floor gallery resting on slender pillars, making an attractive arcade on the ground floor. This roof has made the Hôtel Dieu a symbol of Burgundy.

It was founded in 1443 by Nicolas Rolin, the fantastically wealthy chancellor of the Dukes of Burgundy, as a palace for 'Les Pôvres' (*les pauvres*, 'the poor'). The Hôtel Dieu – the name means 'charity hospital' – has continued to be used as a charitable hospice ever since. It served as a general hospital for over 500 years, right up to 1948, and is now a geriatric hospital. It is considered one of Europe's best

Hospices de Beaune – hospitals and wine

The Hospices de Beaune is an ancient charity that owns and runs the historic Hôtel Dieu and the Hospices de la Charité geriatric hospitals, as well as the town's state-of-the-art Philippe le Bon general hospital and the modern Nicolas Rolin care home. The Hospices also owns extensive high-quality vineyards, especially in the distinguished area between Aloxe-Corton and Meursault.

The annual Hospices de Beaune wine auction, continuing until a candle has burnt out, colourfully conveys all of Burgundy's love of tradition, of ritual … and of wine. The auction, on the second day of the *Trois Glorieuses* (see *page 126*), takes place in the cellars of the Hôtel Dieu on the 3rd Sunday in November, and is followed by a gala dinner for the wine trade and its guests.

All profits go to charity. The auction of the Hospices' 39 vintages raises the money for the medical services of the Hospices, as well as for the maintenance of its historic building. In addition, it plays an important role in establishing prices for each year's new vintage, with a knock-on effect for prices of wines from other regions of France and all around the world.

The auctioneer is not selling bottles of wine, but the newly harvested wine of the year that's just ended. The buyers are all traders and merchants, who must mature, bottle and market the wines themselves. Two days before the auction, winetasting takes place in the Hôtel Dieu cellars. To buy a case of Hospices de Beaunes wines, contact Syndicat des Négociants en Vins Fins de Bourgogne (Burgundy Fine Wines Traders' Association) (*7 pl. Carnot, 21200 Beaune; tel: 03 80 22 19 60, fax: 03 80 24 03 88*).

Right
Hôtel Dieu

surviving examples of medieval civic architecture. The residents' meals are still made in the original kitchens, which have been thoroughly modernised.

Centrepiece of the Hôtel Dieu is its Great Hall, or Salle des Pôvres, a huge ward – 46m long – with stone walls and a flagstone floor under a magnificent timber ceiling. The immaculate beds, within heavy curtains and each with its polished table and chair, may look rather inviting, but all was not as it seems – when Louis XIV visited the hospital he was amazed and shocked to find up to four patients in each bed and he immediately ordered that women and men patients should not be placed in beds together! All beds face the altar at one end, where a lifelike (but larger-than-life) 15th-century painted woodcarving of Christ stands.

Continue into the Salle de Polyptyque, specially made to house a polyptych altarpiece of *The Last Judgement* by Rogier van der Weyden. Commissioned by Nicolas Rolin himself, this work was completed in 1443. It depicts, in fine detail (a magnifying glass is supplied so you can get a good look), several contemporary dignitaries including Rolin himself, his wife and Duke Philippe le Bon, amid portraits of Biblical characters. The bottom of the panel shows the naked dead making their way to Heaven and Hell. Medieval tapestries hang opposite the tryptych. There's a spectacular **son et lumière**** in the Cour d'Honneur every summer evening.

Above
Hôtel Dieu at night

Les Trois Glorieuses

The third Saturday, Sunday and Monday in November make a whole weekend of feasting and doing business, when the *viticulteurs* and their merchants get together. It starts with the big *chapitre* (banquet) at the Château du Clos de Vougeot (see page 118). The second day sees the sale by auction, in the Halles opposite the Hôtel Dieu at Beaune, of the new wines of the Hospices de Beaune vineyards – an important occasion which establishes the prices for most of the other wines in the region – which concludes with another banquet. The third night is the *Paulée* at Meursault (see page 116), a huge party and banquet to which growers bring their own wine. For information, tel: 03 80 26 21 30.

Right
Église de Beaune

Marché aux Vins €€
*Pl. de la Halle; tel: 03
80 25 08 20.*

Other markets: the
Grand Marché is the
big, lively main market in
pl. Camot – Sat am; the
Marché Gourmand is a
smaller specialist food
market – Wed am.

Marché aux Vins*

For a winetasting experience with less pressure and more choice, step
into the atmospheric old Marché aux Vins, inside a former 13th-
century church, where you can sample (without obligation) some of
the finest Côte d'Or wines. You pay a deposit for a *tastevin* – a shallow
drinking cup for winetasting – and are given the run of the place.
More than 25 vintages, some grand and in dusty old bottles, stand
about for your enjoyment and education. Afterwards you can buy
some wine, while the *tastevin* makes a perfect souvenir of the occasion
and of Beaune.

Musées des Beaux-Arts et Marey €€ *R. de l'Hôtel de Ville/r. de Lorraine; tel: 03 80 24 56 92; open Mar–Oct 1400–1800, also open 3rd weekend in Nov.* Ticket also valid for Musée du Vin.

Musées des Beaux-Arts et Marey (Fine Arts and Marey Museums)*
These two connected museums occupy part of the former 17th-century convent, which also houses today's town hall. The Fine Arts collection includes a lot of work by the local artist Félix Ziem, as well as several 16th- and 17th-century Flemish paintings and some medieval and Renaissance sculpture. The Marey museum records the work and ideas of local doctor Étienne-Jules Marey, whose special interest was the measurement and study of movement. Among his achievements was the so-called 'rifle camera', which took several photos in quick succession, producing a prototype movie.

Remparts (Ramparts)**
The near-complete circle of Beaune's 13th- to 16th-century ramparts seems now to be protecting the historic town centre from invading cars and coaches, which hurtle around the perimeter. The ramparts are fortified with a succession of sturdy 'bastions' and towers and are draped with greenery in places. The ancient moat, now largely filled in, and much of the ramparts have become a shady, pleasant, park-like walk. The former Château (or Bastion St-Jean) is an imposing double bastion – just north of it, Tour Blondeau sticks out from the walls. Clockwise from here, Rempart St-Jean keeps its medieval flavour, with the arrow-slits of Tour Renard. Rempart Madeleine is studded by the greenery of Bastion Ste-Anne, the Grosse Tour (Great Tower) and Tour des Billes or Jolibois. The approach to Tour des Dames is an agreeable walkway. The triangular Place des Lions, just beyond, is a filled-in bastion. The ramparts are broken at this point, and resume at the 18th-century archway, Porte St-Nicolas. On both sides of Bastion Nôtre-Dame, with its little turret, there's a broad, wooded area. The perimeter walk is about 2km.

Accommodation and food in Beaune

Beaune has an exceptionally large number of hotels and restaurants, both independent and chains, de luxe and low budget. Though rates are a little lower outside the walls, it's worth staying in the town centre if possible, where there are dozens of decent family-run hotels and restaurants. Surprisingly, considering that the town is creaking with tourists, even in the centre the general price level is not high.

Auberge Bourguignonne €€ *4 pl. Madeleine; tel: 03 80 22 23 53, fax: 03 80 22 51 64.* Located outside the walls not far from Rempart Madeleine, this is a good restaurant with reasonable prices and a few modest bedrooms.

Hôtel Bleu Marine and Restaurant Le Clos du Cedre €€€ *10–12 boulevard Foch; tel: 03 80 24 01 01, fax: 03 80 24 09 90.* One of the

Opposite
Renaissance architecture, Beaune

Above
View of Beaune

most appealing places in town. Comfortable, modern, efficient and stylish, with good breakfasts, useful brunch, nice garden and an excellent restaurant for lunch or dinner.

Hôtel Grillon €€ *21 route de Seurre; tel: 03 80 22 44 25, fax: 03 80 24 94 89.* Convenient for the *autoroute* exit, yet only about 1km from the town centre, this is a charming family-run hotel and restaurant with its own grounds.

Hôtel Le Cep €€€ *27 r. Maufoux; tel: 03 80 22 35 48.* Extremely elegant rooms open on to an arcaded courtyard at this town-centre Renaissance mansion.

Bernard Morillon €€€ *31 r. Maufoux; tel: 03 80 24 12 06, fax: 03 80 22 66 22.* Grand, celebratory, luxurious: classic dishes are prepared with skill and are noted for Breton langoustines done *à la Brillat Savarin*, and pigeon from Bresse. Delicious desserts.

La Ciboulette € *69 r. de Lorraine; tel: 03 80 24 70 72, fax: 03 80 22 79 71.* Unpretentious but stylish little town-centre restaurant with excellent food at affordable prices, not yet discovered by tourists.

Jardin des Remparts €€€ *19 r. de l'Hôtel Dieu; tel: 03 80 24 79 41, fax. 03 80 24 92 79.* Debates about which is the best restaurant in Beaune generally end with agreement that it's chef Rolan Henrion's congenial, welcoming and stylish place near the Hôtel Dieu. *Foie gras*, fresh fish, delicious sauces: try the asparagus and haddock gelée with asparagus coulis. Good value set menu on weekdays.

Restaurant les Tontons € *22 faubourg Madeleine; tel: 03 80 24 19 64, closed Sun and Mon pm.* Outside the walls at place de la Madeleine, this amiable bistro-style restaurant offers excellent cooking at affordable prices.

Walking tour

Total distance: About 2km, or 4km including the detour.

Time: Though only an hour's walk, allow a full day to visit museums and sights.

Links: Beaune is on the Côte d'Or driving tour (*see page 119*).

Route: Start from place de la Halle, at the heart of town. On one corner is the tourist office, the **Halles** (covered market) and the **MARCHÉ AUX VINS** ❶. Across the road is the **HÔTEL DIEU** ❷. Walk from one *place* into another – place Fleury. Turn down r.

Maufoux, passing several handsome Renaissance buildings. Reaching the **REMPARTS** ❸ at Bastion Condé, turn right to follow the shady park-like ramparts' path past the imposing stonework of the Bastion des Dames. Go down the steps into avenue de la République and turn left for place Leclerc and **COLLÉGIALE NÔTRE-DAME** ❹.

Detour: Instead of leaving the ramparts here, follow them all the way round. The section after Bastion des Dames is the least satisfying, for here the fortifications have been filled in and much altered. At the 18th-century triumphal arch, Porte St-Nicolas, the ramparts resume and circle the town centre. Returning to r. Maufoux, or r. Cloutier just beyond, leave the ramparts and turn right to reach place Leclerc and Église Nôtre-Dame.

From the church, take r. d'Enfer – the strangely named Hell Street – for a few paces to the entrance of the **HÔTEL DES DUCS DE BOURGOGNE** ❺. On the other side of the building is the equally oddly named r. Paradis (Paradise Street). Turn right into place au Beurre, the one-time Butter Market, and the adjoining place Monge. Notice here the 16th-century mansion **Hôtel de la Rochepot** with its Gothic façade of mullioned windows, and the typically Flemish 14th-century belfry, clear evidence of Burgundy's medieval connections with Flanders. Walk up r. de Lorraine, which has much Renaissance architecture, to **MUSÉES DES BEAUX-ARTS ET MAREY** ❻. Return via place au Beurre, r. Carnot and r. Monge to place de la Halle.

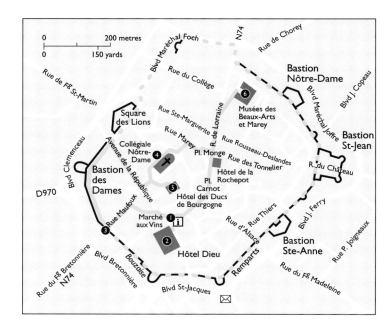

The Chalonnais

Ratings

Restaurants	●●●●●
Winetasting	●●●●●
Activities	●●●○○
Architecture	●●●○○
Museums	●●●○○
Children	●●○○○
History	●●○○○
Scenery	●●○○○

Prestigious vines lie like a thick-pile carpet across the Côte Chalonnaise countryside. This is the narrow strip of rolling, pretty vineyard-covered landscape extending south of the Côte d'Or. Like the 'Golden Slope', from which it is notionally separated by the little River Dheume, the Chalonnais is acclaimed for fine wines. The area's best-known names are Rully, Mercurey, Givry, Buxy, Bouzeron and Montagny-les-Buxy – all are hardworking little villages, admittedly not the prettiest in Burgundy, but producing connoisseur wines. The D981, the Chalonnais wine road, runs through the middle of the district, with good views to the east. The main town, Chalon, is busy, preoccupied and lacking much picturesque charm. On the other hand, it thinks of itself as 'between *langue d'oil* and *langue d'oc*' – between northern and southern France – and considers that this area is quintessential Burgundy, enjoying the best of everything.

W Many villages in the area have a page on *www.cc-chalon-val-de-bourgogne.fr/*.

Z The whole Côte Chalonnaise area lies alongside the *Autoroute du Soleil*, the A6. Almost all the villages on our route are less than 20 minutes from an *autoroute* exit.

Wines of Chalonnais

Though not reaching the level of the finest from the Côte d'Or, the village *appellations* or *appellations communales* of La Côte Chalonnaise (the Chalonnais slope) are considered great wines. The best are designated as *Premiers Crus*. Both red and white are produced: the one rich, strong and dark, the other crisp, fruity and golden. Pre-eminent for reds are the *appellations* Mercurey and Givry, while for white wine Montagny is the most outstanding. The village of Bouzeron is noted for the crisply dry white Aligoté, while Rully makes both red and white, and is best known for sparkling wine. Usually bracketed together with Chalonnais are the wines of Couchois, a tiny, separate area lying on the other side of the Canal du Centre, west of Rully. Much of Chalonnais wine does not reach the standard of a village *appellation*, and comes into the more general Côte Chalonnaise, Bourgogne and Bourgogne Aligoté *appellations*, or is used to make sparkling Crémant de Bourgogne.

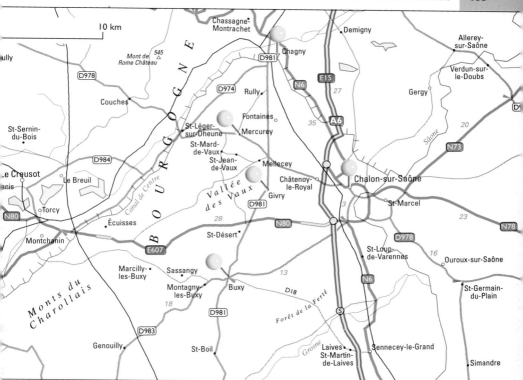

BUXY*

Rising on a hillside, fortified Buxy (pronounced 'Bussy') is one of the district's more attractive small towns. Its old defensive Tour Rouge (not red, despite the name) stands in the centre, and here you can buy and taste the excellent local wines, both red and white, notably the Montagny *appellation*. As well as numerous private growers and winemakers, the village has two *caves coopératives* (co-operative wineries). At the **Chai de Buxy ('Les Vignes de la Croix')*** co-operative, a wide range of Burgundy wines can be tasted and bought. Other local produce includes *foie gras* and goats' cheeses, featured on the menus of local restaurants. **The Musée du Vigneron***, inside a vaulted wine cellar in the village, shows a year in the life of a *vigneron* (grape farmer).

Food in Buxy

Aux Années Vins €€ *Pl. Carcabot; tel: 03 85 92 15 76.* This really excellent little village restaurant serves tasty, well-prepared dishes and local wines.

Chagny✢

ℹ Chagny Tourist Office 2 r. des Halles; tel: 03 85 87 25 95, fax: 03 85 87 14 44; open Mon–Sat 1000–1200, 1400–1800 (1500–1900 in summer), Sun 0940–1300, in July and Aug according to demand.

 Market: Sun am.

The first village of the Chalonnais and the last village on the Côte d'Or (it lies in Saône-et-Loire *département* rather than in Côte d'Or) is now a busy little industrial centre where Burgundy's great wines are not so much made as bought and sold … and drunk. The town preserves a few charming old buildings, but is better known as a well-placed stopover with some good hotels and a gastronomic restaurant.

Accommodation and food in Chagny

Auberge la Musardière €–€€ *30 route de Chalon; tel: 03 85 87 04 97, fax: 03 85 87 20 51.* Exceptional value for decent, comfortable accommodation, with a garden, a terrace and a good restaurant.

Hôtel-Restaurant Lameloise €€€ *36 pl. d'Armes; tel: 03 85 87 65 65, fax: 03 85 87 03 57.* World-famous Burgundian chef Jaques Lameloise prepares classic dishes with consummate skill and finesse at this grand old Burgundian mansion. It's also a small, luxurious hotel, with memorable breakfasts.

Chalon-sur-Saône✢

ℹ Main Chalon Tourist Office Pl. Chabas, blvd de la République; tel: 03 85 48 37 97, fax: 03 85 48 63 55; open Mon–Sat 0900–1200, 1330–1830 (till 1930 in July and Aug), Sun 1000–1200 (1030–1230, 1500–1800 in July and Aug).

Annexe Galerie du Châtelet, 1 r. du Pont; tel: 03 85 48 79 56; open July and Aug, Tue–Sat 1400–1800.

⊘ There are exits from autoroute A6 for north Chalon and south Chalon. The N6 leads into the centre of town. A maze of one-way streets makes driving difficult in the town centre.

Although it has become a large, industrial town and business centre, this Saône river port has an upbeat, good-life feel to it. The old quarter on the right bank, bound by a triangle of *remparts* (ramparts – though now they are streets running where the old fortifications used to be), keeps many of its historic timbered houses, an impressive Gothic cathedral and cloister and several other traces of a long history. Chalon was a bishopric from the 4th century right up to the French Revolution, and in the 6th century was the residence of the Burgundian kings (as they then were).

The town's two most eminent sons were both here in the same era: the archaeologist and engraver Baron Denont (1747–1825) and Joseph-Nicéphore Niepce, the inventor of photography (1755–1833). Both have museums dedicated to them. **Musée Denon✢✢** has several different types of collections, including 17th- to 19th-century paintings on one floor and local folk culture on another. The ground floor is devoted to extensive local archaeological collections. The best of them are Gallo-Roman, though the highlight is a set of beautiful 18,000-year-old flint tools from nearby Volgu. **Musée Nicéphore Niepce✢✢** contains an intriguing collection of early forms of photography and copying, as well as cameras ranging from the earliest models to the equipment used on the Apollo spacecraft.

From the Musée Nicéphore you can see the river island where there is a 16th-century hospital, full of the Flemish-Burgundian

P Use car parks on the edge of the town centre, just outside the *remparts*.

Guided tours are available from the tourist office.

Musée Denon € *Pl. de l'Hôtel de Ville; tel: 03 85 90 50 50; open daily 0930–1200, 1400–1730, closed Tue.*

Musée Nicéphore Niepce € *28 quai des Messageries; tel: 03 85 48 41 98, fax: 03 85 48 63 20; open daily 0930–1130, 1430–1730 (July and Aug 1000–1200, 1400–1830), closed Tue.*

Roseraie St-Nicolas € *R. Julien Leneuveu, tel: 03 85 41 63 80, fax: 03 85 93 45 96; open daily.*

Winetasting For a taste of all the region's wines, and a chance to buy at a good price, visit the Maison des Vins de la Côte Chalonnaise (*Promenade Ste-Marie; tel: 03 85 41 64 00; open daily 0900–1900*).

craftsmanship and design of the period. A 15th-century tower, Tour du Doyenné, rises from the tip of the island, but don't be deceived: it originally stood by the cathedral on the right bank and was moved here in the 1920s. Flower-lovers should continue on to the left bank and turn left to reach the **Roseraie St-Nicolas✦✦**, where a 5km-footpath winds through a riverside park with a huge rose-garden of 25,000 rose bushes, as well as other flowers, lawns and trees. To enjoy the full effect, visit in June or July.

Accommodation and food in Chalon

Hôtel St-Georges and **Restaurant Le Petit Comptoir** €€€ *32 av. Jean Jaurès; tel: 03 85 48 27 05, fax: 03 85 93 23 88; closed Sat midday.* Best hotel in town and by far the best restaurant, with accomplished preparation of fresh local meat and fish.

Le Bourgogne €€ *28 r. Strasbourg; tel: 03 85 48 89 18, fax: 03 85 93 39 10; closed 4–22 July, Fri, Sun pm and Sat midday.* The name says it all – here's a classic, solid, traditional restaurant serving favourite regional dishes, adequately prepared, in a 17th-century mansion.

Chez Jules € *11 r. Strasbourg; tel: 03 85 48 08 34; closed half of Aug, Sat pm and Sun.* A down-to-earth bistro dishing up delicious terrines, fish dishes and wonderful desserts.

Restaurant Marché € *7 pl. St-Vincent; tel: 03 85 48 62 00; closed Sun pm and Mon.* Nicely placed by the river and the cathedral, this unpretentious eating place excels at popular local specialities such as *oeufs en meurette* and *andouillettes* in mustard sauce.

Above
Mercurey vineyards

Festivals: *Foire Froide* – a huge, ancient trade fair for the buying and selling of furs, pelts and leather at the end of Feb; *Carnaval* – huge street festival with music, parades and a children's costume ball, all from 16–24 Mar; *Foire aux Sauvagines* – an ancient fair again buying and selling furs and pelts at the end of June; *Chalon dans la Rue (Festival Transnational des Artistes de la Rue)* – brilliant dreamlike mix of music and street theatre in the parks, squares and streets of the town at the end of July. The festival has its own creative and beautiful French and English website: *www. chalondanslarue.com/*; International Film Festival in October.

The origins of photography

Press the button and think of Joseph-Nicéphore Niepce. This retired army officer, living in his native Chalon, wondered if an image copied on to a piece of glass, using a lens and a dark box, could be reproduced. In 1822, he proved that it could. Working with Louis Daguerre, the two created the first photograph – now in a museum in Texas. Niepce also invented a prototype jet engine and devised the bicycle brake. There's a statue of Joseph-Nicéphore Niepce on quai Gambetta, in Chalon.

GIVRY✧

Givry Tourist Office *Halle Ronde; tel: 03 85 44 43 36; open in season.*

Follow signs to the *Mairie*, or better, park by the church and walk to the village centre across the road.

Givry was the everyday drink of Henri IV and its name became synonymous with Chalonnais wine, though Mercurey perhaps plays that role today. There are many private cellars for winetasting. Enter the village through an unusual, pompous 18th-century gateway that houses the town hall, and head up to the main street. Givry's oddity is the **Halle Ronde✧**, a 19th-century, circular, two-storey covered market standing on the main street. Built of pale stone, originally a corn market, it's an attractive sight. Inside, a corkscrew of stone steps in the centre leads up to the upper floor. It still serves as a market-place and a winetasting cellar, as well as a tourist office. The village **church✧** is another curiosity. Designed by a civil engineer, Emilan Gauthey (who built the Canal du Centre, which passes close by), it's in the form of a rotunda adorned with domes and semi-domes.

Accommodation and food in Givry

Right
Chalonnais vineyards near Montagny

Hôtellerie de la Halle €€ *2 pl. de la Halle; tel: 03 85 44 32 45, fax: 03 85 44 49 45.* Opposite the Halle Ronde, this *restaurant avec chambres* offers an excellent menu and a wonderfully short wine list of just the five top wines at modest prices. There are four simple bedrooms.

MERCUREY*

ℹ️ **Mercurey Tourist Office** Tel: 03 85 45 22 99, fax: 03 85 45 24 88.

🍷 **Les Vignerons du Caveau de Mercurey** Tel: 03 85 47 20 01; open daily in summer, otherwise at weekends.

🎉 **Festivals:** La St-Vincent – wine festival in Jan; Summer Solstice – ancient festivities on about 19 June; La Paulée – the end-of-harvest celebrations in early Nov.

A large village devoted to making arguably the best red wine of the Côte Chalonnaise and one of the best in Burgundy, Mercurey's wine-making traditions go back at least to the 6th century. The whole of the Côte Chalonnaise district is often known as the Région de Mercurey. There are numerous private winemakers' cellars in the parish. To taste the local produce, pause at the village wine cellars, **Les Vignerons du Caveau de Mercurey***.

Accommodation and food in Mercurey

Hôtellerie du Val d'Or €€ Grande Rue; tel: 03 85 45 13 70; closed most of Dec and Jan. Sumptuous, serious, top-quality rural eating, with duck's liver, fine Charolais beef, good local wines. It's a small hotel as well, with spacious, comfortable and unpretentious rooms.

Suggested tour

Total distance: 81km.

Time: Half a day to 1 day.

Links: At Chagny the route links with the Côte d'Or route (see page 119). The two routes could easily be combined into one longer tour.

Route: From **CHALON-SUR-SAÔNE** ❶, take the N6 to **CHAGNY** ❷. Leave the little town on the D981 travelling southwards and turn off at the sign to enter the tranquil wine village of **Rully**, with its 12th-century fortress. This is the first of the important Chalonnais *appellations*. Stay on the road out of the village on the other side (follow the signs carefully) to reach **MERCUREY** ❸. Leave the village up a hill on the D978, then down the slope for a minute before turning left to **St-Mard-de-Vaux**. You are now in the wonderfully picturesque, old-fashioned area known as the Vallée des Vaux, although the river valley itself is the Upper Orbise. Dedicated to wines, the villages rest on the hillside overlooking a lovely landscape. Follow the lane to the next pretty village, **St-Jean-de-Vaux**. Notice the houses with their neighbouring wine cellars. Cross the Orbise and return via Mellecey to the through road, the D981. Turn right on to the D981 and drive into larger **GIVRY** ❹. Continue on the D981 into **BUXY** ❺, at the end of the Côte Chalonnaise.

Getting out of the car: La Voie Verte (The Green Way) makes an enjoyable outing on foot from either Givry or Buxy. This former rural railway line that runs for 44km through the Charollais and Mâconnais countryside from Givry to Cluny has become a popular leisure activity for residents and visitors. Renamed *La Voie Verte*, it has been transformed by the departmental council into a surfaced rural route, which is ideal for walkers, cyclists and riders. Motor vehicles are forbidden.

Take the D18 from Buxy, through the **Forêt de la Ferté** towards the Saône. Just after Laives is the tiny village of Sermaizey. Take the track on the right up to **St-Martin-de-Laives**, a lovely little 11th-century Romanesque church with fantastic views over Bresse and Charollais. Back on the D18, go under the *autoroute* and into **Sennecey-le-Grand**. Though too close to the *autoroute* for comfort, it's easy to see that this attractive river port on the Saône once cut a grander figure. It still has signs of its feudal Château de Ruffey, now occupied by the town hall. The neo-classical church was also built on part of the castle site. There's a much older church too, the Romanesque and Gothic St-Julien. On the N6 return northward. Beside the road at St-Loup-de-Varennes there's a monument to Joseph-Nicéphore Niepce (*see page 136*). Stay on the N6 back into Chalon.

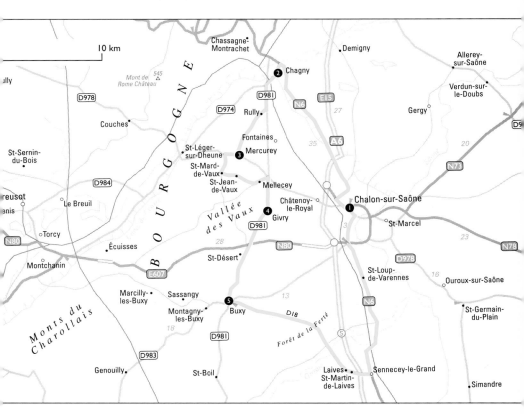

The Mâconnais

Ratings

Medieval architecture	●●●●●
Restaurants	●●●●●
Winetasting	●●●●●
Children	●●●
History	●●●
Museums	●●●
Scenery	●●●
Villages	●●●

The journey from Toumus to Mâcon, both ancient towns on the banks of the broad River Saône, takes less than half an hour to drive. As the river approaches Mâcon, there's an early hint of southern warmth in the air. Mâcon itself, a town which has destroyed much of its heritage, brims with activity and the enjoyment of life. Yet just to the west the hills of the Mâconnais deserve a thorough exploration. Cluny, once so important in European religion and politics, today rests quietly among these green woods, rolling fields and vineyards. Attractive, agricultural, rich in history, this is also one of France's most eminent winemaking regions, producing first-rate whites and modest reds. The greatest of the wines come from a handful of small villages around the enigmatic Solutré rock, jutting like a gigantic monument from the vines.

BRANCION✦✦

Château € *In village; tel: 03 85 51 03 83; open Mar–Nov daily 0900–1900, rest of the year Sun and hols only, 1000–1800.*

A picture-perfect walled village poised on a rocky ridge between two ravines, Brancion makes a striking sight. Walk through the gateway in the ramparts into a wonderful tangle of lanes reaching a medieval **château**✦ of the Dukes of Burgundy, a 15th-century covered market, many lovely old houses and a simple 12th-century Romanesque church clinging to the limit of the spur.

Accommodation and food in Brancion

Hôtel-Restaurant La Montagne de Brancion €€–€€€ *Col de Brancion; tel: 03 85 51 12 40, fax: 03 85 51 18 64; open mid-Mar–mid-Nov only.* Just outside the village, set up high with wonderful panoramic views over the Mâconnais, this immaculate, well-equipped country hotel also has an outstanding restaurant.

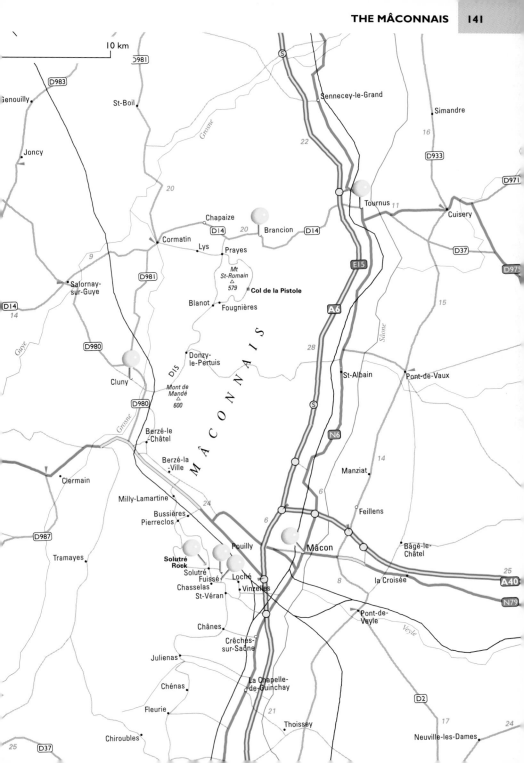

10 km

D983

Genouilly

Joncy

St-Boil

D981

D981

20

Chapaize

Cormatin

D14

20

Brancion

D14

Lys

Prayes

Mt
St-Romain
△
579

Col de la Pistole

Salornay-
sur-Guye

9

D14

14

Blanot

Fougnières

Guye

D980

MÂCONNAIS

Donzy-
le-Pertuis

D15

Cluny

Mont de
Mandé
△
600

D980

Grosne

Berzé-le-
-Châtel

Berzé-la-
-Ville

Clermain

Milly-Lamartine

24

Bussières

Pierreclos

D987

Tramayes

Solutré
Rock

Solutré

Fuissé

Chasselas

St-Véran

Pouilly

Loché

Vinzelles

6

Mâcon

Chânes

Crêches-
sur-Saône

Julienas

Chénas

La Chapelle-
de-Guinchay

Fleurie

21

Thoissey

Chiroubles

D37

25

Grosne

Sennecey-le-Grand

Simandre

16

D933

22

20

Tournus

11

Cuisery

D37

E15

D971

A6

Saône

15

28

St-Albain

Pont-de-Vaux

S

N6

14

Manziat

6

Feillens

8

la Croisée

Bâgé-le-
Châtel

25

A40

N79

Pont-de-
Veyle

Veyle

D2

17

24

Neuville-les-Dames

S

CLUNY✧✧✧

Little is left of the Benedictines' **Abbaye de Cluny**✧✧✧, but it still dominates this village on the River Grosne. The building itself was immense, its church the largest in the world until St Peter's in Rome was built just a few metres longer. All that's left is a handful of ruins and a small, undamaged fragment, yet the minute fraction that remains is not disappointing. Pillars, doorways, corridors, vaults of such celestial proportions speak volumes about the grandeur of the place as it was. The south section of the main transept, with the lovely octagonal *Clocher de l'Eau Benite* ('Holy Water Belfry') and the 13th-century *Farinier* ('Granary'), remains unscathed. Surviving towers mark the edges of the abbey and the **Tour des Fromages**✧✧✧ offers an ideal vantage point from which to imagine how it once looked, in its green, rolling countryside.

To visit the abbey, apply at the **Musée Ochier**✧, the museum of art and archaeology housed in the 15th-century former abbots' palace, Palais de Jean de Bourbon. Several Romanesque houses in the village have superb design and decoration dating from as far back as the 12th century. Alongside the abbey ruins, the **Haras National (National Stud)**✧ has made Cluny a centre of racing and horse trials.

Accommodation and food in Cluny

Bourgogne €€€ *Pl. de l'Abbaye; tel: 03 85 59 00 58, fax: 03 85 59 03 73.* One of Cluny's better but dearer hotel-restaurants, in a green setting right beside the abbey ruins, with opulent rooms and classic Burgundian cuisine served in the elegant restaurant.

Hôtel de l'Abbaye €–€€ *Av. Charles de Gaulle; tel: 03 85 59 11 14, fax: 03 85 59 09 76.* A decent family-run two-star with character, offering good value accommodation and meals.

St-Odilon €€ *Belle Croix; tel: 03 85 59 25 00, fax: 03 85 59 06 18.* Modern building of churchy inspiration, this pleasant, good-value hotel stands quietly amongst the greenery, across the river a short distance from the village.

The power of Cluny

All over Burgundy, dignified Romanesque religious buildings were built in 'the Cluny style'. Now hardly more than a village, agreeably situated beside the little River Grosne, Cluny was once the seat of the largest and most powerful abbey in western Christendom, at a time when kings and emperors could hardly move without religious sanction for their acts, when every act of naked personal ambition could be camouflaged by seeming to be condoned by God. In those days approval gained from Cluny was such a moral victory that it could virtually ensure the triumph of one party over another. Only the Pope had greater influence – but even he would not have risked a split with the Abbot of Cluny, who frequently undertook the role of the Pope's adviser. A number of Popes were themselves from Cluny. Of course, vying for Cluny's intervention was all on the material level, often through generous gifts made to the abbey. Thanks to these donations, it had become immensely wealthy by the 13th century, and the life of the abbots was extremely comfortable.

Cluny Abbey was founded in 910. Benedictine rule was introduced in 926. Cluny's influence reached its height about 200 years later, and remained supreme for centuries. Eventually excessive wealth jeopardised its moral superiority, and in the 15th century the abbey came completely under the control of the French monarchy, who 'appointed' the abbots it wanted and destroyed their influence. The buildings were damaged during the Wars of Religion (1562–98), and finally, during and after the French Revolution, were totally destroyed, being in fact mainly dismantled for their fine dressed stone.

MÂCON**

ℹ **Mâcon Tourist Office** 1 pl. St-Pierre; tel: 03 85 21 07 07, fax: 03 85 40 96 00, e-mail: communication@mairie-macon.fr, www.macon-bourgogne.com/; open June–Sept, Mon–Sat 1000–1900, Sun and hols 1400–1800, rest of the year daily 1000–1800, closed Sun.

🏛 **Musée des Ursulines** € 5 r. des Ursulines/allée de Matisco; tel: 03 85 39 90 38, fax: 03 85 38 20 60; open Tue–Sat 1000–1200, 1400–1800, Sun 1400–1800. Ticket also allows access to Musée Lamartine.

Musée Lamartine € 41 r. Sigorgne; tel: 03 85 30 90 58; open same times as Musée des Ursulines, with joint ticket.

Maison Mâconnaise des Vins € 484 av. Maréchal de Lattre de Tassigny; tel: 03 85 38 36 70; daily 0800–2100.

A large and industrial town, centre of the region's wine trade, Mâcon might not seem an obvious place to pause. It has long had a proletarian and anti-authoritarian image – it embraced Protestantism during the Religious Wars (1562–98), keenly supported the French Revolution, and it was a trader from Mâcon who bought and demolished Cluny Abbey. Nowadays it has enticing riverside quays lined with cafés, and plenty of enjoyable events, especially street theatre and jazz concerts. It has good value shops, hotels and restaurants and makes an excellent base for a tour of Beaujolais or Bresse, as well as the Mâconnais.

For an inspiring overview, stand on the Pont St-Laurent, the long, fortified medieval bridge across the Saône. A few other historic buildings survived the town's French Revolutionary fervour. It's worth visiting the **Musée des Ursulines (Ursuline Museum)***, housed in a lovely 17th-century Ursuline convent. Across the street, **Musée Lamartine (Lamartine Museum)*** honours Mâcon's most famous son, the aristocratic but radical Romantic poet Alphonse Lamartine (1790–1869), much admired in France. The museum, in the 18th-century mansion Hôtel Senecé, one of the family's homes, today houses not only memorabilia of the great poet but a wide range of artworks, tapestries and period furniture. **Maison Mâconnaise des Vins****, alongside the rousingly named Place de la Déclaration des Droits de l'Homme (Declaration of the Rights of Man Square), is the place to learn about, taste or buy Burgundy's wines.

Accommodation and food in Mâcon

Hôtel Bellevue €€€ 416 quai Lamartine; tel: 03 85 21 04 04, fax: 03 85 21 04 02. A little pricey, but this is the place if you want to be close to the best of Mâcon – the river, quai Lamartine, the old quarter. Well-equipped, with traditional comfort, and a good restaurant.

Hôtel Terminus €€ 91 r. Victor Hugo; tel: 03 85 39 17 11, fax: 03 85 38 02 75. Modern, family-run hotel with pool, garden and restaurant, close to the town centre.

Restaurant Le Charollais € 71 r. Rambuteau; tel: 03 85 38 36 23; closed Sun pm and Mon, and end July. Excellent classic Burgundian cooking at modest prices, served in a traditional ambience with beamed ceilings and copperware hanging on the walls.

Restaurant Pierre €€ 7–9 r. Dufour; tel: 03 85 38 14 23, fax: 03 85 39 84 04, closed Sun pm and Mon. Arguably Mâcon's best, yet prices are reasonable at this rustic-style restaurant specialising in rich, luxurious cooking, with quenelles de brochet and Charolais beef.

Opposite
Solutré Rock

POUILLY-FUISSÉ AND THE VINEYARDS❖❖

Pouilly-Fuissé Tourist Information *Office de Tourisme de la Route des Vins Mâconnais-Beaujolais, 6 r. Dufour, Mâcon; tel: 03 85 38 09 99, fax: 03 85 39 88 48.*

This southern corner of the Mâconnais, clustered around Solutré Rock (*see below*), merges into northern Beaujolais (*see page 158*). This is pretty countryside: steep, plunging hills cut into hundreds of oddly shaped vineyards, all cultivating Chardonnay grapes. From these fields come the finest of the region's wines. The district is centred on the village of Pouilly, an unassuming hamlet below picturesque Solutré village. Pouilly, with its neighbour Fuissé, is one of the great white wine *appellations* of France – though great whites come from several surrounding communes as well, such as Chaintré, Vergisson, Vinzelles and Loché. Rustic little Chasselas has given its name not to a wine but to a variety of eating grape now found on dinner tables throughout the world. One of the villages, the hillside hamlet of St-Véran, with a pretty church and lovely views, produces excellent Chardonnay wine (spelled 'St-Vérand').

SOLUTRÉ ROCK❖❖

Musée Départementale de Préhistoire €€ *Tel: 03 85 35 85 24, fax: 03 85 35 86 83; open Feb–Apr and Oct–Nov 1000–1200, 1400–1700 (closed Tue), May 1000–1200, 1400–1800 (closed Tue), June–Sept daily 1000–1900, closed Dec and Jan.*

Sharply piercing the Pouilly vineyards and soaring 500m into the air, the narrow wedge-shaped Solutré Rock is the centre of a mystery. Around the base of the rock a phenomenal quantity of animal bones has been discovered. Mammoth and bison, reindeer and especially horse skeletons were found in a layer up to 2m thick and covering an area of 4 000 sq m. The explanation remains the subject of academic debate, but the rock was clearly of importance to prehistoric people, if only as a hunting site. Dug into the base of the rock, the **Musée Départementale de Préhistoire (Departmental Prehistory Museum)**❖❖ displays the finds and reveals that the site was used for ambushing animals for over 25,000 years.

Tournus❖❖

ℹ **Tournus Tourist Office** 2 pl. Camot; tel: 03 85 51 13 10, fax: 03 85 32 18 21, www.perso. wanadoo.fr/tournus/; open Mon–Sat 0900–1200, 1400–1800.

🏨 **Hôtel Dieu and Musée Greuze** €€ 21 r. de l'Hôpital; tel: 03 85 51 23 50; open Apr–Oct 1100–1800 (closed Tue).

Ancienne Abbaye/Église St-Philibert € R. Thibaudet; tel: 03 85 51 13 10; open daily: variable opening times. Guided tours in summer.

Musée Bourgignon € Pl. de l'Abbaye; tel: 03 85 51 29 68; open Apr–Oct 0900–1200, 1400–1800 (closed Tue), rest of the year closed.

Walled Tournus (the 's' is silent) is a small, quiet and old-fashioned town, once a Roman fort, which looks from its riverside *quais* over the curving Saône. Arcaded sidewalks and shopfronts, and some imposing mansions, make the town centre an attractive place to stroll or shop at its delicious *pâtisseries* and *épiceries*. Close to quai du Midi, modest little 12th- to 15th-century Église Madeleine has a superbly simple interior: whitewashed, almost without decoration. The 17th-century **Hôtel Dieu (Charity Hospital)**❖❖❖ preserves many of its original features, including a traditional apothecary, and served as a hospital right up to 1982. The patients' neat, heavily curtained wooden beds are arranged in three wards, one for women, another for men, the third for soldiers, all set around a chapel. The building also provides the setting for the **Musée Greuze**❖, where works by the artist Jean-Baptiste Greuze (1725–1805), son of the hospital's builder, are displayed.

At the other end of town stands the huge **Ancienne Abbaye**❖❖❖. Its **Église St-Philibert** is unusual: three churches built on top of each other in the course of a couple of centuries – 9th to 11th – creating a single curious and original building in pure Romanesque style, though with castellations as if to repel attackers. Enter through a lovely dark vestibule, a forest of pillars under a low ceiling, which opens out into the light, tall, magnificently sturdy, yet elegant church with thick, unadorned brick columns. The central nave is barrel-vaulted strangely, crosswise, but the side aisles are rib-vaulted, an odd combination. And the stained glass, though modern and out of keeping, is not unattractive either. Standing on top of the vestibule is another church, St-Michel, reached by an outdoor staircase. Extraordinarily, this part of the abbey was built before the nave of the main church. Don't miss the cloisters and other abbey buildings.

Musée Bourgignon (Burgundy Museum)❖, alongside the abbey, is a collection of displays on peasant life, folk costume and traditional interiors spread through the rooms of a 17th-century mansion.

Right
Église St-Philibert cloister

Accommodation and food in Tournus

Hôtel-Restaurant de Greuze €€€ *5–6 pl. de l'Abbaye; tel: 03 85 51 77 77, fax: 03 85 51 77 23.* Grandiose eating and luxurious accommodation at this long-established hotel close to the abbey. It's expensive but has character and excellent *pâté en croûte, quenelles de brochet* and *poulet de Bresse.*

Hôtel-Restaurant Le Rempart €€ *2–4 av. Gambetta; tel: 03 85 51 10 56, fax: 03 85 51 77 22, www.lerempart.com/.* Closer to the abbey is a pricier, solidly reliable mid-range hotel with a classy restaurant acclaimed for superb Burgundian cuisine. Frogs' legs, pigs' trotters and Bresse chicken are specialities. There's also a cheaper bistro-style alternative.

Hôtel-Restaurant Le Sauvage €–€€ *Pl. Champ de Mars, tel: 03 85 51 14 45, fax: 03 85 32 10 27.* A little more modest than the others, but comfortable and satisfying and not badly placed. Good value.

Suggested tour

Total distance: 60km, plus a 15km detour.

Time: 1 day.

Links: At Mâcon and at the village of St-Véran on the D31 this route connects with the Beaujolais (*see page 158*).

Route: From **TOURNUS** ❶, take the winding D14 for 13km west to **BRANCION** ❷. Further on (passing a dolmen on the right), at the end of a forest drive, turn left (for the D187 via Prayes).

Detour: Stay on the D14 to **Chapaize**, dominated by an 11th-century church with a distinctive square bell tower. Keep going into **Cormatin** and visit the town's elegant château. Take the D187 through **Lys**, a small and very traditional village, back to the main route.

The D187 climbs up and down through a handsome *forêt* around **Mont-St-Romain**. At **Col de la Pistole**, where the road forks, follow the D446 on the right. Soon after, on the right, there's a steep access road to the summit of Mont-St-Romain, 579m high and with good views. Deep caves and grottoes underneath the mountain can be entered just by **Fougnières**. The road reaches **Blanot**, where, among the narrow lanes, old cottages and stone walls of the tiny village, are a 12th-century Romanesque church and remnants of a 14th-century abbey in the Cluny style. You reach the D15 at **Donzy-le-Pertuis**, an interesting village with very old houses, an 11th-century church and a ruined 12th-century Cluniac priory. Turn right for **CLUNY** ❸.

The D980 runs south 5km to the N79, where you turn left (direction Mâcon) for the left turn into **Berzé-le-Châtel** with its 13th-century feudal castle. From here take the minor D17 into **Berzé-la-Ville**. A few moments from the village on the D220, passing under the main road (N79), you reach **Milly-Lamartine**. Driving through Milly-Lamartine, you come to Pierreclos, with its château, and take the left turn to continue through villages on narrow lanes to the massive and intriguing **SOLUTRÉ ROCK** ❹.

It's hard to find the right road among the twisting lanes of this steep and varied countryside. It's not important to see every wine village, but rather to explore this acclaimed vineyard country. Aim for **POUILLY** village ❺, join the D172 into **FUISSÉ** ❻, then to little **Chasselas** and **St-Véran**. Either take the D31 to the busy N6 for a return into **MÂCON** ❼, or find your way back to the town on the country roads through wine villages **Loché** and **Vinzelles**.

10 km

D981

D983

nouilly

St-Boil

Sennecey-le-Grand

Simandre

16

Joncy

22

D933

D971

20

Chapaize

20 Brancion

D14

Tournus

1

11

Cuisery

D14

Cormatin

Lys

Prayes

E15

D37

D975

9

Mt St-Romain
△
579 **Col de la Pistole**

Salornay-
sur-Guye

D981

A6

15

D14

14

Blanot

Fougnières

MÂCONNAIS

28

D980

Donzy-
le-Pertuis

St-Albain

Pont-de-Vaux

D15

Cluny 3

Mont de
Mandé
△
600

D980

Berzé-le-
Châtel

N6

S

Berzé-la-
Ville

14

Manziat

Clermain

6

Milly-Lamartine

24

Bussières

Pierreclos

6

Feillens

D987

Mâcon

Bâgé-le-
Châtel

Tramayes

**Solutré
Rock** 4

Pouilly

Solutré 5
Fuissé 6

Loché

la Croisée

25

A40

Chasselas

St-Véran

Vinzelles

8

N79

Pont-de-
Veyle

Chânes

Crêches-
sur-Saône

Julienas

Chénas

La Chapelle-
de-Guinchay

D2

Fleurie

21

17

24

Thoissey

Chiroubles

Neuville-les-Dames

25

D37

Beaujolais

Ratings

Restaurants	●●●●●
Winetasting	●●●●●
History	●●●●○
Scenery	●●●●○
Villages	●●●●○
Children	●●●○○
Folklore	●●●○○
Shopping	●●●○○

A confusing tangle of tiny meandering lanes covers the charming hills and vineyards like lace. Many of the great names of wine turn out to be hamlets rather than villages, or even a cluster of cottages at a crossroads. Rising from the west bank of the great valley of the Saône, Beaujolais is a long narrow massif, its hills and terraces pretty with woods and vineyards in which Gamay is almost the only grape variety grown. Make a point of calling in at some of the *crus*, those ten small villages that produce the finest of the region's wines. A signposted *Route du Beaujolais* makes its way among the villages where local wine can be tasted. The multitude of narrow roads provides any number of alternative routes. Handsome wooded hills, ideal for walking and cycling, rise above the vine country.

BEAUJEU❖❖

ℹ️ **Tourist offices in Beaujolais** There are all-year-round tourist offices at Beaujeu and Villefranche-sur-Saône. There are summer-season tourist offices in some larger Beaujolais villages.

A long, narrow little town attractively sited between vines and woods, Beaujeu was the old château-village from which the whole region took its name. The town has the remains of the castle of the local Beaujolais nobility, who possessed Beaujolais from the 9th century onwards. The most renowned member of the family was Anne de Beaujeu, who acquired Beaujolais by marrying its then owner, Pierre de Bourbon. The daughter of Louis XI, Anne was a 15th-century regent of France while her brother Charles VIII was too young to take the throne.

Focal point for the visitor is pl. de l'Hôtel de Ville, the square beside the town's 12th-century church. In an attractive half-timbered building, **Les Sources du Beaujolais**❖ is an intriguing and entertaining family attraction telling the story of Beaujeu and the Beaujolais. Across the road is the Hôtel de Ville, housing the **Musée Marius Audin**❖❖, an eclectic museum of folk culture with a good collection of antique dolls

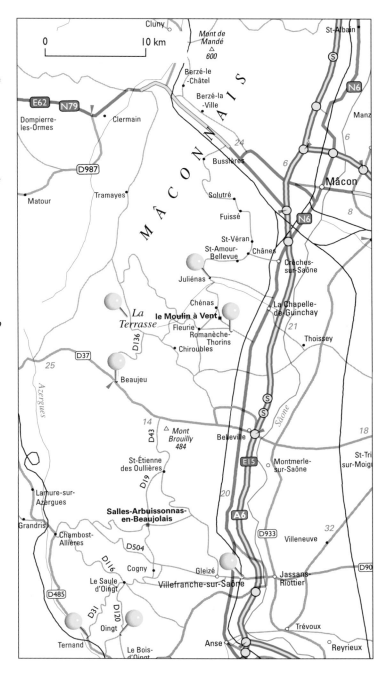

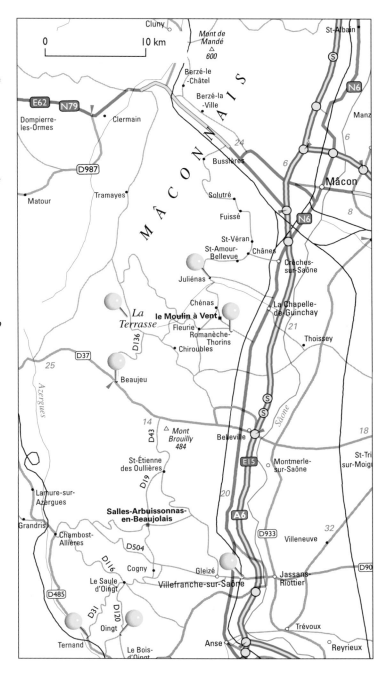 *www.beaujolais.
net/eng/page* (masses
of information, facts, news
about Beaujolais, in
English); *www.beaujolais-
wines.com/* (informative site
of online wine merchants
Les Vins du Beaujolais);
www.francebeaujolais.com
(commercial site with lots
of information and a
search engine).

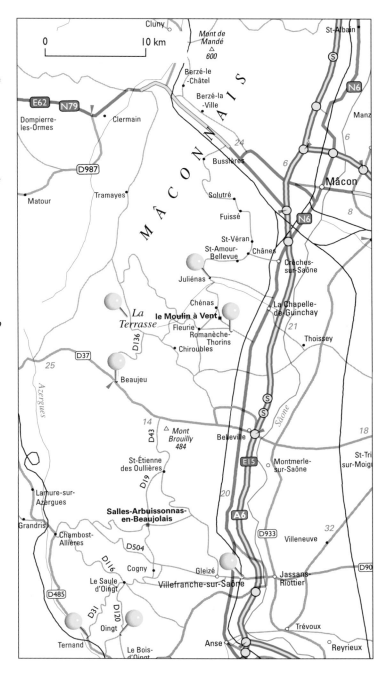 **Beaujeu Tourist
Office** *Pl. de l'Hôtel de
Ville; tel/fax: 04 74 69 22
88, e-mail: beaujeu.
beaujolais@wanadoo.fr,
www.perso.wanadoo.fr/
beaujeu.beaujolais; open
Mar–Dec 1000–1200,
1400–1800, closed Tue,
Jan–Feb office closed but all
queries are answered.*

 **Les Sources du
Beaujolais** €€ *Pl. de
l'Hôtel de Ville; tel: 04 74 69
20 56, e-mail: sources.
beaujolais@wanadoo.fr;
open same hours as Musée
Marius Audin.*

Musée Marius Audin €
*Pl. de l'Hôtel de Ville
(entrance in pl. Grand'han);
tel/fax: 04 74 69 22 88;
open Mar–Apr and Oct–Dec
1000–1200, 1400–1800,
closed Tue, May–Sept daily
1000–1900, Jan and Feb
closed.*

Map:

0   10 km

Cluny
Mont de
Mandé
△
600
St-Albain

Berzé-le
-Châtel

Berzé-la
-Ville

E62 N79
N6

Dompierre-
les-Ormes
Clermain
Manz

D987

Bussières

6

Matour
Tramayes
Solutré
Mâcon

Fuissé

8

St-Véran
St-Amour-
Bellevue
Chânes

N6

Crèches-
sur-Saône

Juliénas

Chénas
La Chapelle-
de-Guinchay

*La
Terrasse*
le Moulin à Vent
Fleurie
Romanèche-
Thorins
Thoissey

21

Chiroubles

D37

25
D136

Beaujeu

Azergues

14

Mont
Brouilly
484

Belleville

S
S

Saône

18

St-Étienne
des Oullières

D43
D19

Montmerle-
sur-Saône

St-Tri
sur-Moig

E15

20

Lamure-sur-
Azergues

A6

Grandris

Salles-Arbuissonnas-
en-Beaujolais

D933
Villeneuve

32

Chambost-
Allières
D504

D116
Cogny
Gleizé
Jassans
Riottier

D90

Le Saule
d'Oingt
Villefranche-sur-Saône

D485

D31
D120

Oingt

Ternand
Le Bois-
d'Oingt
Anse
Trévoux
Reyrieux

MACONNAIS

24

6

Manz

Caveau des Beaujolais-Villages
€€ *Underneath tourist office and museum, pl. de l'Hôtel de Ville; tel: 04 74 04 81 18; open daily 1030–1300, 1400–1930.*

An inclusive ticket (€€) can be purchased at either of the Beaujeu attractions giving entrance to both, plus a free tasting at the Caveau.

Festivals: last Sun in Mar – *Fête des Conscrits* (Army Conscripts Festival); last Sun in Apr – *Foire de Printemps* (Spring Fair): wine, local produce and crafts; 3rd Sun in July – *Foire à la Brocante* (Secondhand Fair); eve of 3rd Thur in Nov – *Les Sarmentelles de Beaujeu*, the Beaujolais Nouveau celebration; 2nd Sun in Dec – auction of the wines of the Hospices de Beaujeu.

Beaujolais Nouveau

Every year, at midnight on the third Thursday in November, the new Beaujolais wine, made from the freshly harvested grapes, is released. It's a time of celebration. The festive mood continues to the end of December, when one is supposed to stop drinking Beaujolais Nouveau and get to work on the region's proper wine. Not all Beaujolais producers make Nouveau, and Beaujolais Nouveau can only come from the two *appellations* Beaujolais and Beaujolais-Villages. There's nothing new about Beaujolais Nouveau: it's been around for centuries. In fact, until the invention of the airtight wine bottle and cork stopper 300 years ago, most wine was drunk *en primeur*. So Beaujolais Nouveau, with its dew-fresh taste, cherry-red colour and bunch-of-flowers aroma, is the authentic traditional Beaujolais. Unlike most reds, it should be drunk chilled, and doesn't need to breathe. Just uncork and enjoy.

and displays of 'snapshots' of life in Beaujeu, such as the interior of a peasant home. Underneath it, the **Caveau des Beaujolais-Villages****, beneath a low vaulted stone ceiling, is an atmospheric spot to sample the Beaujolais *crus*.

Right
Beaujolais vineyards

Accommodation and food in Beaujeu

Hôtel-Restaurant Anne de Beaujeu €€ *28 r. de la République; tel: 04 74 04 87 58, fax: 04 74 69 22 13.* Anne de Beaujeu will be remembered thanks to this good, reliable *restaurant avec chambres* named after her. In the heart of Beaujeu, it's in a fine 19th-century mansion with lovely grounds.

JULIÉNAS✥

Le Cellier de la Vieille Église €
In village centre; tel/fax: 04 74 04 42 98; open daily (Oct–May closed Tue) 0945–1200, 1430–1830.

At the entrance to pleasant Juliénas, visitors may be startled by the large image of a reclining Dionysus. **Le Cellier de la Vieille Église**✥ – the wine cellars inside the old deconsecrated church – is now the main place to taste and buy the wines of the village. Juliénas is one of the top Beaujolais *crus*, and one of the local wines which can be aged for a year or two as well as being enjoyed young and fresh.

The 12 Beaujolais *appellations*

The 10 *crus* – Brouilly, Chénas (the smallest, with 260 hectares), Chiroubles, Côte de Brouilly, Fleurie, Juliénas, Morgon, Moulin à Vent, Regnié, St-Amour.

The 2 non-*crus* – Most of the region's wine is in these *appellations*: Beaujolais (by far the largest, with nearly 10,000 hectares) and Beaujolais-Villages. (*Cru*, literally 'growth', means a particular place or vineyard and its wines.)

Right
Cave de Juliénas

Accommodation and food in Juliénas

Chez La Rose €€ *Village centre; tel: 04 74 04 41 20, fax: 04 74 04 49 29, e-mail: chez-la-rose@wanadoo.fr, www.chez-la-rose.fr.* This appealing hotel-restaurant in the centre of the village offers elegant local cooking at affordable prices; the accommodation is set back behind a courtyard.

OINGT✦✦✦

The tiny village of Oingt captures all the charm of the Pays des Pierres Dorées ('the land of golden stone') in the southern part of Beaujolais. Its narrow streets, lined with beautiful old houses, climb to the circular tower and the old church which was once the chapel of the ruined castle. Walk into the enclosed medieval village through a fine gateway and inside find a visual delight of lanes, steps and houses, everything made of the rough, dark yellow stone looking like gold ore. At the top of the village, by the church, there's a wonderful vista of the vine-draped lower country and the wooded crests of the hills.

ROMANÈCHE-THORINS✦✦✦

Musée du Compagnonnage € Village centre; tel: 03 85 35 22 02, fax: 03 85 35 86 83; open Apr–Oct 1400–1800 daily except Tue, July and Aug daily 1000–1800.

Moulin à Vent € Domaine du Moulin à Vent; tel: 03 85 35 58 91, fax: 03 85 35 59 39; open approximately 0900–1700.

Hameau du Vin €€€ La Gare; tel: 03 85 35 22 22, fax: 03 85 35 21 18, e-mail: info@hameau-du-vin.tm.fr, www.hameau-du-vin.tm.fr; open daily 0900–1800 for guided visits lasting around 2 hours. Winetasting included in the entrance fee. Bistro-style restaurant with snacks and drinks on site.

Touro-Parc €€€ La Maison Blanche; tel: 03 85 35 51 53, fax: 03 85 35 52 34, e-mail: touroparc@ wanadoo.fr, www.touroparc. com; open Mar–Oct, daily 0900–1900, rest of the year zoo only, 0900–1200, 1330–1730.

This large *commune* is the most prestigious wine name in Beaujolais, even though there is no wine actually called Romanèche-Thorins. In the village, the Musée Départemental du Compagnonnage Pierre-François Guillon, usually known simply as the **Musée du Compagnonnage (Museum of Trade Guilds)**✦, has documents on the history of the travelling, skilled craftsmen of the past. Away from the centre, on the road to Chénas, stands the famed **Moulin à Vent**✦✦✦, the 15th-century windmill which gives its name to the greatest of Beaujolais wines. Beautifully restored and maintained, today it's a listed *Monument Historique*.

At the other end of the village, in the restored turn-of-the-century former Romanèche-Thorins railway station, the **Hameau du Vin**✦✦✦ (**The Wine Hamlet**) is one of the most interesting and enjoyable attractions in Beaujolais. Run by wine merchants Georges Duboeuf, its lavish and fascinating displays arranged in 16 rooms tell the whole story of Beaujolais wine, complete with props and tasting.

Also within this surprising commune, although it is on the other side of the N6 in the district called La Maison Blanche, is **Touro-Parc**✦, a big and popular family leisure park divided into five *Rêves* (dreams). These are devoted to rare animals (over 1 000 species, including a pair of white tigers), water rides, a museum, tropical birds and a restaurant complex.

Accommodation and food in Romanèche-Thorins

Les Maritonnes €€ *Rte de Fleurie; tel: 03 85 35 51 70, fax: 03 85 35 58 14, e-mail: mariton@wanadoo.fr, www.maritonnes.com.* This is a long-established favourite with French food lovers. Well placed and easy to get to, with a pretty garden, comfortable accommodation and swimming pool.

˙ERNAND✠✠

Quiet and unspoiled on its hill, medieval Ternand is a haven of tranquil history. Wander up its lanes between ancient houses. At the top of the village stands a fortified church – inside, there's a 13th-century Virgin Mary in painted wood. The Ternand Ville d'Antan (Ternand of Yesteryear) Association is restoring and reviving the historic folk traditions, including December's *Fête des Lampions* (Candlelight Festival), a colourful procession in medieval costume honouring the Virgin Mary.

ˍA TERRASSE✠✠

This remarkable viewpoint, on a bend in the D18 just east of the village of Avenas, is a lovely spot, but almost too high to give a perspective on Beaujolais: from here the pretty vine-covered hills look like a patch of flattish land far below, while instead the eye drifts over more distant hills and valleys – the Saône Valley, the Bresse *plateau*, the Jura, sometimes the Alps. A few paces from the viewing table, the *vignerons* (vinegrowers and winemakers) of Chiroubles have a *chalet de dégustation* for tasting their Beaujolais *crus* wines.

Accommodation and food in La Terrasse

La Terrasse €€ *On the D18; tel: 04 74 69 90 79; open daily Mar–Sept but may be closed during the rest of the year.* Numerous dishes, large and small, are available at this well-placed roadside eatery at the La Terrasse viewpoint.

Right
Village of Oingt

VILLEFRANCHE-SUR-SAÔNE**

ⓘ Villefranche Tourist Office *290 rte de Thizy; tel: 04 74 68 05 18, fax: 04 74 68 44 91; open Mon–Sat 0900–1200, 1330–1800 (July and Aug 0900–1200, 1430–1900), Sun 0900–1200 (summer only). Guided tours every Sat in July and Aug at 1000.*

🅷 Le Nautile €€ *Opposite Géant Casino hypermarket off the N6; tel: 04 74 68 01 16; open daily.*

A big, bustling, yet rather handsome walled town on the busy Saône Valley highway into Lyon, this became the regional capital of the Lords of Beaujeu after the 13th century. In its old centre, and especially along the main street, r. Nationale, Villefranche retains much charm and a good deal of local importance as the commercial centre of the Beaujolais wine trade. Along the r. Nationale you'll find fine food and wine specialist stores and scores of stylish clothes boutiques are housed in tall, narrow, historic buildings. The street passes right in front of the Flamboyant Gothic façade of Église Nôtre Dame-des-Marais. Note too the Renaissance 'Maison d'Italien' complete with a *Cour d'Honneur* (No 407), and the 15th-century staircase round the corner at 17 r. Grenette. Other attractions in and around town include **Le Nautile***, a water fun park with slides, toboggans, pools and sauna.

Accommodation and food in Villefranche-sur Saône

Right
Beaujolais vineyards

Below
Asparagus on a market stall in Villefranche-sur-Saône

Hotels and restaurants are clustered around r. d'Anse and av. de la Libération, at the south end of r. Nationale. For cheaper, chain hotels look along av. Théodore Braun, east of *autoroute* A6.

Hôtel Plaisance €€ *96 av. de la Libération; tel: 04 74 65 33 52, fax: 04 74 62 02 89.* A popular town-centre hotel, welcoming and comfortable, with secure parking and decent dining room.

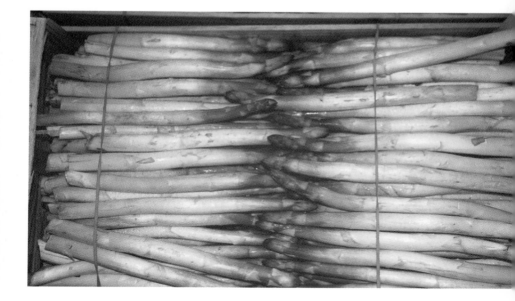

Suggested tour

Auberge du Cep €€
Pl. de l'Église, Fleurie;
tel: 04 74 04 10 77, fax: 04
74 04 10 28. A modest-
looking restaurant in the
centre of this acclaimed
wine village, Le Cep has a
selection of interesting
menus, each based on the
local areas – for example,
De Bresse en Dombes or *De
Bourgogne en Val de Saône*
or, cheapest and closest to
home, *Comme en
Beaujolais*, with a *fricassée
de boudin*, roasted
andouillette à la moutarde
and local cheeses. The
standard is exceptionally
high and booking is
essential.

Total distance: About 60km, plus a 30km detour.

Time: Touring in Beaujolais takes patience. Driving is slow on the narrow, winding roads of the area. This route can be completed quickly in one long day, or more comfortably in two or three days, allowing time for a couple of winetastings and to visit the sights.

Links: At Mâcon and on the D31 this route connects with the Mâconnais (*see page 148*). At Villefranche-sur-Saône it links with the West of Lyon route (*see page 183*).

Route: Leave Mâcon heading south on the N6. At Crêches-sur-Saône, about 10km from Mâcon, turn right on to the D31 for **St-Véran**, considered to be in the Mâconnais rather than Beaujolais, to cover the white wine of the surrounding villages (*see The Mâconnais, page 145*). The D31 may be considered the approximate northern limit of the Beaujolais, which has no clearly defined boundaries. Turn left here (D17e) for rustic **St-Amour-Bellevue**, the most northerly village within the Beaujolais. It's one of the 10 Beaujolais *crus*, even though it produces mainly Beaujolais Blanc, white wines of style. Continue into **JULIÉNAS** ❶. Take the road to **Chénas**, a small community – another of the Beaujolais *crus* – and on via the D266, signposted Romanèche. The road passes the famed **Moulin à Vent**, the windmill that gives its name to the greatest of Beaujolais *appellations* (pause for winetasting inside); it stands within the *commune* of **ROMANÈCHE-THORINS** ❷, where the road now arrives. Follow signs to reach the Hameau du Vin (*see page 154*).

The Hameau du Vin is just off the route de Fleurie, leading into the old wine village of **Fleurie**. The distinctive little chapel perched high on a ridge above the village is called La Madone. To reach it, take the D32 uphill from the village, then take a sharp turn left for the chapel – it gives dramatic views. Now stay on the D32 as it climbs up, and follow it round on to the lofty D26. Where this meets the D18, turn right. The road soars up, reaching the **LA TERRASSE** ❸ viewpoint at a sharp bend. The restaurant and snackbar here make a good place to pause.

You're now in the wooded hills of Beaujolais' higher ground. Reaching the winding and attractive D136, turn left through pleasant woods down to **BEAUJEU** ❹. Either on the D37 or on one of the parallel lesser roads follow the valley down, out of the woods again, towards the foot of **Mont Brouilly** (Brouilly and Côtes de Brouilly are Beaujolais *crus*). Access to the summit of the little 'mountain' – once part of a volcano – is by a steep road off the D43. At the top there's a small chapel to which the local vinegrowers make a pilgrimage each year on 8 September.

Right
Wine mural

Follow the D43 south, turning right on to the D19 at St-Étienne de Oullières. Stay resolutely on this road through all its twists and turns. Go through Salles-Arbuissonnas-en-Beaujolais, cross the D504 and continue past Cogny: this is a lovely road of trees and views. Soon you'll come to the meeting of five minor roads at **Le Saule d'Oingt**. This is not a village, simply a high, attractive pass among peaceful meadows. Here, take the D120 into **OINGT** ❺ .

Just south of Oingt, don't miss the right turn, the D96, to descend through St-Laurent d'Oingt to the Azergues Valley. Turn right on to the D485, the wide, fast road that runs along the wooded valley, and drive just 2km to reach **TERNAND** ❻ . The part of the village on the main road is called Les Grandes Planches, and although the tourist office is here, this is not what we have come to see. Turn left here at the sign for the Village Médiéval to reach the historic village 2km away.

Return straight to Le Saule d'Oingt on the D31, or take the short detour.

Detour: From Ternand, continue along the pleasant D485 to Chambost-Allières. Here there are few vines as this part of Beaujolais lives on timber, not wine. At the entrance to the village turn right on to the steep D116, which climbs quickly to higher ground. You might think you had left the Beaujolais and crossed directly into the Auvergne or the Pyrenees, with cattle grazing in airy green meadows among pine forests and not a grape in sight. The winding road gives a succession of wonderful views. Pause, and there is perfect silence but for the whispering of the air itself. After 23km the detour arrives at Le Saule d'Oingt.

Below
Central market in Villefranche-sur-Saône

Following the signs to Villefranche, use either the D31 or D504 (via Cogny) to drive through attractive 'golden stone' country into **VILLEFRANCHE-SUR-SAÔNE** ❼ .

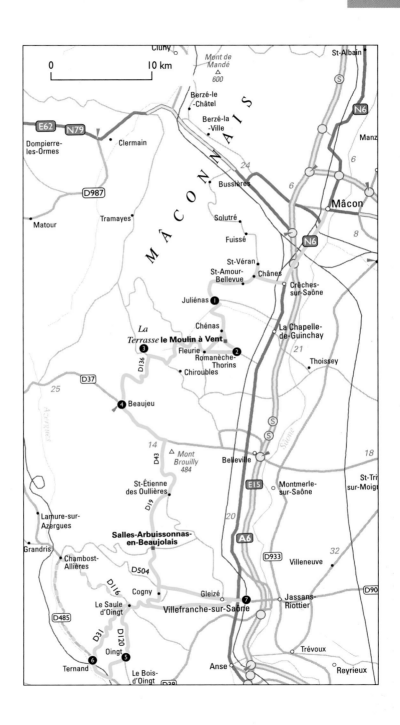

0   10 km

Cluny

Mont de Mandé △ 600

St-Albain

Berzé-le-Châtel

Berzé-la-Ville

E62   N79

Dompierre-les-Ormes

Clermain

Manz

N6

D987

24

Bussières

6

6

Mâcon

Matour

Tramayes

Solutré

8

Fuissé

St-Véran

St-Amour-Bellevue

Chânes

Crêches-sur-Saône

N6

Juliénas ❶

La Terrasse le Moulin à Vent ❸

Chénas

Fleurie

Romanèche-Thorins

Chiroubles

Chânes

La Chapelle-de-Guinchay

21

Thoissey

D36

D37

25

❹ Beaujeu

Azergues

14

△ Mont Brouilly 484

Belleville

S

S

Saône

18

D43

St-Étienne des Oullières

St-Tri sur-Moig

E15

Montmerle-sur-Saône

D19

20

Lamure-sur-Azergues

A6

Salles-Arbuissonnas-en-Beaujolais

Grandris

Chambost-Allières

D933

Villeneuve

32

D90

D504

Cogny

Gleizé

Jassans-Riottier

D116

Le Saule d'Oingt

❼

Villefranche-sur-Saône

D485

D31

D120

Oingt ❺

Trévoux

❻

Ternand

Anse

Reyrieux

Le Bois-d'Oingt

D28

M Â C O N N A I S

The Loire in Burgundy

Ratings

River views	●●●●●
Museums	●●●●○
Restaurants	●●●●○
Children	●●●○○
History	●●●○○
Scenery	●●●○○
Wildlife	●●●○○
Winetasting	●●●○○

Upstream from the famed westward-flowing Loire Valley of islands and châteaux and royal history, the Loire first flows north for hundreds of miles from the Massif Central, and marks the western limit of Burgundy and the Loire Valley region. Our riverside route is mostly in the Nièvre *département*, occasionally crossing into the Cher *département* on the other side to taste the local wines. All the way up to Nevers, the regional capital, the river is wide and brisk, spanned by fine old bridges, edged by industrious small towns with dignified stone embankments and quaysides. Once teeming with small businesses and busy docks, today the Loire runs peacefully under its pearly skies. In the backcountry rise wild, wooded hills and the Morvan plateau, but down by the water's edge are gently undulating pastures and vineyards and small farms, and an air of centuries-old civilisation and refinement.

BRIARE✦✦✦

ⓘ **Regional Tourist Office** Most of the route runs through the area covered by the Comité Départementale du Tourisme de la Nièvre: *3 r. du Sort, Nevers; tel: 03 86 36 39 80, fax: 03 86 36 36 63, e-mail: cdt-nièvre58@wanadoo.fr.*

A tranquil town clinging to the east bank of the Loire, at the meeting point of handsome 17th-century canals, Briare (sometimes now calling itself Briare-le-Canal) has become a centre for boating. Its loveliest sight is the great Pont Canal (Canal Bridge) that carries the calm waters of a canal over the fast swirl of the River Loire. The imposing wrought-iron bridge (662m long) dates from 1890, and has an elegance and style that belies its purely functional purpose. The waterside pavement makes a pleasing and unusual stroll to the other side of the Loire and back.

The waterways, which linked the Atlantic, the Mediterranean and Paris, made Briare a prosperous small town. **La Maison des Deux Marines (House of the Two Waterways)✦** is all about the role of the canals and the river in the fortunes of the town, which in the 18th and 19th centuries became a great centre of trade and transportation as every type of merchandise was carried through here. About a

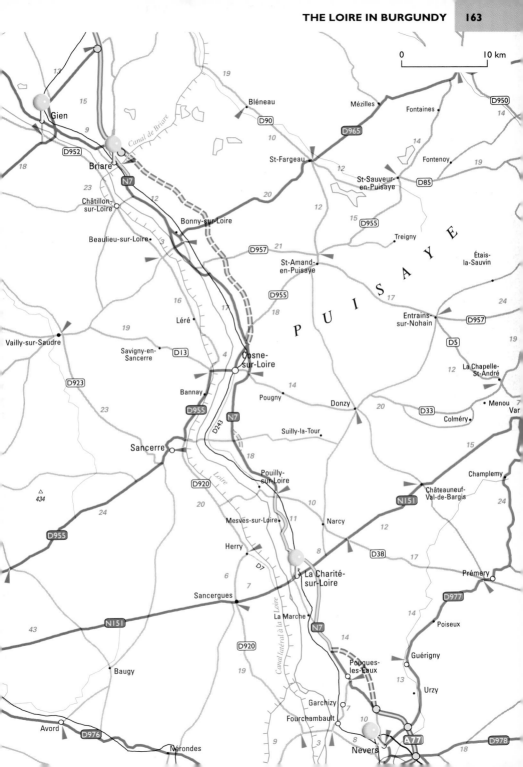

0   10 km

Gien
Bléneau   Mézilles   Fontaines
D90   D950
D952   D965   14
Briare   St-Fargeau   14
N7   St-Sauveur-
Châtillon-   en-Puisaye   Fontenoy
sur-Loire   D85   19
Bonny-sur-Loire   D955
Beaulieu-sur-Loire   Treigny
D957   21   Étais-
St-Amand-   la-Sauvin
en-Puisaye
P U I S A Y E
D955
Léré   Entrains-   D957
sur-Nohain   24
Vailly-sur-Saudre   D5   19
Savigny-en-   D13   La Chapelle-
Sancerre   Cosne-   St-André
D923   sur-Loire   Menou
Bannay   Pougny   Donzy   D33   Colméry   Var
N7   Suilly-la-Tour   Champlemy
Sancerre   Châteauneuf-
D920   Pouilly-   Val-de-Bargis
D955   sur-Loire   N151
△   Mesves-sur-Loire   Narcy   Prémery
434   Herry   D38   D977
D955   La Charité-   Poiseux
sur-Loire
Sancergues   La Marche   Guérigny
N151   N7   Urzy
Baugy   D977
D920   Pougues-
les-Eaux
Avord   Garchizy
D976   Fourchambault
Nérondes   Nevers   A77   D978

Canal de Briare
Canal latéral à la Loire
Loire
D243
D7

ℹ **Briare Tourist Office** 1 pl. Charles de Gaulle; tel: 02 38 31 24 51, fax: 02 38 37 15 16; open Apr–Sept, Mon–Sat 1000–1830, Sun 1000–1200, Oct–Mar, Mon–Sat 1000–1200, 1400–1800.

🛏 **La Maison des Deux Marines** € 58 blvd Buyser; tel: 02 38 31 28 27, fax: 02 38 37 07 45; open 1 June–30 Sept 1000–1230, 1330–1830, 1 Oct–31 Dec and 1 Mar–31 May 1400–1800.

Musée de la Mosaïque et des Émaux €€ Blvd Loreau; tel: 02 38 31 20 51; open 1 June–30 Sept, daily 1000–1830, 1 Oct–31 Dec and 1 Mar–31 May 1400–1800.

century ago, Briare's wealth came from high-quality enamelware. In particular, Briare had a factory that could mass-produce buttons – an innovation that other firms around the world could not compete with. Another development here was the use of machinery to create artworks, especially in ironwork and in mosaic, heralding the beginnings of art nouveau. A still-operating enamel factory is the setting for the town's interesting **Musée de la Mosaïque et des Émaux (Museum of Mosaic and Enamel)**✦, including a mosaic by art-nouveau artist Eugène Grasset.

Wildlife on the Loire

The broad River Loire, threatened by dams and development, is home to 240 species of birds. River swallows dart from the banks, crested warblers drift on the stream, herons and partridges and hoopoes fly by. Under the surface, catfish, eels, bream and perch number among a myriad of fish. Beside the river, wildlife thrives in shallow lakes, streams and deciduous woods. The Forêt de Bertranges, near La Charité-sur-Loire, is a forest of oak, beech, maple, cherry and other varieties, providing shelter for deer, wild boar, badgers and wild cats.

LA CHARITÉ-SUR-LOIRE✦✧

ℹ **La Charité Tourist Office** Pl. Ste-Croix; tel: 03 86 70 15 06, fax: 03 86 70 21 55; open in season 0900–1900, rest of the year varying hours.

🌐 www.perso.wanadoo. fr/marianne/indchar; www.mairie-charite-sur-loire.icar.fr/.

The first place (or the last, heading upriver) where the true grandeur of the Loire can be seen and felt is at La Charité. This small and picturesque former monastic town, once a bustling river port, has kept its curious old ramparts with a commanding walkway. An abbey was first founded here in the 8th century, and reconstructed in the 11th. So generous were the abbey fathers that the needy used to crowd here asking for help, and the town changed its name from Seyr to 'Charity'. Remnants of the abbey, entered through a splendid gateway, have become private dwellings. The town's handsome Romanesque **Église Nôtre-Dame**✦✧ with its octagonal tower is just a fraction that survives of the original abbey-church. **Excavations**✦ on the old abbey site produced many finds, now exhibited – along with a variety of other artworks and local memorabilia – in the town's **Museum**✦. Best of all here are the riverside walks and quays, which give thrillingly beautiful views, of the town with its towers and of the historic stone bridge over the water.

Right
The Loire river at Nevers

Accommodation and food in La Charité

Église Nôtre-Dame
€ *Tel: 03 86 70 15 06;
open daily.*

Excavations € *Entrance
via 47 Grande Rue; guided
visits in July and Aug 1000,
1100, 1500, 1600 and
1700.*

Museum €€ *R. des
Chapelains; tel: 03 86 70 34
83; open Mar–Nov (daily
except Tue) 1000–1200,
1400–1800 (1900 in July
and Aug), closed mid-
Dec–mid-Jan, rest of the year
weekends only.*

As well as enjoying
the famous white
wine from Sancerre,
across the river, La
Charité makes a decent
red wine of its own.

Le Grand Monarque €€ *33 quai Clémenceau; tel: 03 86 70 21 73, fax: 03 86 69 62 32.* A good hotel and substantial traditional restaurant, relaxed and peaceful, set in its own courtyard, down by the riverside.

Gîtes and *chambres d'hôte* – ask the tourist office for a list of local hosts.

Memories of the old Loire

The River Loire was once one of the busiest highways in France, and created a whole culture with it. Along the banks were thousands of families whose livelihood for centuries came from the river trade – tradition has it that River Loire people were renowned for roughness and ill manners. As early as the 4th century, the boatmen of the Loire had a powerful organisation to protect their interests. In the Middle Ages the Loire Merchants Company, granted the right to charge tolls on traders, became very wealthy. Up into the 19th century, Burgundy's foods, wines and fine chinaware were exported downstream by freelance boatmen who would then dismantle their craft, sell the wood and walk back upstream. In the last 100 years, all that life has vanished. Along the riverbanks today one sees abandoned inns and, in places, churches with a boat hanging above the aisle.

GIEN❖❖

ℹ **Gien Tourist Office**
Centre Anne de Beaujeu, Pl. Jean-Jaurès; tel: 02 38 29 85 54, fax: 02 38 29 80 09.

🏛 **Musée de la Faïencerie €€** *78 pl. de la Victoire; tel: 02 38 67 00 05, fax: 02 38 67 44; open May–Sept, daily 0900–1830 (from 1000 on Sun), Oct–Apr (except Jan and Feb) Mon–Sat 0900–1200, 1400–1800 (from 1000 on Sun), Jan and Feb Mon–Sat 1400–1800.*

Château de Gien/Musée International de la Chasse €€ *Pl. du Château; tel: 02 38 67 69 69, fax: 02 38 38 07 32; open Nov–Apr, daily 0900–1200, 1400–1700, May–Oct, daily 0930–1830.*

Église Ste-Jeanne-d'Arc € *Pl. du Château; open daily.*

Ⓦ *www.rivernet.org/loire* (economics, politics, conservation and ecology); *www.lagauche.free.fr/* (canoeing and kayaking on the upper Loire and its tributaries); *www.lvo.com/* (Loire Valley Online, a commercial site about the region, in English).

How very odd! A noble château built mainly of bricks, while the ordinary houses and cottages all around are built mainly of handsome stone. Flower-filled cobbled streets and restored historic townhouses – all recreated after heavy wartime destruction – make the town attractive. The best view is from the handsome, pale stone bridge, which spans the Loire. The River Loire is at its best here, stately and wide, yet not inaccessibly vast. Ordinary little bars line its quayside, and you can walk right beside the flowing river. Traditionally, the Gien Faïence Works was one of the world's leading manufacturers of *faïence*, or glazed earthenware (*see page 168*). The factory is still in business, and this important part of the town's art and history can be explored at its excellent **Musée de la Faïencerie (Chinaware Museum)❖❖**. Housed in atmospheric cellars beneath the workshops, the museum explores everything ceramic, from inexpensive household crockery to the most elegant chinaware commissioned by aristocratic families. Flights of steps lead up to Gien's star attraction, the very striking 15th-century **Château de Gien❖❖** with its geometric pattern of red and black brickwork. Originally 9th century, the castle was reconstructed in this way by Anne of Beaujeu (*see page 150*), daughter of Louis XI, in 1484. Here young King Louis XIV, along with his new queen, Anne of Austria, took shelter during the turmoil of the aristocratic Fronde rebellion of 1652. Inside the castle today is a comprehensive **Musée International de la Chasse (International Hunting Museum)❖❖**. If hunting upsets you, don't go in – the museum looks at the whole process of chasing and killing animals and birds and how it has inspired, entertained and fed people. Over 3000 artworks depicting the hunt are displayed along with numerous stuffed specimens. While in town, visit the modern reconstruction of the 15th-century **Église Ste-Jeanne-d'Arc❖**, which has beautiful stained glass by Max Ingrand.

Accommodation and food in Gien

Hôtel-Restaurant du Rivage €€ *1 quai de Nice; tel: 02 38 37 79 00, fax: 02 38 38 10 21.* Have a cocktail at the bar and enjoy dinner on the terrace at this outstanding restaurant specialising in local dishes, skilfully made from fresh ingredients. There's also a small hotel in this handsome building looking over the Loire.

NEVERS***

....

ℹ Nevers Tourist Office *Palais Ducal, r. Sabatier; tel: 03 86 68 46 00, fax: 03 86 68 45 98, www.ville-nevers.fr/.* The tourist office runs a programme of short guided tours. In summer, a mini 'train' makes a tour of the main sights.

🚗 The town is bypassed by a *voie express* (expressway) on the N7, with four exits leading into the centre. The N81 (from Autun) also runs into the town. The modern town is focused on the meeting point of av. Beregovoy, av. Charles de Gaulle and r. du 14-juillet at pl. Carnot.

🅿 Head for the riverbank and park in one of the car parks near the Loire bridge. More parking places can be found in the modern town alongside pl. Roger Salengro, north of the old quarter.

🏛 Ateliers Montagnon € *10 r. de la Porte-du-Croux; tel: 03 86 71 96 90.* Free guided tour (in French) at 1430 on first Wed of each month.

Cathédrale St-Cyr et Ste-Julitte € *R. du Cloître St-Cyr; tel: 03 86 21 25 07; open all year, daily 0900–1900.*

Église St-Gildard € *In St-Gildard convent, entrance in r. St-Gildard; open Apr–Oct, daily 0700–1930, Nov–Mar, daily 0730–1200, 1400–1900.*

Deep in the heart of the burgeoning modern industrial town is an attractive ancient quarter, with remnants of its old fortifications, rising in terraces from the place where the Nièvre flows into the Loire. In the Middle Ages, a twist of fate caused Nevers, as the seat of a small duchy, to end up in Italian hands. In 1565 it was inherited by the noble Gonzaga family of Mantua, who brought artists and craftsmen to Nevers from Italy and so introduced the knowledge of how to make *faïence*, or glazed earthenware and fine porcelain. From then on, the town's economic future was secure, and the high-quality, richly decorated Nevers porcelain – especially its exquisite *Bleu de Nevers* (Nevers Blue) colouring – became famous throughout Europe. It's still made and sold in three small *faïence* workshops – **Ateliers Montagnon**✦ gives guided tours.

The best view of the medieval old town is from the handsome Loire bridge. Then wander up the lanes and steps of the historic centre to the immense **Cathédrale St-Cyr et Ste-Julitte**✦✦, a strange-looking building with sections in every style of French architecture from the 10th century to the 20th. It even has two apses, Romanesque at the west end, Gothic at the east, because it was originally two separate churches. Across pl. de l'Hôtel de Ville, the 15th- to 16th-century Palais Ducal, now housing the tourist office, exhibitions and an aquarium, was originally the home of the Dukes of Nevers. It's a sumptuous Renaissance building with octagonal turrets and an elegant sculptured central tower. Église St-Étienne, on the east side of the town centre, is a simple 11th-century Cluny priory church in pure Romanesque style. Although partly destroyed during the Revolution, it has an appealing, if grimly austere, interior, with three vaulted chapels off the apse.

North of the big central municipal park, Parc Roger Salengro, is the convent chapel of **St-Gildard**✦ where the embalmed, intact body of Bernadette Soubirous (1844–79) – Ste-Bernadette of Lourdes – has been eerily contained in a glass-fronted shrine since 1925, when it was dug up. Bernadette retired to the convent at the age of 22 from her native Lourdes after her series of teenage visions of the Virgin, which made Lourdes one of the major Catholic pilgrimage places of the 20th century. Around half a million pilgrims visit Église St-Gildard each summer, so it can be crowded on occasions.

Over on the western side of the old quarter, a surviving section of 12th-century town wall leads to Porte du Croux, an imposing square tower gateway added to the walls in 1393. Inside it, the **Musée Archéologique (Archaeological Museum)**✦ contains Greek and Roman sculptures among the finds made in the area. Alongside a pleasant ramparts walk, the **Jardin et Musée Blandin (Blandin Museum and Gardens)**✦✦ has a superb collection of antique Nevers *faïence* and glassware.

Musée Archéologique €
Porte du Croux; tel: 03 86 59 17 85; open Mar–Nov Wed–Sun 1400–1800, rest of the year closed.

Jardin et Musée Blandin
€ Access via Promenade des Remparts; tel: 03 86 71 67 90; open May–Sept, daily (except Tue) 1000–1830, Oct–Apr Mon–Fri 1330–1730, Sat, Sun and hols 1000–1200, 1400–1730.

Nevers is proud of its traditional local cuisine and specialities, making good use of local Charolais beef, Loire fish in Loire wine sauces, and nougatine confectionery.

Summer **market** – every second Wed from end June to early Sept – with regional produce, arts and crafts, entertainment.

Faïence

Faïence means 'chinaware' and is a general term for decorated glazed or enamelled earthenware. Faïence-making comes (in Europe) from the pottery town Faënza in Italy. Several places along the Loire had the right clay soils to develop faïence-making with great success. Gien is best known for fine dinner services and tableware, while Nevers specialises in an elegant, highly decorated majolica porcelain.

Accommodation and food in Nevers

The town has many budget and mid-priced chain hotels.

Hôtel Loire €€ Quai de Médine; tel: 03 86 61 50 92, fax: 03 86 59 43 29. Modern and functional hotel with a restaurant, in the town centre next to the river.

Restaurant Jean-Michel Couron €–€€ 21 r. St-Étienne; tel: 03 86 61 19 28, fax: 03 86 36 02 96, closed Sun pm and Mon and for 3 weeks in summer. The best Nevers restaurant in the heart of the old quarter, arranged in three stylish, attractive small rooms, is the place to enjoy a brilliant, unpretentious approach to Burgundian and Loire cooking that keeps menu prices as low as possible. Specialities include snails, roast Charolais and chocolate-and-spice soup.

Suggested tour

Total distance: 133km one way.

Time: 1–2 days.

Links: This route links with Puisaye (see page 56).

Route: From **GIEN ❶**, take the D952 to **BRIARE ❷**. Take the N7 – or seek out the tiny lanes closer to the river – to **Cosne-sur-Loire**, a largish and busy but likeable riverside town. Leave Cosne and return on to the N7, or perhaps choose the D243 for a route closer to the river.

Detour: At Cosne, or on the St-Thibault bridge 10km south from Cosne, cross the Loire and continue into **Sancerre**. This good-looking town is poised on a round hill gazing across its neat vineyards, its tangled old streets and lanes guarded by a 14th-century tower. It's well known for excellent, world-class fragrant dry white wines, regarded as the local wine everywhere along this route. Try, too, some of the district's highly praised goats' cheese called crottin, perfectly delicious despite the name (it means 'goat droppings'). Continuing on the left bank, take the D920 and D7 until you can cross the river again into **LA CHARITÉ-SUR-LOIRE ❸**.

The main route runs to **Pouilly-sur-Loire** and La Charité-sur-Loire. Follow the main road out of town, meeting the N7. You pass by **Pougues-les-Eaux**, an attractive spa with good views, and reach **NEVERS ❹**.

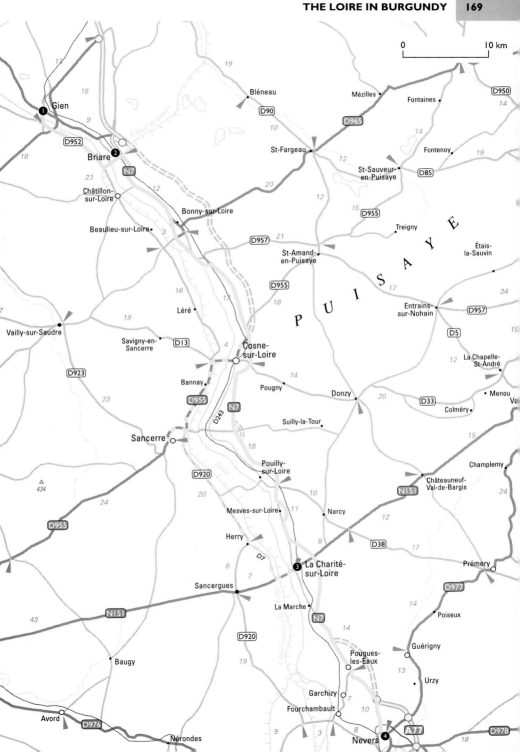

0   10 km

Gien

D952

Briare

N7

Châtillon-
sur-Loire

Beaulieu-sur-Loire

Bonny-sur-Loire

Bléneau

D90

Mézilles

Fontaines

D950

St-Fargeau

D965

St-Sauveur-
en-Puisaye

D85

Fontenoy

D955

Treigny

Étais-
la-Sauvin

D957

St-Amand-
en-Puisaye

D955

P U I S A Y E

Léré

Vailly-sur-Saudre

Savigny-en-
Sancerre

D13

Cosne-
sur-Loire

Entrains-
sur-Nohain

D957

D5

D923

Bannay

D955

N7

D243

Pougny

Donzy

D33

Menou

Colméry

La Chapelle-
St-André

Sancerre

Suilly-la-Tour

Champlemy

D920

Pouilly-
sur-Loire

Châteauneuf-
Val-de-Bargis

N151

Mesves-sur-Loire

Narcy

D38

Prémery

Herry

D7

La Charité-
sur-Loire

D977

Sancergues

Poiseux

N151

La Marche

N7

Guérigny

D920

Urzy

Baugy

Pougues-
les-Eaux

Garchizy

Fourchambault

Avord

D976

Nérondes

Nevers

A77

D978

The Charollais and Brionnais

Ratings

Medieval architecture	●●●●●
Restaurants	●●●●○
Villages	●●●●○
History	●●●○○
Markets	●●●○○
Museums	●●●○○
Children	●●○○○
Scenery	●●○○○

Across the whole of Burgundy, Romanesque churches imitating the once-great abbey at Cluny rise from tiny, unknown villages. One of the most intriguing concentrations of all is in the Brionnais. This southern corner of the ancient duchy broadly overlaps with another area equally tranquil and rustic, yet with a name well-enough known to cattle farmers – the Charollais. For here a breed of cattle (properly known as Charolais with a single 'l') was developed, completely white and exceptionally heavy with their lean meat. The nearer one approaches to the small market town of Charolles, the more numerous are these impressive white animals standing in their green fields. Without a map it would be no easy matter to find one's way around these two small regions. Together they constitute a veritable 'kingdom of little roads', with lovely tangled lanes and plenty of junctions without signposts!

ANZY-LE-DUC❖❖

For guided walks on llamas from Anzy-le-Duc, *tel: 03 85 25 26 09.*

This little village has one of the best of all the Brionnais churches, a lovely golden-hued building with unchristian-looking frescos. Note especially the fine tympanum, capitals and bell tower. It's believed to be the model for the huge abbey church at Vézelay (*see page 80*).

BOURBON-LANCY❖

Thermal spa €€ *Tel: 03 85 89 18 84, fax: 03 85 89 25 45.*

A short distance from the Charollais, this little town overlooking the Loire Valley is three things in one: a small manufacturing centre, a historic country town with some old houses and a belfry beside the town gates, and a well-established **thermal spa**❖ specialising in the treatment of rheumatism and cardio-vascular complaints. Around half-a-million litres of water a day pour from its five hot springs, with temperatures ranging from 46° to 58°C.

0   10 km

Bourbon-Lancy

Chalmoux

D60

Gueugnon

25

12

Perrecy-
les-Forges

Ciry-le-
Noble

Neuvy-
Grandchamp

Génelard

Marizy

D994

E607

20

Martigny-le-Comte

15

22

D979

St-Agnan

Arroux

Digoin

N79

E62

29

Molinet

Canal du Centre

Bourbince

D985

Paray-le-
Monial

13

Charolles

St-Yan

19

D985

Plaines de la Loire et de l'Allier

24

Canal de Roanne à Digoin

26

29

Changy

St-Julien-
de-Civry

Dyo

D982

Montceaux-
l'Étoile

D10

Arconce

20

Bois-Ste-
Marie

22

D989

Anzy-le-Duc

Varenne-
l'Arconce

D34

Château de Drée

D79

Vareilles

1

St-Christophe-
en-Brionnais

D989

La Clayette

Marcigny

23

△
549

Semur-en-
Brionnais

B R I O N N A I S

Urbise

St-Julien-
de-Jonzy

D987

D985

Châteauneuf

24

14

C H A R O L L A I S

Loire

18

La Montagne

Sornin

Chauffailles

D4

Iguerande

D227

D987

21

Belmont-de-
la-Loire

36

La Pacaudière

Charlieu

R o a n n a i s

N7

14

Briennon

D31

Pouilly-sous-
Charlieu

D4

Cours-
la-Ville

21

Ambierle

12

12

D482

Monts de la Madelei...

St-Haon-le-Châtel

Roanne

Monts du Beaujolais

Renaison

Riorges

Perreux

Montagny

Thizy

D8

D53

CHARLIEU✦✦✦

ⓘ Charlieu Tourist Office *Pl. St-Philibert; tel: 04 77 60 12 42, fax: 04 77 60 16 91, e-mail: office.tourisme.charlieu@wanadoo.fr; open all year various hours, Mar–Sept closed Mon am, Oct–Feb also closed Sun.*

Ⓦ *www.boizet.com/a_index; www.welcome.to/charlieu.*

ⓘ Abbaye Bénédictine €€ *Pl. de l'Abbaye; tel: 04 77 60 08 17; open mid-June–mid-Sept 0930–1900, Mar–mid-June and mid-Sept–Dec 0930–1230, 1400–1830, closed Mon, Feb, Nov and Dec 1000–1230, 1400–1730, closed Mon. Closed Jan.*

Hôtel Dieu and Musée de la Soierie €€ *R. Morel; tel: 04 77 60 28 84; open mid-June–mid-Sept 1000–1300, 1400–1900, rest of the year 1400–1800.*

Couvent des Cordeliers cloisters €€ *R. Rouillier; tel: 04 77 60 07 42; open mid-June–mid-Sept 1000–1930, Mar–mid-June and mid-Sept–Oct Tue–Sun 1000–1230, 1430–1800, closed Mon, Feb and Nov 1000–1230, 1400–1700, closed Dec and Jan.*

A small and ancient cattle market town with many attractive medieval houses, Charlieu preserves at its centre remnants of a fine Cluniac fortified **Abbaye Bénédictine (Benedictine Abbey)✦✦✦**, founded as long ago as the 9th century, although nothing survives from that period. The exceptional 12th-century vestibule and carved doorway called *Le Grand Portail* (the Great Doorway) is the most outstanding feature, but notice, too, the smaller doorway and tympanum on its right, which are from the same era. Just inside is the two-storey narthex, whose east wall is the west wall of another 11th-century church, St-Fortunat. A lot of what remains of the abbey today – the cloisters, chapter-house and prior's chapel, for example – dates from the 15th or 16th centuries, but is well worth seeing.

Close by, in the 18th-century **Hôtel Dieu (Charity Hospital)✦** you can see how the hospital looked from about 1850 to 1950 – it was still a working hospital until 1981. Today it also houses a **Musée de la Soierie (Silkmaking Museum)✦**, with working equipment of this important local industry. A short walk away along r. Rouillier is the curious 15th-century **Couvent des Cordeliers cloisters✦✦**, all that's left of a monastery which, foolishly and tragically, has been dismembered and taken away to the United States. In fact the cloisters were also sold, but were saved at the last minute when the French government managed to buy them back before they were dismantled.

Accommodation and food in Charlieu

Relais de l'Abbaye €€ *Le Pont de Pierre Charlieu; tel: 04 77 60 00 88, fax: 04 77 60 14 60.* This modest and reasonable family-run hotel on the other side of the river has a good restaurant with Charollais specialities.

Right
Château de le Clayette

CHAROLLES*

Charolles Tourist Office In Ancien Couvent des Clarisses, r. Baudinot; tel/fax: 03 85 24 05 95; open 0900–1200, 1400–1800, closed Sun.

On the menu

Charolais beef, of course. But the other local speciality is goats' cheese, sold at several local markets. Look out too for local *andouilles* and *andouillettes* (chitterlings), farm-made jams and *coulis*, and fish freshly caught from the Loire and other rivers.

The Arconce and Semence rivers and the Canal du Moulin twist and wind throughout this sedate, charming old town in green and hilly countryside. Altogether it has 30 little bridges. Charolles has few 'sights', though, other than the remnants of the castle of the counts of Charollais, which now houses the town hall. Through one of the former gateways, at the foot of a 14th-century tower, Le Tour de Charles le Téméraire, a pleasant public garden now covers part of the ramparts and gives agreeable views across the surrounding rolling country. The 16th-century Ancien Couvent des Clarisses – now home to the tourist office – is where Marguerite-Marie Alacoque (*see page 175*) had her first communion, in 1656.

Accommodation and food in Charolles

Hôtel de France €–€€ *Av. J. Furtin; tel: 03 85 24 06 66, fax: 03 85 24 05 54.* Decent, simple, family-run hotel with no restaurant.

Hôtel-Restaurant Moderne €€ *Av. J. Furtin; tel: 03 85 24 07 02, fax: 03 85 24 05 21.* A comfortable family-run hotel with a good traditional restaurant.

Hôtel-Restaurant de la Poste €€ *2 av. de la Libération; tel: 03 85 24 11 32, fax: 03 85 24 05 74.* More of a *restaurant avec chambres*, this appealing place has a small number of comfortable rooms, as well as a charming dining room with excellent food and wine at moderate prices.

LA CLAYETTE**

La Clayette Tourist Office 3 rte de Charolles; tel: 03 85 28 16 35, fax: 03 85 26 87 25; open July–Aug 1000–1200, 1430–1800 (closed Sun and Mon am), rest of the year 1400–1700 (or 1800), closed Sun and Mon.

Château No entry except for Musée Automobile.

Musée Automobile €€ Château; tel: 03 85 28 22 07, fax: 03 85 26 84 65. Variable times.

La Clayette (pronounced 'La Clett') is a bustling local centre, a small market town on the bank of the Genette, which broadens here to make a lake, attractive with plane trees: a suitably impressive setting for a 14th-century moated **château**** with sturdy round towers (extensively restored in the 19th century). The 15th-century outbuildings rather incongruously house a good **Musée Automobile (Automobile Museum)*** with grand old Rolls-Royces, dashing pre-war Bugattis and sleek newer Ferraris and Maseratis.

Accommodation and food in La Clayette

Hôtel-Restaurant de la Gare € *In village; tel: 03 85 28 01 65, closed Sun pm and Mon, except in July and Aug.* Good, satisfyingly inexpensive restaurant with a small number of comfortable rooms.

PARAY-LE-MONIAL✦✦✦

Right
Grounds of Basilique de Nôtre-Dame

'Paray of the monks', a lovely country town on the banks of the poplar-lined River Bourbince, is rather remarkably the second most popular place of religious pilgrimage in France (after Lourdes), and is the capital of the Brionnais. For it was here that the Catholic cult of the 'Sacred Heart' originated. The town's beautiful **Basilique de Nôtre-Dame (Nôtre-Dame Basilica)**✦✦✦, although now generally known to pilgrims as the Basilique du Sacré-Coeur, has nothing to do with the cult and predates it by many hundreds of years. Built in the early 1100s, it was intended as a smaller copy of the huge abbey-church at Cluny *(see page 142)*, no longer standing, and reveals something of why Cluny was so much praised. The building is dignified, strong, sturdy, massive yet elegant. The secret of its beauty is simplicity. The curve of the ambulatory is exquisite, the columns delightfully slender.

Some of Paray's other popular sights have less to recommend them! Behind the basilica is a small museum about Ste-Marguerite-Marie, called the **Chambre des Reliques (Room of Relics)**✦. It contains a jumble of items connected with her, such as an ordinary table fork said to have been hers and several awful pictures. The room where it is alleged that she had visions has become the Chapelle de la Visitation, object of much veneration. **Musée Hiéron**✦ is a museum of religious art with little of interest apart from an impressive 12th-century tympanum in good condition that comes from Anzy-le-Duc. In contrast to the simple finesse of the basilica, Paray's Hôtel de Ville is gorgeously tasteless. A 16th-century building, originally named Maison Jayet, it was at one time the private house of a wealthy cloth merchant. It has an absolutely extraordinary façade, heavily covered with sculpted ornamentation, including odd little figurines, either naked, or clothed in improbable outfits.

The Sacré-Coeur

In 1673 Marguerite-Marie Alacoque, a young novice nun and daughter of a prominent local lawyer, told her fellow nuns, her confessor and the Mother Superior that Christ had physically appeared before her with his chest ripped open and the heart visible inside. He had said to her 'Here is the heart which so loved Man'. The Mother Superior, for one, did not believe this story. So many others did, though (the confessor proved a useful ally), that the Mother Superior declared that she had moved from incredulity to uncertainty. Thus began the cult of the Sacré-Coeur. Marguerite-Marie Alacoque had the same vision again and again until her death in 1690. Strangely though, the devotion to the Sacred Heart only really took off in earnest over a century later, during an 18th-century religious backlash against the Revolution. As a result, Marguerite-Marie was beatified in 1864, and in 1873 it was decided 'to consecrate France to the Sacred Heart of Jesus', hence the building of the impressive Sacré-Coeur basilica in Paris. Marguerite-Marie was made a saint in 1920.

Accommodation and food in Paray

Aux Vendanges de Bourgogne €–€€ *5 r. Papin; tel: 03 85 81 13 43, fax: 03 85 88 87 59.* There are many hotels and restaurants in town, but as is often the case with places of pilgrimage, such earthly considerations as food and shelter leave something to be desired. This is one of the most acceptable, and very reasonably priced.

Le Charollais €–€€ *On the N74, 3km out of town towards Digion; tel: 03 85 81 03 35, fax: 03 85 81 50 31.* This characterless but adequate motel is conveniently placed and has a decent, inexpensive grill restaurant.

SEMUR-EN-BRIONNAIS❖❖

Château de St-Hugues € *Tel: 03 85 25 13 57; open Mon–Sat 1000–1200, 1400–1900 (or 1800), Sun pm only.*

Bourbon-Lancy Tourist Office *Pl. d'Aligre; tel: 03 85 89 18 27, fax: 03 85 89 28 38, e-mail: Bourbon.Tourisme @wanadoo.fr; open Mar–Oct Mon–Fri 0900–1200, 1400–1900 (Sat, Sun and hols 1400–1800), Nov–Feb Mon–Fri 1000–1200, 1430–1630.*

Handsome Semur, raised high among vines and orchards, has one of the most beautiful examples of the Brionnais churches. Romanesque arcades decorate the lovely octagonal Cluny-style bell tower, and the west doorway is exceptionally richly carved. Close by is the so-called **Château de St-Hugues❖**. In this castle keep, a sturdy rectangle with two round towers dating back to the 9th century, St-Hugues de Semur was born in 1024. He went on to become the abbot who built up Cluny into a major centre of spiritual influence and power, and it was he who started the construction of the famous abbey buildings.

Suggested tour

Total distance: About 150km, plus two detours totalling 80km.

Time: 1 to 2 days.

Route: From **CHAROLLES** ❶ (55km west of Mâcon on the N79) take the D985, heading south (direction La Clayette), turning right after 8km on to the D20. Continue through St-Julien-de-Civry and take a right turn (D108) to **Varenne-l'Arconce**. This tiny village has a fine Cluniac church dating from the early 12th century, made of local sandstone with the simplest design, dominated by an elegant four-sided belfry. Running through pretty pastoral country, the D34 goes to tiny **St-Christophe-en-Brionnais** ❷, noted for its huge Thursday morning cattle market. The road to La Clayette (D989) passes by **Vareilles**, with its simple but graceful Romanesque church and interesting bell tower. The road continues into **LA CLAYETTE** ❸.

Detour: It's worth making the short detour from here to the splendid 17th-century **Château de Drée** 4km north. Built in classical style from golden stone, it stands alone in a wood. Beyond is the village of **Bois-Ste-Marie**, where the 11th-century church is one of the oldest in the Brionnais, unusual in that it predates Cluny. Head back from here to La Clayette.

Make your way on the D987 to attractive **Châteauneuf**, on a peaceful wooded hillside overlooking the Sornin. Here stands a château, together with one of the last Romanesque churches ever built, a fascinating example of the style, with sturdy grace and some intriguing sculpture. Follow the Sornin (still on the D987) down to **CHARLIEU** ❹.

Setting out from Charlieu (now on the D227) follow the signs of the marked *Circuit des Églises Romanes du Brionnais* (Circuit of Romanesque Churches of Brionnais) all the way up to **Paray-le-Monial**. Not only does this take in several more of the region's Romanesque churches, but it also follows an attractive route along minor roads most of the way. There's something of interest at nearly every village church: **La Montagne, Iguerande**, overlooking the River Loire (concerts in the church in Sept), St-Julien-de-Jonzy and **SEMUR-EN-BRIONNAIS** ❺. In **Marcigny** ❻, the church is less interesting, but it does house a simple Musée de Faïences (Faïence Museum). Finally, drive via **ANZY-LE-DUC** ❼ and **Montceaux-l'Étoile** to join the slightly busier and faster D982. This leads through uninteresting St-Yan to **Digoin** ❽, with its impressive 16-arch canal bridge of 1836.

Detour: If you'd like to see more of the Loire, from Digoin, take the D979 and follow it downstream. Continue, eventually leaving the Charollais and Brionnais region, to **BOURBON-LANCY** ❾. Return to Digoin.

Continue into **PARAY-LE-MONIAL** ❿. To complete the circle, Charolles lies 12km east of Paray on the busy N79.

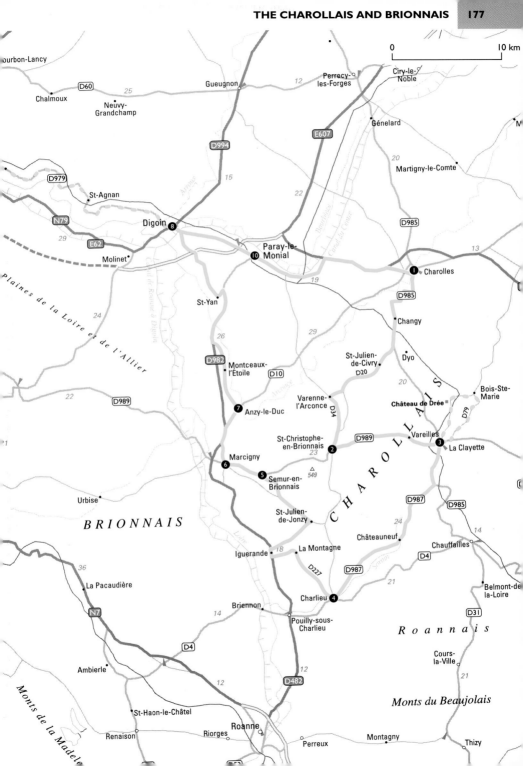

West of Lyon

Ratings

Restaurants	●●●●●
Scenery	●●●●●
Activities	●●●●○
Museums	●●●●○
Shopping	●●●●○
Children	●●●○○
Entertainment	●●●○○
Medieval architecture	●●●○○

The countryside west of Lyon, stretching from the Rhône to the Loire, has always provided the gastronomic city with much of its produce, just as Beaujolais has provided much of its wine. Mixing rocky peaks, gentler steep green hills of farms, forests and cherry orchards, and many small industrial and developed corners, combining rustic villages, suburbs and large towns, this is one of the most diverse parts of the region. It provides a breath of fresh air for daytrippers from Lyon. Above all, it is a favourite for gourmets. As well as the many gastronomic restaurants in Lyon itself, this Lyonnais countryside abounds with high-quality places to enjoy the refined regional cuisine. Stop off to enjoy a variety of local museums, sights and attractions. In addition, it's a region geared to leisure activities: ask tourist offices for details of riding centres, walks or bike hire.

CHAZELLES-SUR-LYON✤

ⓘ Most of this tour is within the *département* of Le Rhône. For information, contact: *CDT du Rhône; tel: 04 72 61 78 90, fax: 04 72 77 52 05, e-mail: rhone. tourisme@asi.fr.*

Chazelles Tourist Office *Pl. J-B Galland; tel: 04 77 54 98 86, fax: 04 77 54 94 58; open Mon–Sat 0900–1800.*

Felt-making was apparently introduced to this village by the 12th-century Knights Templars, who once had a castle here (of which only a hexagonal tower survives). The felt-making turned Chazelles into a veritable capital of millinery. A century ago, two dozen factories were turning out vast numbers of hats. The industry has all but vanished today, but a **Musée du Chapeau (Hat Museum)✤** remains, with displays on hat design and some top people's hats on show.

Musée du Chapeau €€ *In village; tel: 04 77 94 23 29; open 1400–1800 (closed Tue, except in July and Aug).*

Accommodation and food in Chazelles-sur-Lyon

Château Blanchard €€ *36 rte St-Galmier; tel: 04 77 54 28 88, fax: 04 77 54 36 03.* Appealing, peaceful, family-run place with a garden and a good restaurant serving regional dishes all at reasonable prices.

MONTROND-LES-BAINS❖

Montrond Tourist Office *Av. Philibert Gary; tel: 04 77 94 64 74; variable seasonal opening hours.*

Casino €€ *Tel: 04 77 52 70 70, fax: 04 77 52 70 79; open daily 1100–1600.*

A busy, commercial, main road stopover in the green Forez hills, with ruins of a medieval château, Montrond is also a small spa town. Its mineral waters are used in the treatment of diabetes and obesity. Here too are discos, nightlife and a casino.

Accommodation and food in Montrond-les-Bains

Hostellerie de la Poularde €€–€€€ *2 r. St-Étienne; tel: 04 77 54 40 06, fax: 04 77 54 53 14.* This high-quality hotel and restaurant is close to the town's casino and spa treatment centre. It's a *Relais et Châteaux*, with superbly comfortable rooms and an outstanding gastronomic restaurant. Richly succulent dishes include *foie gras* in wine, bass with fennel and limes, crayfish and oyster roast and black-and-white chocolate dessert.

Le Bougainvillier €–€€ *Pré-Château, St-Galmier (10km south of Montrond); tel: 04 77 54 03 31; closed Sun pm and Mon.* The cheapest menu here is a marvel of flair and four courses of good eating at a really affordable price. Pay more to discover what the chef is capable of.

MONTS D'OR LYONNAIS❖

Distances are small. Allow about 2 hours to make a short tour of the area.

Maison d'Ampère € *Poleymieux; tel: 04 78 91 90 77; open 0900–1200, 1400–1800 (closed Tue).*

Immediately north of Lyon, on the west bank of the Saône, the Monts d'Or is a magical cluster of limestone hills rising from the river plain. Dry and sparse on the south-facing slopes, richly wooded on the north slopes, abundantly farmed in the fertile valleys, the area is idyllically rustic in places, almost suburban in other parts. Little roads climb to the peaks, from which the views are a delight. Mont Thou (609m) is at the centre of the range, with a vista over the Saône and Lyon. Near the small town of Limonest, there's an 18th-century mansion, Château de la Barollière with good views. Close to the village of Poleymieux, the Croix Rampau summit (463m) gives panoramic views. South of the village, the **Maison d'Ampère**❖❖ was the home of André-Marie Ampère (1775–1836), the great scientist, mathematician and discoverer whose name became a unit of measure for electricity. A small museum in the house deals with the history of the use of electricity.

www.leroannais.com
(Roanne Tourist
Office site); www.monts-du-
yonnais.org (website of the
rural canton of St-Laurent-
de-Chamousset).

Accommodation and food in Monts d'Or Lyonnais

Le Cellier €€ *Quai Saône, Albigney-sur-Saône; tel: 04 78 98 26 16; closed Sun pm and Mon.* A terrace by the Saône is the setting for the skilful classic cuisine offered here. The emphasis is on fresh fish, but you can also try dishes such as beef in Béarnaise sauce.

Paul Bocuse €€€ *40 r. de la Plage, Collonges au Mont d'Or; tel: 04 72 42 90 90, fax: 04 72 27 85 87.* The most famous chef, and perhaps still the most famous restaurant, in France, as well as one of the most expensive. The aged Bocuse is the Grand Old Man of modern French *haute cuisine* and the creator of *nouvelle cuisine*, whose dishes have been described as 'masterpieces of simplicity, freshness, technique, honesty and good taste'.

Restaurant Guy Lassausaie €€ *Rte de Belle Cize, Chasselay; tel: 04 78 47 62 59, fax: 04 78 47 06 19; closed Tue pm and Wed.* An outstanding up-and-coming chef, at this lovely spot, offers accomplished and satisfying cooking at a remarkably affordable price. Braised *foie gras* in *sauternes* and pigeon cooked in herbs, are specialities.

ROANNE*

Roanne Tourist Office *I cours de la République; tel: 04 77 71 51 77, fax: 04 77 70 96 62, e-mail: roannais@avo.fr; open Mon–Sat 0900–1800.*

A ring of boulevards surrounds the town centre. Promenade Populle, on the ring road, is a popular park close to the tourist office.

A canalboat trip from Roanne towards Digoin makes a peaceful outing. Choose between a couple of hours, a full day, or more. Details from the tourist office.

Although 2000 years old, the town has few attractions, yet it is a must for all those who love French gastronomy. Thanks to being in the midst of richly productive agricultural regions producing the highest quality ingredients, Roanne has a high reputation for its cooking. It's essentially an industrial town, though, and stands at the highest navigable point on the River Loire. Freelance watermen who shipped goods downstream from here would then (having dismantled their craft and sold the wood) return on foot. Near the docks, there's a 17th-century chapel dedicated to the patron saint of watermen, St Nicolas. At the centre of town is a ruined castle keep. The fine arts and archaeology museum **Musée Déchelette***, housed in an 18th-century mansion, has a mix of collections, including interesting decorated chinaware made during the Revolutionary period and some Gallo-Roman antiquities.

Accommodation and food in Roanne

Musée Déchelette
€€ *R. Anatole-France;*
tel: 04 77 70 00 90; open
Mon, Wed, Thur, Sat
1000–1200, 1400–1800,
Fri 1000–1800, Sun
1400–2000, closed Tue.

Hôtel-Restaurant Troisgros €€€ *Pl. Jean Troisgros (or pl. Gare); tel: 04 77 71 66 97, fax: 04 77 70 39 77.* With set menus up to 800F or more, and rooms at double that, this place is reckoned one of the best restaurants in France, with a hotel of a dreamlike luxury.

Auberge Costelloise €€ *2 av. de la Libération, Le Coteau; tel: 04 77 68 12 71, fax: 04 77 72 26 78.* This highly rated restaurant offers imaginative cooking on classic Burgundian and Loire themes, and at surprisingly modest prices. Try the local delicacy *sandre* (pike-perch) in parsley, calf sweetbreads in lobster sauce and delicious desserts.

ST-ÉTIENNE*

**St-Étienne Tourist
Offices** *3 Place
Roannelle; tel: 04 77 25 12
14, fax: 04 77 32 71 28;
open Mon–Sat 0900–1230,
1330–1900, Sun
1000–1300. 16 av. de la
Libération; tel: 04 77 49 39
00, fax: 04 77 49 39 03, e-
mail: information@
tourisme-st-etienne.com;
open Mon–Sat 0900–1900,
Sun 1000–1300.*

*www.tourisme-st-
etienne.com (tourist office
site, in English and French);
www.emse.fr/STETIENNE/
ENGLISH/ (one of several
St-Étienne sites with
masses of information
about the city. In English,
French and other
languages).*

There are big town-
centre car parks at pl.
de l'Hôtel de Ville and pl.
Antonin Moine.

In the town centre
use the tram.

This large, modern industrial town has a good atmosphere, a sense of thoroughly enjoying life. All around, even in the centre of town, green hills are within view. The town sprung up almost entirely in the wake of 20th-century large-scale coal-mining and steel manufacturing, albeit around an older small town (today's place du Peuple was once a medieval market square). From the Middle Ages onwards, St-Étienne was known for two contrasting high-quality local products – ribbons and guns.

Heavily bombed during the Second World War, its historical centre has all but vanished, although the 15th-century church in local Gothic style called the Grande Église St-Étienne-St-Laurent still stands near the centre, and there are some old houses nearby. More interesting, perhaps, are several buildings in early 20th-century styles and some experimental 1930s architecture, for example on r. Michelet. On the main street, not far from the church, **Musée du Vieux St-Étienne (Museum of Old St-Étienne)*** uses old documents to evoke the history of the town. There are several other museums. The **Musée d'Art et d'Industrie (Art and Industry Museum)*** has an interesting and imaginative array of local products from the 16th century to today, especially weapons and bicycles. Southeast of the town centre, there's an entertaining **planetarium***, while to the west, the **Musée de la Mine (Mining Museum)**** gives a fascinating hour-long tour of a coal mine (closed in 1973) which once employed 1500 men to produce 3000 tonnes of coal a day. The best of the St-Étienne museums, 5km north of the town centre, is the **Musée d'Art Moderne (Museum of Modern Art)****, housing the most important collection of 20th-century art in France outside Paris. The building, clad in black tiles, suggests a grim, ironic link to the district's coal mining. Examples of all the modern schools are here, with works by artists from Monet and Picasso to Warhol.

Musée du Vieux St-Étienne € *13 bis r. Gambetta; tel: 04 77 25 74 32, fax: 04 77 38 17 28; open Mon–Sat 1430–1800.*

Musée d'Art et d'Industrie €€ *2 r. Louis Comte; tel: 04 77 33 04 85. Call for latest opening times.*

Planetarium €€ *Espace Fauriel, av. Fauriel; tel: 04 77 25 54 92, fax: 04 77 33 35 70, website: www.sideral. com; open pm on Wed and weekend for 90-min shows at 1415 and 1535 in winter, 1500 and 1630 in summer.*

Musée de la Mine €€ *Blvd Franchet d'Esperey; tel: 04 77 43 83 23, fax: 04 77 43 83 29; open generally 1000–1130, 1400–1715 (1800 at weekends). May be closed Mon and some hols. Different hours for certain dates in school holidays.*

Musée d'Art Moderne €€ *La Terrasse; tel: 04 77 79 52 52, fax: 04 77 79 52 50; open daily 1000–1800, closed hols.*

St-Étienne's local specialities include potato pancake.

There's good-quality shopping on the main avenue (r. du Géneral Foy and r. Gambetta) and its side streets.

There are many late-night restaurants, bars and discos in the area around central pl. Jean-Jaurès and adjacent r. Dormoy.

Accommodation and food in St-Étienne

Le Clos Fleuri €€ *76 av. Albert Raimond, St-Priest-en-Jarez (on northern edge of town, 4km north of centre); tel: 04 77 74 63 24, fax: 04 77 79 06 70; closed Sun pm.* Close to the Museum of Modern Art, and offering satisfying, imaginative, high-quality cooking of classic dishes.

Hôtel-Restaurant Terminus du Forez €€ *29–31 av. Denfert Rochereau; tel: 04 77 32 48 47, fax: 04 77 34 03 30.* This modern family-run hotel near the station, east of the town centre, is full of character and charm, with moderate prices, individualised rooms and good service and facilities.

Allez Les Verts!

St-Étienne is best known in France for its once-great football team, known as *Les Verts* (the Greens) because of their strip. Les Verts were hard hit by a fraud scandal several years ago. Fans deserted them and performance has plummeted. You'll still see car stickers saying *Allez Les Verts!* (Go Greens!).

Suggested tour

Total distance: 210km, or 241km with St-Étienne detour, and another 10km to detour into the Monts d'Or Lyonnais.

Time: 2 days, or selected highlights in 1 day.

Links: For Lyon, *see page 202*. At Villefranche-sur-Saône this route links with Beaujolais (*see page 158*). At Trévoux it links with La Dombes (*see page 200*). At St-Étienne it links with Haut-Vivarais (*see page 227*).

Route: Start from **Lyon** or, to by-pass Lyon, it would be simple to start and finish this route from either Villefranche-sur-Saône or Roanne.

From Lyon, cross the Saône and head west out of the city centre. Aim at first for the big Place Vauboin junction in **Tassin-la-Demi-Lune**. Follow signs for Yzeron and Chazelles-sur-Lyon on the D489. Straight away, you are following the Yzeron Valley up into the **Monts du Lyonnais**, the Lyon hills. You may like to continue a short distance past Tassin on the N7, then the D7, to visit **Charbonnières-les-Bains**, a popular spa resort in an attractive wooded vale.

Stay on the D489 as it winds and zigzags through the hills. Here and

La Rotonde €€–€€€
*200 av. du Casino, La
Tour de Salvagny (on the
N7); tel: 04 78 87 00 97,
fax: 04 78 87 81 39; closed
Sun pm and Mon.* The
gourmets of Lyon argue
about this attractive art-
deco restaurant – is it (or
will it be) one of the best
in France, or just very
good? Cooking is rich in
Mediterranean flavours,
and chef Philippe Gauvreau
is fond of vegetables,
which are beautifully
prepared. Good wine list
and, at the end, an
interesting coffee menu.

there are glorious viewpoints off the road, for example close to the high, picturesque rock-perched village of **Yzeron**. At **Duerne**, turn on to the D34 for **CHAZELLES-SUR-LYON ❶**. Here the hill country has come to an end and ahead lies the watery Forez plain. Continue via the D12A and N89 to meet the River Loire at **MONTROND-LES BAINS ❷**.

Detour: From Chazelles-sur-Lyon drive via St-Symphorien-sur-Coise to **ST-ÉTIENNE ❸**. Leave the sights on the north side of town – such as the Museum of Modern Art – until last, as that's the way out of St Étienne on to the main N82 (direction Roanne). The railway line beside the road on the left is the oldest in France, and has been in use since 1827. **St-Galmier**, off to the right, has a good restaurant, which is listed under Montrond. The road continues into Montrond-les Bains.

From Montrond, the N82 passes via the crossroads town of **Feurs**, through **Balbigny**, to meet the N7 and continue into **ROANNE ❹**.

Return from Roanne on the N7 towards Lyon. Although a busy road, this is an attractive hill drive. Turn off left at Nuelles or soon after at Le Grand-Chemin (the Rotonde Restaurant at **La Tour-de-Salvagny** is just beyond). Pick up the D70 and follow this road into **Villefranche-sur-Saône** (*see Beaujolais, page 156*). Turn right on to the N6 as far as **Anse**, where you can cross the Saône to **Trévoux** (*see La Dombes, page 198*). From here follow the D933 (becomes the D433) to prettily located **Neuville-sur-Saône**, standing by a bend in the river. Just beyond, at **Rochetaillée**, it's worth pausing to admire the restored 15th-century château and its terraced river-view gardens. Inside the château there's a superb vintage car museum. The 150 cars on display span the period 1890–1990. Eighteen of the vehicles were made in Lyon. At Rochetaillée, cross to the west side of the Saône again.

Detour: Having crossed the river, take the small roads to explore the hills of the **MONTS D'OR LYONNAIS ❺**.

The D51 follows the west bank of the Saône back into Lyon.

10 km

D985

Chauffailles
D4
D487
D31
Belmont-de-la-Loire
Charlieu
Briennon
Pouilly-sous-Charlieu
D482
Roanne
D53
N7
Perreux
Régny
St-Symphorien-de-Lay
N7
Neulise
N82
Néronde
Balbigny
D1
Nervieux
Panissières
E70
Feurs
D60
D89
ouzan
es-en-an
D8
Montrond-les-Bains
N89
Virigneux
D12
Savigneux
Montbrison
Moingt
Veauche
A72
Andrézieux-Bouthéon
St-Galmier
St-Héand
Bonson
N82
Villars
L'Étrat
St-Just-St-Rambert
St-Étienne
La Ricamarie
Roche-la-Molière
St-Bonnet-le-Château
Unieux
Le Chambon-Feugerolles
Firminy
D46
Monistrol-sur-Loire
St-Didier-en-Velay
St-Pal-de-Mons
Beauzac
D23

Roannais
Montagny
Thizy
Monts du Beaujolais
Cours-la-Ville
917
Ampleuis
Tarare
D8
Violay
Tour Matagrin
999
560
Plaine du Forez

La Chapelle-de-Guinchay
Chénas
Fleurie
Thoissey
Chiroubles
D2
Beaujeu
D37
Mont St-Rigaud
1009
25
Belleville
Montmerle-sur-Saône
Marlieux
St-Trivier-sur-Moignans
Gleizé
Jassans-Riottier
D933
Villeneuve
D904
Villefranche-sur-Saône
Oingt
Trévoux
Reyrieux
St-André-de-Corcy
D485
Le Bois-d'Oingt
Anse
D38
Nuelles
L'Arbresle
D485
D596
N7
La Tour-de-Salvagny
Neuville-sur-Saône
Monts d'Or Lyonnais
Rochetaillée
Rillieux-la-Pape
Mionnay
Miribel
Charbonnières-les-Bains
Caluire-et-Cuire
Tassin-la-Demi-Lune
Lyon
St-Fons
D489
Ste-Foy-l'Argentière
Yzeron
D34
Duerne
Thurins
Brignais
Irigny
A46
St-Martin-en-Haut
Signal de St-André
934
N7
St-Symphorien-d'Ozon
St-Symphorien-sur-Coise
D2
Givors
D42
N86
E15
Chuzelles
Chasse-sur-Rhône
A47
Rive-de-Gier
Loire-sur-Rhône
Pont-Évêque
Vienne
La Grand-Croix
D59
Jardin
L'Horme
Condrieu
St-Chamond
A7
St-Clair-du-Rhône
E70
D7
Pélussin
Mont Pilat
1432
Chavanay
St-Maurice-l'Exil
E15
Le Péage-de-Roussillon
Roussillon
St-Genest-Malifaux
Col de la République
1161
N86
Serrières
N7
D519
Chanas
Bourg-Argental
St-Rambert-d'Albon
Marlhes
Andance
Anneyron
Châteauneuf-de-Galaure
Annonay
D82
Albon

N89
Chazelles-sur-Lyon

D503

Monts du Lyonnais

Bresse

Ratings

Medieval architecture	●●●●●
Restaurants	●●●●●
Towns and villages	●●●●●
Crafts and traditions	●●●●
Markets	●●●●
Children	●●●
Museums	●●●
Scenery	●●●

In the French mind, and perhaps to true gourmets everywhere, Bresse means just one thing: poultry. The only chicken to have its own *appellation contrôlée*, it is judged to be the most delicious in the world. It is hardly possible to drive through Bresse without seeing its famous free-range hens, pullets and capons out in all weathers (notice how they shelter inside the hedges on rainy days). All around are the region's traditional, broad, low farmhouses. Made of timbers and narrow bricks under wide, shallow roofs, each stands comfortably in its own space among fields and copses. The gently rolling lush countryside has the most rustic, old-fashioned feel. Many villages and small farms have kept their old arcaded pavements, and the village markets are full of calm, old-world character (and if you miss them this far you're sure to come across some Bresse chickens here!).

BOURG-EN-BRESSE AND BROU✦✦✦

W *www.inter communalites.com/ bourgenbresse/* (Bourg and its region, in French); *www.bresse.com/* (comprehensive regional site, in French).

The town is pronounced 'Bourk', and its people are called 'Bourgeois'.

Neither the busy commercial market town of Bourg nor its suburban village of Brou are especially appealing. Bourg does have at its heart – just south of the church – a small old quarter with some 15th- to 17th-century houses. However, just outside the centre, the **Église de Brou✦✦✦** is a glorious white wedding-cake of fine Flamboyant Gothic stonework and accomplished craftsmanship that even those with little interest in architecture will love. Or hate – its heavy, complex ornamentation, tracery and refinement repelled the writer Aldous Huxley, among others. Built in the 16th century by Margaret of Austria, it was actually intended as a mausoleum for herself and her beloved husband, Philibert le Beau of Savoy, and also for Philibert's mother, Margaret of Bourbon. Philibert had died at the age of just 24. Money was no object, and for 26 years (1506–32) the greatest Flemish

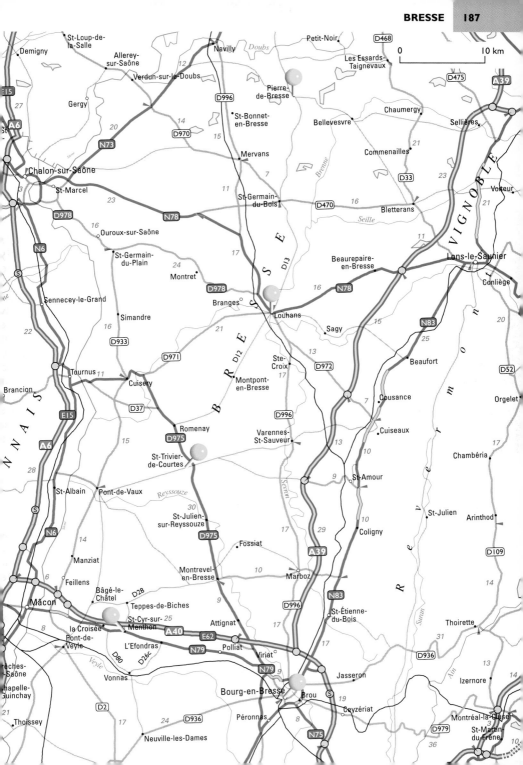

0   10 km

Demigny
St-Loup-de-la-Salle
Allerey-sur-Saône
Verdun-sur-le-Doubs
Navilly
Doubs
Petit-Noir
Les Essards-Taignevaux
D468
D475
A39
Gergy
12
Pierre-de-Bresse
St-Bonnet-en-Bresse
Bellevesvre
Chaumergy
Sellières
Vokeur
27
N73
20
14
D996
D970
15
Mervans
Commenailles
Brenne
21
VIGNOBLE
Chalon-sur-Saône
St-Marcel
23
11
7
St-Germain-du-Bois
D470
16
Bletterans
23
D33
D978
16
N78
St-Germain-du-Plain
Ouroux-sur-Saône
Seille
11
N6
S
17
24
Montret
B R E S S E
D13
Beaurepaire-en-Bresse
Lons-le-Saunier
Conliège
Sennecey-le-Grand
Simandre
16
D978
Branges
16
N78
Louhans
22
21
Sagy
15
N83
25
20
D933
Beaufort
Brancion
D971
Cuisery
Tournus
11
13
D972
D52
E15
Ste-Croix
Cousance
Orgelet
D37
17
Montpont-en-Bresse
7
A6
15
D996
Cuiseaux
17
Romenay
D975
Varennes-St-Sauveur
10
Chambéria
St-Trivier-de-Courtes
13
St-Albain
28
9
St-Amour
Pont-de-Vaux
Reyssouze
St-Julien
Arinthod
S
30
St-Julien-sur-Reyssouze
N6
Sevron
10
14
D975
D109
Manziat
Fossiat
29
Coligny
Feillens
6
Montrevel-en-Bresse
10
A39
14
Bâgé-le-Châtel
D28
Marboz
N83
Mâcon
Teppes-de-Biches
9
D996
St-Étienne-du-Bois
8
St-Cyr-sur-Menthon
25
Attignat
17
Thoirette
D936
la Croisée
A40
E62
Polliat
31
Pont-de-Veyle
N79
Viriat
Izernore
L'Efondras
D80
D26c
Veyle
Vonnas
N79
Jasseron
S
19
13
Bourg-en-Bresse
Brou
Ceyzériat
Montréal-la-Cluse
Thoissey
D2
D936
Péronnas
8
D979
St-Martin-du-Frêne
21
17
24
Neuville-les-Dames
N75
36

artists and craftsmen of the day were employed to create the church. The pale interior is beautifully lit. The rood screen is exceptionally finely carved. The Flamboyant choir doors and exquisitely carved oak choirstalls are remarkable. You can see Margaret's sad face in the church's beautiful stained-glass windows and in sculpture on her tomb. The three elaborately carved tombs lie on the south side of the choir. All around are chapels or oratories, some with outstanding altarpieces and other workmanship.

Beside the church stands Brou's **monastery**, built at the same time, with three attractive galleried cloisters. By being swathed in straw and used as a pig farm, the church and monastery managed to survive untouched during the French Revolution. Later they saw service as a prison, a vagrants' hostel, a barracks and a lunatic asylum. Today, the monastery houses the **Musée de Brou**, which has good collections of 16th- to 20th-century paintings and 12th- to 17th-century sculpture.

Accommodation and food in Bourg and Brou

Hôtel de France €–€€ *19 pl. Bernard, Bourg; tel: 04 74 23 30 24, fax: 04 74 23 69 90.* On a lovely little square at the heart of town, and just upstairs from Jacques Guy's famed restaurant, this 100-year-old hotel mixes faded glory, real luxury and unpretentious affordability!

La Petite Croûte € *9 r. Jules Migonney, Bourg; tel: 04 74 45 34 86, fax: 04 74 23 21 15; closed Sat pm and Sun.* In an atmospheric old house at the heart of town, this restaurant goes for the rustic look, with beams and bare stone. The set menus offer good regional cooking at modest prices.

Restaurant Jacques Guy €€–€€€ *19 pl. Bernard, Bourg; tel: 04 74 45 29 11, fax: 04 74 24 73 69.* A wide variety of imaginative beautifully prepared dishes at the best restaurant in Bourg. The lowest priced set three-course menu is an exceptional bargain.

Bresse poultry – beware of imitations!

Bresse is the champagne of chicken. And like champagne, it has many imitators and substitutes for the real thing. That's why the famed poultry of Bresse has its own wine-style *appellation d'origine contrôlée*, making it an offence to describe chicken as Bresse poultry unless it meets several strict requirements. Bresse poultry is recognisable by its colours: pure white plumage, skin and flesh; ears white or lightly reddened; pure, sleek blue feet; bright red crest and 'beard'. No *Poulet de Bresse* chicken must be younger than four months at slaughter. In addition, all Bresse poultry must be: pure Bresse breed; raised in Bresse; completely free-range, living on lush grass until the last two to four weeks of life; fattened in special cages for the last two to four weeks; given only unadulterated sweetcorn, cereals and dairy products to eat; identifiable with a ring showing the name and address of the farmer, attached to its left leg; after slaughter, certified by the merchant's tricolour seal at the base of its neck, in addition to the *Volaille de Bresse appellation d'origine contrôlée* label.

LOUHANS✧✧

Louhans Tourist Office / Arcades St-Jean, Place St-Jean; tel: 03 85 75 05 02, fax: 03 85 76 01 84, e-mail: otlouhans@wanadoo.fr; open Mon–Sat 0930–1200, 1400–1900, Sun in summer only, approx 1015–1200. In summer, guided town visits start from the tourist office at 1400 on Tue, Thur and Sat. The tourist office also arranges guided tours of the villages and country sights around Louhans.

This important local centre stands at the meeting of southern and northern Bresse, beside the confluence of the Seille and Solnan rivers. It's the ideal of a busy, well-to-do market town, with commerce and industry both old and new. Picturesque and historic, it thrives on sales of its dairy produce, pigs and, of course, poultry. It's a centre for local craft sales too. Country people from all around the region come for its weekly poultry market. Walk along Grande Rue, with its lovely ensemble of 15th-century wood and stone arcades and façades, down to the riverside, then back along Rue des Dôdanes, stepping into the old lanes linking these two central streets. Historical highlights of the town are its late 17th-century **Hôtel Dieu (Charity Hospital)**✧✧, with a magnificent **apothecary**✧✧✧, with carved wood and glassware immaculately polished and gleaming, and the former print workshop of the 19th-century local Bresse newspaper *L'Indépendant*, now preserved as a fascinating **Musée de l'Imprimerie (Printing Museum)**✧✧.

Hôtel Dieu et Apothicaire €€ *R. du Capitaine Vic; tel: 03 85 75 54 32; open Mar–Sept. Guided visits (in French) daily at 1030 (not Sun), 1430 and 1600, closed Tue, Oct–Feb same times, but on Mon, Thur and Sat only.*

Musée de l'Imprimerie € *29 r. des Dôdanes; tel: 03 85 76 27 16; open 15 May–end Sept, daily 1500–1900, rest of the year Mon–Fri 1400–1800.*

Markets: *Bresse poultry market – Mon am; market fair – twice monthly.*

Festivals: *Concours de Volailles de Bresse ('La Glorieuse') – poultry fair in Dec; Fête de Pentecôte – local festival at Whitsun.*

Accommodation and food in Louhans

Hôtel-Restaurant Le Moulin de Bourgchâteau €€ *Rte de Chalons; tel: 03 85 75 37 12, fax: 03 85 75 45 11; closed Mon midday and Sun in winter.* It's a real *moulin* (mill), dating to the 18th century and standing on the River Seille. Tranquil, simple, rustic with bare wood and stone, full of charm and cosy comfort. Generous breakfasts. The first-floor restaurant is traditional, and serves local specialities to a high standard, at a very moderate price.

Six Ecomusées de la Bresse Bourguignonne

The Ecomuseum has six other 'branches' in the region, open on summer afternoons only (closed Tue). They are the wine and winemaking museum at Cuiseaux, the former print workshop at Louhans (see page 189), a traditional chair-maker's at Rancy, a museum of Bresse farming at St-Germain-du-Bois (see page 192), a museum of traditional forestry at St-Martin-en-Bresse and the museum of traditional breadmaking at Verdun-sur-le-Doubs.

Chicken shows

Every year on about 15 Dec *Poulet de Bresse* farmers show off their birds at traditional shows in Louhans, Pont de Vaux, Montrevel and Bourg-en-Bresse.

PIERRE-DE-BRESSE❖❖

Pierre-de-Bresse Tourist Office *Pl. du Château; tel: 03 85 76 24 95.*

Château and Ecomusée de la Bresse Bourguignonne €€ *On the D13, south of town; tel: 03 85 76 27 16, fax: 03 85 72 84 33; open 15 May–15 Sept, daily 1000–1900, rest of the year, daily 1400–1800.*

An astonishingly grand 17th-century moated **château**❖❖❖ stands on the edge of this country town in the north of Bresse. Dignified and pale under an ornate black roof, in a huge formal park, it was constructed by the Counts of Thiard. Today, the château belongs to the local municipality and is home to the excellent **Ecomusée de la Bresse Bourguignonne (Bresse Bourguignonne Ecomuseum)**❖❖❖. A wide variety of permanent and temporary displays and videos evoke the daily life, traditions, customs and culture of northern Bresse. It's also a good place to buy local products.

St-Cyr-sur-Menthon*

Domaine des Planons €€ Tel: 03 85 36 31 22; open 1st Sun in Apr to 11 Nov. Guided visits (1½ hours) are available in French.

There are many attractive old buildings in and around this little town (only 12km from Mâcon). It's at the heart of a 'Saracen chimneys' area (see below), and one of the best examples can be seen on the nearby farm museum of **Domaine des Planons**. A working farm until 1984 – although it was already a listed building and a historic site – this is a picture-perfect example of the traditional farmhouse. Dating from 1490, it has preserved most of its original features, and, thanks to an inventory of the farm dated 1784, it has been possible to recreate the farm as it was at that time. Parts of the farm and grounds are family entertainment as much as museum, with sound-effect tapes in some of the buildings, a duckpond and living displays on poultry-raising today.

Saracen chimneys

A number of the older houses in the Bresse have odd, ornate chimneys called Saracen chimneys. Mostly 200 or 300 years old, these are topped with a hood that makes them look like miniature belfries. A few are indeed tall enough to be belfries. It is not clear what their purpose was, but seems unlikely that they have anything to do with the Moors or Arabs, who were called Saracens. Saracen chimneys tend to be found in a cluster together – a number can be seen near St-Trivier-de-Courtes.

Above
Domaine des Planons

St-Trivier-de-Courtes ❖❖

Above
Ferme-Musée de la Forêt, St-Trivier-de-Courtes

This village has a supremely picturesque ancient centre, all cobbles and old cottages. Wander about to discover many 15th- and 16th-century buildings, some humble cottages, others grand residences. There are remnants of 12th-century fortifications, a former salt warehouse and a hospice with a Renaissance tower. Just outside the village, the **Ferme-Musée de la Forêt** gives you a chance to take a look inside 16th-century farm buildings, now arranged as a museum of Bresse country life.

Suggested tour

Total distance: 87km, or 120km if you take the detour.

Time: An easy 1 day.

Links: At Bourg-en-Bresse the route links with La Dombes (*see page 200*).

Route: Leave **BOURG-EN-BRESSE** ❶ on the N79 northwards. The N79 veers west (towards Mâcon) 4km out of Bourg, but our route continues straight, on the D975, to **Montrevel-en-Bresse** ❷.

Detour: Where the N79 turns left, stay with it. Pass through a succession of main-road villages until L'Efondras, where you turn left on to the D26c to go into **Vonnas**. Leave on the D80 and follow this country road as far as **ST-CYR-SUR-MENTHON** ❸. Turn off right here, on the D80, to **Teppes-de-Biches** on the D28. Turn right here to reach Montrevel-en-Bresse.

Stay on the road to **ST-TRIVIER-DE-COURTES** ❹. Continue on the D975 to **Romenay**, where you turn off the main road on to the D12, on the right. You are now entering the more varied and wooded country of the Bresse Bourguignonne. The road runs to **LOUHANS** ❺. Leave Louhans on the country road (D13) for **St-Germain-du-Bois**, where there is an interesting and varied farm museum, open in summer only (*tel: 03 85 76 27 16*). This road at last reaches **PIERRE-DE-BRESSE** ❻, at the northern edge of the Bresse.

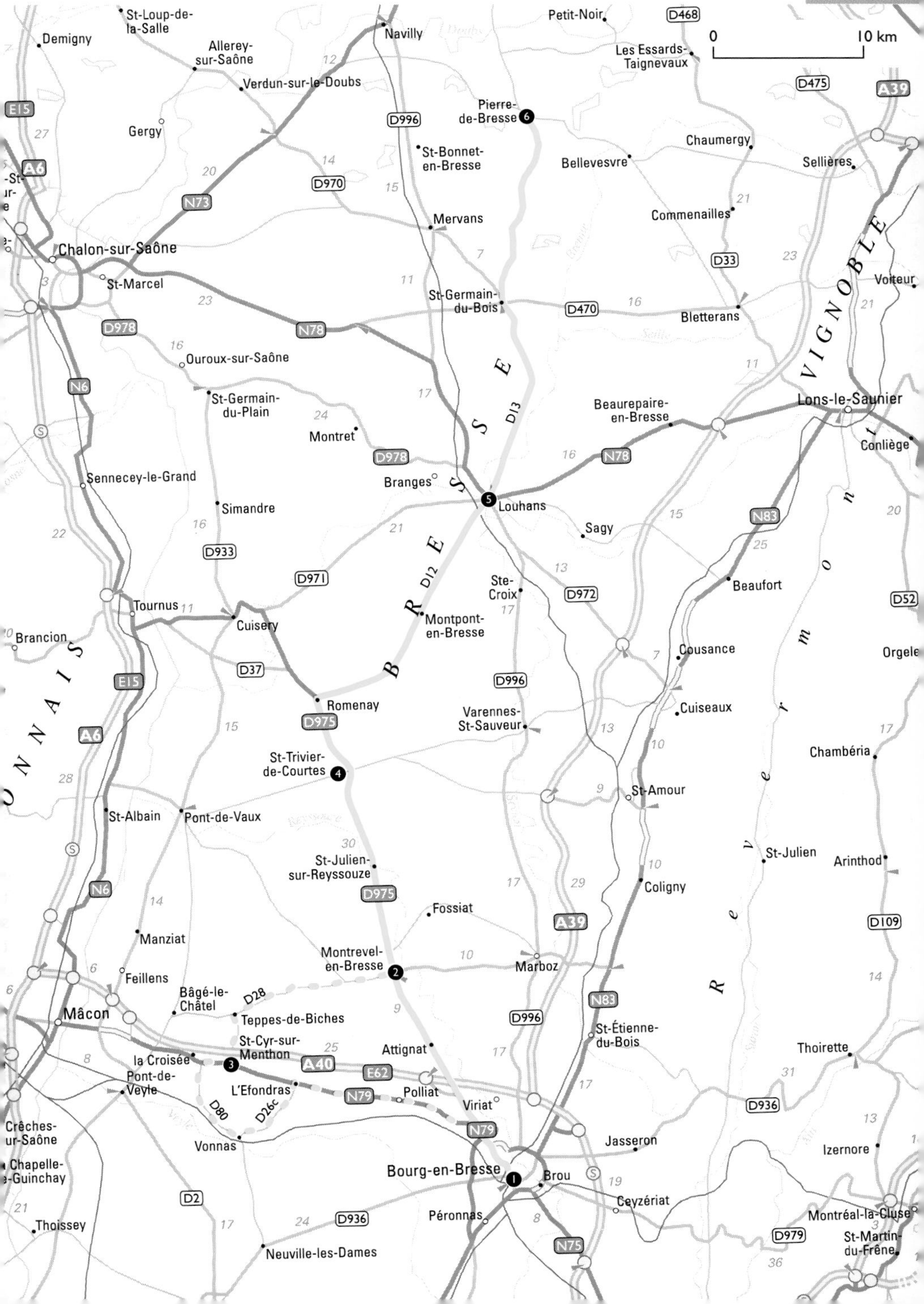

St-Loup-de-la-Salle
Demigny
Allerey-sur-Saône
Navilly
Petit-Noir
D468
0   10 km
Les Essards-Taignevaux
D475
A39
Verdun-sur-le-Doubs
E15
Gergy
D996
Pierre-de-Bresse 6
Chaumergy
Sellières
N73
D970
St-Bonnet-en-Bresse
Bellevesvre
Commenailles
D33
Voiteur
A6
-St-
ure-
e
3
Chalon-sur-Saône
St-Marcel
Mervans
St-Germain-du-Bois
D470
Bletterans
Lons-le-Saunier
D978
Ouroux-sur-Saône
N78
St-Germain-du-Plain
Conliège
N6
Montret
D978
Beaurepaire-en-Bresse
Branges
N78
Sennecey-le-Grand
Simandre
Louhans 5
Sagy
N83
Beaufort
D933
D971
D52
Tournus
Cuisery
Ste-Croix
D972
Cousance
Orgele
Brancion
D37
Montpont-en-Bresse
Cuiseaux
E15
A6
Romenay
D996
Chambéria
D975
Varennes-St-Sauveur
St-Trivier-de-Courtes 4
St-Amour
St-Albain
Pont-de-Vaux
St-Julien
Arinthod
St-Julien-sur-Reyssouze
D109
D975
Coligny
N6
Fossiat
Manziat
Montrevel-en-Bresse 2
Marboz
A39
Feillens
Bâge-le-Châtel
D28
Teppes-de-Biches
N83
St-Étienne-du-Bois
Thoirette
Mâcon
St-Cyr-sur-Menthon
A40
D996
D936
la Croisée 3
E62
Pont-de-Veyle
L'Efondras
Polliat
Izernore
Crêches-sur-Saône
D80
D26c
N79
Viriat
N79
Vonnas
Bourg-en-Bresse 1
Brou
Jasseron
Chapelle-Guinchay
Attignat
Montréal-la-Cluse
D2
Ceyzériat
D979
St-Martin-du-Frêne
Thoissey
D936
Péronnas
N75
Neuville-les-Dames

BRESSE
VIGNOBLE
BRIONNAIS
Revermont

La Dombes

Ratings

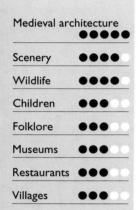

Medieval architecture	●●●●●
Scenery	●●●●○
Wildlife	●●●●○
Children	●●●○○
Folklore	●●●○○
Museums	●●●○○
Restaurants	●●●○○
Villages	●●●○○

A calm, quiet, almost flat land of shallow lakes, rough meadows, copses and tiny farms, La Dombes is rustic and unpolished. Apart from a few small towns and isolated farmhouses, it often appears strangely empty, like a sort of lush, green desert. La Dombes has over 1000 lakes, most artificially created centuries ago from marshy, waterlogged terrain. Before the huge 19th-century drainage programme, there were twice as many. A complicated system of drainage allows farmers to drain one lake into another to refresh the water. At the region's centre is a large Ornithological Park, a reserve for wildfowl. The region's simple country buildings, mainly constructed of uncut stone or terracotta bricks, have a rough, attractive quality. At the edges of La Dombes are fine, prosperous old towns, which derived great wealth from the lakes without having to get their own feet wet!

CHÂTILLON-SUR-CHALARONNE✦✦

ⓘ Châtillon Tourist Office *Pavillon du Tourisme, Place du Champ de Foire; tel: 04 74 55 02 27, fax: 04 74 55 34 78; winter hours Tue–Sat 0900–1200, 1400–1800 (closed Sun and Mon), summer hours Mon–Sat 0900–1200, 1400–1830, Sun 1500–1800. Summer annexe Apothicaire, pl. St-Vincent de Paul; open Sun and Mon.*

One of the region's larger towns, Châtillon stands at the meeting of La Dombes and La Bresse regions. It's a busy local commercial focal point, bustling and pretty with flowers, though with many modern buildings to match the old. At its centre, though, there are whole streets of attractive historic buildings in irregular brick and exposed timber. It's especially lovely beside the River Chalaronne, crossed by picturesque, flower-covered bridges. Beside the river, the 17th-century Ancien Hôpital is one of the most appealing of the town's old, low, brick buildings, arranged around a courtyard. Installed inside is the **Centre Culturel des Dombes✦**, which has a succession of small exhibitions and displays about the region. In the same building, the **Apothicaire✦✦**, the hospital's pharmacy constructed in 1814 and never changed, preserves in immaculate condition the rows of fine ceramic jars in their polished wood cabinets in Directoire style (an 18th-century style, current during and after the reign of Louis XVI,

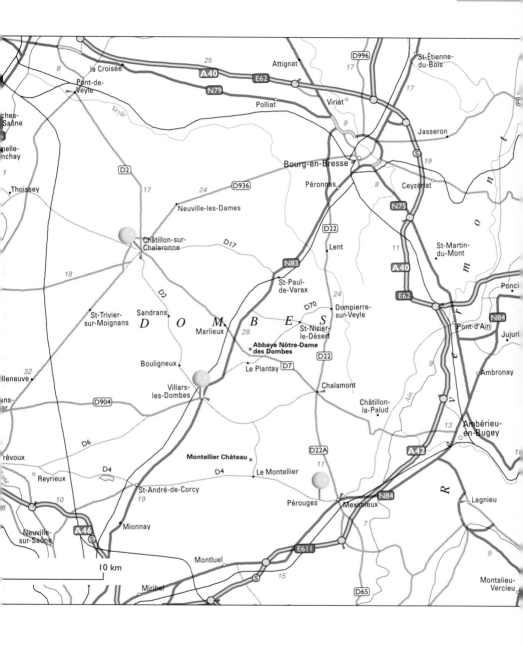

La Croisée
Pont-de-Veyle
25
8
Attignat
D996
St-Étienne-du-Bois
17
A40
E62
N79
Polliat
Viriat
17
Veyle
9
ches-Saône
pelle-nchay
1
Thoissey
D2
Bourg-en-Bresse
Jasseron
19
17
24
D936
Péronnas
Ceyzériat
8
Neuville-les-Dames
N75
Châtillon-sur-Chalaronne
D17
D22
Lent
St-Martin-du-Mont
11
18
St-Paul-de-Varax
N83
A40
Ponci
St-Trivier-sur-Moignans
Sandrans
D2
D70
24
Dompierre-sur-Veyle
E62
D O M B E S
Marlieux
28
St-Nizier-le-Désert
Pont-d'Ain
N84
Jujuri
Bouligneux
Abbaye Nôtre-Dame des Dombes
D22
32
lleneuve
ns-r
Le Plantay
D7
Chalamont
Ambronay
Villars-les-Dombes
D904
Châtillon-la-Palud
13
Amberieu-en-Bugey
D6
D22A
A42
1
révoux
Reyrieux
D4
Montellier Château
D4
Le Montellier
11
9
St-André-de-Corcy
19
Pérouges
Meximieux
N84
R
Lagnieu
A46
Neuville-sur-Saône
Mionnay
10
7
Montluel
E611
9
10 km
Miribel
15
D65
Montalieu-Vercieu

www.amitel:fr/
vdepaul/depaul1
(website of the annual St-
Vincent de Paul festival).

**Centre Culturel
des Dombes** €
Ancien Hôpital, pl. St-Vincent
de Paul; tel: 04 74 55 03
70; Mon–Sat 0900–1200,
1400–1800.

Apothicaire € Ancien
Hôpital, pl. St-Vincent de
Paul; tel/fax: 04 74 55 15
70; open 1000–1200,
1400–1800 (1900
June–Aug), closed Tue.

Musée Tradition et Vie
€ 24 impasse des Remparts;
tel/fax: 04 74 55 15 70;
open 1000–1200,
1400–1800 (1900
June–Aug), closed Tue.

Maison St-Vincent € Pl.
des Halles; tel: 04 74 55 26
64. Guided tours on Sun am.
Phone to check first.

There are several
simple chambres
d'hôtes (bed and
breakfasts) and gîtes ruraux
(rental cottages) available
in the area. Ask local
tourist offices for details.

A large, colourful
market with flowers,
poultry and local produce
takes place on Sat am in
the historic Halles.

embracing Revolutionary emblems and civic symbols). Also displayed in the apothecary is Châtillon's remarkable triptych (a religious painting on three wooden panels) of 1527.

Châtillon was once fortified. Rising behind the Ancien Hôpital are ruins of a medieval castle. On its access road, the **Musée Tradition et Vie (Museum of Traditional Life)***, using eclectic, evocative tableaux with models and authentic tools and equipment, depicts rural life and work in past times in the Dombes and the Bresse. In r. Victor Hugo, the impressive 14th-century Porte de Villars is a surviving town gate made all of rough bricks. The revered St-Vincent de Paul, founder of worldwide charitable missions to the poor, lodged in the town in 1617, and while here created the Order of the Sisters of Charity. The house is now known as the **Maison St-Vincent***. The **Halles**, or covered marketplace, opposite his house (but constructed about 50 years after his stay), is a magnificent structure of massive wooden beams supported by 32 pillars, each of which is the whole trunk of an oak tree. It's still in use for the weekly market.

Accommodation and food in Châtillon-sur-Chalaronne

Hôtel-Restaurant de la Tour €–€€ Pl. de la République; tel: 04 74 55 05 12, fax: 04 74 55 09 19; closed Wed and Sun pm. A decent, family-run restaurant avec chambres in the main square offering good value for money.

Right
Window display in Châtillon-sur-Chalaronne

PÉROUGES✦✦✦

Pérouges Tourist Office *Town entrance; tel: 04 74 61 01 14.* One-hour guided tours in English and French available all year.

www.perouges.org/ (official site about the town, in English and French); *www.festival-perouges.org/* (Pérouges Festival site).

The town is reached from junction 7 of *autoroute* A42, or directly from N84.

No vehicles are allowed in the historic centre; parking is provided outside.

Museum € *Tel: 04 74 61 00 88; open Easter to end Oct 1000–1200, 1400–1800.*

Pérouges music festival takes place in late May and early June.

It's not surprising that a number of French movies have been filmed here, including *The Three Musketeers* and *Monsieur Vincent*. A film director might have had the whole place especially built. Houses with overhanging eaves, narrow steps, twisting lanes and a fortified church from the Middle Ages are perfectly preserved in this wonderfully picturesque little hilltop town at the southeast edge of La Dombes. Almost everything is constructed from the local flint, and dates from the 13th to 16th centuries. In that period (apart from the siege of 1468), the town prospered from its clothmaking and weaving. After the industrial revolution and the start of the railway age, rustic, isolated Pérouges began a decline which meant that by the first decade of the 20th century many houses fell into ruin and were demolished. In 1909 journalist Anthelme Thibault wrote a moving article about the death of the medieval village. Immediately taken up by artists and historians from Lyon, it began a dramatic revival.

R. des Rondes, encircling the old heart of the town, has managed to keep most of its medieval character. The main street, r. du Prince, leads round the Grand Maison des Princes de Savoy (now a **museum✦** of the folk culture of La Dombes and La Bresse), to pl. de la Halle, the delightful old market square dominated by its lime tree, planted during the Revolution. A marked walking tour meanders through the town, and another path (Promenade des Terreaux) follows the former moat from Porte d'en Haut (the Upper Gateway) round to the Porte d'En Bas (the Lower Gateway).

Accommodation and food in Pérouges

Hostellerie du Vieux Pérouges €€–€€€ *Pl. du Tilleul; tel: 04 74 61 00 88, fax: 04 74 34 77 90.* Enjoy great comfort and style at this perfectly located historic inn, on the beautiful little main square of the town. When the tourists have all gone for the night, it's utterly tranquil.

TRÉVOUX❖❖

ⓘ Trévoux Tourist Office *Maison des Sires de Villars, Place du Pont; tel: 04 74 00 36 32, fax: 04 74 00 08 05, e-mail: office.tourisme@mairie-trevoux.fr; open Mon–Sat 1000–1200, 1400–1900 (1800 in winter), Sun 1400–1800, closed Dec and Sun in Jan. Guided tours take place throughout the summer.*

Ⓦ *www.mairie-trevoux.fr/ (official site, in English and French).*

ⓘ Palais du Parlement € *R. du Palais. No phone enquiries except regarding court cases. Open June–Sept, Sat–Sun 1430–1830, and at any other time during court sessions.*

Ⓜ The **market** takes place on Sat am.

A historic and very attractive little town, Trévoux rises on terraces looking south across a curve in the Saône. It was an important place in medieval times, when it was the capital of La Dombes and an independent principality with its own parliament. Rising over the town are the three towers of its ruined 14th-century castle. In the 17th century it was decided that all members of parliament and other officials had to reside in the town, or at least have a house here. That's why many grand homes were constructed at that time, still handsome today. It was also a well-known Jesuit centre with its own printing press. The 17th-century **Palais du Parlement**❖❖❖ – now the regional law courts – has some impressive rooms, notably the courtroom with its beamed ceiling. R. du Gouvernement is the attractive main street with the Jesuit printing press and several other fine old buildings. The 17th-century hospital preserves its wood-panelled pharmacy and a lovely collection of *faïence* from Nevers and Gien. R. de l'Herberie was for Jews only – numerous here until the expulsion of Jews from Burgundy in the 15th century.

VILLARS-LES-DOMBES❖❖

ⓘ Villars-les-Dombes Tourist Office *3 pl. de l'Hôtel de Ville; tel: 04 74 98 06 29, fax: 04 74 98 12 77; open summer Mon–Sat 0900–1230, 1400–1800, winter Mon–Fri 0900–1230, 1400–1800, Sat 0900–1230. The office here covers villages in the whole central area of the Dombes.*

Ⓦ *www.tourisme.fr/ villarslesdombes/ (good site about the town and its region, in English and French).*

At the watery heart of the region, the principal visitor attraction of La Dombes is here: the bird park, or **Parc des Oiseaux**❖❖, on the edge of Villars. This is partly serious wildlife conservation and education, partly family entertainment. A 'little train' makes a very enjoyable tour in the park, or you can stroll at leisure among the easy pathways that lead to different areas and climate houses around two lakes. In the park, many varieties of local herons, egrets, ducks and other waterfowl can be spotted; in addition, you'll see scores of colourful foreign varieties. There are play areas, snackbars and a picnic area in the park. The same site also accommodates (at the entrance) the **Maison de la Dombes**❖❖, with information and displays about the region and its heritage. It has a shop, too, which is a treat in itself, with its wide range of gourmet and farm-made produce from the Dombes.

Accommodation and food in Villars-les-Dombes

Parc des Oiseaux
€€ *On the N83; tel: 04
74 98 05 54, fax: 04 74 98
27 74, www.easypark.
com/francais/regions/01/oise
aux; open daily 0900–1900
(1730 in winter).*

Maison de la Dombes €
*Parc des Oiseaux; tel: 04 74
98 16 66; open Mon–Sat
1000–1300, 1400–1800,
Sun 1000–1900. The shop
is open 0900–1800 (daily in
summer, Mon–Fri in winter).*

On the menu

You'll be plied with fish,
fowl and frogs – all fresh
from the wild. Other
specialities are local
cream, butter, beef, and
duck *foie gras*. Bresse
chicken, too, features
on Dombes menus.

Ribotel Le Parc €€ *34 av. Charles de Gaulle (route de Lyon); tel: 04 74 98
08 03, fax: 04 74 98 29 55.* The uninviting name masks a capable,
comfortable, family-run hotel and restaurant, well-equipped and
friendly.

Restaurant Jean-Claude Bouvier €€ *83 rte de Lyon; tel: 04 74 98 11 91,
fax: 04 74 98 24 42; closed Sun pm and Mon.* The classic Dombes and
Bresse specialities are prepared and served with flair and skill here.
There's a pretty terrace for outdoor summer eating.

Suggested tour

Auberge des Chasseurs €€ *On main road through the village of Bouligneux; tel: 04 74 98 10 02, fax: 04 74 98 28 87; closed Tue pm and Wed.* Large, interesting, spacious premises house this good-quality restaurant where the emphasis is on Dombes game and fish. On the north edge of the village close to the lake and castle.

Le Thou €€ *On main road through the village of Bouligneux; tel: 04 74 98 15 25, fax: 04 74 98 13 57; closed Mon and Tue.* Hearty, meaty Dombes specialities are served at this good quality, moderately priced restaurant beside the road on the edge of the village. It's near the castle and the lake.

W *www.multimania.com/ sandrans/* (introduction to the village of Sandrans, with information on local events, in French only).

Total distance: 107km, or 144km if you take the detour.

Time: 1 day.

Links: At Bourg-en-Bresse the route links with the Bresse region (*see page 192*). At Trévoux, it links with the West of Lyon route (*see page 183*).

Route: Leave **Bourg-en-Bresse** on the N83 (the main road to Lyon), but just 5km out of town veer off left on to the D22 (direction Pérouges). The road follows the little River Veyle. Pass through **Lent**, which has some old timber houses, and reach **Dompierre-sur-Veyle**, which has a Romanesque church at its centre. Turn right here on to a smaller lane, the D70, that straight away leads into the watery, marshy terrain of the Grand Marais. Follow the road through the village of **St-Nizier-le-Désert** – the name implies loneliness and isolation – to reach **Le Plantay**. The sturdy circular tower beside this rather dull little village among the lakes has become a symbol of La Dombes. Also here (2km away) is the **Abbaye Nôtre-Dame des Dombes**, a Trappist community, which in 1863 successfully undertook the task of draining and reclaiming large areas of La Dombes. Double back a few metres to get on to the D7, which ascends to **Chalamont**. At just 334m, this is a high point for La Dombes. The village has an old *lavoir* (wash house) and several old houses, especially along r. des Halles. Follow the D22A to **PÉROUGES** ❶. Head westward from Pérouges on the D4. At **Le Montellier** turn off to the right towards Villars-les-Dombes – off the road stands the redbrick **Montellier Château**, the largest castle in La Dombes.

Detour: Instead of turning off at Le Montellier, continue along the D4 away from the lakeland to **TRÉVOUX** ❷, on the bank of the River Saône. Return from Trévoux on the same road: it is called the D6 just here. After 4km, where the road forks into the D6 and D4, take the D6 to **VILLARS-LES-DOMBES** ❸.

From Villars, take the D2. It's worth pausing at **Bouligneux** to see the impressive brick fortress, a 14th-century feudal castle (and there are a couple of good restaurants here, too). Continue to Sandrans, a small village with some more brick fortifications, and a fine pale church of stone and river pebbles. The road soon arrives at CHÂTILLON-SUR-CHALARONNE ❹. Return on the D17 into the watery heart of the region. Continue all the way to **St-Paul-de-Varax**, a popular little lakeside resort, with a fine old manor house and a Romanesque church. Rejoin the N83 here and return into Bourg.

10 km

Lyon

Ratings

Architecture	●●●●●
Children	●●●●●
Entertainment	●●●●●
History	●●●●●
Museums	●●●●●
Restaurants	●●●●●
Shopping	●●●●●
Street life	●●●●●

Built on silk and socialism, modern Lyon even now combines luxury with earthy directness. The air, light and sense of good living lift the spirit immediately on arrival. Explore the lanes and squares and the curious *traboules*, short-cuts through courtyards and beneath houses. Originally Greek, then Roman, Lyon is now a World Heritage Site and the second largest conurbation in France. Its excellent museums all tell chapters in the city's dramatic, often painful story. The setting on two large rivers is striking too: the Rhône pours from the Alps into Lyon to meet the darker Saône coming from Burgundy. Of the two, the Saône is the more approachable. On its right bank rises the city's atmospheric old quarter. Above all, Lyon is France's great gastronomic city. The old streets and lanes are packed with discreet little high-quality, modestly priced restaurants, called *bouchons* or *mères*.

Getting there and getting around

ⓘ **Lyon Tourist Office**
Office du Tourisme et des Congrès du Grand Lyon, *Pavillon du Tourisme, Place Bellecour; tel: 04 72 77 69 69, fax: 04 78 42 04 32, e-mail: lyoncvb@lyon-france.com, www.lyon-france.com; open daily all year.*

By road
The city is circled on the east side by the A46. There is also a complicated *périphérique* (ring road), partly in tunnels, whose closest point to the city centre is at Perrache. Expect heavy congestion.

By rail
Lyon's two principal city centre stations – Part-Dieu and Perrache – have TGV links direct to Paris, Dijon, Lille, Marseille and Montpellier.

200 metres
150 yards

Musée d'Art
Contemporain
and La Cité
Internationale

Parc de la
Tête d'Or

Pont de Winston
Churchill

LA CROIX-ROUSSE

Maison
des Canuts

Place de
la Croix-
Rousse

Rhône

Avenue de Grande Bretagne

Boulevard des Belges

Musée
d'Histoire
Naturelle

Boulevard de la Croix Rousse

TUNNEL DE LA CROIX ROUSSE

de la Croix Rousse

Place de la
Croix-Rousse

Rue Duquesne

Avenue du Maréchal Foch

Rue Sully

Rue Créqui

Rue Garibaldi

Rue Dupont

Montée de la Grande Côte

Pont
de Lattre
Tassigny

Rue Tronchet

Cours Vitton

Amphithéâtre
des Trois Gaules

Quai André Lassagne

Cours du Général Giraud

Jardin des Chartreux

TERREAUX

Place de la
Comédie

Place du
Maréchal
Lyautey

Cours Franklin Roosevelt

Massén

Quai St-Vincent

Notre-Dame-
St-Vincent

Hôtel
de Ville

Opéra
de Lyon

Quai Jean Moulin

Pont
Morand

Avenue du Maréchal de Saxe

Saône

Quai Pierre Scize

Église
St-Paul

Place des
Terreaux

Quai de Bondy

Quai de la Pêcherie

Musée des
Beaux-Arts

Quai du Général Sarrail

Rue Bugeaud

Rue Juliette Récamier

Gare St-Paul

Rue Franklin

Théâtre
Guignol

St-Nizier

FOURVIÈRE

Rue St-Jean

Musée de
l'Imprimerie

Pont
Alphonse Juin

Palais du
Commerce

Rue de la République

Rue du Président Édouard Herriot

Pont
La Fayette

Cours La Fayette

Basilique
Notre-Dame
de Fourvière

Funiculaire

Palais de
Justice

Rue Rolland

St-Bonaventure

Rue du Président Carnot

Quai Victor Augagneur

EAST
BANK

Cathédrale
St-Jean

Rue Romain

Place des
Jacobins

Place de la
République

Pont
Wilson

Rue de la République

Quai Jules Courmont

Cours Gambetta

Avenue du Maréchal de Saxe

Rue Moncey

de la
isation
maine

Hôpital de
l'Antiquaille

VIEUX
LYON

Quai des Célestins autrefois du-Retz

Rue du Col. Chambonnet

Rue Bonaparte

Quai St-Antoine

LA PRESQU'
ÎLE

Place de
l'Hôpital

Cours de la Liberté

Pont
St-Georges

Quai Tilsitt

Place Bellecour

Hôtel Dieu

St-Just

Rue A. Fochier

Rue Sala

Place
Antonin
Poncet

Pont de la
Guillotière

Place
A. Jutard

Place
A. Vollon

St-François

Place
G. Péri

St-Martin
d'Ainay

Rue Victor Hugo

Rue Ste-Hélène

Hôtel des
Postes

Rue Sala

Cours Gambetta

Quai Maréchal Joffre

Rue Vaubecour

Rue de la Charité

Musée des
Tissus

Rue Pasteur

Rue de Marseille

Quai Fulchiron

Saône

Musée des
Arts Décoratifs

Quai du Dr. Gailleton

Pont de
l'Université

Rue de Condé

Place
Carnot

Ste-Croix

Rhône

Quai Claude Bernard

Avenue Jean Jaurès

D487

Pont
Kitchener
Marchand

J. Moulin
Lyon III
Universités

Rue de l'Université

Quai Rambaud

Pont
Galliéni

A7

Gare de
Perrache

Centre d'Histoire
de la Résistance
et de la Déportation

www.ec-lyon.fr/ (good city site prepared by Ecole Centrale de Lyon); *www.mairie-lyon.fr/* (comprehensive city site from Lyon Town Hall; click 'tourism'); *www.welcome.to/lyon/* (Danish-run guide to Lyon); *www.lyon-france.com* (the city's comprehensive official site for visitors); *www.leprogres.fr/* (*Le Progrès* online, with practical and current affairs and what's on info about the Lyon region).

Most Lyon museums are closed Mon and some public holidays.

Lyon City Card

The Lyon City Card covers 14 of Lyon's top museums and is valid for one, two or three days at differing prices. It's also valid for city tours, river cruises and access to Fourvière. *Contact the tourist office or see www.lyon-france.com.*

What's on

Weekly *Lyon Poche* and *Lyon Cap* and monthly *Lyon Mag* from news-stands have full listings.

Right
La Croix-Rousse quarter

By air

There are dozens of internal and international flights daily to Lyon-Saint Exupéry International Airport, about 25km from the city centre.

Parking

There is metered street parking, as well as car parks at pl. Bellecour, pl. des Terreaux and other main squares along the Saône quays, and on the Rhône's east bank.

Getting around the city

The Metro runs on four lines. Most useful to visitors are Line A (Perrache–Bellecour–Hôtel de Ville) and Line D (Bellecour–Vieux Lyon). The bus service is comprehensive. The very inexpensive *Ticket Liberté* (the same price as just three single journeys) gives unlimited travel for a whole day.

City tours and trips out of town

The tourist office organises or takes bookings for the following sightseeing tours:

- guided walking tours of Vieux-Lyon, Croix-Rousse and the city centre (some themed – eg silk, *traboules*, etc);
- two-hour guided bus tours of the city;
- cruises on the rivers.

You can also hire a walkman for a do-it-yourself city walking tour lasting about three hours.

Sights

Amphithéâtre des Trois Gaules €
Montée de la Grande Côte.

Maison des Canuts €€
10–12 r. d'Ivry; tel: 04 78 28 62 04, fax: 04 78 28 16 93; open 0830–1200, 1400–1830, closed Sun.

Traboules

These curious passageways (often with a front door opening on to the street) are rights of way running beneath or through private buildings – often via a central courtyard. There are hundreds of them altogether, making a secretive maze. The name comes from Latin *transambulare* (walk through), but *traboules* date from the 16th century, when they started as short-cuts for silk carriers. Over the centuries these house-to-house alleys served as escape routes during times of unrest, rebellion and persecution, and helped to make Lyon a centre of resistance during the Second World War.

La Croix-Rousse✦✦

Once the gritty proletarian neighbourhood of the *canuts*, Lyon's hard-bitten and badly paid silk-workers, this characterful 19th-century hillside district north of pl. Terreaux (*see page 207*) remains a run-down clothing district, though it has become almost trendy in parts. The high-ceilinged blocks where families once toiled with their looms are being restored, and today the area has an arty, mixed, leftist chic.

The long, steep Montée de la Grande Côte – down which silk workers marched in 1831 with their black flags and their slogan ('Live Working or Die Fighting') into gunfire (600 died) – climbs up through the centre of the district. On its left lies the **Amphithéâtre des Trois Gaules✦**, the meeting place for delegates of the Gallic tribes under Roman rule, dating from about 19 BC. It's worth turning off to explore the Croix-Rousse alleys and stairways. The *traboules* (*see left*) of this district are especially maze-like and intriguing. Reaching the top of the hill, the **Maison des Canuts✦✦** preserves the craftsmanship of the silk-workers, and you can watch loom operators at work (and buy their products).

Right
Silk machine

Musée d'Histoire Naturelle €€ 28 blvd des Belges; tel: 04 72 69 05 00; open Wed–Sun 1300–1800. In school holidays (except summer holidays) Mon–Sun 1030–1800.

Musée d'Art Contemporain €€ 81 quai Charles de Gaulle; tel: 04 72 69 17 18, fax: 04 72 69 17 00, e-mail: stella@mairie-lyon.fr; open Wed–Sun 1200–1900.

Centre d'Histoire de la Résistance et de la Déportation €€ 12–14 av. Bérthelot; tel: 04 78 72 23 11, fax: 04 72 73 32 98; open Wed–Fri 0900–1730. Not suitable for children.

Fourvière can be reached by climbing the steep stairways called Montées, or more swiftly on funicular railcars from Gare St-Jean in Vieux Lyon.

Basilique Nôtre-Dame € Tel: 04 78 25 13 01; open 0700–1900.

Musée de la Civilisation Gallo-Romaine and Parc Archéologique € 17 r. Cléberg; tel: 04 72 3881 90; open Wed–Sun 0930–1200, 1400–1800.

Right
Basilique Nôtre-Dame

East bank (of the Rhône)✦

Lyon's east bank districts have come to symbolise modernism. The main commercial focus, La Part-Dieu, is dominated by the rocket-shaped 142m-high Tour Crédit Lyonnais, visible all across the city centre. A few hundred metres north is the extensive Parc de la Tête d'Or. With its lake, Guignol shows and superb rose garden, it's a popular outing for Lyon residents. On the edge of the park is Lyon's surprising **Musée d'Histoire Naturelle✦✦**, surprising because it contains not just a first-rate overview of natural history, but also exceptional collections of Egyptian and Oriental art and ethnography.

Between the park and the river a vast new riverside complex is being built. La Cité Internationale, with its red-brick buildings and greenery, includes shops, cultural centres and a cinema complex, as well as residential and hotel areas. Also here is the **Musée d'Art Contemporain✦**, still with the original 1930s façade of the former exhibition building it occupies, dedicated to 20th-century art.

To the south, across the river from the Perrache area, is the harrowing **Centre d'Histoire de la Résistance et de la Déportation✦✦✦**. As a focal point of the Resistance, an important centre of the Gestapo and a city with a large Jewish population, Lyon was deeply marked by the Nazi occupation. The centre is housed in the former Gestapo headquarters (1942–4). There's a permanent exhibition inside the cells and cellars where Jews and suspected Resistance members were tortured and killed. Here you can watch a video (45 minutes) of people who survived, giving their testimony at the trial of Lyon's Gestapo chief, Klaus Barbie.

Fourvière✦✦

Looking down across the city from the heights of Fourvière hill is the **Basilique Nôtre-Dame✦**, built in 1896, a striking landmark, especially at night, but a crazy, tasteless mishmash of multi-coloured marble and mosaic seen close up. The view of the city, though (notably from the belvedere behind the adjoining Vieux Chapelle), is magnificent. A short walk south of the basilica is the site of the Roman city, or **Parc Archéologique✦**, still being excavated and dominated by remnants of two Roman theatres. The site's **Musée de la Civilisation Gallo-Romaine✦✦✦**, partly buried in the hillside, displays the many exceptional finds made at the site.

Musée de l'Imprimerie et de la Banque €€ *13 r. de la Poulaillerie; tel: 04 78 37 65 9, fax: 04 78 38 25 95; open Wed–Sun 0930–1200, 1400–1800 (no midday closing on Fri).*

Musée des Beaux-Arts €€ *20 pl. Terreaux; tel: 04 72 10 17 40, fax: 04 78 28 12 45; open 1020–1800, closed Tue.*

Musée des Tissus €€ *34 r. de la Charité; tel: 04 78 38 42 00, fax: 04 72 40 25 12; open 1000–1200, 1400–1730; closed Mon. Joint ticket and joint entrance with Musée des Arts Décoratifs.*

Musée des Arts Décoratifs *See Musée des Tissus.*

Below
Place des Terreaux

La Presqu'île (city centre)***

On the narrow peninsula (*presqu'île*) between the two great rivers which confine the city centre lies a tangle of narrow old streets and tinier squares, edged with high old buildings and the small restaurants for which the city is famous. Lying in the middle of the peninsula is the broad pedestrianised r. de la République, lined with chic boutiques and grandiose 19th-century façades in pale golden stone, where shoppers stroll between café tables and buskers. There are several more big squares here, like the amusing pl. des Terreaux (Earthwaters) with its wildly ornate lead fountain by Bartholdi and a pavement pierced with a multitude of smaller water spouts which pedestrians must dodge if they want to keep their feet dry.

Housed in the 15th-century Hôtel de la Couronne, the fascinating **Musée de l'Imprimerie et de la Banque (Museum of Printing and Banking)*** ranges across the whole subject from Gutenberg's Bible (1455) to modern print-shop lithography. The **Musée des Beaux-Arts (Fine Arts Museum)****, in an attractive former Benedictine abbey, contains a vast and varied collection of different periods, genres and cultures.

The **Musée des Tissus (Fabrics Museum)**** displays extraordinary, dazzling collections of beautiful fabrics, astonishing not just for the richness of design and quality of workmanship, but for the almost incredible age and pedigree of some of the items. Its neighbour, the **Musée des Arts Décoratifs (Museum of Decorative Arts)****, focuses (mainly) on the opulent, extravagant workmanship of 17th- to 19th-century furnishings, ornaments, wall covering and interior decoration.

Gare St-Jean This station just south of Cathédrale St-Jean is served by the Metro and is the terminal of the two funiculars that climb Fourvière hill.

Musée Historique de Lyon €€ *1 pl. du Petit-Collège; tel: 04 78 42 03 61, fax: 04 78 42 79 71; open 1045–1800, closed Tue.*

Musée International de la Marionnette *Joint ticket and joint entrance with Musée Historique de Lyon.*

Théâtre Guignol *2 r. Louis Carrand; tel: 04 78 28 92 57, fax: 04 78 30 00 52; performances Wed and Sat at 1500 and 1615, and Sun at 1500. Adult shows at 2030 (phone or visit for programme).*

Cathédrale St-Jean € *Pl. St-Jean; tel: 04 78 42 25 75; variable hours.* The **astronomical clock** chimes and automata operate at 1200, 1400 and 1500.

Église St-Paul € *R. St-Paul; tel 04 78 28 34 45; open 1200–1800.*

Above
Théâtre Guignol

Vieux Lyon (Old Quarter)♦♦♦

Six bridges cross from the Presqu'île to Lyon's narrow Old Town on the Saône's steep right bank, which climbs the Fourvière hill. With the recent restorations, it has become clear that many of the quarter's 300 or so magnificent Renaissance houses stand on Roman foundations. The main street of the quarter is r. St-Jean. Other picturesque streets and lanes, running parallel to the river, are cut across by steep stairways called *montées* and vaulted old *traboules* leading into inner courtyards, which often have elaborate 16th-century Renaissance galleries and staircase towers. One of the best of these is at 28 r. St-Jean.

The largest of the old quarter's 16th-century houses, Hôtel de Gadagne, has two museums. The **Musée Historique de Lyon (Lyon Historical Museum)**♦ contains all sorts of old items of pottery, furniture and intriguing historical documents. The **Musée International de la Marionnette (International Puppet Museum)**♦♦ preserves numerous historical marionettes and glove puppets, including, of course, the local Guignol puppets (*see below*).

Vieux Lyon grew around two important churches. The oldest of them, **Cathédrale St-Jean**♦♦♦, built from the 12th century, has an unusual façade, with 320 medallions and ornate carvings. The entertaining 14th-century **astronomical clock**♦♦♦ has figures that pop in and out like cuckoos. The faces tell the time, day and date, and the religious feast days up to the year 2019. Built not long after, **Église St-Paul**♦ has suffered much damage but has an attractive octagonal bell tower.

Guignol

The insolent Guignol, his long-suffering wife Madelon and their boozy, Beaujolais-quaffing friend Gnafron have been fixtures on the Lyon scene for around 200 years. Representing typical Lyonnais characters, these glove puppets – invented by Lyonnais silk-worker Laurent Mourguet – act out their boisterous, bawdy stories at indoor or outdoor puppet shows around town. Pitched at children and adults alike, Guignol is a traditional Lyonnais entertainment. Depending on the venue and the audience, the language can be hard-edged and satirical for grown-ups, or simple and hilarious for kids. It's hard to understand, though, if you don't speak any French. For performances, go to the **Théâtre Guignol** or take a look, too, at the **Petit Musée Fantastique de Guignol (Fantastic Little Guignol Museum)** (*6 r. St-Jean; tel: 04 78 37 01 67; open Wed–Sun 1000–1730*).

Accommodation and food in Lyon

On the menu

Lyon is France's foremost gastronomic city, with over 1 000 restaurants in the central districts. Local cuisine is rich in butter and *charcuterie* (pork products) and uses plenty of Charolais beef, Bresse chicken, Dombes game and fish and high-quality farm produce from country districts all round the city. Onions, too, are essential ingredients in Lyon cooking – *Lyonnaise* usually means cooked with onions. Lyon favourites include *gras-double* (ox tripe) and *cervelas* (garlic-rich pork sausage). One hundred years ago, women chefs running small restaurants, where robust set meals were served at a modest price, gave rise to the tradition of *mères*, traditional Lyonnais bistros. These are still part of the city's life, though now the chefs are men and settings have become more luxurious. Another Lyon tradition is the *bouchon*, the down-to-earth traditional restaurant specialising in local dishes.

Hôtel Globe et Cécil €€ *21 r. Gasparin; tel: 04 78 42 58 95, fax: 04 72 41 99 06.* Excellent value for money, this is one of the most appealing *presqu'île* hotels (it's near pl. Bellecour). Friendly and efficient, it has good service and attractively furnished rooms.

Hôtel Normandie € *R. Béllier; tel: 04 78 37 31 36, fax: 04 72 40 98 56.* Convenient and cheap, right next to Perrache station (but in a fairly quiet adjoining street), this traditional simple hotel offers small but neat and attractive rooms.

Hôtel St-Vincent €€ *9 r. Pareille; tel: 04 78 27 22 56, fax: 04 78 30 92 87.* Some rooms at this characterful traditional place, near pl. Terreaux, have beautiful old fireplaces and all are comfortable.

Mercure Part-Dieu €€€ *Tour Crédit Lyonnais, 129 r. Servient; tel: 04 78 63 55 00, fax: 04 78 63 55 20.* The highest hotel in Europe (they say), located at the top of the eye-catching circular Part-Dieu Tower, also has sky-high prices. But the views are phenomenal.

La Tour Rose €€€ and **Maison de la Tour** €€€ *22 r. du Boeuf; tel: 04 78 37 25 90, fax: 04 78 42 26 02.* This glorious 17th-century Renaissance mansion in the old quarter is the setting for creative Lyonnais gastronomy, prepared by top chef Philippe Chavent. It's also a small, luxurious hotel. In the open courtyard is Chavent's cheaper option, the more informal **Terrasses de la Tour** €€, covered and heated in winter, open air in summer.

Brasserie Georges €–€€ *30 cours de Verdun; tel: 04 72 56 54 54.* Alongside Perrache station, a huge, popular art deco bar-restaurant.

Léon de Lyon €€€ *1 r. Pleney; tel: 04 72 10 11 12, fax: 04 72 10 11 13.* One of the most famous names in France, this relaxed, *bouchon*/bistro-style restaurant belonging to chef Jean-Paul Lacombe is a gastronomic haven, offering classic, hearty Lyonnais dishes. Next door is **Le Petit Léon** €, his much less expensive lunchtime bistro.

Shopping

The main city-centre shopping street is r. de la République from pl. Bellecour to pl. des Cordeliers, and r. Victor Hugo to its south. The streets between pl. Bellecour and pl. des Jacobins have elegant, upmarket designer stores. Across the Saône, the Centre Commercial de Part-Dieu indoor shopping mall has over 250 shops. Lyon souvenirs include local silk, from workshops in La Croix-Rousse, and puppets from workshops in Vieux Lyon.

Markets

Produce markets:
- Halle de Lyon (covered market), *Cours Lafayette; open every day from 0700;*
- Blvd de Croix-Rousse, *open every morning except Mon;*
- Quai St-Antoine (Saône, Presqu'île side), *open every morning except Mon.*

Antiques, books, arts and crafts:
- Cité des Antiquitaires, *Blvd de Stalingrad, Villeurbanne; open Thur, Sat and Sun from 0930;*
- Quai de la Pêcherie (Saône, Presqu'île side), *books every afternoon;*
- Vieux-Lyon river quays, *Sun am;*
- Flea market, *R. du Canal, Villeurbanne; open Thur, Sat and Sun mornings.*

Festivals

- *Vogue* – autumn fair at La Croix-Rousse: chestnuts, crêpes and funfairs;
- *Fête des Lumières* (Festival of Lights) – 8 Dec: all the windows and balconies are decorated with lights;
- *Festival de Musique Ancienne* – 2 weeks in Dec: season of classical concerts.

Nocturnal Lyon

Lyon after dark is full of light and life. Hundreds of buildings and squares are beautifully illuminated. The city has scores of late-night discos, bars, *café-théâtres*, nightclubs, jazz clubs, cabaret shows, a casino and other after-hours venues catering to every taste. Focal points for nightlife are Vieux Lyon, the banks of the Saône and the Presqu'île city centre. All evening venues are listed, with description and details, in the tourist office booklet *Lyon: Hôtels – Restaurants – Nocturne.*

Suggested walk (with the Metro and funicular)

Total distance: In addition to public transport, the main tour includes about 5km on foot. The first detour is up to 3 to 5km more on foot. The second detour is about 1.5km on foot.

Time: 2 full days. The tour breaks naturally into shorter sections, which can be done in any order. It's a good idea to visit Vieux Lyon during the morning if possible, as some *traboules* are closed in the afternoon.

Route: Start from the tourist office in pl. Bellecour in **LA PRESQU'ÎLE** ❶. Walk and window-shop up traffic-free r. de la République. Turn right into r. Confort to pl. de l'Hôpital to see the **Hôtel Dieu** (charity hospital), originally founded in the Middle Ages. Rabelais was a doctor here. It was reconstructed in the 18th century, and now houses a Medical Museum. Return to r. de la République and keep walking up to pl. de la République and continue to pl. de la Bourse. Here turn into r. de la Poulaillerie for the **Musée de l'Imprimerie et de la Banque** (*see page 207*). A few paces further along, turn right into r. du Président Herriot. Walk up here for a few minutes to reach the **Musée des Beaux-Arts** (*see page 207*). Beside it lies pl. des Terreaux. This is a convenient spot to take a break.

Behind the Hôtel de Ville, in pl. de la Comédie, catch the Metro (Line C) to **LA CROIX-ROUSSE** ❷. You emerge into pl. de la Croix-Rousse. Leave the square on r. du Mail, and take the second right, r. d'Ivry, for the **Maison des Canuts** (*see page 205*). Go back to pl. de la Croix-Rousse and leave on **Montée de la Grande Côte**. Take side-turns that catch your eye, and explore the lanes and alleys to either side, but keep heading downhill. On the right of the Montée, see the **Amphithéâtre des Trois Gaules** (*see page 205*). Reaching the bottom of the Montée, turn right, left and second left to return to pl. des Terreaux.

Detour: Again take the Metro from the Hôtel de Ville station, catching a Line A train (direction Bonnevay) to Masséna station on the **EAST BANK** ❸. Leaving the station, walk a few minutes north to the **Parc de la Tête d'Or** (*see page 206*) entrance on blvd des Belges. Visit the park and the **Cité Internationale** with its **Musée d'Art Contemporain** (*see page 206*), and return via the **Musée d'Histoire Naturelle** (*see page 206*) on blvd des Belges. Return on the Metro to Hôtel de Ville station and pl. des Terreaux.

Leave pl. des Terreaux from the southwest corner, on r. Chenavard. Follow this to pl. St-Nizier. The 15th-century **Église St-Nizier** (restored in the 19th century) was the scene of a massacre in 1834 when troops entered the church to fire on striking silk-workers who were taking refuge there. Across the square, take **r. Mercière**, the main commercial street of a historic trade district with plenty of character. Head off right to explore r. de la Monnaie, another interesting street with old houses and façades. Go as far as quai des Célestins beside the Saône. Walk along the riverside to **Passerelle du Palais de Justice** and cross the river.

The route through **VIEUX LYON** ❹ is simply a suggestion – almost every street is tempting. Reaching the Palais de Justice on the far side of the bridge, walk round to **r. St-Jean** on the other side of the building. Turn right and walk along this main street of Old Lyon. *Traboules* and openings to inner courtyards lead off at several points – nos 27, 24 and 19 and others. At **pl. du Gouvernement**, with several fine restored houses, the door at no 3 opens up a quick route to the riverside *quai*. The street continues past this point to beautiful **pl. du Change**, with an exceptional medieval house at no 2. Continue on r. Lainerie to pl. St-Paul. Turn back from the square on **r. Juiverie**, a Jewish street in the Middle Ages, with several exceptional houses. At the end, turn left and right into r. de Gadagne. At the next corner, **Hôtel de Gadagne** (*see page 208*) houses the Marionette and Old Lyon museums. Cross pl. du Petit-Collège to r. du Boeuf, where houses no 14 and 16 have good courtyards. Reaching r. de la Bombarde, turn left and right to reach pl. St-Jean and the **Cathédrale St-Jean** (*see page 208*). Cross the square (and adjoining pl. E. Commette) and on the right is Vieux Lyon station. Beside it is the long **Montée du Gourguillon**, the steep walkway up the Fourvière hill to the Roman town. It follows the original Roman track.

From Vieux Lyon station, take the St-Just funicular up to the Minimes stop. This gives access to the **Théâtre Gallo-Romaine** and the **Musée de la Civilisation Gallo-Romaine** (*see page 206*) of **FOURVIÈRE** ❺. Walk from here to pl. de Fourvière and the **Basilique Nôtre-Dame** (*see page 206*). Return on the funicular to the Vieux Lyon station. Return by bus, Metro or on foot to pl. Bellecour.

From pl. Bellecour, walk south along pedestrianised r. Victor Hugo. Turn left into r. des Remparts d'Ainay and left again into r. de la Charité. On the next corner are the **Musée des Arts Décoratifs** and **Musée des Tissus** (*see page 207*) in La Presqu'île, next door to one another.

Detour: By taxi or on foot, continue to the Rhône and cross the river on Pont de l'Université back to the East Bank. Turn right on the far side and follow the Rhône quayside to the next bridge. Don't cross the bridge; turn left into av. Berthelot to reach the **Centre d'Histoire de la Résistance et de la Déportation** (*see page 206*). Turn back towards the river, cross it on Pont Galliéni, and continue to pl. Carnot (in front of Perrache station).

Return to pl. Bellecour either on foot or by Metro (from Perrache or Ampère-Victor Hugo stations).

200 metres
150 yards

Musée d'Art
Contemporain
and La Cité
Internationale

Pont de Winston
Churchill

Parc de la
Tête d'Or

Maison
des Canuts

2 LA CROIX-ROUSSE

Place de
la Croix-
Rousse

Rhône

Avenue de Grande Bretagne

Musée
d'Histoire
Naturelle

Boulevard des Belges

Boulevard de la Croix Rousse

TUNNEL DE LA CROIX ROUSSE

Place de la
Croix-Rousse

Rue Duquesne

e la Croix Rousse

Montée de la
Grande Côte

Pont
de Lattre
Tassigny

Avenue du Maréchal Foch

Rue Sully

Rue Créqui

Rue Garibaldi

Dupont

Montée de la Grande Côte

Quai André Lassagne

Rue Tronchet

Cours Vitton

Amphithéâtre
des Trois Gaules

Masséna

TERREAUX

Pont
Morand

Place du
Maréchal
Lyautey

Cours Franklin Roosevelt

s du Général Giraud
ardin des Chartreux

Nôtre-Dame-
St-Vincent

Place de la
Comédie

Hôtel
de Ville

Opéra
de Lyon

Avenue du Général Sarrail

Avenue du Maréchal de Saxe

Rue Bugeaud

Quai St-Vincent

Place des
Terreaux

Saône
Quai Pierre Scize

Église
St-Paul

Quai de Bondy

Quai de la Pêcherie

Musée des
Beaux-Arts

Rue Juliette Récamier

Gare St-Paul

Quai Fr. Vernay

Rue Fr. Vernay

Théâtre
Guignol

St-Nizier

5 FOURVIÈRE

Musée de
l'Imprimerie

Palais du
Commerce

Quai Jean Moulin

Pont
La Fayette

Cours La Fayette

Rue St-Jean

Rue du Président Edouard Herriot

Pont
Alphonse Juin

Rue de la République

St-Bonaventure

3 EAST BANK

Basilique
Nôtre-Dame
de Fourvière

Rue St-Jean

Rue du Président Carnot

Quai Victor Augagneur

Palais de
Justice

Rue Romain Rolland

Rue du Col. Chambonnet

Pont
Wilson

Cours Gambetta

Rue Moncey

de la
sation
maine

Funicular

Cathédrale
St-Jean

Pont
Bonaparte

Rue St-Antoine

Place des
Jacobins

Place de la
République

Cours Jules Courmont

Cours de la Liberté

Avenue du Maréchal de Saxe

Hôpital de
l'Antiquaille

4 VIEUX LYON

Rue Tilsitt

1 LA PRESQU' ÎLE

Rue de la République

Place de
l'Hôpital

St-Georges

St-Just

Rue Sala

Rue A. Fochier

Hôtel Dieu

Pont de la
Guillotière

Place
A. Jutard

Place
Antonin
Poncet

Place
A. Vollon

St-François

Hôtel des
Postes

Place
G. Pèri

Cours Gambetta

Quai Fulchiron

Saône

Rue Maréchal Joffre

Rue Vauban

St-Martin
d'Ainay

Rue Victor Hugo

Rue Ste-Hélène

Rue Sala

Musée des
Tissus

Rue Pasteur

Musée des
Arts Décoratifs

Rue de la Charité

Place
Bellecour

Rue de Condé

Ste-Croix

Place
Carnot

Quai du Dr. Gailleton

Pont de
l'Université

Rhône

Rue de Marseille

Rue de l'Université

Avenue Jean Jaurès

Pont
Kitchener
Marchand

D487

Quai Rambaud

Gare de
Perrache

A7

Pont
Galliéni

Quai Claude Bernard

Rue Pasteur

J. Moulin
Lyon III
Universités

Centre d'Histoire
de la Résistance
et de la Déportation

Vienne

Ratings

History	●●●●●
Museums	●●●●●
Roman remains	●●●●●
Architecture	●●●●○
Restaurants	●●●○○
Street life	●●●○○
Children	●●○○○
Shopping	●●○○○

Despite Vienne's striking setting, between the broad, turning Rhône and the pressing hills, it may be hard to persuade yourself to turn off the highway while barely outside Lyon's unsightly industrial fringe. Do so, if you enjoy a quiet, civilised town with a hint of the South and classical ruins and abundant treasures left by the passing centuries. Behind the grim riverside through-roads, lies a little city scattered with remnants of its illustrious period as capital of Roman Gaul. All the sites are well signposted, and near enough to each other that most of Vienne can be visited simply by parking the car and strolling around town for a few hours. If you decide to linger longer, there are convivial bars, restaurants, and more to see a little further from the centre. The town makes an ideal base for touring to either side of the Rhône.

Getting there and getting around

ⓘ Vienne Tourist Office *Cours Brillier (at Rhône end); tel: 04 74 53 80 30, fax: 04 74 53 80 31; open mid-June–mid-Sept, Mon–Sat 0900–1230, 1330–1900, Sun 1000–1200, 1430–1800, rest of the year Mon–Sat 0830–1200, 1400–1800, Sun 1000–1200.* The tourist office organises a choice of 90-min town tours in several languages throughout July and Aug.

Vienne is highly accessible by road, rail and air. It is on *autoroute* A7 and the N7, just 32km south of Lyon and 6km south of the junction between the A7 and the Lyon ring road A40. Lyon-Saint Exupéry Airport is 36km away. There are frequent TGVs to Vienne from Paris, Dijon and Lyon and from the south.

From the riverside N7, at the section called quai Jean-Jaurès, turn left into Cours Brillier to enter the town centre. Turn left into Cours Romestang, which leads into the central square, pl. de Miremont.

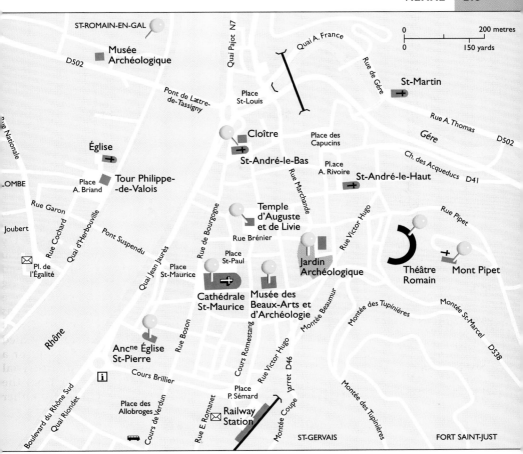

www.culture.fr/culture/arcnat/vienne/fr/ (mainly about the antiquities, in English and French); www.district-vienne.fr/ (official site for residents and visitors, in French only).

Vienne's history

100 BC: The town is the main settlement of the Gaulish *Allobroges* tribe.

0 AD: Roman Vienne founded as *Vienna Senatoria*.

177: Vienne is a wealthy and cosmopolitan city, with a large Christian and Jewish presence.

413–534: Vienne is capital of the Burgundian territories in the Rhône Valley.

879–1032: Vienne is capital of the Provençal kingdom of Arles.

12th to 14th centuries: Vienne is an important ecclesiastical centre.

15th century: Vienne, now part of Dauphiné, becomes French.

From the 16th and 17th centuries: Lyon overtakes Vienne in importance; the town declines.

Museum ticket The Théâtre Antique (Roman theatre), Musée des Beaux-Arts et d'Archéologie, Église St-André-le-Bas and cloister, and Église St-Pierre and museum may all be visited on a single cheaper ticket from any of the sites.

Museum information

Call the Musées de Vienne tel: 04 74 85 50 42 for information about the town's museums.

There's a big weekly market every Sat in the town centre.

Festival de l'Humour – Mar; theatre season – summer, at the Théâtre Antique; jazz festival 'Jazz à Vienne', the city's major festival – first half of July, at the Théâtre Antique.

Sights

Cathédrale St-Maurice € *Pl. St-Maurice; open daily.*

Église et Cloître St-André-le-Bas € *Pl. du Jeu de Paume; tel: 04 74 85 18 49, fax: 04 74 53 34 59; open Apr–Oct Tue–Sat 0930–1300, 1400–1800, Nov–Mar Tue–Sat 0930–1230, 1400–1700, Sun 1330–1730, closed Mon and hols all year.*

Cathédrale St-Maurice (St-Maurice Cathedral)••
Steps climb from the riverside square to the Flamboyant west front of the town's large cathedral. A curious, rather uneasy blend of Romanesque and Gothic, hemmed in by houses, the building originally dates from the 12th century. It was much added to, and much damaged, and sometimes repaired, over the centuries. Still, it contains a prolific quantity of fine stonework and decoration from the Romanesque period as well as the later centuries. The interior is vast: 97m long, and without transepts.

Église et Cloître St-André-le-Bas (Lower St-André Church and cloister)••
The origins of this appealing church go back to the first Christians in Vienne. The present building is partly 9th and mainly 12th century, with some later additions. The handsome belfry, for example, is 12th century except for an older base and a later top. Notice that some of the church's stonework is Roman, for example two columns in the chancel. On the south side is a collection of stonework, and on the north side a lovely Romanesque cloister with fascinating carved capitals that all seem to tell a story.

Above
Église St-André-le-Bas

Église St-Pierre et Musée Lapidaire €
*Pl. St-Pierre; tel: 04 74 85
20 35; open Apr–Oct
Tue–Sat 0930–1300,
1400–1800, Nov–Mar
Tue–Sat 0930–1230,
1400–1700, Sun
1330–1730, closed Mon
and hols all year.*

Jardin Archéologique €
Pl. Albert Vassy.

**Musée des Beaux-Arts
et d'Archéologie €** *Pl. de
Miremont; tel: 04 74 85 50
42, fax: 04 74 53 34 59;
open Nov–Mar Tue–Sat
0930–1230, 1400–1700,
Sun 1330–1730, Apr–Oct
Tue–Sun 0930–1300,
1400–1800, closed public
hols.*

The footpath to the
top of Mont Pipet is
on the east side of the hill
(the other side from the
Roman theatre). It takes
around 15 minutes each
way to walk to the top and
back.

Église St-Pierre et Musée Lapidaire (St-Pierre Church and Stonework Museum)✦

This ancient, sturdy building is one of the most charming in town. A church and abbey dedicated to Saint Peter was first constructed here in the 5th century. Built outside the town walls, it served mainly as the burial place for the bishops of Vienne. Having been damaged by Saracens five hundred years later, the church was repaired and reconstructed partly using stonework taken from the dilapidated Roman monuments. Then in the 12th century, with the abbey prospering, it was enlarged and restored once more, the west tower added and the south door put in to connect with the abbey cloisters. In the 19th century the building was restored and turned into a museum of stone carvings. Among some remarkable Roman pieces there are extensive mosaics, a head of Juno and a marble statue of the Roman town's protective goddess Tutela.

Jardin Archéologique (Archaeological Gardens)✦

An archaeological site in the centre of town, this was a focal point of the Roman town. Although the surviving pieces convey little of their original purpose, the ruins are of a *forum* – a portico is still standing – and an open-air theatre dedicated to the cult of Cybele.

Mont Pipet✦

Half city park, half archaeological site, this steep hill at the back of the town centre has the Roman theatre (*see page 218*) carved into its lower slope, and ruins of a Roman citadel on the summit. Also on top there's a chapel, a 19th-century religious statue and an esplanade with a thrilling view over the town and river.

Musée des Beaux-Arts et d'Archéologie (Museum of Fine Arts and Archaeology)✦

In a former covered market, this large city-centre museum holds Vienne's major collections of prehistoric and Gallo-Roman objects, including beautiful 3rd-century silver goblets and an engraved plate and some bronze dolphins, perhaps part of a bridge (found in the river). There are Roman coins, glassware and ceramics, and an imposing bronze statue of Julius Pacantianus, a Roman official.

On the menu

Regional dishes include *gratin dauphinoise, matelotte d'anguille* (eel stew), chicken and fish *quenelles*, goats' cheese and fruit and wines of the Rhône Valley. Try a nip of the area's *eau de vie de poire* (pear brandy).

Site et Musée Archéologique St-Romain-en-Gal et Vienne €€ *Off the D502, by west end of Pont de Lattre de Tassigny; tel: 04 74 53 74 00; open 0930–1830, closed Mon.*

Temple d'Auguste et de Livie € *Pl. Charles-de-Gaulle.*

Théâtre Antique € *7 r. du Cirque (colline de Pipet); tel: 04 74 85 39 23; open Nov–Mar Tue–Sat 0930–1230, 1400–1700, Sun 1330–1730, Apr–Aug daily 0930–1300, 1400–1800, Sept and Oct Tue–Sun 0930–1300, 1400–1800, closed public hols.*

Odeon *Montée des Tupinières. Not open to the public, but visible from the Terrasse de Pipet.*

Ste-Colombe and St-Romain-en-Gal**

In Roman times a bridge crossed the Rhône and reached the far shore close to the **Tour Philippe de Valois***. Philippe constructed the tower in 1343 to protect the bridge, which was eventually destroyed in 1651. Roman Vienne had two suburbs across the river. **Ste-Colombe*** is thought to be the site of a wealthy quarter of sumptuous villas. A built-up area today, it has been impossible to excavate. **St-Romain-en-Gal***, to its north, was a larger commercial area of villas, ordinary streets, houses, bathhouses, craftsmen's workshops and traders' warehouses. An area of two hectares of this neighbourhood has been excavated continuously since 1967, and hundreds of valuable finds made. Most of these date from the 1st to 3rd century period. The most striking discoveries have been beautiful mosaics – considered the best yet uncovered in Gaul. Three roads made of granite paving, covering a sewage system, are being restored. The grandest building has been called the **House of the Ocean Gods***, where an exquisite mosaic shows water gods with flowing hair and beards. The **House of Five Mosaics***, close by, is a large residence with more good mosaics. A **viewpoint**** has been made, allowing visitors to get a good overall view of the buildings and streets. At the entrance to the site, the **Musée Archéologique St-Romain-en-Gal et Vienne*** displays scores of intriguing items that have been uncovered here, with everyday objects, vases and ceramics, monuments, mosaics and murals. Using the finds, the museum sets out to convey vividly what everyday life was like in Roman Vienne and its suburbs.

Temple d'Auguste et de Livie (Temple of Augustus and Livia)***

Standing elegantly in a square, this visually pleasing 1st-century Roman temple closely resembles the more famous Maison Carrée in Nîmes. The structure has had an eventful life – constantly altered and damaged, it saw service as a church, a Revolutionary meeting place, a Temple to Reason, a courthouse, a museum and a library. It was restored to its Roman form in 1840.

Théâtre Antique or Théâtre Romain (Ancient or Roman Theatre)**

A large semicircle of seat-terraces cut into the side of Mont Pipet and facing towards the town, the theatre at Vienne is one of the biggest known (larger than the one at Orange, for example). As many as 13,500 people would sit here for the various spectacular open-air performances. Though not by any means the best preserved of Roman theatres, it's an evocative site, and the top rows of seats give good views over the town. Completely excavated in 1922, after a full 1500 years buried in earth, it is now the scene of Vienne's top-name annual Jazz Festival. Just south is the site of an **Odeon**, a Roman venue for smaller performances.

Accommodation and food in Vienne

Hôtel Central €€ *7 rue de l'Archevêché; tel: 04 74 85 18 38, fax: 04 74 31 96 33.* The simple name says it all – this decent, modest hotel is in a backstreet right in the middle of the old town near all the sights.

La Pyramide €€€ *14 blvd Fernand Point; tel: 04 74 53 01 96, fax: 04 74 85 69 73; closed Tue and Wed.* Never mind the Roman ruins. Vienne's other historic site, for gastronomes, is the Restaurant La Pyramide, where Fernand Point taught the chefs who pioneered *nouvelle cuisine* – notably Bocuse and the Troisgros brothers. It's hard to believe that it's some 40 years since he died. The street is named in his honour. Some way out of the town centre on the Valence road, it's an excellent, imaginative restaurant serving pricey, lavish dishes. Good selection of top Côtes du Rhône wines. It's a hotel, too, with 20 expensive, luxurious, pretty rooms, a garden and terrace.

Le Bec Fin €€ *7 pl. St-Maurice; tel: 04 74 85 76 72, fax: 04 74 85 15 30; closed Sun pm and Mon.* Best of the town-centre restaurants, by the cathedral, this locals' favourite serves classic, well-prepared dishes. The lunchtime menu is very reasonably priced.

L'Estancot € *4 r. Table Ronde; tel: 04 74 85 12 09; closed Sun and Mon.* Tucked away in a town-centre backstreet, a good place to come for a variety of ambitious, tasty dishes at low prices. If it's full, there are several similar establishments nearby.

Walking tour

Total distance: About 3.5km, or 4km including the detour.

Time: The tour could take all day, allowing time to visit museums and sites. Alternatively, done at a brisk pace, the walk could be completed in little over an hour.

Links: Vienne is the starting point for the Bas Dauphiné route (*see page 260*) and the Côtes du Rhône route (*see page 250*).

Route: Start from the tourist office in Cours Brillier. In the park behind, a section of the Roman road *Via Aurelia* has been uncovered. Walk along Cours Brillier and turn into Cours Romestang to reach pl. de Miremont: these are the main town-centre streets. The **MUSÉE DES BEAUX-ARTS ET D'ARCHÉOLOGIE ❶** occupies the former grain market in pl. de Miremont. Leave the square on r. Clémentine and walk to the **TEMPLE D'AUGUSTE ET DE LIVIE ❷** (can be seen later in the tour if preferred). Turn back on to r. Brénier and r. Chantelouve to reach the **JARDIN ARCHÉOLOGIQUE ❸**. Walk round to r. Victor Hugo and turn up Montée St-Marcel. Take a left into r. du Cirque (but if you'd like a view of the traces of a Roman **Odeon**, first go a few paces into Montée des Tupinières on the right). R. du Cirque leads past

Below
Temple d'Auguste et de Livie

the **THÉÂTRE ROMAIN ❹** to its entrance, with Mont Pipet rising behind. For a little extra exertion – rewarded by a good view – after leaving the theatre, you may wish to follow the road round to the top of **MONT PIPET ❺**.

From the Roman theatre take r. des Ursulines, which leads to **Porte de l'Ambulance** – which refers not to ambulances but to the ambulatory: this monumental gateway was once the entrance to the Benedictine abbey of St-André-le-Haut. Facing the portal is r. St-André-le-Haut, which leads alongside the abbey-church of **St-André-le-Haut**. Reaching the front of the building, turn right into pl. A. Rivoire (notice the church's classical façade) and left down some steps. This quarter of town has several stepped alleys. Reaching r. Marchande, turn right and go to pl. A. Briand. Turn left to reach the church and cloisters of **ST-ANDRÉ-LE-BAS. ❻**

Either take the detour or follow r. des Clercs to pl. du Palais, past the Temple of Augustus and Livia, and continue via r. Clémentine and pl. St-Paul to go round to the entrance of **CATHÉDRALE ST-MAURICE** ❼.

Detour to the west bank: (You may prefer to visit the west bank by car.) From St-André-le-Bas, brave the busy roads to cross the Rhône on Pont de Lattre-de-Tassigny. On the other side, turn down on the right to reach the site of **ST-ROMAIN-EN-GAL** ❽. Follow the riverside to see the square tower, **Tour Philippe-de-Valois**, built in the 14th century to guard the river crossing, which was then still on a Roman bridge. Carry on to get up to the suspension bridge (pedestrians only) back over the Rhône. It arrives at pl. St-Maurice. Go up to the front of Cathédrale St-Maurice.

Leave the square on the right to reach the attractive former church (and now museum) of **ST-PIERRE** ❾. Walk round the block to find Cours Brillier and the tourist office again.

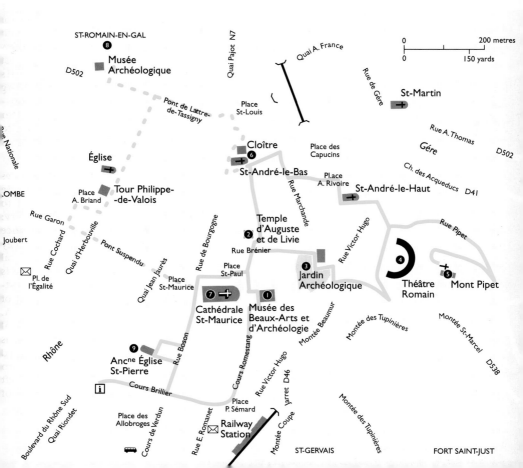

The Haut-Vivarais

Ratings

Scenery	●●●●●
Walks	●●●●●
Activities	●●●●○
Children	●●●○○
Historic railways	●●●○○
Medieval architecture	●●●○○
Nature parks	●●●○○
Restaurants	●●●○○

The Ardèche, or Vivarais, is the enticing land of green mountains, plunging valleys and old-fashioned villages that rises west of the Rhône. The northern part is called Haut-Vivarais. Millions of travellers on the Rhône Valley *autoroute* and rail lines, emerging from the industrial development south of Lyon, have gazed at the long line of green crests and wondered what lies among those hills. The answer is simple – mountain scenery laced with a multitude of tiny lanes. Broad rocky plateaux step down from the heights of Mont Pilat (1432m) and Gerbier de Jonc (1551m) to the Rhône, while beyond rises the volcanic Auvergne region. Indeed, dark basalt lava running down from prehistoric volcanoes there created the Vivarais. Few towns of any size have grown up here, and the area retains a profound rusticity, although many small-scale traditional manufacturing districts have survived in the valleys.

ANNONAY✧✧

ℹ **Comité Départementale du Tourisme de l'Ardèche (Ardèche Tourism)** *4 cours du Palais, Privas; tel: 04 75 64 04 66, fax: 04 75 64 23 93, e-mail: cdt07@ardeche-guide.com.*

Ⓦ *www.ardeche-guide.com/ (official tourist office site); www.guideweb.com/ardeche/index; www.i-sf.com/tourism/index.*

A large town of business and industry, Annonay is a focal point for both residents and tourists in the northern Ardèche. The most popular local attraction is the **Peaugres Safari Park✧✧✧**, 10 minutes away. The town itself – ravaged during the Wars of Religion (1562–98), when it sided strongly with Protestantism – has a long history as a manufacturing centre. In contrast to the surrounding factories, its Old Quarter, lying between the Cance and Deûme rivers close to their confluence, has plenty of low-key charm and history, with lanes and steps and vaulted passageways. The old town below the Ancien Château was entered via the two Portes Fortifiés, fortified medieval gateways on r. de Bourgville. The tall 16th-century stone spire of the 14th-century Gothic Chapelle de Trachin, on main street r. Boissy d'Anglas, is a useful landmark. Adjacent to it is the central market

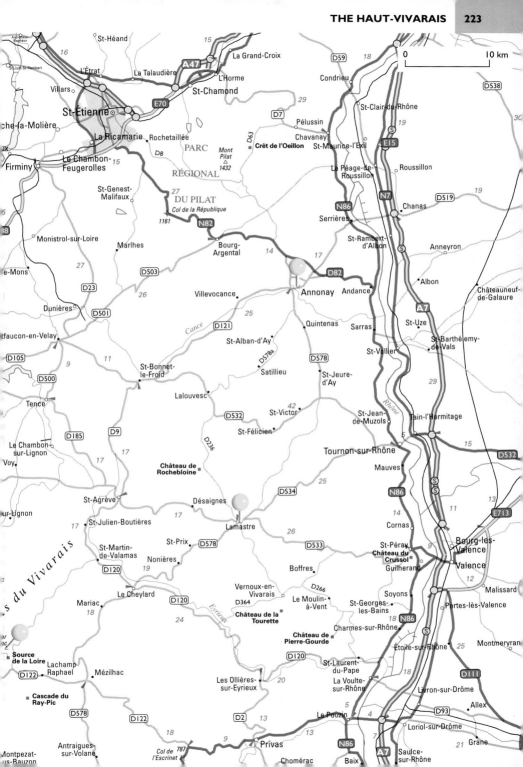

ℹ Annonay Tourist Office *Pl. des Cordeliers; tel: 04 75 33 24 51, fax: 04 75 32 47 79, e-mail: annonay-Tour@ inforoutes-ardeche.fr; open all year – varying hours.*

Ⓦ *www.mairie-annonay.fr/ (excellent official site of the local town hall); www.inforoutes-ardeche.fr/~annotour/Menu (tourist office site).*

⇄ The town is 14km from the A7, and lies 5km off the busy N82/D82 connecting St-Étienne to the Rhône Valley. The main street is r. Boissy d'Anglais. There are plenty of car parks around town.

🏛 Peaugres Safari Park €€€ *8km NE of Annonay on N82; tel: 04 75 33 00 32, fax: 04 75 67 78 75, e-mail:safari@safari-peaugres.com; website: www.safari-peaugres.com/; open 0930–1800 in summer, 1100–1700 in winter.*

Musée Vivarois César Filhol € *15 r. Jean-Baptiste Béchetoille; tel: 04 75 33 24 51; open Wed, Sat and Sun 1400–1800 (July and Aug daily).*

Musée des Papeteries Canson et Montgolfier € *2km N at Vidalon (beside Davézieu industrial estate); tel: 04 75 69 88 00; open July–31 Aug, daily 1430–1800, rest of the year Wed and Sun only.*

square, pl. de la Liberté, from which curious old lanes descend to the River Deûme.

The main river bridge is Pont Mongolfier, which gives a good view of the older bridge, medieval Pont Valgelas. On that side of the river Pl. des Cordeliers was the scene of the world's first-ever hot-air balloon experiment. Its inventors were the wealthy local paper manufacturers Joseph and Étienne de Montgolfier (*see below*), and a plaque in the square commemorates the event. Most of modern Annonay lies on this side of the Deûme.

Annonay and the hot-air balloon

In the 18th century, Annonay paper manufacturers Joseph and Étienne de Montgolfier noticed that paper floated upwards in hot air. From this simple observation they created the hot-air balloon, still known in French as a *montgolfière*. Their successful launch of the first-ever hot-air balloon – held together by ordinary buttons – took place in Annonay in June 1783. It rose to 2000m and stayed there for half an hour. That first trial is celebrated every year, and hot-air ballooning has remained popular at Annonay ever since – it's a great way to see the local countryside. One Annonay company offering balloon excursions is Ardèche Montgolfières. *Tel: 04 75 69 39 39, fax: 04 75 69 69 40.*

Above
Mural, Annonay

Festival International du Premier Film International First Film Festival) – Feb; theatre season – in summer; re-enactment of the first hot-air balloon flight – 1st weekend in June; *Les Gourmandises d'Ardèche* (local gastronomic fair) – 3rd weekend in Nov.

Ten marked walks run through the countryside around town. The Bassin d'Annonay marked trail allows walkers, horseback riders and mountain bikers to explore the narrow, wooded Deûme Valley area.

Downstream, the Deûme narrows and rushes through a tight, rocky section called the Défilé des Fouines. There are former cloth workshops along here. From Pont Valgelas, curious little r. de la Mure and a covered passage called the Voûtes Soubise climb back up to the heart of town, where attractive old houses stand along the town's original main street, Rue Franki-Kramer. This leads to the **Musée Vivarois César Filhol***, where a royal bailiwick of 1700 now houses a diverse array of Ardèche and Annonay sacred art, folk culture and history, including a model of the pioneering steam locomotive made by local engineer and inventor Marc Séguin in 1828. Those with an interest in papermaking past and present should head out of the town centre to the house where the Montgolfier brothers were born. It's now the **Musée des Papeteries Canson et Montgolfier***, a historical museum of their prestigious 18th-century paper works.

Accommodation and food in Annonay

La Halle €–€€ *17 pl. des Cordeliers; tel: 04 75 32 04 62; closed Sun pm and Mon.* Good imaginative cooking with clean, sharp, savoury flavours is offered at this friendly place with its terrace and courtyard, in the main square just across the Deûme from the old quarter.

Right
Mont Gerbier de Jonc

GERBIER DE JONC***

What's in a name?

The evocative name of the Gerbier de Jonc means nothing in French. Some speculate that Gerbier may come from *ger*, an ancient word for 'rock', and *jonc* from the Latin *jugum*, 'a mountain'.

This curious, dark, rounded high point projects oddly from the surrounding green mountain countryside. From a distance, the summit resembles a nipple on a breast, but closer to the top, it looks more like a haystack, with its flaky, shaley surface. A stiff 30-minute hike brings you to the top (1550m), where you are rewarded by an astonishing view, stretching clear across central Ardèche in all directions. The mountain stands on an awesome watershed where a multitude of springs emerge and are drawn either all the way to the Atlantic or all the way to the Mediterranean. Most famous of all is the source of the Loire, the longest river in France, which rises from a series of springs on the mountain's south side.

LAMASTRE*

ⓘ Lamastre Tourist Office *Pl. Montgolfier; tel: 04 75 06 48 99, fax: 04 75 06 37 53; open Mon–Sat 1000–1200, 1500–1700 (summer Mon–Sat 1000–1230, 1400–1800, Sun 1030–1230).*

Ⓦ *www.multimania.com/ lamastre/* (Lamastre site with attitude).

ⓘ Vivarais Railway *Tel: 04 78 28 83 34 for details.*

Today a centre of diverse small manufacturing, Lamastre is a long standing craft town and the terminus of the popular **Vivarais Railway**** The 33-km Tournon–Lamastre line is the longest steam train journey in France. It was built in the 1880s and is served today by a jolly little train with steam engine and bright colourful, wooden carriages. The journey along the Doux Valley passes through pretty, pastoral countryside in places, or chestnut woods, and at other points passes through dramatic gorges. The one-way journey takes 1 hour.

Accommodation and food in Lamastre

Château d'Urbilhac €€€ *On D2 SE of village; tel: 04 75 06 42 11, fax: 04 75 06 52 75; open May–Oct only.* This authentic old fortress is now an atmospheric, peaceful and comfortable hotel furnished with antiques There's a terrace and garden, a good restaurant, and lovely views.

Hôtel-Restaurant du Midi €€ *Pl. Seignobos; tel: 04 75 06 41 50, fax: 04 75 06 49 75; closed Jan to mid-Feb, Fri pm, Sun pm and Mon.* A small, comfortable hotel, the Midi is also a thoroughly enjoyable restaurant offering first-class cooking, using the best of local ingredients.

Historic trains of the Ardèche

Several historic private rail services have been kept going in the Ardèche. The Vivarais train runs from Tournon to Lamastre along the Doux Valley (tel: 04 78 28 83 34). Others are the 1950s 'Viaduc 07' train from St-Germain to St-Jean-le-Centenier (tel: 04 75 37 03 52), south of Aubenas, and the Velay train in the Lignon Valley from Le Chambon to Tence (tel: 04 71 61 94 44).

Pilat Regional Nature Park

Although close to the urban districts of St-Étienne, Lyon and the Rhône Valley, the green Pilat uplands are cool and refreshing, and full of diversity. There are farms, forests, open heathlands, vineyards and orchards, and trees ranging from Mediterranean almonds to Norway pine. The region is sparsely populated now, but before the industrial revolution its forests and abundant water sustained numerous rural communities. Silk-making was a local trade. Today, the rivers and springs in the Pilat region contribute significantly to the water supplies of the surrounding urban areas, and it also serves as a major outdoor leisure resource for the nearby towns. Some 65,000 hectares of the Pilat upland – including about 50 villages – are contained within the Regional Nature Park, which is threaded by numerous well-marked footpaths, trails and long-distance paths GR7 and GR42; in winter, there are ski trails. The Park's head office is in the village of Pélussin. *Website: www.parcs-naturels-regionaux.tm.fr/lesparcs/pilab.*

Suggested tour

La Poste €–€€ 28 r.
des Cévennes,
Lalouvesc; tel: 04 75 67 82
84, fax: 04 75 67 85 08.
This simple, long-
established hotel-
restaurant, or restaurant
avec chambres, is open only
from Easter to November.
Set menus feature the
classic traditional dishes,
with wine included, at
modest prices.

Total distance: 170km, or 305km if you take the detours. Add 1 hour for the walks, and 2 hours for the train excursion to Tournon.

Time: Mountain driving can be tiring and time-consuming. Allow 1 day for the main route only, 2 days with the detours. (A shorter tour can be made by ignoring detours, and by heading straight into Valence from Lamastre on D533.)

Links: At Valence the route links with the Côtes du Rhône: Vienne to Valence (*see page 250*).

Route: Start from **St-Étienne** (*see page 182*), taking the D8 into the **Pilat Regional Nature Park (Parc Régional du Pilat)** ❶ (*see page 226*). 7km out of St-Étienne, **Rochetaillée** is a village sited above two ravines and beneath the ruins of a medieval castle.

Getting out of the car: A side turn opposite Rochetaillée drops down to a footpath. Following a riverbed, the path enters a tight, narrow ravine – the **Gouffre d'Enfer**. The walk takes about 30 minutes each way.

The D8 continues, and joins the D63, which leads right up to the **Crêt de l'Oeillon** (1 370m), one of the most famous viewpoints in the Rhône Valley region. The phenomenal view here reaches to the Alps to the east, and to Mont Ventoux in Provence. Head back down the D63, veering left on to the D34A towards **ANNONAY** ❷.

Leave Annonay on the D578A, heading south into the hills and the valley of the River Ay (many village names end in 'd'Ay' along here). Continue all the way to **Lalouvesc** (pronounced 'Lalouvay'), between two tree-covered volcanic peaks. In front of its 19th-century basilica, there's a viewpoint with a huge panorama. (If you are looking for a good hotel or restaurant, consider making the 11km drive west, on the D532, to the little mountain resort of St-Bonnet-le-Froid, over the border in the Haute-Loire département.) The D236 twists and turns south, climbing up to Col du Buisson, where the **Village Miniature** is one man's obsessive creation – a tiny version of a typical Ardèche village made of granite stones (*tel: 04 75 23 14 77*). Continuing, the road skirts the ruins of the old **Château de Rochebloine** fortress: a footpath leads to the ruins themselves, and from here there's a superb view of mountain scenery. Around 11km further on is **LAMASTRE** ❸.

Getting out of the car: Take the little steam train from Lamastre along the pretty Doux Valley and gorge to **Tournon** (*see page 226*) and back. The round trip takes an hour or so.

Detour: This long, scenic detour from Lamastre goes via rivers, waterfalls, rocks and mountains to the **GERBIER DE JONC** ❹. In Lamastre, turn right on to the bigger D533, but at the edge of the

village continue straight on the D578, and follow this, through Le Cheylard, to the Mézilhac junction. Continue towards Gerbier de Jonc/Source de la Loire on the D122. Some of the strange little hills are reminiscent of the volcanic Auvergne region whose borders are close to here. Hills called *sucs* are remnants of volcanic eruptions. At Lachamp Raphael, you may wish to take the side road to the **Cascade du Ray-Pic**: you must park and walk (15 to 20 minutes) to reach this dramatic waterfall pouring between two dark volcanic rocks at the bottom of a ravine. In summer, you won't have it to yourself: this is a popular outing for walkers, and sometimes even for coach parties. Continuing on the D122, another 9km brings you to the **Source de la Loire**, right of the road: it is several modest springs rather than a single source. To the right, you can walk up to the top of the Gerbier de Jonc. Return the way you came, to Le Cheylard. There, turn right (D120) along the valley of the Eyrieux. After 14km turn left on to the D364 for **Vernoux-en-Vivarais**, rejoining the main tour.

From Lamastre, take the D2 to Vernoux-en-Vivarais, beautifully sited around its church in a vale among the hills. If you decide to linger here, there's an enjoyable excursion – on foot or by car – from the village up to the evocative ruins of the **Château de la Tourette**, a medieval fortress perched on a hilltop with superb views. Take the D14 from Vernoux, turning right on to the D232, and then, at **Le Moulin-à-Vent**, head round on to the D266, a mountain road with lovely views.

Detour: Turn right on to the track to reach the evocative hilltop ruins of the village and castle of **Château de Pierre-Gourde**, a spectacular viewpoint.

Continuing on the D266, the road descends towards the Eyrieux Valley, giving impressive vistas, before arriving at St-Laurent-du-Pape. It's worth taking the D120 to the well-placed neighbouring village, **La Voulte-sur-Rhône**, guarded by its 14th- to 16th-century château and with a strategic view of both the Rhône and its broad tributary, the Drôme. Drive down to the main Rhône Valley road, N86. Turn left towards Valence (*see page 248*). Either continue into town, perhaps pausing to see the archaeological site at **Soyons**; or, for some more Vivarois scenery, take a left turn to the village of **St-Georges-les-Bains** and follow the backroad to St-Péray and the **Château de Crussol** (*see page 244*), descending into Valence from there.

Above
Pétanque set in a shop in the Haut-Vivarais

St-Héand

André-ezieux-Bouthéon

St-Just-St-Rambert

La Grand-Croix

D59 18

Condrieu

0   10 km

D538

L'Étrat

La Talaudière

A47

L'Horme

St-Clair-du-Rhône

Villars

E70

St-Chamond

29

Pélussin

19

D7

E15

St-Étienne

Rochetaillée

Chavanay

Crêt de l'Oeillon

St-Maurice-l'Exil

che-la-Molière

PARC

Mont
Pilat
1432

Le Péage-de-
Roussillon

Roussillon

La Ricamarie

D8

❶

RÉGIONAL

N7

Le Chambon-
Feugerolles

15

St-Genest-
Malifaux

27

N86

Chanas

D519

19

Firminy

DU PILAT

Serrières

15

Col de la République
1161

N82

St-Rambert-
d'Albon

Anneyron

88

Monistrol-sur-Loire

Marlhes

Bourg-
Argental

14

D82

St-Uze

Albon

Châteauneuf-
de-Galaure

de-Mons

27

D503

17

❷ Annonay

Andance

A7

D23

26

Villevocance

25

St-Barthélemy-
de-Vals

Dunières

D501

D121

Quintenas

Sarras

St-Vallier

tfaucon-en-Velay

St-Alban-d'Ay

D578a

D578

D105

11

St-Bonnet-
le-Froid

Satillieu

St-Jeure-
d'Ay

29

D500

9

St-Jean-
de-Muzols

Tence

Lalouvesc

42

St-Victor

Tain-l'Hermitage

D185

D9

D532

St-Félicien

Tournon-sur-Rhône

15

D532

Le Chambon-
sur-Lignon

17

Mauves

-Voy

17

Château de
Rochebloine

Désaignes

D534

25

N86

11

E713

13

sur-Lignon

17

St-Julien-Boutières

17

❸ Lamastre

26

14

Cornas

Bourg-les-
Valence

St-Prix

D578

D533

St-Péray

9

St-Martin-
de-Valamas

Nonières

19

Boffres

Château du
Crussol
Guilherand

Valence

12

D120

Le Cheylard

D120

Vernoux-en-
Vivarais

D266

Soyons

Malissard

Mariac

18

D364

Le Moulin-
à-Vent

St-Georges-
les-Bains

Portes-lès-Valence

Gerbier
de Jonc
1551

24

Château de la
Tourette

Charmes-sur-Rhône

18

N86

❹ Source
de la Loire

Château de
Pierre-Gourde

Étoile-sur-Rhône

25

Montmeyra

Lachamp-
Raphael

Mézilhac

D120

St-Laurent-
du-Pape

18

D111

D122

Les Ollières-
sur-Eyrieux

20

La Voulte-
sur-Rhône

Livron-sur-Drôme

Cascade du
Ray-Pic

Allex

D578

D122

D2

13

Le Pouzin

4

D93

Loriol-sur-Drôme

Montpezat-
ous-Bauzon

18

Col de
l'Escrinet

787

9

Privas

N86

13

21

Grane

Antraigues-
sur-Volane

Chomérac

Baix

A7

Saulce-
sur-Rhône

ts du Vivarais

The southern Ardèche

Ratings

Activities	●●●●●
Rocks and caves	●●●●●
Scenery	●●●●●
Children	●●●●○
History	●●●●○
Prehistory	●●●●○
Villages	●●●●○
Restaurants	●●●○○

For scenery and character, southern Ardèche is the jewel of the Rhône region. Below Valence, the landscapes, vegetation and climate suddenly become much more Mediterranean. At Pont-St-Esprit, the Rhône enters Provence. Between these two towns, there is much development along the river itself, including nuclear power stations. But rising away from the Rhône's left bank is a place of mountainous greenery and peace. The southern Ardèche, created by volcanic basalt carving a path through limestone, is a world of fantastic weatherworn rockscapes and caves, as well as ordinary hills, woods and rough heat. This landscape has ruined fortresses, tranquil small farms and family-run vineyards producing palatable *vins de pays*. To the south rise high plateaux cut by streams and rivers. Historically, the only way into this countryside was along the dramatic valley of the River Ardèche, still the highlight of the region.

ALBA-LA-ROMAINE❖

ⓘ **Fortress** € *Tel: 04 75 52 42 90; open for visits at certain times in July and Aug.*

Archaeological site €
On other side of D107 from the village; tel: 04 75 52 46 42. Guided visit available by appointment.

An awesome basalt rock and a 15th-century **fortress**❖❖ dominate La Roche, the picturesque medieval part of Alba beside the River Escoutay. This little village – formerly called Aps – was once the important Roman provincial town of *Alba Helviorum*, built over the main settlement of the *Helvii* tribe of Gauls. Look closely, and you'll see the pieces of Roman masonry used in the later houses. Close by is the **archaeological site**❖, with remnants of a 2nd-century Roman theatre and the mosaic floor of a Roman villa, both currently being restored. In the 4th century invading Visigoths entirely destroyed the Roman town.

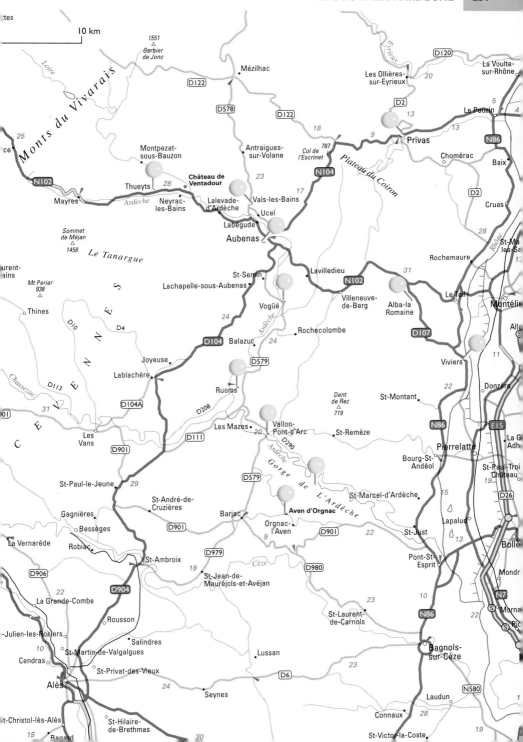

10 km

1551
△
Gerbier
de Jonc

Mézilhac

Les Ollières-
sur-Eyrieux

La Voulte-
sur-Rhône

D120

D122

D578

D122

18

20

D2

13

Le Pouzin

4

5

Monts du Vivarais

25

Privas

13

N86

ce

Montpezat-
sous-Bauzon

Antraigues-
sur-Volane

Col de
l'Escrinet

787

9

Chomérac

Baix

Château de
Ventadour

23

N104

Plateau du Coiron

Loire

N102

Thueyts

28

Lalevade-
d'Ardèche

17

Mayres

Ardèche

Neyrac-
les-Bains

Vals-les-Bains

Cruas

D2

Sommet
de Méjan
△
1458

Le Tanargue

Ucel

Labégude

Rochemaure

28

St-Ma
les-S

Aubenas

Mt Perier
938

St-Semin

Lachapelle-sous-Aubenas

Lavilledieu

31

Alba-la
Romaine

Le Teil

Montéli

urent-
ains

Vogüé

N102

Villeneuve-
de-Berg

Thines

Ardèche

24

Rochecolombe

24

D107

Viviers

11

Donzère

Joyeuse

Balazuc

D104

D579

St-Montant

22

Les
Vans

Lablachère

Chassezac

D113

31

D10

D4

Ruoms

Dent
de Rez
△
719

N86

E15

La G
Adh

St-Paul-le-Jeune

D104A

D208

Les Mazes

20

Vallon-
Pont-d'Arc

St-Remèze

Pierrelatte

St-Paul-Troi
Château

19

D901

D111

D290

Bourg-St-
Andéol

29

St-André-de-
Cruzières

D579

Gorge de L'Ardèche

St-Marcel-d'Ardèche

15

D26

Gagnières

Barjac

Aven d'Orgnac

Lapalud

13

Bollè

Bessèges

D901

Orgnac-
l'Aven

9

D901

22

St-Just

La Vernarède

Robiac

D979

Cèze

D980

Pont-St-
Esprit

Mondr

St-Ambroix

18

St-Jean-de-
Mauréjols-et-Avéjan

N7

D906

23

10

Morna

D904

22

La Grande-Combe

Rousson

St-Laurent-
de-Carnols

N86

22

Pic

-Julien-les-Rosiers

10

Salindres

Lussan

Bagnols-
sur-Cèze

Cendras

St-Martin-de-Valgalgues

St-Privat-des-Vieux

D6

Alès

24

Seynes

Laudun

N580

-Christol-lès-Alès

15

St-Hilaire-
de-Brethmas

Bagard

30

Connaux

28

St-Victor-la-Coste

19

ARDÈCHE GORGE***

Aven de Marzal €€
Tel: 04 75 04 12 45,
fax: 04 75 55 28 20; open
Apr–Oct daily, rest of the
year Sun and hols only.

Zoo Préhistorique €€
Combined ticket with
Aven de Marzal available.

Just below the village of Vallon-Pont-d'Arc (*see page 236*) the Ardèche river enters the most spectacular part of its course, where it has hewn countless caves, potholes and bizarre rock formations in the limestone. One of the most amazing sights is the arch of rock over the river known as Pont-d'Arc, best seen from the viewing area on the D290, or from the riverside at its foot. The arch is 59m across, and soars 34m above the average water level. Downstream from this point, the Ardèche is trapped within a spectacular gorge of red-tinted cliffs. Along the top, the many striking *belvédères*, or viewpoints, on the D290 give dramatic views down into the rock and forest of the ravine. The Belvédère du Serre de Tourre looks straight down on to an immense turn in the river; on the promontory stands the ruined Château d'Ebbo. The impressive **Aven de Marzal**** prehistoric stalactite caves are reached via the D590 side-road, 10km out of Vallon. Originally explored in 1892, the caves were filled in and forgotten; their breathtaking colours and forms were rediscovered in 1949. Run jointly with the Aven is the **Zoo Préhistorique***, a family attraction with reconstructions of prehistoric humans and animals, including dinosaurs. Beyond this point the clifftop road reaches its most impressive section, the Haute-Corniche. The road then leaves the river briefly, returning to it at the Grande Belvédère for a final view of the end of the gorge.

AUBENAS❖❖

Aubenas Tourist Office *4 blvd Gambetta; tel: 04 75 89 02 03, fax: 04 75 89 02 04, e-mail: ot.aubenas.ardeche @en-france.com, www. inforoutes-ardeche.fr/ tourisme/AUBENAS1; open Mon–Sat 0900–1200, 1400–1800 (daily in July and Aug). Organises guided walks in the old quarter.*

Château € *Pl. de l'Hôtel-de-Ville; tel: 04 75 87 81 11; open July and Aug daily at 1100, 1500, 1600, 1700, 1800. Rest of year Tue–Sat at 1500 and 1600 (additional tour at 1100 in June and Sept). 45-min guided tours.*

St-Benoît *Pl. de la Grenette; tel: 04 75 87 81 11; open July and Aug 1500–1830.*

The historic capital of southern Ardèche is built on a steep hilltop, with broad vistas over a wide area along the River Ardèche. At the heart of town, the **château**❖ was begun in the 12th century, though much of today's fine, decorative edifice dates from the 15th and 18th centuries. Opposite, the House of the Gargoyles is a richly adorned 16th-century townhouse, one of several old dwellings in the neighbourhood. The dome rising over the rooftops crowns a hexagonal Benedictine chapel, **St-Benoît**❖. On 30 April 1670 local peasants were massacred by royal troops for rioting against tax increases. The people of this area have never been strangers to rebellion, and remained staunchly Protestant throughout the Religious Wars.

Accommodation and food in Aubenas

Le Cévenol €€ *77 blvd Gambetta; tel: 04 75 35 00 10, fax: 04 75 35 03 29.* On a main street edging the town centre, this traditional provincial hotel has comfortable, well-kept rooms. No restaurant, but there is a bar.

La Pinède €€ *R. du Camping des Pins, on D235; tel: 04 75 35 25 88.* This out-of-town family-run hotel stands in a pine wood above a valley. It's simple and quiet, but has plenty of facilities, including a pool and a good restaurant.

On the menu

Southern Ardèche products include *marrons glacés* (glazed chestnuts) and numerous other chestnut preparations, as well as rough, tasty pâtés, hams and *charcuterie*, local wines and cheeses, wild mushrooms and wild fruits such as *myrtilles* (bilberries) and wild raspberries. There are peaches and cherries from the area's orchards, and you may also come across local country fare such as *maouche* (port haggis), *caillettes* (meatballs) and *criques* (potato pancakes).

AVEN D'ORGNAC✥✥✥

ℹ Aven d'Orgnac €€
Take the D579 across the Ardèche river from Vallon-Pont-d'Arc (heading south). At Barjac, turn left on to the D176 (becomes the D317) to reach the site; tel: 04 75 38 62 51, www.guideweb.com/ardeche/ orgnac/; 1-hour or 3-hour guided tours 0930–1200, 1400–1800 (July and Aug – no midday closing; Mar, Oct and Nov closes 1700), closed mid-Nov to Feb. Also at the site: a **Museum of Prehistory €€**, *with local prehistoric finds.*

One of the largest and most impressive stalactite caverns in Europe, this *aven* was always known to the locals – who called it Le Bertras – as a large hole in the ground. In 1935 experienced potholer Robert de Joly went down inside, and discovered a world of majestic chambers, curious colours, eerie half-light and rock formations. Today, a guided walk takes in the highlights, including the urn, placed in an impressive rock formation, that now contains de Joly's heart.

Avens and grottes

Hollows, caves, grottoes and other subterranean phenomena pepper the Ardèche limestone. Some are called *avens* and others *grottes*. Aven, translated variously as 'swallow-hole' or 'pothole', refers to large natural holes or cavities in the ground, generally an underground chamber whose roof has collapsed. *Grotte*, sometimes translated as 'grotto' or 'cave', is a tunnel-like formation into the earth's rock. Don't be tempted to call either of them a *cave* in French – that means 'cellar'.

PRIVAS✥

ℹ Privas Tourist Office *Pl. du Général de Gaulle; tel: 04 75 64 33 35, fax: 04 75 64 73 95, e-mail: ot.privas.ardeche@ en-france.com; open Mon–Sat (and Sun in July and Aug).*

Musée de la Terre Ardèchoise € *Pl. des Récollets; tel: 04 75 64 43 69; open July and Aug 0900–1200, 1500–1900, rest of the year 1400–1800, closed Mon and Tue.*

Privas, with its vistas and its wonderful site on a volcanic wedge between two valleys, is a fine base for the southern Ardèche. Get a good view of the town from its old Pont Louis XIII, south of the town centre. The **Musée de la Terre Ardèchoise (Museum of the Ardèche Land)**✥ is housed in a former convent. Staunchly Protestant Privas was all but destroyed in 1629 during the Religious Wars, and only a few houses pre-date that time. The village of Pranles, 12km north, is a focal point of this strongly Protestant district, with a small museum and an annual religious gathering for French Protestants on Whit Monday.

Accommodation and food in Privas

Hôtel de la Chaumette €€ *Av. du Vanel; tel: 04 75 64 30 66, fax: 04 75 64 88 25.* Usefully placed near the centre of town, on the road leading out to the *autoroute*, this is a good, family-run place with an above-average restaurant, good facilities and reasonable prices.

Le Panoramic Escrinet €–€€ *Col de l'Escrinet; tel: 04 75 87 10 11, fax: 04 75 87 10 34; open Mar–Nov only, closed Mon (except in season).* A relaxed atmosphere and well-equipped, comfortable rooms at this hotel on a high pass with the panoramic views of its name. The restaurant capably prepares a range of dishes ranging from classic favourites to imaginative innovations.

RUOMS*

ⓘ Ruoms Tourist Office R. Alphonse Daudet; tel: 04 75 93 91 90, fax: 04 75 39 78 91; open winter Mon–Sat 0830–1200, 1330–1730, summer Mon–Sat 0900–1300, 1500–1900, Sun 1000–1300.

A modern little town on the Ardèche river, with a historic, walled Old Quarter. The ramparts form a rectangle with seven round towers. Within the walled town, the 11th- to 12th-century Romanesque church has a curious arcaded belfry patterned with volcanic stones. Cross the water and head up to exquisite **Labeaume****, at one end of the Gorges de la Beaume ravine.

Accommodation and food in Ruoms

La Chapoulière €€ *Rte de St-Ambroix, about 3km from Ruoms on D111; tel: 04 75 39 65 43, fax: 04 75 39 75 82; closed Sun pm.* A good, mid-priced hotel and restaurant. It's small and family-run, close to the River Ardèche, and very well placed for the gorge and other sights. There's a pretty garden and terrace, and play area for children. Book well ahead.

Above
Sausage display in Ruoms

Thueyts❖❖

ℹ️ **Thueyts Tourist Office** *Pavillon d'Accueil, pl. du Champs de Mars; tel: 04 75 36 46 79, fax: 04 75 36 46 79; open summer 0800–1200, 1400–1800, winter 0800–1200, 1330–1730.*

🏛️ **Musée d'Ardèche d'Autrefois €€** *Pl. du Champs de Mars; tel: 04 75 36 46 27; open Mar–Oct 0900–1200, 1400–1800; closed Wed.*

This appealing old village stands at the foot of an extinct volcano beside the upper River Ardèche, amid scenery combining bizarre rocks with pretty pastures, orchards and farms. Thueyts has a well-preserved little medieval quarter. The **Musée d'Ardèche d'Autrefois (Museum of the Ardèche of Yesteryear)❖** displays local artefacts in an 18th-century house. Out of the centre, the old stone Pont du Diable (Devil's Bridge) leads over the Ardèche to a broad terrace of volcanic basalt. Many strange rock formations between the river and the village have evocative names – look out for the Chaussée des Géants (Giants' Way) and the Cascade de la Gueule d'Escade (Waterfall of the Jaws of Hell). The viewpoint on N102 just east of town gives a great overview. There are exciting, sometimes challenging, marked walks in the volcanic terrain, and it is also possible to climb to the top of the basalt flow.

Vallon-Pont-d'Arc❖

ℹ️ **Vallon-Pont-d'Arc Tourist Office** *1 pl. de l'Ancienne Gare; tel: 04 75 88 04 01, fax: 04 75 88 41 09, e-mail: tourisme. vallon@wanadoo.fr, www.vallon-pont-darc.com. Organises free guided tours of the village, every Fri 0900.*

🏛️ **Expo Grotte Chauvet-Pont-d'Arc €€** *R. Miarou; tel: 04 75 37 17 68, fax: 04 75 88 11 76, www.culture.fr/ culture/arcnat/chauvet/fr/ -gvpda-d; open Mar–Nov.*

Aubusson Tapestries € *Mairie; tel: 04 75 88 02 06; open Mon–Fri 1000–1200, 1500–1700.*

The small resort town of Vallon is the point of departure for kayak trips along the Ardèche Gorge and excursions to Aven d'Orgnac, and a popular base for campers. In 1995 the French Minister of Culture announced a major new discovery at Chauvet-Pont-d'Arc cave near here – some 300 black and red prehistoric paintings and hundreds of engravings, representing many different species of animals, as well as owls and outlined human hands. The work appears to be about 31,000 years old. There is also a huge amount of important archaeological material, giving insight into the culture of the artists. The caves are closed while studies continue, but the **Expo Grotte Chauvet-Pont-d'Arc (Chauvet Cave Exhibition)❖❖❖**, in Vallon-Pont-d'Arc, offers a first sight of what has been found, through photos and videos. Vallon's town hall, formerly a grand 18th-century château, houses a group of seven fine 300-year-old **Aubusson tapestries❖**. On a hillside beside today's Vallon are the ruins of the medieval village and feudal castle of Vieux-Vallon.

VALS-LES-BAINS*

Vals-les-Bains Tourist Office 116 bis r. Jean Jaurès; tel: 04 75 37 49 27, fax: 04 75 94 67 00, e-mail: tourisme@vals-les-bains.com, ot.vals. ardeche@en-france.com; variable opening times.

W www.vals-les-bains.com.

Intermittent Spring In a park on the east bank, near the south end of town, on av. Dr. Héritier. The water flow reaches its height every six hours: 1030 and 1630 (add an hour during summer time).

Établissement Thermal (Spa) Av. Dr Héritier; tel: 04 75 37 46 68 (morning only).

Produce markets every Thur and Sun morning. Evening markets on Thur in July and Aug. Craft markets on Wed in July and Aug.

This traditional little spa town, which lies along the high-sided, narrow Volane Valley, has 145 springs. The **Intermittent Spring*** varies considerably, and predictably, during the day. Vals' waters – cold, and high in bicarbonate of soda – are mainly for drinking rather than bathing, and are sold all over France. There are several parks, a casino and, of course, an **Établissement Thermal (Spa)***. The town makes a good starting point for drives in some fascinating scenery, particularly to the dramatic gorges further upstream.

Accommodation and food in Vals-les-Bains

Le Vivarais €€ 5 r. Claude-Expilly; tel: 04 75 94 65 85, fax: 04 75 37 65 47. By the river, the park, the Intermittent Spring and the Casino, this grand, traditional hotel has attractive gardens and a superb restaurant. You'll find some of the most delicious and imaginative Ardèche cooking here, with such dishes as chestnut soup, snails and crique (the local potato dish), and good local wines.

VIVIERS✧

ⓘ **Viviers Tourist Office** *Pl. Riquet (in Ville Basse); tel: 04 75 52 77 00, fax: 04 75 52 81 63; variable opening hours. Details of guided tours available.*

ⓘ **Cathédrale St-Vincent** € *Pl. St-Jean; open daily.*

Maison des Chevaliers *R. de la République. No entry – exterior only.*

Belvédère de Châteauvieux *At north end of ramparts, via r. de Châteauvieux. Free access.*

The Romans built Viviers on a rock beside the Rhône as a lookout and river port for Alba. Alba was subsequently totally destroyed, and the invading Germanic tribes built up Viviers as their new regional capital. The centre of their settlement is now the Vieille Ville (Old Quarter), also known as the Ville Ecclesiastique (Ecclesiastical Town), around pl. de la Plaine and the cathedral. Their gateways, Porte de l'Abri and Porte de la Gache, survive. Originally 12th century, the **Cathédrale St-Vincent**✧ was badly damaged in the Religious Wars. Viviers has been an episcopal seat since the 5th century. The bishop's palace (now the town hall) and the former town hall (now the palace) stand across the road from each other at the south end of the Vieille Ville. The Grande Rue has some fine 18th-century façades and – at Place République – a river view. A few paces from here, the 16th-century **Maison des Chevaliers**✧✧ has a beautiful Renaissance façade. For more impressive vistas over the Rhône, take the steps up from Grande Rue to the **Belvédère de Châteauvieux**✧ (try to ignore the cement works and nuclear power station). The medieval area of the Ville Basse (Lower Town), at the foot of the cliff, used to have its own ramparts. A tree-shaded walk goes from here to the little harbour at the mouth of the Escoutay.

VOGÜÉ✧

ⓘ **Vogüé Tourist Office** *Grande Rue; tel: 04 75 37 01 17, fax: 04 75 37 01 17; variable hours, but available by phone all year.*

ⓘ **Château de Vogüé** €€ *Tel: 04 75 35 76 50; open mid-June–mid-Sept 1000–1200, 1530–1930 (closed Tue), Easter–mid-June Sun and hols only 1400–1800.*

Viaduc 07 €€ *For information, tel: 04 75 37 03 52; open May, June and Sept Sun only, July and Aug every day except Sat.*

Picturesque Vogüé seems to be dug right into an escarpment alongside the River Ardèche. This, and the next village, Rochecolombe, were the twin fortresses of the Lords of Vogüé, who eventually became Barons of Languedoc and Governors of Provence. The Vogüé family still owns the 16th-century **Château de Vogüé**✧, which has a Romanesque chapel and hanging garden. Vogüé has become a popular tourist centre, and there are lots of campsites nearby. An appealing historical railway called **Viaduc 07**✧✧ runs from here up to St-Jean-le-Centenier.

Activities in the Ardèche

- Canoeing – particularly down the Ardèche gorge from Vallon-Pont-d'Arc;

- Walks and hikes – on GR4, and many other marked paths around the towns and villages, such as the Bois de Païolive in Les Vans or the gorge from Pont-d'Arc to the village of Aiguèze;

- Exploring caves and grottoes – guided tours or serious potholing or caving (at other *avens* and *grottes* around the Ardèche gorge);

- Rock climbing – the Ardèche is France's leading region, with over 50 locations and 1500 maintained itineraries;

- Riding – there are 30 riding centres; ask at local tourist offices.

Suggested tour

Le Grangousier
€–€€ *R. Courte, Les Vans; tel: 04 75 94 90 86; open Mar–Nov only, closed Wed and Sun pm (except uly and Aug).* A smart, accomplished restaurant in a 16th-century mansion opposite the church. Sumptuous and skilful dishes making good use of local ingredients.

Le Mas de l'Espaïïre €€ *On D901, Les Vans; tel: 04 75 94 95 01, fax: 04 75 37 21 00.* Well placed for the Ardèche Gorge and for our detours starting from Les Vans, this former silk farm lies south of town near the Bois de Païolive. It's a quiet, charming, rustic place, with comfortable, well-kept rooms, a pool and a shaded terrace.

Total distance: 248km, plus detours of 30km, 40km, 42km and 28km.

Time: The main route can be done in 1–2 days. With all the detours, it would be better to take at least 2–3 days. Many people touring the area spend a week, allowing time to walk, explore, linger over lunch and maybe take a dip in the river.

Links: At Montelimar the tour connects with the Border of Provence route (*see page 280*).

Route: From **PRIVAS** ❶ , take the main road, N104, through countryside of rocky hills and chestnut woods towards Aubenas. Two or three old castles can be glimpsed along the way. The road climbs up and over **Col de l'Escrinet**, below **Roc de Gourdon** (1061m). Before entering Aubenas turn off for **VALS-LES-BAINS** ❷ .

Detour: From Vals-les-Bains, turn on to the N102 heading west up the narrowing Ardèche Valley. You'll pass the ruins of the medieval **Château de Ventadour**, and the turn into the little spa village of Neyrac-les-Bains, before reaching **THUEYTS** ❸ and, beyond, Mayres. Return to Vals-les-Bains.

From Vals-les-Bains go down the road to neighbouring **AUBENAS** ❹ . Come out of town on the D104, turning left on to the D579 (the Ruoms road). The wider, cultivated valley gives attractive perspectives along this road, which reaches the side turn to enter **VOGÜÉ** ❺ . A short distance after, another turn leads to the beautifully sited picturesque village of **Rochecolombe**, with its evocative medieval predecessor standing beside a river alongside. Back on the D579, turn off the road to the right to reach medieval **Balazuc**, clinging to a ledge by a river gorge. It has winding lanes and stairways, pale limestone houses, remnants of fortifications and a Romanesque church. On the D579, continue to **RUOMS** ❻. Travel on the D208 by the Chassezac river – a tributary of the Ardèche – up to **Les Vans**.

Detour 1 from Les Vans: Take the D113, first beside the River Chassezac with its dams and then beside the River Thines, to the remote village of **Thines**. Return the same way.

Detour 2 from Les Vans: Drive up the scenic D10 to Mont Perier, beside the **Corniche du Vivarais Cévenol**. Turn around and descend (sometimes steeply) the spectacular corniche road (D4) all the way to **Lablachère**. Here, take the D104A back to Les Vans.

From Les Vans drive back to the Ardèche Valley road on the D111, reaching it about 2km from Ruoms. Turn right for **VALLON-PONT-D'ARC** ❼. (3km before Vallon, a lane off to the right goes a couple of km up to **Les Mazes**, where you can visit one of the last silkworm farms still operating, together with a museum.)

Detour: Cross the Ardèche river on the D579 to **Barjac**. Turn on the winding road here for **AVEN D'ORGNAC** ❽. Continue to the village of **Orgnac-l'Aven**, where you can turn on to the D217 to head back to Vallon-Pont-d'Arc.

Leave Vallon-Pont-d'Arc on the D290, the left-bank road which follows the **ARDÈCHE GORGE** ❾. Emerging from the gorge, continue to **Pont-St-Esprit** on the Rhône, which flows shallow and fast just here. The town is an ancient crossing place on the river and its name comes from a 13th-century bridge that was almost 1000m long from one side to the other. The bridge was widened and extended in 1860, two arches being replaced; of its original 25 arches, 19 are still there. Old houses and mansions in town include the 15th-century Maison du Roi, which has a fresco of the bridge.

Take the N86 (the west-bank road) up the Rhône Valley. The road passes through a succession of beautiful old villages, dramatic scenery and unsightly industrial developments. At **Bourg-St-Andéol**, there's a good 12th-century Romanesque church. A side-turn shortly after leads up to the fortified old village of **St-Montant**. Continue into **VIVIERS** ❿, and on towards **Le Teil**.

Detour: Just after Viviers, take the turn to **ALBA-LA-ROMAINE** ⓫. Leaving Alba, continue further in that direction to meet the N102, where you can turn right to descend directly to Le Teil.

North of this point, there are ugly quarries. On the other side of the Rhône, 5km away, is **Montélimar** (*see page 275*). At **Rochemaure** are juxtaposed striking volcanic scenery, the ruins of an ancient, impressive castle, a Romanesque church – and the cooling towers of a power station. A left turn just after climbs back up to Privas.

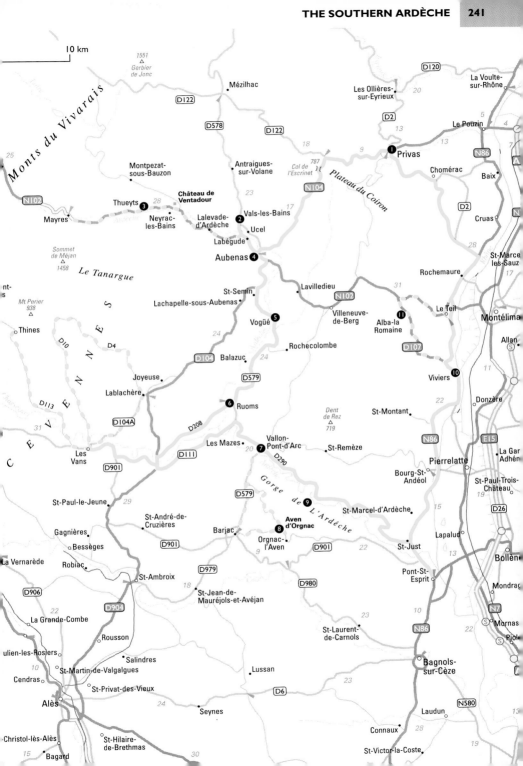

Côtes du Rhône: Vienne to Valence

Ratings

Restaurants	●●●●●
Scenery and river views	●●●●●
Winetasting	●●●●●
Castles	●●●●
Medieval architecture	●●●●
Children	●●●
History	●●●
Museums	●●●

The Côtes du Rhône vineyards almost come through the town gates at Vienne's southern tip, then, all the way from Vienne to Valence, they dominate the landscape. At first the vines are mainly on the river's right bank, but beyond Tain-l'Hermitage and Tournon, they climb the banks on both sides. There are orchards, too, and vast market gardens, as well as some industrial stretches, and an air of abundance and activity. The river and its valley become immense at times, then they narrow again, and there are more homely, historic towns and villages. There's no need, though, to stay beside the river. South of Tournon, the Corniche du Rhône is a winding hilltop road west of the valley – the views are immense if the weather is clear (and it usually is). To the east, far beyond Valence, the Alps rise like a jagged-topped solid wall.

ALBON*

ⓘ Albon Tourist Office On N7 at Le Creux de la Thine; tel: 04 75 03 17 05, fax: 04 75 03 17 13; open 15 June–31 Aug Mon–Thur 1000–1200, 1345–1745; Fri–Sat 1000–1200, 1400–1800, rest of the year, same hours, but afternoons only on Mon–Thur, all day Fri and Sat.

The Counts of Albon – whose now-ruined castle was a few kilometres north at St-Rambert d'Albon – started out in the Middle Ages as local feudal lords, and eventually carved out a territory that became Dauphiny. The **Tour d'Albon (Albon Tower)**, just outside the village, is the counts' ruined watchtower, also known as the Belvédère du Dauphiné. Even from its foot, it commands the most amazing view. Some of the inscriptions and graffiti date back hundreds of years. One refers to 'the Republicans of Albon on the 100th anniversary of the Revolution'. Boson (brother-in-law of Charles the Bald, son of Charlemagne, and the original inheritor of Burgundy) was crowned King of Burgundy in 879 in the now-ruined **Mantaille Castle**, which stands beside a calm valley 4km further east. Boson was also King of Provence.

ⓘ Comité Régional du Tourisme Rhône-Alpes *104 rte de Paris, Charbonnières-les-Bains; tel: 04 72 59 21 59, fax: 04 72 59 21 60, e-mail: crt@rhonealpes-tourisme.com, www.rhonealpes-tourisme.com.*

🏛 Tour d'Albon and Mantaille Castle €.

🧺 Le Panier Fermier in the village sells local produce direct from the farm *(tel: 04 75 03 07 21).*

Rhône or Loire?

In a curious bureaucratic anomaly, the stretch of the Rhône flowing south of Condrieu comes within the Loire *département.* At the same time, the whole of the Loire *département* is part of the Rhône-Alpes region. The Loire region is hundreds of kilometres to the north.

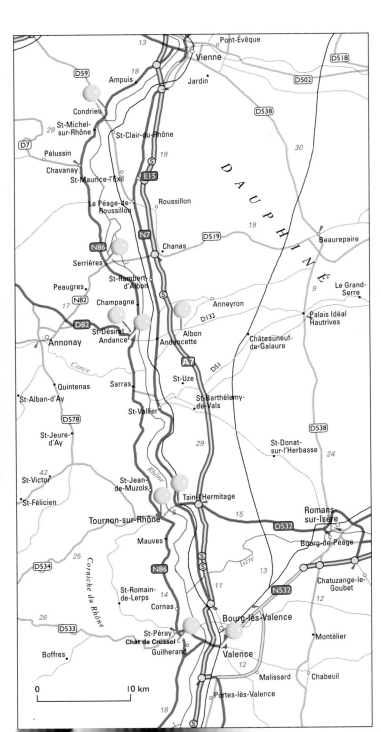

ANDANCE❖

🛈 Andance Tourist Office *Information from the Mairie; tel: 04 75 34 22 33.*

Ⓦ *www.inforoutes-ardeche.fr/ tourisme/ANDANCE1* (in French only).

Formerly a working river port, Andance still has a navigable harbour and is now a stop for river cruises. It has an appealing waterside quay and a beautiful cast-iron mariners' cross. Crossing the river here is a suspension bridge of 1827 – the oldest in France still in use. The village was a possession of the left-bank Counts of Albon, and still has part of its old fortifications. Historic buildings in the heart of the village include the striking 13th-century church, entered by steps under an elaborate porch. Inside, there's an exceptional *croix des équipages* (crews' cross) in the right chapel.

CHÂTEAU DE CRUSSOL❖❖

➋ The ruins of the Château de Crussol are only accessible on foot. From St-Péray pass the Château de Beauregard and continue to the car park alongside the statue of the Virgin. Take the footpath GR42B. It takes about 30 minutes to reach the site.

The impressive white ruins of the mighty 12th-century Château de Crussol perch on a high rock along the Rhône Valley, above the restored Château de Beauregard and overlooking Valence on the opposite side of the river. The path up to it passes the Villette, where locals came for safety when there was danger on the river plain, and continues to the crest of the Montagne de Crussol. After gaining great power and glory in the royal court, and inheriting domains in Provence, the Lords of Crussol eventually partly demolished their castle in the 17th century.

CONDRIEU❖

The little town of Condrieu, at the foot of its vineyards and surrounded by fruit and vegetables, was a thriving river port before the industrial revolution. It remains attached to its 'river' memories, and retains an appealing port area. In the higher part of town, the Maison de la Gabelle (by the church) has an interesting 15th- to 16th-century façade. Condrieu has won great renown for its unusual, fragrant white wine made from the local Viognier grape. The district is small (about 15 hectares), the grape variety unpredictable, and the wine must be drunk young and fresh, so Condrieu wine has a scarcity value that pushes its price way up. There is also a cheese, in a soft, round shape, and properly made of raw goats' milk (although it is often imitated using cows' milk).

Above
Fishermen at Condrieu

Accommodation and food in Condrieu

Hôtellerie Beau Rivage €€€ *R. du Beau-Rivage; tel: 04 74 56 82 82, fax: 04 74 59 59 36.* There's a lovely river view from the terrace, and first-rate cooking of regional classics, at this sumptuous, enjoyable hotel-restaurant.

The Côtes du Rhône vineyards

The vineyards of the Rhône are believed to be the oldest in France, with some being introduced by Greek settlers in the 4th century BC. The Côtes du Rhône forms a long, narrow and very varied wine region, extending from Vienne to Avignon. The Côtes du Rhône Septentrionales, or Northern Côtes du Rhône, run from Vienne to Valence. Here, some of the grandest Côtes du Rhône vineyards cling to steep, terraced hills rising from the valley. The highest ranking of these is Condrieu among the whites, and Côte Rôtie, Crozes-Hermitage and Hermitage among the reds. Close behind follow St-Joseph, Château-Grillet, St-Péray and Cornas. After a short gap south of Valence, the Côtes du Rhône vineyards resume again in a more Provençal climate, with a multitude of different regions (some of them quite a long way from the Rhône) known collectively as the Côtes du Rhône Méridionales.

St-Désirat✧✧

Musée de l'Alambic
€ *Distillerie Jean Gauthier, in village; tel: 04 75 34 23 11, fax: 04 75 34 28 81; open all year – call to check hours.*

Cave de St-Désirat
Tel: 04 75 34 22 05, fax: 04 75 34 30 10, www.cave-saint-desirat.com; open daily – varying hours.

This village is at the heart of the St-Joseph *appellation* vineyards, producing good red (using only Syrah grapes) and white wines (from Marsanne and Rousanne). Grander whites are made from the Viognier grape, and a more down-to-earth Gamay red is also produced. Look out too for Le Domaine Rochevine wines, producing Condrieu and St-Joséph *appellation* wines from 19 hectares of steep slopes arranged in little walled terraces. All can be tried and bought at the local *cave*. In the village, try a tot of traditional local pear liqueur at the **Musée de l'Alambic (Distillers Museum)**, which deals with the history of the region's *gnoliers*, or travelling distillers.

Right
Cherry trees at St-Désirat

The grape varieties of the northern Côtes du Rhône

Syrah – for the great reds.

Gamay – for some of the more modest reds.

Viognier – on its own for the greatest whites, or blending in reds.

Roussane, Marsanne, Clairette, Muscat, Chardonnay and Aligoté – for whites.

SERRIÈRES-SUR-RHÔNE**❖❖**

❶ **Serrières Tourist Office** *Pavillon du Tourisme, Quai Jules Roche; tel: 04 75 34 06 01; open 15 June–15 Sept, daily 1000–1230, 1500–1900, rest of the year office closed, but all written queries will be answered.*

🏛 **Musée des Mariniers du Rhône** € *St Sornin Chapel; tel: 04 75 34 01 26; open Apr–Oct weekends and hols 1500–1800 for 1-hr guided tours.*

Serrières is an old river boatmen's town, with a riverside footpath, a suspension bridge to Sablons and summertime jousting tournaments on the river. **The Musée des Mariniers du Rhône (Museum of Rhône Mariners)❖❖**, in the 12th- to 14th-century St-Sornin chapel, contains a mass of nostalgic items recalling the work and daily life of the bargemen of Serrières. Just 7km out of town is the popular family attraction, Peaugres Safari Park (*see page 224*).

Accommodation and food in Serrières

Hôtel-Restaurant Schaeffer €€ *Quai Jules Roche; tel: 04 75 34 00 07, fax: 04 75 34 08 79; closed Sun pm and Mon, Tue in July and Aug.* Comfortable riverside *restaurant avec chambres* on the main road, offering skilful cooking of Lyonnais dishes and other classics, accompanied by the famous local Condrieu and St-Joseph wines.

TAIN-L'HERMITAGE**❖**

❶ **Tain Tourist Office** *70 av. Jean Jaurès; tel: 04 75 08 06 81, fax: 04 75 08 34 59; open Mon–Sat 0900–1200, 1400–1800.*

Tain is an old town on the Rhône riverbank, at the foot of rocky slopes. In AD 184, while other towns were becoming Christianised, Tain was installing a new altar for the sacrifice of bulls. Today it stands in the main square, Place Taurobole. Tain is a commercial centre for northern Rhône wines, being the nearest town to the vineyards of the great Hermitage and Crozes-Hermitage labels. Visit the local *cave** for a taste, or ask the tourist office for details of the individual producers. **Chocolatier Valrhona❖❖❖**, one of the world's top creators of gourmet chocolate delicacies, is also based here. A footbridge crosses the Rhône to Tournon.

Accommodation and food in Tain-l'Hermitage

Caves de Tain l'Hermitage *22 rte le Larnage; tel: 04 75 08 20 87; open 0800–1200, 1400–1800 (from 0900 on Sun).*

Chocolatier Valrhona *av. Président Roosevelt; no phone enquiries; open 0900–1900 (Sat closes at 1800. Sun closed).*

Hôtel-Restaurant Jean-Marc Reynaud €€ *82 av. Président Roosevelt; tel: 04 75 07 22 10, fax: 04 75 08 03 53.* The best restaurant in town overlooks the Rhône from the riverside boulevard, and serves plenty of fish and local vegetables capably prepared. The comfortable hotel, with pool and other facilities, also benefits from the riverside views.

The *appellations*

The wines of the Côtes du Rhône – north and south – have several distinct *appellations*, depending on their place of origin, type of grapes and quality, among other factors. Broadly, they are:

Côtes du Rhône – the region's catch-all name for its varied *vins ordinaires*.

Côtes du Rhône Villages – wine from 77 superior southern villages, of which 16 may add their own name to the label.

Les Crus – 13 exceptional locations with their own *appellations* (8 in the north, 5 in the south).

Right
Medieval festival in Tain-l'Hermitage

TOURNON (SUR RHÔNE)**

ⓘ Tournon Tourist Office *Hôtel de la Tourette, Quai Farconnet; tel: 04 75 08 10 23, fax: 04 75 08 41 28, e-mail: ot.tournon.ardeche@en-france.com; open Mon–Sat 0930–1200, 1400–1830 (July and Aug until 1900 and open Sun 0930–1200).*

ⓗ Château and Musée Rhodanien € *Quai Marc Séguin; open June–Aug 1000–1200, 1400–1800 (closed Tue), Apr, May, Sept, Oct, pm only (closes 1700 in Oct and closed Tue), rest of the year closed.*

Église St-Julien € *Quai Marc Séguin; open daily.*

Lycée Gabriel-Fauré € *Off r. Thiers; open on request, if convenient, during term time.*

Vivarais Railway *Tel: 04 78 28 83 34 for details.*

◖ Festivals and events: *June–July – Music Festival; July – Jousting on the Rhône; Aug – Les Soirées d'Hélène, historical shows at the castle.*

With steep slopes rising behind it, busy, congenial Tournon has a harbour on the river, and a shaded quay. Most of the town's charm is focused around Quai Farconnet at the historic north end of the town centre. Rising behind are the two beautiful terraced gardens of the imposing old **château*** – the main attraction. One day in 1536, the poet Pierre de Ronsard, then aged 12, arrived here to start work as a page boy for the eldest son of François I. Sent up to the room, he found the 19-year-old prince dead in bed. Today, the castle houses the **Musée Rhodanien (Museum of the Rhône)***, covering local history. Close by, two towers – Tour de l'Hôpital and Tour de Pierregousde – are remnants of the town's medieval ramparts. **Église St-Julien*** (14th to 17th century) has a coffered ceiling and good medieval artwork, including a 16th-century triptych. **Lycée Gabriel-Fauré***, set back from the waterfront, has a fine Renaissance doorway; the public may request to see its attractive 16th- and 17th-century décor, carvings and tapestries. A footbridge goes from the quayside to Tain-l'Hermitage (*see page 246*), across the Rhône. The 100-year-old **Vivarais Railway*** steam train runs from Tournon, along the Doux Valley, to Lamastre (*see page 226*).

Accommodation and food in Tournon

Hôtel-Restaurant Les Azalées €–€€ *6 av. de la Gare; tel: 04 75 08 05 23, fax: 04 75 08 18 27.* High in the town near central pl. de la Résistance, this modern, comfortable, family-run hotel is close to the steam railway station. The restaurant offers good, local cooking at moderate prices.

VALENCE**

ⓘ Valence Tourist Office *Parvis de la Gare; tel: 04 75 44 90 40, fax: 04 75 44 90 41, e-mail: info@tourisme-valence.com; open summer daily 0900–1900, off-season Mon 1400–1830, Tue–Sat 0900–1230, 1400–1830.*

ⓦ *www.tourisme-valence.com/ (official site, in French and English).*

A bright, busy river port, ancient Valence rises in terraces from the east shore of the Rhône. Across the water, the castle ruins on the high ridge of the Crussol mountains make a handsome sight from Parc Jouvet or the Champs de Mars *esplanade*. The town is industrialised on the east side, a major centre of the Rhône Valley's fruit and vegetable trade, and the administrative capital of the Drôme *département*. *Valentia Julia* was founded in 123 BC, but little or nothing remains from its Roman days, and its historic ramparts were replaced by boulevards 100 years ago. There are, however, reminders of the medieval and Renaissance periods. The heart of town has an atmospheric tangle of steps and lanes – known as *côtes* – lined with old

The N7 and A7 run together between the town and riverbank. Double boulevards encircle the old town centre.

There is plenty of parking in Champs de Mars, off av. Gambetta, and in the space between blvds Bancel and Charles de Gaulle, and between blvds Alsace and Sidi Carnot.

Cathédrale St-Apollinaire *Pl. des Ormeaux; open daily.*

Musée de Valence (or des Beaux-Arts) € *Pl. des Ormeaux; tel: 04 75 79 20 80; open daily 1415–1745 and also Wed, Sat and Sun 0900–1145.*

Côtes du Rhône wine Designed to promote or sell the region's wines, these English-language sites have useful vineyard information: *www.vivarhone.com/VRAnglais/StructureSommaire; www.opali.fr/decouverte/anglais/cepages; www.french-wine-shop.com/rhone.*

houses, near **Cathédrale St-Apollinaire**✤. The cathedral, Romanesque, and dating from the 11th century, was largely rebuilt (in the same style) in the 17th century. The incongruous belfry was added in 1862. Beside the church on the south side, the **Musée de Valence (or des Beaux-Arts)**✤ occupies the former bishop's palace. On the other side of the cathedral is an odd classical-style funerary monument of 1548 called the Pendetif. Across pl. des Clercs and a few paces down Grande Rue, on the worn façade of 16th-century Maison des Têtes, four large carved heads represent the four winds. A teenage Napoleon lived opposite this house, when he was a student at the town's School of Artillery. Another distinguished resident was François Rabelais, who attended the university here in the 15th century.

Accommodation and food in Valence

Hôtel-Restaurant Pic €€€ *285 av. Victor Hugo; tel: 04 75 44 15 32, fax: 04 75 40 96 03; closed Sun pm, Tue midday, and Mon out of season.* The Pic (named after the chef-proprietor), a member of the *Relais et Châteaux* group, has a fistful of stars and accolades – and has served the Aga Khan and the King of Morocco, among others. The setting and service are luxurious, and menus offer *foie gras*, caviar, truffles and high-priced classic Burgundian and Rhône dishes. The hotel has characterful, individualised rooms. The same family runs the affordable **Auberge du Pin restaurant** (€€) at the same address.

Right
Cathédrale St-Apollinaire

Suggested tour

Dégustez!

You will see *Dégustation* (tasting) inscribed on scores of signboards along this route. Follow the signs to try out local wines.

W Hautrives: *www.aricie.fr/facteur-cheval.*

Total distance: 150km, or 206km if you take the detours to Annona and Hautrives. Add 1 hour for the Crussol walk, and 2 hours for the train excursion to Lamastre.

Time: 1–2 days. At a minimum, allow half a day for the drive and quick look at the main sights on the way, and another half-day to explore Valence. To include one or two of the suggested detours an excursions, add at least another half-day.

Links: At Vienne the route links with the Bas-Dauphiné tour (*see pag 260*). At Valence the route links with the Haut-Vivarais tour (*see pag 227*).

Route: From **Vienne** (*see page 214*), cross to the west bank of th Rhône and head south on the N86. This route now stays on the N8 most of the way. The vineyards beside the road at the start are amon the most prestigious in France. Pass through several villages, includin **Ampuis**. First stop is **CONDRIEU** ❶, a separate distinguishe *appellation*. After leaving the town, go a few minutes up the steep winding D34 to the church of St-Michel-sur-Rhône, for a broad viev over this section of the Rhône Valley. The N86 continues sout through a less charming section into **SERRIÈRES-SUR-RHÔNE** ❷.

Detour: Take a trip up to **Annonay** (*see page 222*) on the N82, perhap stopping at **Peaugres Safari Park** (*see page 224*). Take the D82 t return to the main route at **ANDANCE** ❸.

From Serrières, the N86 passes through **Champagne**, where there's ar unusual 11th-century church with Roman stonework, a nave vaultec with domes and beautiful 15th-century choirstalls. Although on th right bank of the river, the town used to be part of Dauphiny. A righ turn leads into **ST-DÉSIRAT** ❹, where you can try traditional loca pear liqueur at the **Musée de l'Alambic (Distillers Museum)**. The N8 reaches Andance.

Cross the Rhône here on the suspension bridge to **Andancette**, the bear right on to the D122A. Cross the N7 and go under the *autorout* to reach the village and tower of **ALBON** ❺.

Detour: Continue via the D132, left on to the D53 and right on to th D187, under the railway line, to flowery **Hautrives**. The **Palais Idéa (Fanciful Palace)**, a sort of surreal temple, is a 19th-centur architectural folly in the back garden of its creator, local postma Ferdinand Cheval. He spent 33 years constructing it out of pebbles and adorning it with words of wisdom. He constructed his own grav in the same style, and completed it just before his death, in 1924. Tak the D51 to return to the main route at St-Vallier.

Opposite
Shop sign in Valence

From **Tour d'Albon**, the D122 leads to the N7 and **St-Vallier**. There'

some striking scenery here, and the Rhône itself contracts into a narrow defile. Just east, off the D51, are gorges, prehistoric standing stones and eerily balanced 'trembling rocks'. Steep slopes or sheer cliffs rise beside the road as the N7 continues south, sometimes right on the water's edge, to the towns of **TAIN-L'HERMITAGE** ❻ and **TOURNON** ❼. Ruined feudal castles perch on rocky ledges. Growers bearing the Hermitage *appellation* have emblazoned their names across the vine-covered left-bank slopes.

La Côte Rôtie €€ *Pl. de l'Église, Ampuis; tel: 04 74 56 12 05, fax: 04 74 56 12 05.* Strongly tipped young chef Manuel Viron prepares delicious, vivid, imaginative dishes, unusually spiced and seasoned, using the finest ingredients. Prices are modest, and at his lunchtime-only winebar **Serine (€)**, next door, they are even less for a memorable set three courses.

Restaurant Lecomte and Hôtel Terminus €€ *116 av. Jean-Jaurès (route de Lyon), St-Vallier; tel: 04 75 23 01 12, fax: 04 75 23 38 82; closed Sun pm and Mon, and most of Aug.* The comfortable little station hotel at St-Vallier (soundproofed rooms) has a wonderful restaurant with good, classic Burgundian cooking – and with an emphasis on desserts. Good wine list.

Getting out of the car: Take the old steam railway from Tournon to Lamastre (*see page 226*). The 33-km ride along the pretty Doux Valley takes 1 hour.

At Tournon, abandon the riverbanks to climb the **Corniche du Rhône** road. Leave town behind the château on the northwest side (r. du Dr Cadet), with a sharp turn left (south), signposted *Route Panoramique*, direction St-Romain-de-Lerps. Immediately, there is a string of dizzying hairpins. Part of the road is also designated as the GR42 footpath. From the viewpoints on the Corniche road outside **St-Romains-de-Lerps**, you can sometimes see into a dozen *départements* – from Mont Pilat, near Lyon, to Mont Blanc in the east and to Mont Ventoux in Provence. The road winds down into the small villages of **St-Péray** and Cornas, in a prestigious wine district, and on to **CRUSSOL** ❽ (1 hour's walk to visit the château ruins). Drive 4km down to the Rhône and cross the river into **VALENCE** ❾.

Also worth exploring

As an alternative or addition to the Rhône Valley tour, travel through the rolling country **east of the Rhône**, on the river's left bank. The D538 runs all the way from Vienne to Romans-sur-Isère, and the N532 goes from there to Valence. On the way you'll pass through pleasant country towns: **Beaurepaire**, which has some 15th-century houses, **Hautrives** (*see page 250*), and **St-Donat-sur-l'Herbasse**, with its ruined 12th-century château, and an annual Bach organ festival. **Romans-sur-Isère** has a centuries-long history of shoe-making.

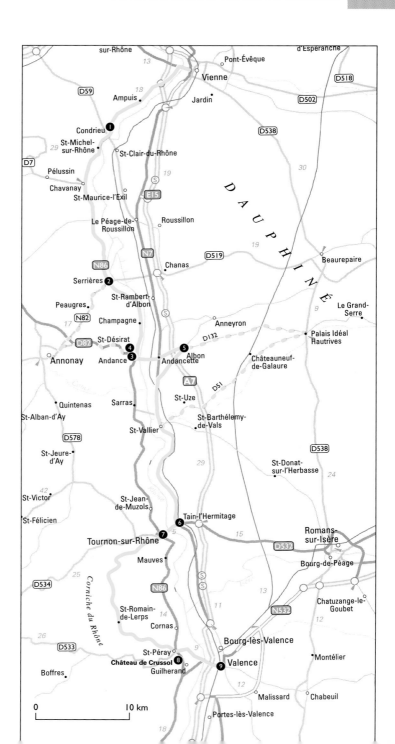

Bas-Dauphiné

Ratings

Medieval architecture
●●●●

Restaurants ●●●●

Rural tradition
●●●●

Activities ●●●

Children ●●●

History ●●●

Roman remains
●●●

Scenery ●●●

Abroad, rolling green landscape extends eastwards from the busy Rhône Valley as the river sweeps south from Lyon and Vienne. Bas Dauphiné, or Lower Dauphiny, reaches to the Alps in a series of plateaux and valleys dominated by the higher crests and peaks of the Vercors and Chartreuse nature parks. For visitors, the higher ground is a place of clean air, inspiring exploration and activity. The lower ground, though mostly within the Isère, is not at all typical of that Alpine *département*. Dubbed *plaines et collines* ('plains and hills'), it's cut across by *autoroutes* and railway lines, but it does contain many of the *département's* best museums, attractions and historical monuments. The region continues south, with little change of scene, across the border into the Drôme *département*, but to the east it ends abruptly at the steep slopes of the Pré-Alpes.

LA BALME-LES-GROTTES✦✦

ℹ️ **La Balme Tourist Office** At the Mairie; tel: 04 74 90 60 49, fax: 04 74 90 67 03.

🌐 www.voiron.com/ (local site that covers much of the region).

🏛️ **Grottes de la Balme** €€ Tel: 04 74 90 63 76; open Apr–Sept 1000–1200, 1400–1800, rest of the year, Sun and hols 1400–1700.

This village stands near the tip of the Île de Crémieu, a plateau peninsula around which the Rhône makes a hairpin on its way to Lyon. It's worth visiting for its fascinating **Grottes de la Balme (La Balme Caves)✦✦✦** which dig into the base of the Crémieu plateau. The caves have been much visited and explored since the Middle Ages, and are entered through an arrangement of two chapels one on top of the other, with a large porch. Inside are spacious caverns with a labyrinth of tortuous galleries and dramatic rock formations. 'Lake Gallery' has a series of waterfalls descending into pools and an underground river.

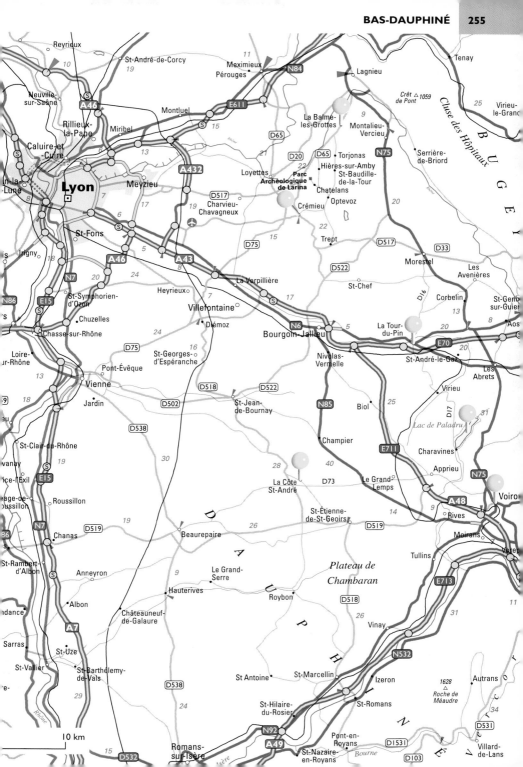

Reyrieux
St-André-de-Corcy
19
11
Meximieux
Pérouges
Tenay

N84
Lagnieu
Crêt de Pont △ 1059
25
Virieu-le-Grand

Neuville-sur-Saône
A46
Montluel
E611
15
La Balme-les-Grottes
9
Montalieu-Vercieu
B U G E Y
Cluse des Hôpitaux

Rillieux-la-Pape
Miribel
D65
D65
Torjonas
N75
Serrière-de-Briord

Caluire-et-Cuire
13
A432
D20
Hières-sur-Amby
St-Baudille-de-la-Tour
Chatelans

In-la-Lune
8
Lyon
7
Meyzieu
17
19
D517
Charvieu-Chavagneux
21
Loyettes
22
Parc Archéologique de Larina
Crémieu
Optevoz
20

6
St-Fons
D75
22
Trept
D517
D33
Morestel

A46
A43
5
8
Heyrieux
La Verpillière
15
D522
St-Chef
Corbelin
Les Avenières
St-Genix-sur-Guiers

N7
20
24
7
547
17
13
Aos

E15
St-Symphorien-d'Ozon
Chuzelles
Diémoz
N6
Bourgoin-Jallieu
5
La Tour-du-Pin
E70
20

N86
Chasse-sur-Rhône
24
Villefontaine
Nivolas-Vermelle
St-André-le-Gaz
Les Abrets

Loire-sur-Rhône
D75
16
St-Georges-d'Espéranche
Virieu
D17
31

13
Pont-Évêque
D518
D522
N85
Biol
25
Lac de Paladru

18
Vienne
Jardin
D502
St-Jean-de-Bournay
Champier
E711
Charavines
Apprieu
N75

vaney
D538
28
40
Le Grand-Lemps
A48
Voiro

ice-l'Exil
E15
30
La Côte St-André
D73
14
9
Rives

age-de-ussillon
Roussillon
19
St-Étienne-de-St-Geoirs
D519
Moirans

N7
Chanas
D519
26
Tullins
E713
11

St-Rambert-d'Albon
Anneyron
9
Le Grand-Serre
Roybon
D518
26
Vinay
31

Albon
Hauterives
Plateau de Chambaran
N532

A7
Châteauneuf-de-Galaure
Autrans
Roche de Méaudre
1628 △

Sarras
St-Uze
St Antoine
St-Marcellin
Izeron
D531
34

St-Vallier
St-Barthélemy-de-Vals
D538
29
24
St-Hilaire-du-Rosier
St-Romans
N E

10 km
15
D532
Romans-sur-Isère
N92
A49
Pont-en-Royans
St-Nazaire-en-Royans
D1531
Bourne
D103
Villard-de-Lans

LA CÔTE ST-ANDRÉ**

ⓘ La Côte St-André Tourist Office *Pl. H. Berlioz; tel: 04 74 20 61 43, fax: 04 74 20 56 25; open all year – variable hours.*

Ⓦ *www.standrews.u-net.com/Berlioz Lacote (La Côte St-André site in English maintained by Berlioz fans).*

Ⓜ Musée Berlioz €€ *69 r. de la République; tel: 04 74 20 24 88; open Mar–Dec 0900–1200, 1500–1800, Feb 1400–1700, closed Tue, and Jan.*

Château *By appointment only, tel: 04 74 20 27 00.*

Palais du Chocolat € *Château; tel: 04 74 20 35 89. Phone first.*

Musée des Liqueurs € *Av. Camille Rocher; tel: 04 74 93 38 10. Open for free 1hr guided tours June–Sept 0900–1200, 1500–1800 (closed Mon).*

❍ There's a **market** every Thur morning in the ancient Halles.

Several artists and writers used to frequent this ancient, hillside town overlooking the Bièvre plain, and it was the birthplace and childhood home of the orchestral composer Hector Berlioz (1803–69). The musician described his town in these words: 'It overlooks a wide, rich plain, green and golden and in its stillness filled with a sense of dreamlike grandeur – a grandeur enhanced by the chain of mountains bounding the plain to the south and east, behind which, far off, gleaming with glaciers, rise the towering peaks of the Alps'. The painter Jean-Barthold Jongkind (1819–91) lived here at the end of his life, and is buried in the parish cemetery. The **Musée Berlioz (Berlioz Museum)***, in the 17th-century town house where he grew up, displays memorabilia of the composer, as well as a few Jongkind paintings. The town's large 500-year-old Halles (covered market) has fine timbers and a huge shallow roof. Note, too, the beautiful Renaissance interior courtyard of the town hall and the attractive and unusual old church. Rising over all is the medieval fortress rebuilt in the 16th century as a handsome Renaissance **château*** (there's a wonderful view from its upper terrace). Pause to visit and enjoy the **Palais du Chocolat*** at the château, where artisan chocolatiers tell the story of chocolate. For more flavours, the **Musée des Liqueurs (Liqueur Museum)***, in the 18th-century Rocher distillery, deals with another important local product: fruit spirits and cordials. There's a free tasting when you visit.

Accommodation and food in La Côte St-André

Hôtel de France €€–€€€ *Pl. Église; tel: 04 74 20 25 99, fax: 04 74 20 35 30.* Madame France, of course, owns and runs the old-fashioned Hôtel de France, which has an excellent, highly rated, traditional restaurant serving such classics as calf sweetbreads with truffles, frogs' legs, and saddle of hare *à la crème*. Modest prices.

CRÉMIEU**

ⓘ Crémieu Tourist Office *Pl. de la Nation Charles de Gaulle; tel: 04 74 90 45 13, fax: 04 74 90 02 25, e-mail: office.tourisme cremieu@wanadoo.fr; open 1000–1200, 1400–1730.*

Once a heavily guarded gateway to the Dauphiné region, Crémieu has become a tourist centre, with plenty of campsites and other budget accommodation nearby. It's a popular jumping off point for trips around the Plateau de Crémieu, whether by car, bike or on horseback. Crémieu is an intriguing medieval town, physically shaped by a fascinating setting, in a narrow valley with a horseshoe of hills rising above. The town keeps impressive sections of its 14th- to 16th-century fortifications, including four 'city gates' (note especially the daunting 14th-century Porte de la Loi) and the 12th-century hilltop **Château** www.ville-cremieu.fr/.

Château Delphinal
€ At top of Montée St
Laurent; no phone.

Cloister € Pl. de la Nation;
no phone.

Halles € R. Porcherie; no
phone.

Delphinal* fortress. The *mairie*, or town hall, occupies a former Augustine monastery, and still has its attractive **cloister***. There are remains of several other monasteries in the area. In the town-centre streets, lanes and stairways there are many old craft workshops and artisans' houses as well as grander homes. At 14 r. du Marché-Vieux, notice the strange Fenêtre des Trois Pendus (Window of the Three Hanged Men): it dates back to the 14th century. The town's most remarkable medieval survival is its huge 14th-century **Halles***, or covered market, with hefty rafters, and divided into three aisles, each formerly serving a different trade. It's still the scene of Crémieu's weekly market.

Accommodation and food in Crémieu

Auberge de la Chaite €–€€ *Cours Baron Raverat, tel: 04 74 90 76 36, fax: 04 74 90 88 08. Closed Sun pm and Mon.* This quiet, comfortable, traditional little hotel also has a good restaurant with an outdoor terrace, offering value for money.

LAC DE PALADRU**

**Musée du Lac de
Paladru** € Charavines;
tel: 04 76 55 77 47, fax: 04
76 55 63 13; open May,
Oct, Nov Sat and Sun
1400–1800, June and Sept
daily 1000–1200,
1400–1800, July and Aug
1000–1200, 1500–1900.

This beautiful, narrow stretch of water, 6km long, lies serenely among rustic hills. The slopes are partly wooded, partly farmed, dotted with picturesque traditional farmhouses with broad eaves. It makes a highly enjoyable walk to go right around the lake, and there are several other waymarked trails and paths heading into the hills from the main village of Charavines, at the southern end. The lake is popular with anglers, too. The site has great historical interest, with two underwater archaeological sites revealing traces of former lakeside communities now submerged. One site (at Baigneurs) dates back about 4 700 years, while another (at Colletière) is only 1 000 years old. At Colletière large numbers of tools, weapons, and ordinary household objects of the time have been preserved, as well as play things such as a chess set and a toy crossbow. It seems that the communities displaced by rising water levels moved up the shore slopes and founded the villages of today. The lakeside **Musée du Lac de Paladru*** at Charavines displays finds from the sites and explains their significance.

Accommodation and food in Lac de Paladru

Hôtel de la Poste €€ *965 r. Principale, Charavines; tel: 04 76 06 60 41, fax: 04 76 55 62 42.* Just 500m from the lakeside, this one-time coaching inn is today a comfortable, relaxing, well-equipped country hotel. Its restaurant too is traditional, with generous, expertly prepared dishes making good use of local ingredients.

LA TOUR-DU-PIN❖

ⓘ La Tour du Pin Tourist Office
Maison des Dauphins, r. de Châbons; tel: 04 74 9714 87, fax: 04 74 83 34 74; open 0930–1130, 1500–1730 (closed Sat pm, Sun, and Mon).

A busy little junction, and a useful stopover, close to the branching of two *autoroutes* (A48 and A43). With the busy N6 running through town and a railway station too, this is no tranquil country town. Yet it has the pleasant feel of a long-established local capital, with local art and crafts amenities, and a theatre and cultural centre. The town hall is in a former 17th-century monastery, and there are several fine 16th and 17th-century Renaissance houses in town, especially along r. d'Italie. Inside the church there's an important 16th-century triptych of *The Entombment* by Georges Penez, a pupil of Dürer.

Accommodation and food in La Tour du Pin

Le Château €€€ *at Faverges de la Tour, 10km NE; tel: 04 74 97 42 52 fax: 04 74 88 86 40, e-mail: relaischateau@faverges.com.* Glorious rural luxury in a genuine château, this pricey *Relais et Châteaux* hideaway is also an above-average restaurant with imaginative dishes, including a vegetarian menu.

Le Relais de la Tour €–€€ *Av. Gén. de Gaulle; tel: 04 74 83 31 31, fax 04 74 97 87 01.* This is a thoroughly quiet and restful, moderately priced hotel-restaurant with good views over the town.

Below
Voiron Cathedral

VOIRON❖

ⓘ Voiron Tourist Office *58 cours Becquart Castelbon; tel: 04 76 05 00 38, fax: 04 76 65 63 21; open Mon–Sat 0830–1200, 1400–1800.*

Ⓦ *www.ville-voiron.fr/ (official site, in English and French).*

🏛 Grande-Chartreuse Distillery € 10 *boulevard Edgar Kofler; tel: 04 76 05 81 77; open Jan–Mar and Nov–Dec Mon–Fri 0830–1130, 1400–1730, Easter–June and Sept–Oct, daily 0830–1130, 1400–1830, July and Aug, daily 0830–1830.*

A historic manufacturing and commercial town in a valley at the foot of Dauphiné's mountain regions, Voiron stands beneath the Vouise peak. It has an attractive 19th-century 'cathedral', and is known for its factories making skis and chocolates. The town is an ideal starting point for tours by car or on foot into the Parc Naturel Régional de la Chartreuse. For a shorter walk, three marked trails reach the Vouise summit (737m) in about thirty minutes. At the top stands the 7-m Nôtre-Dame de Vouise, a copy of the statue overlooking Le Puy in the Auvergne. For many, though, Voiron's main attraction is the **Grande-Chartreuse Distillery❖❖**, the largest liqueur cellar in the world, offering free guided tours and tasting.

Accommodation and food in Voiron

Hôtel-Restaurant de la Chaumière €–€€ *R. de la Chaumière; tel: 04 76 05 16 24, fax: 04 76 05 13 27.* This modest family-run establishment is quiet and inexpensive. It's a little away from the centre.

Restaurant la Serratrice €€ *3 av. Tardy, tel: 04 76 05 29 88, closed Sun pm and Mon.* Arguably the town's best restaurant, the style is classic and highly accomplished. There's a variety of dishes, but the emphasis is on top-class fresh fish and shellfish.

Below
Chartreuse Distillery

The secret elixir

The name Chartreuse has been known for centuries as a powerful liqueur, originally made by the Chartreuse monks at their remote monastery in the hills above Voiron. The story of the liqueur is that in 1605 the Maréchal d'Estrées gave the Chartreuse monks a curious secret recipe for the 'Elixir of Life'. Not until 1737 did the monks succeed in making the 71°-proof elixir, a blend of wine distilled several times with powerful local aromatic herbs, aged with honey in oak barrels. They then developed this into the widely available 55°-proof Chartreuse Verte liqueur that made fame and fortune for the austere monastic community. About 100 years later, the 40°-proof yellow Chartreuse was created. After another century, in 1935, the distillery was moved to Voiron where it has continued to make all three versions of the elixir. The process is still in the hands of the Chartreuse monks, and the recipe remains a secret.

Suggested tour

Walibi €€€ *At Les Avenières (via N75); tel: 04 74 33 71 80; open mid-June–Aug 1000–1900 (sometimes 1800 in June), Apr–mid-June Wed, Sat, Sun only, 1000–1800, Sept Sat, Sun only, 1000–1800, closed Oct–mid April.*

Hôtel de France and Restaurant Le Diligence €€ *319 Grande Rue, Morestel; tel: 04 74 80 04 77, fax: 04 74 33 07 47.* This is a really satisfying, comfortable little hotel, with an excellent, unassuming restaurant (closed Sun pm and Mon) offering value-for-money set menus.

Total distance: 200km.

Time: 1–2 days.

Links: At Vienne (*see page 220*) the route links with Côtes du Rhône Vienne to Valence (*see page 250*).

Route: If you want to reach the route from **Lyon**, cross the Rhône and take the D517 to **CRÉMIEU ①**. Otherwise, start from Vienne (*see page 250*). From Vienne, take the D75 through an unappealing area. The TGV line crosses the road, then D75 crosses the *autoroute* (A43) and reaches N6. Go straight over to Crémieu.

From Crémieu take the D52 east. The road gives good views. Pass the Étang de Ry (Ry Lake) and modern Château St-Julien, and follow the road round to penetrate the peninsula known as the **Île de Crémieu**. Notice the traditional roofs of *lauzes* (thin stone slabs) in this area. First of all, continue to Optevoz and beyond. Turn left on to the D52A, a steeply descending, and pretty, winding lane following the rocky green **Gorges d'Amby**. Take the steep left turn up to **Chatelans** from where there's a narrow access road (about 2.5 km long) to the precipitously sited **Parc Archéologique de Larina**, a large and impressive archaeological site, with information panels. Return to the Gorges d'Amby road and continue down into the village of **Hières-sur-Amby**, where the **Maison du Patrimoine** displays finds made at Larina, as well as an interesting model of a Merovingian farm, based on the excavations.

Reaching the bigger, busier D65, turn right to **LA BALME-LES-GROTTES ②** and its *grottes* (caves). Return out of the village along the D65, and at once turn left on to the D52B (note not A or C), which passes through appealing, rustic **Torjonas** and **St-Baudille-de-la-Tour** (the *tour* is part of a 15th-century house) to return to the D52 and Optevoz. At the branch of the D52 and D54, take the D54 to the D517 and turn left for **Morestel** and its **Walibi** theme park. There's a good view of the village on the approach. Leave Morestel on the N75, but at once heading away on the D16 to **LA TOUR-DU-PIN ③**. Continue on the D17 to **Virieu**. The imposing fortress-château just outside the village was originally 11th century. Go in and see the 15th-century arched kitchen, and the bedroom where Louis XIII spent the night in 1622. A little further on the same road, you'll see **LAC DE PALADRU ④** stretching away on the left. It's enjoyable to make the small detour right round the lake, with good views from the road. Failing that, pause at **Charavines**, at the end of the lake. Carry on south to **VOIRON ⑤**.

Travel back 7km on the same road, then veer off westward to **LA CÔTE ST-ANDRÉ ⑥**. Take the D518, then the D502, back to Vienne.

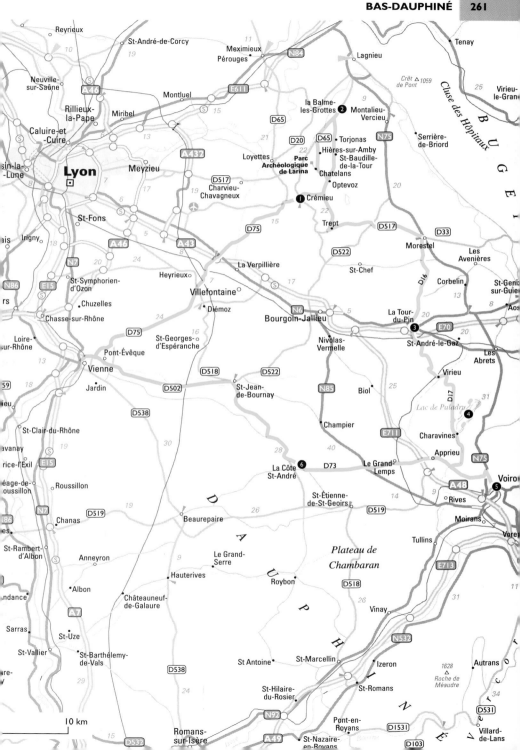

Reyrieux
St-André-de-Corcy
Neuville-sur-Saône
Rillieux-la-Pape
Miribel
Caluire-et-Cuire
Meyzieu
Lyon
St-Fons
Irigny
St-Symphorien-d'Ozon
Chuzelles
Chasse-sur-Rhône
Heyrieux
Villefontaine
Diémoz
St-Georges-d'Espéranche
Pont-Évêque
Vienne
Jardin
St-Clair-du-Rhône
Roussillon
Chanas
St-Rambert-d'Albon
Anneyron
Albon
Châteauneuf-de-Galaure
Sarras
St-Uze
St-Vallier
St-Barthélemy-de-Vals

Meximieux
Pérouges
Lagnieu
Crêt de Pont △ 1059
Virieu-le-Gran
la Balme-les-Grottes ❷ Montalieu-Vercieu
Torjonas
Serrière-de-Briord
Hières-sur-Amby
St-Baudille-de-la-Tour
Loyettes
Parc Archéologique de Larina
Chatelans
Charvieu-Chavagneux
Optevoz
❶ Crémieu
Trept
Morestel
Les Avenières
St-Chef
Corbelin
St-Geni sur-Guie
Ao
La Verpillière
Bourgoin-Jallieu
La Tour-du-Pin ❸
St-André-le-Gaz
Les Abrets
Nivolas-Vermelle
Virieu
St-Jean-de-Bournay
Biol
Lac de Paladru ❹
St-Geni
Champier
Charavines
Apprieu
La Côte ❻ D73 Le Grand-
St-André Lemps
Voiro ❺
St-Étienne-de-St-Geoirs
Rives
Beaurepaire
Moirans
Le Grand-Serre
Vere
Hauterives
Tullins
Roybon
Plateau de Chambaran
Vinay
Autrans
Roche de Méaudre
1628 △
St Antoine
St-Marcellin
Izeron
St-Hilaire-du-Rosier
St-Romans
Pont-en-Royans
Villard-de-Lans
Romans-sur-Isère
St-Nazaire-en-Royans

Road numbers: A46, E611, N84, N75, D65, D20, D517, D75, D522, D33, D16, A432, A43, N7, N86, E15, N6, E70, N85, E711, N75, A48, D518, D502, D538, D519, A7, E713, N532, A49, N92, D1531, D531, D103

10 km

Diois

Ratings

Activities	●●●●●
Scenery	●●●●●
History	●●●●○
Wildlife	●●●●○
Castle ruins	●●●○○
Crafts	●●●○○
Winetasting	●●●○○
Children	●●○○○

South of Valence, and east of the Rhône river plain, soars a mountainous landscape intriguingly marrying the high Alps with the warm south. Country roads wind through high meadows looking up at frosty peaks, then plummet down into shaded villages savouring Provençal warmth and fragrance. Snowy in winter, yet this is a southern scene of lavender and vines – here shepherds and winemakers are neighbours. The main road into this region clings closely to the banks of the River Drôme, and most of its people live along the valley. On both sides, the landscape rises into pale limestone plateaux and hills deeply scored with little ravines and fast-flowing clear waters. The rough heath is scented with wild rosemary and thyme. In winter, there are rustic, unpretentious ski resorts. Even in the peak summer season, you can have this quiet upland world almost to yourself.

CHÂTILLON-EN-DIOIS✦✦

ⓘ **Châtillon Tourist Office** Pl. Jean Giono; tel: 04 75 21 10 07, fax: 04 75 21 10 07; opening hours variable, but phone enquiries will always be answered.

Comité du Tourisme de la Drôme 31 av. Président Herriot, Valence; tel: 04 75 82 19 26, fax: 04 75 56 01 65, e-mail: info@ drometourisme.com, www.drometourisme. com/.

This fortified village, attractively placed among orchards beside the River Bez, is pretty with flowers and fountains. The castle at the centre disappeared long ago, but there remains a powerful sense of history. Several 16th-century buildings survive, such as the belfry and the *mairie*, and narrow, atmospheric alleys (called *viols*) link the old streets. Located at the southern tip of the Vercors mountains, Châtillon-en-Diois is the starting point for trips up to the Cirque d'Archiane.

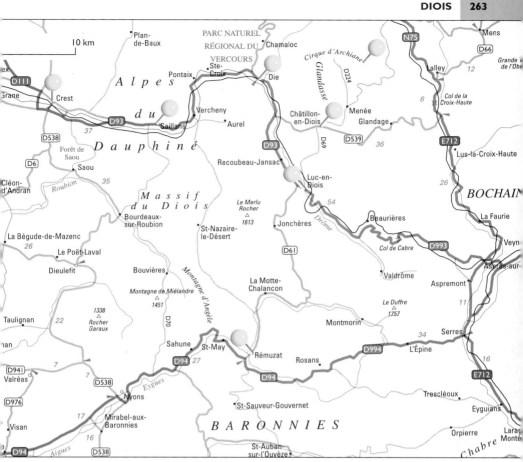

10 km

Plan-de-Baux

PARC NATUREL
RÉGIONAL DU
VERCOURS

Chamaloc

Mens

N75

D66

Cirque d'Archiane

Grande
de l'Ob

D111

ex

Grane

Crest

Alpes

Pontaix
Ste-Croix

Die

Glandasse

D224

Lalley

12

Col de la
Croix-Haute

6

du

Vercheny

Châtillon-en-Diois

Menée

Glandage

Lus-la-Croix-Haute

Saillans

D93

37

Aurel

D93

D69

D539

36

E712

Dauphiné

Forêt de
Saou

D538

D6

Saou

Recoubeau-Jansac

26

BOCHAIN

Cléon-d'Andran

Roubion

35

Massif
du Diois

Luc-en-Diois

La Bégude-de-Mazenc

26

Bourdeaux-sur-Roubion

St-Nazaire-le-Désert

Le Merlu
Rocher
1613

Jonchères

Beaurières

Drôme

54

La Faurie

Le Poët-Laval

Col de Cabre

D993

Veyn

Dieulefit

Bouvières

Aspres-sur-

Montagne d'Angèle

La Motte-Chalancon

D61

Valdrôme

Aspremont

Taulignan

22

Montagne de Miélandre
1451

1338
Rocher
Garaux

D70

Le Duffre
1757

Montmorin

11

Serres

34

nan

Sahune

St-May

Rémuzat

Rosans

D994

L'Épine

16

D941

7

Valréas

7

D538

D94

27

D94

Eygues

E712

D976

Nyons

St-Sauveur-Gouvernet

Trescléoux

Eyguians

Visan

17

Mirabel-aux-Baronnies

16

BARONNIES

Orpierre

Larag
Monté

D94

Aigues

D538

St-Auban-sur-l'Ouvèze

Chabre

Right
View of the Alps

CIRQUE D'ARCHIANE❖❖

 To reach the Cirque d'Archiane, leave Châtillon-en-Diois on the D120 and pass through Mensac village to Menée. Here turn on to the D224 for Archiane. The total distance is 10km.

A majestic scene of high cliffs forming a giant horseshoe around a valley, the Archiane *cirque* is one of the most easily accessible of the dramatic Vercors sights. It's part of the Glandasse massif, which overlooks the Diois. In the midst of this setting is the end-of-the-road hamlet of Archiane, a popular starting point for walkers. Long-distance path GR93 climbs from here, up the valley of the Archiane stream, to the Col de Rousset (1254m), which can also be reached by road from Die.

CREST❖❖

Crest Tourist Office *Pl. Dr-Maurice-Rozier; tel: 04 75 25 11 38, fax: 04 75 76 79 65, e-mail: ot-crest@vallee-drome.com; open all year – variable hours.*

W *www.vallee-drome.com/ot.crest.*

Tour €€ *At top of steps via r. de la Tour; tel: 04 75 25 11 38; open June–Sept, daily 0930–1900, Jan same hours, weekends only, rest of the year daily 1400–1800.*

At the very foot of the hills, just where the Drôme reaches the plain, stands this medieval city with its imposing castle keep – known to locals as the **Tour ('Tower')❖❖**. It's reached on 184 rough, rock-carved steps starting out from the central square beside the church of St-Sauveur. Parallel is another flight of stone steps called the Escalier des Cordeliers, which reaches the Portique des Cordeliers gateway with its five arches. The castle is what remains of a huge fortress built from the 11th to 15th centuries, eventually partly dismantled in 1632. Inside are vaulted rooms and cells, which were used as a political prison in the 19th century. The upper terrace has extensive views from the Auvergne to the Alps. Down in the old town there are grand 16th- and 17th-century mansions, especially in the streets below the church.

On the menu

The region produces crisp, clean-tasting, sparkling golden white wine, Clairette de Die (see page 266). Foods of the region include Défarde tripe stew from Crest, blue cheeses such as Bleu de Sassenage-Vercors and the goats' cheeses called Picodon, pâtés and *charcuterie* made with wild game, trout from the mountain rivers and *foie gras*.

Accommodation and food in Crest

La Grande Hôtel €–€€ *60 r. Hôtel-de-Ville; tel: 04 75 25 08 17, fax: 04 75 25 46 42; closed Sun pm and Mon out of season.* This simple, inexpensive, family-run hotel near the main sights is clean, comfortable and has good local cooking.

Hôtel-Restaurant Kléber €–€€ *6 r. Aristide-Dumont; tel: 04 75 25 11 69, fax: 04 75 76 82 82; closed Sun pm and Mon.* In the centre of town, the Kléber is a classic provincial *restaurant avec chambres* of the best type. It serves traditional regional cooking, well prepared, on modestly priced set menus ranging from simple to celebratory ... and has a handful of attractive, unpretentious bedrooms, too.

DIE❖❖

ⓘ Die Tourist Office
Pl. St-Pierre; tel: 04 75
22 03 03, fax: 04 75 22 40
46, e-mail: otdie@vallee-
drome.com; open in high
season 0900–1230,
1430–1900 (closed Sun
pm), rest of the year
0900–1200, 1400–1800
(closed Sun and hols).

ⓦ www.vallee-
drome.com/die (French
only – rarely updated).
Growers' website:
www.clairette.com.

**ⓕ Cave Coopérative
de Die and Musée
de la Clairette de Die €**
Av. de la Clairette; tel: 04 75
22 30 00, fax: 04 75 22 21
06, e-mail:
mail@clairette.com; open
daily 0900–1230,
1330–1830.

**Musée d'Histoire et
d'Archéologie de Die**
€€ R. Buffardel; tel: 04 75
22 00 69; open July and Aug
daily 1530–1830, June and
Sept same hours, but Tue
and Fri only, rest of the year
closed except by
appointment.

Cathédrale € Pl. de la
Cathédrale. Open daily.

Chapelle St-Nicolas €
Inside Hôtel de Ville; tel: 04
75 21 08 77; open Mon–Fri
0830–1200, 1330–1600
(closed hols).

On the southwestern foot of the looming pale crags of the Montagne de Glandasse, Die provides access into the Vercors massif, with two roads climbing from here into the high mountains. It's an appealing, ancient, little town, whose long history has been much tied up with religion. Today, Die is best known for its white wine, Clairette de Die (*see page 266*), which can be tasted at the **Cave Coopérative de Die❖**. The *cave* represents 90 per cent of the region's winemakers and also houses the **Musée de la Clairette de Die❖** about the origins and making of the local wines.

An important Roman town on the mountain highway from Italy to the Rhône Valley, Die was a centre of the cult of Cybele, a mother goddess who required bulls to be sacrificed. Some of its taurobolia (bull altars) can be seen in the **Musée d'Histoire et d'Archéologie de Die (Die History and Archaeology Museum)❖** as part of a rich collection of Gallo-Roman and later artefacts found here. The Roman town was devastated in an attack by Germanic tribes in the year 275, but was repaired and the encircling ramparts built. These have largely survived until this day – despite (apparently) a poor method of construction using the masonry of demolished buildings. Some vestiges of other Roman structures survive, notably Porte St-Marcel, a handsome triumphal arch, which became part of the ramparts. The museum, ramparts and Roman arch can all be seen on the main through-street, r. Buffardel.

Turn down r. de l'Armellerie to reach the former **Cathédrale❖**. Die was vigorously Christian from an early period, and became an important bishopric early in the 4th century. It remained so until 1276. During the Wars of Religion (1562–98), the town was staunchly Protestant, which led to the partial destruction of the cathedral in the 16th century. Now, parts of the cathedral date from the original 11th-century building (which incorporates remains of a Roman temple) and parts from the 17th-century reconstruction. The nearby Hôtel de Ville (Town Hall) was once the Bishop's Palace: inside it, the bishop's

Festival: *Rythmes et Diois* – summer concert season; *La Fête de la Transhumance* – second 2 weeks in June: the Transhumance is the traditional moving of herds of sheep to their summer pastures at higher altitudes. As they pass through Die there are festivities and street entertainers; *La Fête de la Clairette* – Sept: the local wine festival; *Festival Est-Ouest* – Sept: cross-cultural arts and entertainment.

Die is pronounced 'Dee', and gets its name from the Roman town, *Dea Augusta Vocontiorum*.

private **Chapelle St-Nicolas**✢ dates from the 11th century and contains its original mosaic floor, in classical style, beautifully crafted and representing various allegorical and Biblical images.

Accommodation and food in Die

La Petite Auberge €–€€ *Av. Sidi-Carnot; tel: 04 75 22 05 91, fax: 04 75 22 24 60; closed Sun pm and Wed out of season, Mon in season.* This small, family-run hotel facing the station has a good quality restaurant, including regional dishes.

Clairette de Die

The fresh, golden, sparkling Clairette wines of the Diois come dry or semi-dry, *crémant* (champagne style) or *pétillant* (slightly sparkling). They have four *appellations* of their own, Clairette de Die and Crémant de Die, and, less distinguished, Côteaux de Die and Châtillon en Diois. The Crémant, made by the Méthode Ancestrale, as it is called here, uses an intriguing and subtle mix of clairette (25 per cent) and muscat (75 per cent) grapes. It is not strongly alcoholic (7 to 9 per cent). Wine has been made here for thousands of years. Pliny the Elder mentioned that he liked the wines of *Dea Augusta Vocontiorum*, describing them as the 'most natural' of all wines in the Empire.

LUC-EN-DIOIS✢

ⓘ **Luc Tourist Office** *Pl. de la Croix; tel/fax: 04 75 21 34 14, e-mail: officetourisme@wanadoo.fr; open in summer daily, 0930–1200, 1500–1900 (Sun am only), rest of the year changeable hours.*

Ⓦ *perso.wanadoo.fr/ lucendiois.*

🏨 **Le Claps** € *3km from Luc on D93.*

Set among lavender fields near the meeting of the Rif and Béouse streams with the River Drôme, Luc is a small, appealing and picturesque resort of lanes and flowery squares. Originally a Gallic settlement, then a small Roman town called *Lucus Augusti*, it has unearthed many Roman finds including an important mosaic (all are displayed in the museums at Valence and Die – *see pages 248 and 265*). Just out of town, the Drôme Valley narrows, and the river drops down in a waterfall (called Saut de la Drôme – the Drôme's Leap) through a fascinating, chaotic, rocky terrain called **Le Claps**❖❖ – or rather, originally, Lou Clapas (Provençal for 'the pile of stones'). This curiosity results from a big landslide in 1442.

Accommodation and food in Luc-en-Diois

Hôtel du Levant € *Rte de Gap; tel: 04 75 21 33 30, fax: 04 75 21 31 42; closed Tue.* Enjoy the garden, pool and mountain views at this bargain-priced former 17th-century coaching inn on the main road. You may be obliged to have *demi-pension* (ie, dinner, bed and breakfast) – but it's no hardship to sample the good, regional cooking in the atmospheric old dining room.

RÉMUZAT❖

ℹ Rémuzat Tourist Office *Pl. du Champ de Mars; tel: 04 75 27 85 71; variable hours.*

❖ If walking here, wear good shoes for the rough limestone terrain, and take water.

Overlooked by its curious Rocher du Caire (Caire Rock) across the River Oule, quiet, simple Rémuzat is a small-scale resort for the wild hills east of Nyons, with campsites, children's holiday camps and *gîtes* around the village. The Rif stream runs through the middle of Rémuzat into the Oule, and the Oule flows into the Eygues just south of the village. At the foot of the Rocher stands the 11th-century Chapelle de St-Michel, alongside traces of an earlier village. There are many good walks starting here, along dry gorges and through the fragrant *garrigue* (Mediterranean heathland) and by lavender fields. Cycling and horse riding are popular options, too, and there is also rock-climbing and canoeing.

SAILLANS❖

ℹ Saillans Tourist Office *Montée de la Soubeyranne; tel: 04 75 21 51 05, fax: 04 75 21 58 83, e-mail: office-tourisme-pays-de-saillans@wanadoo; open usually every day Apr–Sept, and less often for the rest of the year.*

W *www.vallee-drome. com/saillans.info/.*

🏠 Magnanerie de Saillans € *1.5 km from village centre on D93; tel: 04 75 21 56 60, fax: 04 75 21 54 11; open May–Sept.*

The Drôme Valley becomes narrow at this old village, which is overlooked by high rocky escarpments. There's a marked walk around the historic heart of the village, and it's a place to try out Clairette de Die. There's also a *magnanerie* (**silk farm**)❖, though today this is run more for education and entertainment than for serious commercial silkmaking.

Activities in Diois

The Comité
Départmentale du
Tourisme and local
tourist offices have
leaflets about the best
places and facilities for
climbing, canoeing,
horseriding, cycling and
XC cycling (called VTT
in French), walking and
skiing.

Suggested tour

Total distance: 216km, and a 21km detour.

Time: 2 days.

Links: At Nyons the route links with the Border of Provence route (*see page 280*).

Route: From **CREST ❶**, take the D93 upriver along the Drôme Valley to **SAILLANS ❷**. The road – and the valley – here turns sharply north. On the curve is the village of **Vercheny**, the centre of the Clairette de Die *appellation*. The road crosses to the other side of the river at very prettily located wine village **Pontaix**, with a ruined 13th-century castle perched on a rock. At **Ste-Croix** there are more riverside ruins, a castle of the Holy Roman Empire. The D93 now curves round into **DIE ❸**. Travel 6km further on the D93, to the junction with the D539 which turns off left just as the main road crosses the Drôme: turn here and continue to **CHÂTILLON-EN-DIOIS ❹**.

Detour: From Châtillon-en-Diois take the D120 to the village of Menée. Here turn on to the D224 for the **CIRQUE D'ARCHIANE ❺**. Return the same way.

About 1km from Châtillon-en-Diois on the D539, going back in the direction of Die, turn left on to the D69 for **LUC-EN-DIOIS ❻**. Allow time to get out of the car to explore Le Claps and maybe have a dip in the river.

Take the D61 (the junction is 1km from Luc along the D93 heading downstream) on a long, scenic drive through the Diois hills, usually clinging to the valley of a little river or stream, with rocky limestone hills rising alongside, and passing through a succession of small villages. It's tempting to get out and walk: the scents of pine, rosemary and thyme are in the air. You may glimpse chamois or wild boar, and soaring birds of prey, and perhaps the local species of vultures, which have recently been reintroduced to the region. Stay on this road all the way to **RÉMUZAT ❼**. The road through the village reaches the Eygues Valley and the D94, where you turn right, following the river through lovely landscapes. Passing into a short section of gorge, it skirts **St-May**, perched above. Soon the road reaches the olive country of **Nyons** (*see page 276*). This area is known as the Baronnies, once an independent territory with Nyons as its capital.

Return 7km along the Eygues Valley road to a left turn, the D70. It climbs away from the Eygues along the side of another small valley, occasionally narrowing into a gorge. At Col la Sausse, the road passes the Montagne d'Angèle (1 606m) and descends into **Bourdeaux-sur-Roubion**. Carry on down into the old village of **Saou**, noted for its winter fruits. The village was partly destroyed by the Germans, but still has its Romanesque abbey-church. Saou is the best approach to explore the extensive **Forêt de Saou**. Take the D136 to follow a circuitous route through the forest, over a pass and down to the D164 for Crest.

Also worth exploring

The Diois lies along the southern edge, and partly within the borders, of the **Parc Naturel Régional du Vercors (Vercors Regional Natural Park)**. This high mountain natural conservation zone, at 150,000 hectares the largest of the French natural parks, is quickly entered from Die and Châtillon-en-Diois. At its highest altitudes, there's an immense nature reserve where animals like the wild goat and marmot are being reintroduced. At lower altitudes, closer to the Diois, the park's role is to defend the environment and conserve and maintain the traditional appearance and culture of the rural communities within its border.

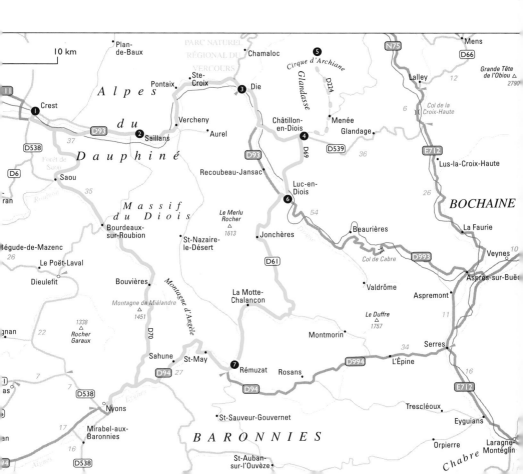

The border of Provence

Ratings

Roman remains	●●●●●
Scenery	●●●●●
Villages	●●●●●
Winetasting	●●●●●
History	●●●●○
Medieval architecture	●●●●○
Restaurants	●●●●○
Children	●●●○○

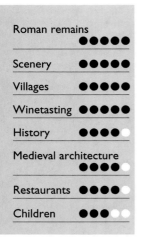

Beyond Valence there's a change. The climate is drier, the light brighter, there's an outdoor feel to life. You can sense the closeness of Provence. Extending east from the Rhône, the villages and valleys of southern Drôme encompass a colourful, evocative diversity. The southern foothills of the Alps bask in sunshine, and in the village squares, café tables are set in the shade of leafy trees while high peaks rise above. Then, at last, it really is Provence. Today's official boundary of the Mediterranean province touches the Rhône at Pont St-Esprit. Beyond this point, our suggested tour reaches two significant Roman towns, Orange and Vaison, before turning back through the olive groves of Nyons. On the return, country roads of the southern Drôme skirt the wild, rocky hills of the Baronnies and Diois areas before arriving again at the banks of the River Rhône.

DENTELLES DE MONTMIRAIL✦✦✦

The D7 passes below the villages; follow signs off the road to enter the village centres.

Rising between towering Mont Ventoux and the hot flatlands of the Rhône, the strange Dentelles – the name means lacework, but sounds too like 'little teeth' – form a line of delicate saws' teeth rocky points. From the vine-covered slopes below them come good Côtes du Rhône wines. A country lane joins pretty, sunlit villages and at almost every village there is *dégustation* (winetasting). One of the prettiest is Gigondas, with its old houses, shaded main square and the best of the local red wines. Séguret, a lovely little medieval village, rests on a steep slope just below the rocky teeth of the Dentelles. There's a 15th-century fountain and 12th-century church, and the village square enjoys an immense view. Walkers are drawn to the village as a starting or finishing point for Dentelles hikes.

10 km

Plateau du Coiron

Cruas

N7

Marsanne

D538

Alpes du
Dauphiné

D6

Saou

28

Cléon-
d'Andran

35

St-Marcel-
lès-Sauzet

Massif
du Diois

Rochemaure

N86

17

Rhône

27

Roubion

Bourdeaux

31

Montélimar

La Bégude-de-Mazenc

St-Nazaire-
le-Désert

Le Teïl

D540

26

Le Poët-Laval

Allan

Bois de
Fonbrenoux

Dieulefit

Bouvières

Viviers

11

Nôtre-Dame-
d'Aiguebelle

Montagne de Miélandre
1451

D107

Donzère

Taulignan

22

1338
Rocher
Garaux

ntant

22

D541

24

Grignan

Montagne
des Vaux

N86

E15

Val-des-Nymphes

Grillon

D941

7

Sahune

Pierrelatte

La Garde-
Adhémar

Valréas

7

27

Bourg-St-
Andéol

19

St-Paul-Trois-
Châteaux

D59

D538

Nyons

Eygues

cel-
che

15

D26

Lèz

12

Visan

D976

17

Mirabel-aux-
Baronnies

ust

Lapalud

13

Bollène

19

Suze-
la-Rousse

D94

Tulette

16

D538

Buis-les-
Baronnies

Pont-St-
Esprit

D976

Aigues

D938

Vaison-la-
Romaine

10

Mondragon

D117

15

9

N86

N7

Sérignan-
du-Comtat

Sablet

Dentelles de
Montmirail

Mont Ventoux
1909

Mornas

22

Piolenc

D975

Violès

D977

Ouvèze

Gigondas

Malaucène

Bagnols-
sur-Cèze

A7

Orange

Vacqueyras

D938

Bédoin

N580

13

Jonquières

Beaumes-
de-Venise

17

28

Laudun

21

Courthézon

Aubignan

Mazan

19

Sarrians

D950

St-Victor-la-coste

Roquemaure

E714

16

Carpentras

D94

ux

Tavel

E15

Sorgues

S

Monteux

Nesque

Pujaut

Entraigues-sur-Sorgues

Pernes-les-Fontaines

14

Villeneuve-lès-Avignon

Vedène

Above
Dentelles de Montmirail

Accommodation and food in Dentelles de Montmirail

Table du Comtat €€ *In village centre, Séguret; tel: 04 90 46 91 49, fax: 04 90 46 94 27.* Housed in a 16th-century former hospice, this peaceful, civilised establishment is a relatively simple hotel and a top-quality restaurant with ambitious cooking of Provençal classic dishes and good selection of local wines. Glorious views.

Le Mesclun € *R. des Poternes, Séguret; tel: 04 90 46 93 43, fax: 04 90 46 93 48; open Apr–Oct only.* Good, classic village restaurant with accomplished cooking at moderate prices. Fantastic view across the vines towards the Rhône.

La Garde-Adhémar✠✠

Adhémar Tourist Office *In the Ancienne Mairie; tel: 04 75 04 40 10; open daily 0900–1100, longer in season. Outside these hours, phone messages will be answered.*

Chapelle des Pénitents € *In the village; tel: 04 75 04 41 21; open Apr–Oct only, Sun and hols, 1500–1800.*

Jardin des Herbes € *In village, beneath the church; tel: 04 75 04 41 09.*

Chapelle du Val-des-Nymphes € *2km east of village on the D472.*

The lofty medieval village of the feudal Adhémars keeps its ramparts, vestiges of its ruined château and its sweeping vista right across the Rhône Valley. The village is a delight, with its lanes and alleys and old stone houses, and the superb Romanesque church. The **Chapelle des Pénitents**✠ – once a meeting hall of the White Penitents brotherhood – has twinned windows dating from the 12th century. It's the setting now for a permanent exhibition about the town. The Chapelle provides access to the **Jardin des Herbes**✠, with an unusual collection of medicinal and aromatic plants. Just east of the village, the Val-des-Nymphes is pretty with many little pools and tiny waterfalls. In a reminder of the Christian takeover of pagan worship, there's a charming 12th-century Romanesque **Chapelle du Val-des-Nymphes**✠.

Accommodation and food in Adhémar

Logis de l'Escalin €€ *R. du Logis-de-Berre; tel: 04 75 04 41 32, fax: 04 75 04 40 05; closed Sun and Mon evenings.* This excellent *restaurant avec chambres* offers imaginative cooking, drawing from cuisines around the world, as well as skilfully prepared Provençal classics. There are just seven bedrooms, comfortable and traditional and utterly peaceful.

Right
Romanesque church, La Garde-Adhémar

GRIGNAN✧✧

The medieval Adhémars became the 16th-century Counts of Grignan. Their beautiful Renaissance **Château de Grignan✧✧**, originally 12th century but radically altered since then, dominates the old village. It deserves a look if only for its opulent period furnishings and the view from its terraces. Lanes and steep *calades* (stone paths), a *lavoir* (public laundry house) and several substantial historic buildings encircle the château.

In the Maison du Bailli, there's a **Musée-Atelier de la Typographie (Printing Workshop Museum)✧**, all about typography down the ages. An unusual attraction in the village is **Village Provençal Miniature✧✧✧**, an entertaining and fascinating collection of tiny tableaux and mini-scenes using 30cm-high figurines to depict Provençal country of a century ago. Local wines of the Coteaux du Tricastin and Côtes du Rhône *appellations* can be tasted at the **Cave Coopérative**.

Accommodation and food in Grignan

Manoir de la Rosaire €€€ *Rte de Valréas; tel: 04 75 46 58 15, fax: 04 75 46 91 55*. Next to the château, this magnificent former manor house is now a pricey little hotel in beautifully kept gardens. It has a brilliant display of roses – hence the name. The rooms have a refreshing, comfortable southern feel. The restaurant is excellent, with substantial and succulent regional dishes.

Right
Grignan

MONTÉLIMAR***

ⓘ Montélimar Tourist Office *Allées Provençales; tel: 04 75 01 00 20, fax: 04 75 52 33 69, e-mail: montelimar. tourisme@wanadoo.fr; open all year – call to check current hours.*

ⓗ Château des Adhémars €€ *At end of r. du Château; tel: 04 75 00 62 30, fax: 04 75 00 62 32; open daily (except Tue from Nov to Mar) 0930–1130, 1400–1730 (1800 in July and Aug).*

Musée de la Miniature €€ *19 r. Pierre Julien; tel: 04 75 53 79 24; open June–mid-Sept, daily 1000–1800, rest of the year Wed–Sun 1400–1800.*

The capital of nougat is obsessed with its subject. Along the length of the N7 through-road, you'd think there was nothing more to the place than the sticky, nutty confectionery that it claims (rather dubiously) to have invented. It comes as a surprise to turn into the centre and discover that Montélimar is an interesting and attractive old town! Its name is said, improbably, to derive from the Adhémars' 12th- to 14th-century fortress, Mont Adhémar, now known as the **Château des Adhémars***. The medieval town was sturdily fortified, but its walls have been replaced by a ring road. Only one of nine town gates survives, Porte St-Martin, at the north end of the main shopping street, r. Pierre

Julien. The street is lined with some good shops, passes the busy marketplace and Gothic church, and close to the other end reaches the extraordinary **Musée de la Miniature (Miniatures Museum)***. Here you can see unbelievably tiny miniaturisations – a portrait and poem on a grain of rice, a chess game set out on a table no bigger than a coin. To either side of the main street there's a tangle of old lanes and little squares.

Accommodation and food in Montélimar

Hôtel Pierre €–€€ *7 pl. des Clercs; tel: 04 75 01 33 16.* A 16th-century town house, right in the heart of old Montélimar, the Pierre has a certain atmosphere. Rooms are simple, and nothing special, but it's inexpensive, family-run and well placed.

Hôtel Sphinx €€ *19 blvd Marre-Desmarais; tel: 04 75 01 86 64, fax: 04 75 52 34 21.* There are many places to stay around the ring of boulevards. This is one of the most convenient, and most appealing – a former 17th-century mansion furnished with antiques, but at moderate prices.

Nougat de Montélimar

In France the word Montélimar has become a synonym for nougat, although the honey-and-nuts sweet was known as *Nux Gatum* (Nut Cake) in the ancient world, and is still made in Italy. Almond trees were planted in the hills around Montélimar in the 17th century. The region's honey was already being used with egg white to make sweets. It didn't take long to discover that adding almonds made them more delicious. From then until the 20th century, small-scale cottage confectioners made nougat over the whole region. They developed a particularly fine, soft product. Production today is mainly in factories. In the town centre, though, skilled confectioners still make their own versions of this sweet and chewy white bar.

NYONS✦✦

ℹ️ **Nyons Tourist Office** *Pavillon du Tourisme, pl. de la Libération; tel: 04 75 26 10 35, fax: 04 75 26 01 57; open in summer Mon–Sat 0900–1230, 1430–1900, Sun 1000–1300, rest of the year Mon–Sat 0900–1230, 1430–1830.*

🌐 *www.guideweb.com/ nyons/index (official tourist office site in English and French).*

🏛️ **Moulin Autrand (or Musée Les Vieux Moulins)** €€ *Promenade de la Digue and Impasse du Moulin; tel: 04 75 26 11 00; closed Jan, and Sun and Mon out of season. Guided tours at 1030, 1130, 1500, 1600, 1700 and 1745.*

Jardin des Arômes € *Promenade de la Digue.*

High-quality black olives of the Tanche variety thrive around Nyons, the only olives with their own *appellation d'origine contrôlée* (official seal of authenticity). You'll notice oil mills in and around town, making traditional cold pressed olive oil and olive products. The most conveniently and centrally placed is **Moulin Autrand✦**, with twin 18th- and 19th-century oil mills still using its traditional processes, and functioning now as a museum. Nyons is known for truffles as well, while lavender distilleries make products from the lavender growing in fields east of the town. Close to the Moulin Autrand, the **Jardin des Arômes (Aromas Garden)✦** features nearly 200 species of scented herbs and medicinal plants. West of the town centre, the **Musée de l'Olivier (Olive Museum)✦** contains tools and equipment used in growing, gathering and pressing this all-important local crop. For another perspective on it, the adjacent **Coopérative Oléicole et Viticole de Nyons (Nyons Oil and Wine Producers' Cooperative)✦** is also open to visitors, and the pressing process can be watched.

Accommodation and food in Nyons

Hôtel la Picholine €€ *Promenade Perrière; tel: 04 75 26 06 21, fax: 04 75 26 40 72.* Just out of town among the olives, this is a modern, comfortable and charming hotel done up in traditional Provençal style. It's quiet and relaxing, with a pool and restaurant.

Restaurant le Petit Caveau €€ *9 r. Victor-Hugo; tel: 04 75 26 20 21, fax: 04 75 26 07 28; closed Sun pm and Mon.* Delicious Provençal and Italian flavours – parmesan, tapenade, duck and seafood – are prepared and presented here with style, at reasonable prices.

Musée de l'Olivier €
Av. des Tilleuls/pl.
Olivier de Serres; tel: 04 75
26 12 12; open Tue–Sat
and Sun in season
1000–1100, 1445–1800
(Nov–May afternoons only).

**Coopérative Oléicole
et Viticole de Nyons €**
Pl. Olivier de Serres; tel: 04
75 26 03 44; open July and
Aug Mon–Sat 0830–1300,
1400–1930, Sun
0930–1230, 1500–1830,
rest of the year Mon–Sat
0830–1230, 1400–1900,
Sun 0930–1200,
1430–1800. 30-min guided
tours.

ORANGE✦✦✦

**Orange Tourist
Office** Cours A. Briand;
tel: 04 90 34 70 88, fax: 04
90 34 99 62; open
Apr–Sept, Mon–Sat
0900–1900, Sun
1000–1800; Oct–Mar,
Mon–Sat 0900–1700.

**Théâtre Antique
(Roman theatre) €€**
Pl. des Frères-Mounet; tel: 04
90 34 70 88; open
Apr–Sept 0900–1830, rest
of the year 0900–1200,
1330–1700 (closed 1 Jan
and 25 Dec). Ticket includes
Musée Municipal, but note
different entry times.

The busy town of Orange, the Catholic principality which came into Dutch hands and whose name subsequently became synonymous with Northern Irish Protestantism, formally became part of France as recently as 1713. It possesses some striking antiquities, including that immense wall which Louis XIV described as 'the finest in my kingdom'. The other side of the wall was the original backdrop for performances in the **Théâtre Antique (Roman theatre)**✦✦✦, which still provides the setting for concerts and plays today.

In the area around it and on the adjacent hill, Colline St-Eutrope, several other Roman relics have been uncovered. From the hill, a viewing platform gives an excellent overview of the Roman district. Across the road, the **Musée Municipal**✦ contains plenty of material excavated here, including the important Roman Land Survey of Orange inscribed on marble.

The medieval central district, called Vieil Orange, is lively and attractive, with little squares, narrow streets and cafés. On the north side of town, standing incongruously on an island encircled by the N7, the Arc de Triomphe is a majestic three-arched monument covered in carvings recalling the defeat of the Gauls, battles, prisoners and naval and military trophies. The north side has survived in

Musée Municipal €€
R. Pontillac; tel: 04 90
51 18 24; open Apr–Sept
0900–1900, rest of the year
0830 (0900 at
weekends)–1200,
1330–1700 (closed 2 Jan
and 26 Dec).

remarkably good condition. Dating from about 20 BC, it honours the victories of Augustus and the setting up of *Arausio* (Orange) as a colony. This triumphant display could result from the fact that at their first attempt to conquer the area, the Romans were trounced by the local Gauls.

Accommodation and food in Orange

Hôtel Arène €€ *Pl. Langes; tel: 04 90 11 40 40, fax: 04 90 11 40 45.* Right in the heart of the old town, yet quiet and peaceful, this traditional and comfortable little provincial hotel would be a first choice for an overnight or longer stay. It doesn't have a restaurant, but there are several *brasseries* in town.

Le Parvis €€ *3 cours Pourtoules; tel: 04 90 34 82 00; closed Sun pm and Mon.* Traditional, reasonably priced, with classic, skilful cooking including *sanglier* (wild boar).

Above
Théâtre Antique, Orange

VAISON-LA-ROMAINE✦✦✦

**Vaison Tourist
Office** Pl. Sautel
(between the two Roman
sites); tel: 04 90 36 02 11,
fax: 04 90 28 76 04.

Vaison, on the River Ouvèze that runs round the northern edges of the Dentelles and Mont Ventoux, is an agreeable small town with a big, colourful weekly market. In fact Vaison is three towns, all of them interesting, the newest lying partly on top of the oldest. On the north bank of the Ouvèze was the Gallo-Roman city *Vasio Vocantiorum*. In the Middle Ages the town moved over to the better defended hill south of the river, where in the 12th century the Counts of Toulouse built the castle. And in the modern era, until 1907, life extended back on to the north bank, and many of the Roman ruins were built over.

Quartier du Puymin, Quartier de la Villasse, Musée Archéologique and the cloisters of Nôtre-Dame de Nazareth €€€
el: 04 90 36 02 11; open un–Aug 0900–1230, 1400–1845, Mar–May and Sept–Oct, 0930–1200, 1400–1745, rest of the year 1000–1200, 1400–1630 Roman ruins closed Tue am Nov–Apr). A single ticket available at any of the sites provides admission to all four of them. The ticket does not have to be used all on one day.

The original Roman bridge, or Pont Romain, an elegant single-arch 2 000-year-old cobbled bridge crossing the Ouvèze, links the medieval Ville Haute with the north bank and is still in use.

Since 1907, in a succession of excavations, the Roman town has been partly uncovered again in two large sites (totalling over 15 hectares, 37 acres) with the modern main road running between them. The huge upper site, **Quartier du Puymin**✦✦✦, is the more interesting, with paved streets, walls, frescos, mosaics, statuary and a complete restored theatre. The best features of the smaller lower site, **Quartier de la Villasse**✦✦✦, are the street of little shops and the mosaic floors of the villas. The **Musée Archéologique (Archaeology Museum)**✦✦ has an impressive collection of Roman sculpture. A few paces west of the Villasse site, the interesting Romanesque former cathedral, **Nôtre-Dame de Nazareth**✦ has attractive 12th-century cloisters.

Accommodation and food in Vaison

Hôtel des Lis €€ *20 cours J. Henri-Fabre; tel: 04 90 36 00 11, fax: 04 90 36 39 05*. Welcoming and attractive, with pleasant, comfortable rooms in a turn-of-the-century house near a square in the centre of town, this moderately priced little hotel decorates the walls with paintings by local artists.

Le Moulin à l'Huile €€ *1 quai Maréchal Foch; tel: 04 90 36 20 67, fax: 04 90 36 20 20*. There are several popular inexpensive *brasseries* in the town centre, and some good restaurants, too, of which this is certainly one of the best. The cooking seems to combine Provence with every other part of the world, with ginger, peppers, soya and spices enlivening fresh local ingredients.

Below
Nôtre-Dame de Nazareth, Vaison-la-Romaine

Suggested tour

Atelier Musée de la Soie *Monboucher sur Jabron; tel: 04 75 01 47 40, fax: 04 75 01 68 50; closed Dec–Feb.*

Total distance: 175km, or 185km if you take the detour.

Time: 2–3 days. Although the drive could be done in 2–3 hours, there is a lot of good sightseeing, winetasting and exploring to be done on this route.

Links: At Montélimar the route links with southern Ardèche (*see page 239*), and at Nyons with the Diois (*see page 268*).

Route: From **MONTÉLIMAR ❶**, take the D4 under the *autoroute* and across country towards Grignan. After the Fonbrenoux woods (about 10km out of Montélimar), you may wish to turn down the D203 on the right to see the Trappist (once Cistercian) monastery of **Nôtre Dame d'Aiguebelle**, which still has its 12th-century church. Otherwise, keep going to **GRIGNAN ❷**. Turn west on the D541 and turn off for La Garde-Adhémar. Before reaching the village, the road passes along the exquisite little **Val-des-Nymphes**, passing the restored Romanesque chapel, just before reaching **LA GARDE ADHÉMAR ❸**. Leave in the direction of Pierrelatte (on the Rhône) but straight away turn left towards **St-Paul-Trois-Châteaux**. Take the D59 to Suze-la-Rousse, where the 14th- to 16th-century castle now houses a wine college. Crossing straight over the D94 on to the D117 follow this attractive country road to **ORANGE ❹**.

From Orange take the D975 out of town and follow it to **VAISON-LA-ROMAINE ❺**.

Detour: After leaving Orange, turn right on to the D8 for the old wine village of **Vacqueyras**. You may want to head another 4km on the road to visit **Beaumes-de-Venise**, producing a well-known sweet dessert (or aperitif) wine. Turn north at Vacqueyras on the little vineyard road (it starts off as the D7) which runs along the slope of the **DENTELLES DE MONTMIRAIL ❻**, with immense views over the vineyards, shimmering in the sunlight. Every village along here is enticing. The road descends to meet the D977, which curves round into Vaison-la-Romaine, then take the D938 into Nyons.

Take the D938 to **NYONS ❼**. For a scenic route out of Nyons, take Promenade des Anglais from pl. J. Buffaven (on the west side of Quartier des Forts) and turn right on to a winding road through the olive groves which eventually descends, at the foot of Montagne des Vaux, on to the D538. Continue round (the road number changes to the D941) to **Valréas**. Leave on the D16 to reach **Dieulefit** in the Jablon Valley. Keep heading towards Montélimar. 4km before the town, at Monboucher-sur-Jabron, **Atelier Musée de la Soie** is an old silkworks preserved as an interesting museum. Carry on back into **Montélimar**.

10 km

A l p e s   d u
D a u p h i n é

M a s s i f
d u   D i o i s

Cruas
Marsanne
St-Marcel-lès-Sauzet
Cléon-d'Andran
Saou
Bourdeaux
St-Nazaire-le-Désert
Rochemaure
Monboucher-sur-Jabron
La Bégude-de-Mazenc
Le Poët-Laval
Le Teil
① Montélimar
Dieulefit
Bouvières
Allan
Bois de Fonbrenoux
Viviers
Montagne de Mielandre
1451
Nôtre-Dame-d'Aiguebelle
Taulignan
1338
Rocher Garaux
Donzère
Montagne des Vaux
Val-des-Nymphes
② Grignan
Sahune
Grillon
Valréas
La Garde-Adhémar **③**
Nyons **⑦**
St-Paul-Trois-Châteaux
Pierrelatte
Mirabel-aux-Baronnies
Visan
Lapalud
Suze-la-Rousse
Tulette
Buis-les-Baronnies
Bollène
Vaison-la-Romaine **⑤**
Pont-St-Esprit
Mondragon
Sablet **⑥**
Dentelles de Montmirail
Mornas
Sérignan-du-Comtat
Violès
Gigondas
Malaucène
Mont Ventoux
1909
Bagnols-sur-Cèze
Piolenc
Vacqueyras
Orange **④**
Beaumes-de-Venise
Bédoin
Jonquières
Aubignan
Laudun
Courthézon
Sarrians
Mazan
St-Victor-la-coste
Roquemaure
Carpentras
Monteux
Tavel
Sorgues
Pujaut
Entraigues-sur-Sorgues
Pernes-les-Fontaines
Villeneuve-lès-Avignon
Vedène

Language

Although English is spoken in most tourist locations it is courteous to attempt to speak some French. The effort is generally appreciated, and may even elicit a reply in perfect English! The following is a very brief list of some useful words and phrases, with approximate pronunciation guides. The *Thomas Cook European Travel Phrasebook* (£4.95/$7.95) lists more than 300 travel phrases in French (and in 11 other European languages).

- **Hello/Goodbye**
  Bonjour/Au revoir *Bawngzhoor/Ohrervwahr*

- **Good evening/Goodnight**
  Bonsoir/Bonne nuit *Bawngswahr/Bon nwee*

- **Yes/No**
  Oui/Non *Wee/Nawng*

- **Please/Thank you (very much)**
  S'il vous plaît/Merci (beaucoup) *Seelvooplay/Mehrsee (bohkoo)*

- **Excuse me, can you help me please?**
  Excusez-moi, vous pouvez m'aider s'il vous plaît? *Ekskewzaymwah, voo poovay mahyday seelvooplay?*

- **Do you speak English?**
  Vous parlez anglais? *Voo pahrlay ahnglay?*

- **I'm sorry, I don't understand.**
  Pardon, je ne comprends pas. *Pahrdawng, zher ner kawngprawng pah.*

- **I am looking for the tourist information office.**
- Je cherche l'office de tourisme. *Zher shaersh lohfeece de tooreezm.*

- **Do you have a map of the town/area?**
  Avez-vous une carte de la ville/région? *Ahveh-voo ewn cart der lah veel/rehzhawng?*

- **Do you have a list of hotels?**
  Vous avez une liste des hôtels? *Vooz ahveh ewn leesst dez ohtehl?*

- **Do you have any rooms free?**
  Vous avez des chambres disponibles? *Voozahveh deh shahngbr deesspohneebl?*

- **I would like to reserve a single/double room with/without bath/shower.**
  Je voudrais réserver une chambre pour une personne/pour deux personnes avec/sans salle de bain/douche. *Zher voudray rehsehrveh ewn shahngbr poor ewn pehrson/poor der pehrson avek/sawns sal der banne/doosh.*

- **I would like bed and breakfast/(room and) half board/(room and) full board.**
  Je voudrais le petit-déjeuner/la demi-pension/la

pension complète. *Zher voodray ler pewtee-dehjewneh/lah dermee-pahngsyawng/lah pahngsyawng kawngplait.*

- **How much is it per night?**
  Quel est le prix pour une nuit? *Khel eh ler pree poor ewn nuwy?*

- **I would like to stay for . . . nights.**
  Je voudrais rester . . . nuits. *Zhe voodray resteh . . . newyh.*

- **Do you accept travellers' cheques/credit cards?**
  Vous acceptez les chèques de voyages/les cartes de crédit? *Voos aksepteh leh sheck der vwoyazh/leh kart der krehdee?*

- **I would like a table for two.**
  Je voudrais une table pour deux personnes. *Zher voodray ewn tabl poor der pehrson.*

- **I would like a cup of/two cups of/another coffee/tea.**
  Je voudrais une tasse de/deux tasses de/encore une tasse de café/thé. *Zher voodray ewn tahss der/der tahss der/oncaw ewn tahss der kafeh/teh.*

- **I would like a bottle/glass/two glasses of mineral water/red wine/white wine, please.**
  Je voudrais une bouteille/un verre/deux verres d'eau minérale/de vin rouge/de vin blanc, s'il vous plaît. *Zhe voodray ewn bootayy/ang vair/der vair doh mynehral/der vang roozh/der vang blahng, seelvooplay*

- **Could I have it well-cooked/medium/rare please?**
  Je le voudrais bien cuit/à point/saignant s'il vous plaît. *Zher ler voodray beeang kwee/ah pwahng/saynyang, seelvooplay?*

- **May I have the bill, please?** L'addition, s'il vous plaît! *Laddyssyawng, seelvooplay!*

- **Where is the toilet (restroom), please?**
- Où sont les toilettes, s'il vous plaît? *Oo sawng leh twahlaitt, seelvooplay?*

- **How much does it/this cost?**
  Quel est le prix? *Kehl eh ler pree?*

- **A (half-) kilo of . . . please.**
  Un (demi-) kilo de . . . s'il vous plaît. *Ang (dermee)keelo der . . . seelvooplay.*

Index

A accidents 24
accommodation 14
airports 15, 30
Alba-la-Romaine 230, 240
Albon 242, 250
Alise-Ste-Reine 68, 74
Aloxe-Corton 112, 120
Ancy-le-Duc 170, 176
Ancy-le-Franc 58–9, 67
Andance 244, 250
Annonay 222, 224–5, 227
Archéodrome de Bourgogne 112, 120
Arcy-sur-Cure 76, 84
Ardèche gorge 232, 240
Aubenas 233, 240
Autun 86, 88, 96
Auxerre 77–8, 84
Avallon 79, 85
Aven d'Orgnac 234, 240

B Baigneux-les-Juifs 74
Beaujeu 150–3, 158
Beaujolais Nouveau 152
Beaune 122–31
  Collégiale Nôtre-Dame 123
  Hospices de Beaune 124
  Hôtel Dieu 124
  Hôtel des Ducs de Bourgogne 123
  Marché aux Vins 127
  Musée des Beaux-Arts 128
  et Marey
  ramparts 128
  wine auction 124
Benedictine Order 142–3
Bibracte 91
Bourbon-Lancy 170, 176
Bourg-en-Bresse 186, 188, 192
Brancion 140, 148
Briare 162, 164, 168
Brou 186, 188
Bussy-Rabutin 70, 74
Buxy 133, 138

C car hire 25, 31
Chablis 60, 66
Chagny 134, 136
Chalon-sur-Saône 134–6, 138
Charlieu 172, 176
Charolles 173, 176
Chartreuse liqueur 258, 259
Châteaurenard 42, 48
Château-Chinon 90, 96
Château de Crussol 244, 252
Châtillon-Coligny 52, 56
Châtillon-en-Diois 262, 268
Châtillon-sur-Chalaronne 194, 196, 200
Châtillon-sur-Seine 70, 74
Chazelles-sur-Lyon 178, 184

Chenôve 113, 119
children 15
Cirque d'Archiane 264, 268
Cistercian Order 62, 72, 114
Cîteaux 114, 120
  Abbaye de Cîteaux 114
climate 15, 33
Cluny 142–3, 148, 174
  Abbaye de Cluny 142
Colette 52, 54
Condrieu 244, 250
Crémieu 256–7, 260
Crest 264, 268
currency 17
customs regulations 17

D Dentelles de Montmirail 270, 280
Dicy 53, 56
Die 265–6, 268
Dijon 98–109
  Cathédrale St-Bénigne 100
  Chartreuse de Champmol 100
  Église Nôtre-Dame 100
  gastronomic capital 105
  Les États de Bourgogne 102
  Musée Archéologique 100
  Musée des Beaux-Arts 102
  Musée Magnin 102
  Palais de Justice 102
  Palais des Ducs 102
  shopping 105

E Epoisses 71, 74

F festivals 18–19
Fontenay, Abbaye de 72, 74

G Gerbier de Jonc 225, 227
Gevry-Chambertin 115, 120
Gien 166, 168
Givry 136, 138
Grignan 274, 280

H health 19

J Joigny 44, 48
Juliénas 153, 158

L La Balme-les-Grottes 254, 260
La Charité-sur-Loire 164, 168
La Clayette 173, 176
La Côte St-André 256, 260
La Garde-Adhémar 273, 280
La Terrasse 155, 158
La Tour-du-Pin 258, 260
Lac de Paladru 257, 260
Lac des Settons 90, 96
Lamastre 226, 227

limestone scenery 234
Loire, River 164, 165
Louhans 189, 192
Luc-en-Diois 266–7, 268
Lyon 202–213
  Amphithéâtre des Trois 205
    Gaules
  astronomical clock 208
  Basilique Nôtre-Dame 206
  Cathédrale St-Jean 208
  Centre d'Histoire de la 206
    Résistance et de la
    Déportation
  Église St-Paul 208
  festivals 210
  Fourvière 206
  gastronomic city 209
  La Croix-Rousse 205
  La Presqu'ile 207
  Maison des Canuts 205
  markets 210
  Musée d'Art Contemporain 206
  Musée de la Civilisation 206
    Gallo-Romaine
  Musée d'Histoire Naturelle 206
  Musée d'l'Imprimerie et de 207
    la Banque
  Musée des Arts Décoratifs 207
  Musée des Beaux-Arts 207
  Musée des Tissus 207
  Musée Historique de Lyon 208
  Musée International de la 208
    Marionnette
  nightlife 210
  Old Quarter 208
  Parc Archéologique 206
  Théâtre Guignol 208

M Mâcon 144, 148
Mercurey 138
Meursault 116, 120, 126
Mitterrand, François (President) 90
Mont Beuvray 91, 96
Montargis 45–6, 48
Montbard 72, 74
Montélimar 275, 276, 280
Montrond-les-Bains 180, 184
Monts d'Or Lyonnais 180, 184

N Nevers 167, 168
Noyers 61, 66
Nuits-St-Georges 116, 120
Nyons 276, 280

O Oingt 154, 160
Orange 277–8, 280

P Paray-le-Monial 174, 176
Pérouges 197, 200
Pierre-de-Bresse 190, 192
Pilat Regional Nature Park 226, 227
Pontigny 62, 67

Pouilly-Fuissé 145, 148
Privas 234, 239

Q Quarré-les-Tombes 92, 96

R regional dishes 36–7, 39
  Bresse chicken 189
  Charolais beef 173
  cheeses 63, 71
  in Dijon 195
  Dombes 199
  Epoisses cheeses 71
  in Lyon 209
  Montélimar nougat 276
  Sénonais 47
  southern Ardèche 233
  in Vienne 217
Rémuzat 267, 268
Roanne 181, 184
Romanèche-Thorins 154, 158
Romanesque architecture 12, 34
Ruoms 235, 240

S Saillans 267, 268
Santenay 116, 120
Saulieu 92, 96
Semur-en-Auxois 73, 74
Semur-en-Brionnais 175, 176
Sens 46–7, 48
Serrières-sur-Rhône 246, 250
Solutré Rock 145, 148
sports activities 22, 239
St-Cyr-sur-Menthon 191, 192
St-Désirat 245, 250
St-Étienne 182–3, 184
St-Fargeau 53, 56
St-Florentin 63, 67
St-Père 94, 96
St-Sauveur-en-Puisaye 54, 56
St-Trivier-de-Courtes 192
steam railways 226

T Tain-l'Hermitage 246, 252
Tanlay 64, 67
telephones 22
Ternand 155, 160
Thueyts 236, 239
Tonnerre 65, 67
Toucy 54, 56
Tournon (sur Rhône) 248, 252
Tournus 146, 148
Treigny-Perreuse 55, 56
Trévoux 198, 200

V Vaison-la-Romaine 278–9, 280
Valence 248–9, 252
Vallon-Pont-d'Arc 236, 240
Vals-les-Bains 237, 239
Vercingetorix 34, 68, 69, 88, 91
Vézelay 80–3, 85, 170
Vienne 214–21
  Cathédrale St-Maurice 216

Église et Cloître St-André-le-Bas	216
Église St-Pierre et Musée Lapidaire	217
Jardin Archéologique	217
Mont Pipet	217
Musée des Beaux-Arts et d'Archéologie	217
Musée Archéologique St-Romain-en-Gal et Vienne	218
Ste-Colombe	218
Temple d'Auguste et Livie	218
Théâtre Antique (Romain)	218
Villars-les-Dombes	198, 200
Villefranche-sur-Saône	156, 160
vineyards	
Beaujolais Nouveau	152
Chablis	60
Clairette de Die	266
Corton-Charlemagne	112
Pouilly-Fuissé	145
Puligny-Montrachet	120
Côtes du Rhône	245, 246, 247
Viviers	238, 240
Vogüé	238, 239
Voiron	258, 260
Vosne-Romanée	118, 120
Vougeot	118, 120
wine festivals	113, 126
wine regions	13, 34–5
Ardèche	35
Auxerrois	34, 84
Beaujolais	35, 153
Chablis	34, 60
Côte Chalonnaise	34, 132
Côte d'Or	34, 110, 112, 118
Côtes du Rhône	35, 245, 246, 247
Mâconnais	35, 145
Val de Loire	35

Acknowledgements

Project Management: Dial House Publishing Services
Series design: Fox Design
Cover design: Pumpkin House
Layout and map work: PDQ Digital Media Solutions Limited and PS Cartography
Repro and image setting: PDQ Digital Media Solutions Limited
Printed and bound in Italy by: Rotolito Lombarda Spa

We would like to thank the following for the photographs used in this book, to whom the copyright belongs:

Cover photographs: front: Michael Busselle, back: Eddy Posthuma De Boer

Michael Busselle (pages 22B, 24, 32, 60, 61, 64, 65, 66, 73, 83, 112, 113, 118, 120, 122, 132, 135, 137, 140, 145, 150, 152, 155, 186, 194, 197 and 271)

Cotes Vues Picture Library (pages 15, 19, 23, 26, 31, 33, 39, 40A, 41B, 42A, 44, 47, 48, 68A, 81, 88, 89, 101, 103, 104, 119, 125, 126, 127, 130, 143, 146, 147, 157, 162, 170, 172, 188, 191, 192, 199, 202A, 202B, 204, 205, 208, 210, 222, 225, 270 and 275)

John Heseltine (pages 12, 13, 14, 28, 29, 30, 34, 41A, 76, 86A, 86B, 90, 93, 110A, 117, 168 and 178A)

Eddy Posthuma De Boer (pages 5, 6, 20, 22A, 36, 37, 40B, 58, 78, 79, 91, 92, 95, 165, 207, 273 and 274)

Neil Setchfield (pages 3, 42B, 50, 52, 53, 56, 62, 63, 68B, 71, 94, 99, 107, 108, 109, 110B, 114, 115, 116, 129, 136, 153, 156, 159, 160, 166, 174, 178B, 181, 196, 198, 214, 216, 219, 220, 224, 226, 228, 230B, 233, 235, 236, 237, 238, 242, 244, 245, 247, 249, 251, 252, 254A, 254B, 258, 259, 262A, 262B, 263, 264, 265, 266, 267, 277 and 279)

Telegraph Colour Library (pages 50B, 70, 98, 142, 184, 206, 211, 214B, 230A, 232 and 278)

Feedback form

If you enjoyed using this book, or even if you didn't, please help us improve future editions by taking part in our reader survey. Every returned form will be acknowledged, and to show our appreciation we will give you £1 off your next purchase of a Thomas Cook guidebook. Just take a few minutes to complete and return this form to us.

When did you buy this book? ....
....

Where did you buy it? (Please give town/city and, if possible, name of retailer)
....
....

When did you/do you intend to travel in Burgundy?...
....

For how long (approx)? ....

How many people in your party? ....

Which cities, national parks and other locations did you/do you intend mainly to visit?
....
....
....
....

Did you/will you:
❏ Make all your travel arrangements independently?
❏ Travel on a fly-drive package?
Please give brief details: ....
....

Did you/do you intend to use this book:
❏ For planning your trip?   ❏ Both?
❏ During the trip itself?

Did you/do you intend also to purchase any of the following travel publications for your trip?
Thomas Cook Travellers: Burgundy...
A road map/atlas (please specify) ....
Other guidebooks (please specify) ....

Have you used any other Thomas Cook guidebooks in the past? If so, which?
....
....

Please rate the following features of 'Signpost Burgundy' for their value to you (Circle VU for 'very useful', U for 'useful', NU for 'little or no use'):

The Travel Facts section on pages 14–23	VU	U	NU
The Driver's Guide section on pages 24–29	VU	U	NU
The Highlights on pages 40–41	VU	U	NU
The recommended driving routes throughout the book	VU	U	NU
Information on towns and cities, National Parks, etc	VU	U	NU
The maps of towns and cities, parks, etc	VU	U	NU

Please use this space to tell us about any features that in your opinion could be changed, improved, or added in future editions of the book, or any other comments you would like to make concerning the book:

....
....
....
....
....
....
....
....
....
....

Your age category: ❏ 21-30   ❏ 31-40   ❏ 41-50   ❏ over 50

Your name: Mr/Mrs/Miss/Ms ....
(First name or initials) ....
(Last name) ....

Your full address: (Please include postal or zip code)

....
....
....
....
....

Your daytime telephone number: ....

Please detach this page and send it to: The Project Editor, Signpost Guides, Thomas Cook Publishing, PO Box 227, Peterborough PE3 6PU, United Kingdom.

We will be pleased to send you details of how to claim your discount upon receipt of this questionnaire.